# British Foreign Policy
## 1945–1973

# British Foreign Policy
## 1945–1973

JOSEPH FRANKEL

*Published for*
THE ROYAL INSTITUTE OF
INTERNATIONAL AFFAIRS
*by*
OXFORD UNIVERSITY PRESS
LONDON   NEW YORK   TORONTO
*1975*

*Oxford University Press, Ely House, London W.1*

GLASGOW   NEW YORK   TORONTO   MELBOURNE   WELLINGTON
CAPE TOWN   IBADAN   NAIROBI   DAR ES SALAAM   LUSAKA   ADDIS ABABA
DELHI   BOMBAY   CALCUTTA   MADRAS   KARACHI   LAHORE   DACCA
KUALA LUMPUR   SINGAPORE   HONG KONG   TOKYO

ISBN 0 19 218306 0

Printed in Great Britain
by W & J Mackay Limited, Chatham

# Contents

# Acknowledgements

First, I would like to thank the Royal Institute of International Affairs for having sponsored this book and offered me its hospitality as a Research Associate in 1971–2, and especially its Deputy Director of Research, Dr Roger Morgan, for initiating the project and chairing the RIIA Study Group on British Foreign Policy, at which early drafts of four chapters were discussed; to all the other members of the Group, to the three RIIA readers for their comments on the draft, to the editor, Miss Katharine Duff, and to the Library staff. My thanks are also due to the University of Southampton for a year's leave; to the SSRC for financing my replacement, and to the Rockefeller Foundation for its hospitality at the Villa Serbelloni, Bellagio.

Furthermore, I would like to acknowledge the useful comments I received on individual sections of the book from several serving members of the Diplomatic Service, and from: Professor Dennis Austin, Mr Robert Cecil, Professor Louis Henkin, Mr Eli Lauterpacht, QC, Dr Peter Lyon, Lord Strang, Miss Susan Strange, Professor D. C. Watt, Mr Duncan Wilson, and for the editorial assistance given to me by my wife and, above all, by my daughter, Mrs Inge Dyson.

Avington, Winchester                                                     J. F.
*January 1974*

# Part One
# The Background of Policy Making
# 1 Introductory

BRITAIN, a member of the victorious Big Three at the end of the second
world war, has in little more than twenty-five years accepted the status
of a major second-rank power, and has decided (or perhaps more pro-
perly resigned herself) to seek entry into a regional grouping. How and
why has this come about? What are the probable lines of her future
evolution? The focus of this study of Britain's problems is national; it
centres upon the decision-makers in foreign policy considered as part of
the British political elite. Foreign policy is not viewed in isolation but as
part and parcel of national policy in the widest sense, set against the
background of the changing international scene. Full allowance will be
made for the impact of international events on Britain's foreign policy.
Conversely, however, any attempt to evaluate the impact of her foreign
policy on the international order would unduly expand the scope of this
enquiry. From so panoramic a point of view, the study of details becomes
relatively less important, the more so as even the principal participants
may not always articulate their real objectives, may sometimes themselves
be unsure of their deeper motives, and cannot fully visualize the part they
are playing in the broad pattern of policy evolution, which seldom
becomes clear till some time has elapsed.

*Patterns in Foreign Policy*
This book is about British foreign policy since the second world war,
not about its theory or philosophy. Nevertheless, as the notion of 'foreign
policy' in general, and of British foreign policy in particular, is by no
means clear, a brief preliminary explanation is necessary. Nobody has
ever formulated a really satisfactory definition of foreign policy, and
probably nobody ever will. At one extreme lies Grant Hugo's behavioural
view that 'British foreign policy is . . . essentially concerned with disputes
between British subjects, British organizations and British governmental
agencies on the one hand, and those of foreign States on the other'.[1]
This definition, which closely corresponds with diplomatic activities, is
by no means unduly narrow—it is not necessarily confined to the work of

the Foreign and Commonwealth Office, and its central notion of disputes need not be restricted to conflicts but may include co-operative efforts to avoid or resolve them.

Usually, however, foreign policy means something more: a mental construct which fits the congeries of specific decisions and actions into an overall pattern. We can refer to the point of time at which specific decisions were made or specific actions taken,[2] and view foreign policy as a system of ideas referring to future action, as a plan or programme of action rather than the action itself. More precisely, but somewhat pedantically, it can be defined as 'a formulation of desired outcomes which are intended (or expected) to be consequent upon decisions adopted (or 'made') by those who have the authority (or ability) to commit the machinery of state or a significant fraction of national resources to the end'.[3]

To the participants, foreign policy of necessity presents itself as a series of more or less disjointed undertakings, the common link between which is that they are dealt with by the same people. All these people naturally endeavour to pursue some particular interests and objectives, and to follow certain principles, but their activities (especially in a country with interests as far-flung and varied as those of Britain) can rarely if ever be subsumed under a coherent overall strategy. The conception of a 'rational', contemplated foreign policy is utterly remote from operational reality. As British foreign policy is marked by pragmatism and an absence of ideology, to analyse it by means of fundamental philosophical structures would force it into a strait-jacket.

One may, however, legitimately assume that British foreign policy, far from being a mere sequence of random improvisations, does reveal some distinctive patterns. This study is, in fact, based on the assumption that whether or not an overall pattern or plan has actually existed, we can nevertheless read *ex post facto* some intelligible patterns into the record of the past. Foreign policy is by no means confined to the Foreign and Commonwealth Office, but, as the major Department concerned with it on whose advice governments generally act, this can justifiably be regarded as the institutional focus for its formulation in the broader sense, not only on specific issues. All decisions and actions by the office refer to specific contexts, but emanate from a climate of opinion within it which evolves through discussion and precedent. By its nature this climate of opinion is generally elusive. Occasionally direction may be prescribed or changed by a definite political decision from above. At intervals, the Permanent Under-Secretary of State may ask for a policy-paper to sum up a position or the climate of Office opinion at a given time—a paper may be wanted for a public statement, a foreign visit, &c.

Even when most of these internal sources become available after the lapse of thirty years, and we can use the occasional systematic statements of the assumptions, the interests, the policy objectives, and the alternatives considered, our reconstruction of the foreign policy to which they all refer will still remain a fairly subjective matter. British foreign policy in the 1930s, on which these materials are now available, is still interpreted quite differently by those opposed to appeasement and those sympathizing with it. Disagreements about the interpretation of the contemporary period are not different in kind except that the time-perspective is, of necessity, much shorter, and the speculative element much greater.

Owing to the pragmatic, non-ideological nature of Britain's foreign policy in the past, we are unable to trace such clear patterns of tradition and principle as we can for other countries whose politicians are more articulate. On recent events, somewhat paradoxically, we suffer both from the lack of information and from its overabundance. The former is perhaps the lesser problem. Full official documentation is not, of course, available, and what is published is frequently less revealing than was the case in the nineteenth century. We have now, however, prompt and often searching analyses by journalists—admittedly speculative, but sometimes based upon leakages and inside information, and often very shrewd. The contemporary fashion of publication results in a spate of memoirs and articles by statesmen and politicians; even civil servants have become more outspoken. Complementary information from abroad is patchy, and particularly limited from the communist countries, but from the United States it is extremely abundant and revealing. Important *lacunae* remain, but these can be temporarily left open or covered by questions and hypotheses.

Interpretation is the real difficulty: to sift out what is important, to discriminate between truth, half-truth, or a deliberately misleading statement. It can also be dangerously misleading to impose an intelligible order upon the chaos of incomplete and at the same time overwhelming information. The official line can be built up from the hints and fragments, but it is much harder to decide about the 'what might have beens', the things that did not happen. We can merely guess and argue about the hidden assumptions, the collective prejudices and emotions; and we cannot hope to identify all the influential individuals and reconstruct the ideas of all of them. Ultimately we need the perspective of time; only the slow and patient process of historical reconstruction will enable us to obtain a fuller and somewhat more reliable picture. Meanwhile, however, we must strive for some provisional understanding, however imperfect.

The present is too bewilderingly obscure—not only for mental comfort but also for clearer thinking about the future.

Britain's foreign policy, as that of other major powers, is concerned both with the maintenance of a reasonably favourable international order and with the pursuit of individual national interests. The traditional categorization into strategic, economic, and political interests can be helpful in dividing foreign policy into three broad, though inevitably somewhat overlapping, areas. First, the creation of conditions conducive to averting war, starting with the establishment and maintenance of strategic alliances but increasingly involving action to discourage major international conflicts. Second, the establishment and maintenance of the structures necessary for international economic activities, especially in the fields of international finance and trade. Third, the extension of the state's influence in relations with other states: to enable it to promote co-operation and to prevent conflict and to secure the maximum possible advantage where its interests clash with those of others. The first two categories may be combined as comprising broadly situational or 'milieu' interests, whereas the third one consists of more specific national interests. Obviously, foreign policy is basically concerned with security and prosperity, but it can scarcely be comprehended as a mere pursuit of vital defence and economic objectives. Its important additional aspects, which will be discussed later, comprise the maintenance of capabilities (see pp. 78–87), considerations of role, status or prestige, or some combination of the three, and the desire to conduct foreign policy according to the correct 'rules of the game' (see chs 4, 6, and 7). Hence the occasional narrow definitions of foreign policy confining it mainly to the activities of the Foreign Office are not satisfactory. Traditionally, the Office has not been concerned with economic matters, although not without some misgivings on this score even before the second world war. Even after 1945, however, though the Office was increasingly aware that the economic and political aspects of foreign policy were becoming ever more closely interwoven (see ch. 11), and that economic matters were central to foreign policy, this awareness had only a limited effect on policy. The Treasury view remained dominant, and economic policies were adopted on superior orders, the more compliantly because until the 1960s the Office lacked any independent economic expertise of its own. The notion that international economic relations are divorced from foreign policy, e.g. that the City operates autonomously, was dispelled on the eve of the last war by E. H. Carr in *The Twenty Years' Crisis* (see p. 258), but only at the beginning of the 1970s have we become able to grasp more fully the implications of the defence of sterling and of the resulting balance-of-payments crises. Our understanding is still deficient but it seems likely that future scholars may effectively compare the post-1945 period to those following the Napoleonic and the first world wars by analysing the security factors which predominate at first but gradually wane in favour of economic priorities which, in turn, result in neglect of security.

It is by no means easy to determine the exact boundaries of foreign policy within the governmental machinery. At the beginning of the post-war period, 'imperial' and 'colonial' and then 'Commonwealth' policies constituted separate categories of departmental activities which fell somewhere between the domestic and the foreign spheres; with the emancipation of dependencies, they gradually became foreign policy proper. With the British entry into the EEC, many European, hitherto foreign, policies may become separated into a category as distinct as the imperial one used to be, or they may become domestic. Moreover, national interests in foreign policy are determined by, and must be understood in their relationship with the domestic areas of national life— we are concerned with problems of incompatibility and complementarity of objectives and with competition for resources. To take a few simple random examples: domestic economic growth depends upon inter- national economic policies; immigration closely relates to British relations with the Commonwealth and the EEC; social welfare competes for resources with defence.

The growing interconnection between defence and economic objectives and between foreign and domestic politics is a world-wide phenomenon but with the variety and complexity of her post-imperial commitments, her widespread commercial interests abroad and the sophistication of her domestic political system, Britain's foreign policy is one of the most complex—if not the most complex—of the foreign policies of all countries. This applies with special force to the immediate postwar period before her commitments had been reduced.

No attempt will be made here to force evidence into some sort of 'rational' mould based on the assumption that to meet all the postwar contingencies, the successive governments were pursuing a coherent policy (or policies) relating to a clearly defined national interest, with occasional 'irrational' disruptions arising from domestic politics and administrative problems. It should, nevertheless, be possible to discern a line of evolution over the whole period from 1945 to 1973, to trace a pattern or patterns. Such patterns, however, which may be compared to a helicopter pilot's view over a crowd, are but a gross simplification of complex reality; they explain little so long as we are ignorant of the details of individual moves. They do, however, enable us to arrange all the confused evidence more systematically, to find general correlations, and to prepare the ground for a fuller and more relevant historical analysis.

The search for such general patterns by a social scientist is by no means identical with a superficially similar search by a historian for historical generalizations. The former has to anticipate more complete historical evidence, whereas the latter generalizes only after such evidence has been collected. Each has his difficulties. A broad synoptic historical view of the contemporary scene is beset by the difficulties of sifting and assessing evidence; isolating a single element deemed to be sufficiently important as a foundation for a definite model for foreign policy inevitably over-simplifies reality.

International theory, which, ideally, should provide us with a suitable perspective, leaves us as remote from a theoretical 'seat in a helicopter' as is a physicist from the Archimedean point of support for holding up the Earth.[4] In recent years the theoreticians have become sufficiently aware of their shortcomings to abandon the search for a grand theory of foreign policy; this would have to be based upon such simplifications as to carry detachment from reality to the point of meaninglessness. The present trend is to concentrate upon the more readily comprehensible and measurable elements of foreign policy, to produce limited models suitable for limited comparison, and to aim for middle-term theories alone. One can doubt 'whether new methods of investigation really allow the political scientist of today to dispense with such traditional tools as impressionistic observation, historical analogy, and common sense judgment'.[5]

Politics cannot aspire to the precision of econometrics. The latter tries to show not simply that particular phenomena are the product of interacting variables, not merely that they interact as a system, but also the precise relationship between the individual variables distinguished. How can one hope to apply anything resembling an econometric model to the interaction, for instance, of the determining factors distinguished by Sir Charles Webster:[6] geography, history, economic development, and the moral and political outlook produced by these conditions? It would be futile to expect as concise and as pregnant a hypothesis about the conduct of foreign policy as about the maximization of profits in the economists' theory of the firm. The former is inevitably much more complex than the behaviour of the management of a firm; the definitions and the operational implications of 'security and prosperity', which are generally regarded as the supreme values pursued in foreign policy, cannot be as precise as those of profit. Well-tested economic techniques can be applied to politics only in the form of general analogies or metaphors. For instance, it may be worth while bearing in mind a notion of 'cost-effectiveness'—that foreign co-operation is advantageous only to the point at which the marginal return equals estimated marginal costs— in estimating the pros and cons of continuing the British alignment with the United States. Not only, however, can we find no reliable indices to be identified and quantified to enable us to make a precise calculation, but we have constantly to bear in mind that restricting Anglo–American co-operation can easily lead to the loss of other, non-marginal benefits with which we do not wish to dispense.

So far, at least, theoretical approaches have only helped to sharpen and systematize the appreciation of foreign policy, and have been useful for partial but not for overall explanation. Take for instance an obvious and reasonably plausible hypothesis that is frequently advanced: that the dominant strand of Britain's post-war foreign policy has been her 'special relationship' with the United States. Theory shows us how to measure systematically several indices, such as the flow of trade, of social communications, of exchanges of personnel; somewhat less precisely, the attitudes of the British public at large as well as of segments of the political elite; or how to subject official statements to analysis of content in order to elucidate official attitudes. We can obtain a fair variety of reasonably reliable measurements, trace fluctuations in attitudes and relations and, to some extent, correlate them with various other factors. Somewhat less convincingly, we can conceptualize the relationship as being—on the British side—based upon the idea of the role of a faithful or subordinate ally, or an ally-cum-mediator. These concepts are often interesting as they single out a major feature of the relationship and help us to focus all the evidence more sharply, but they are not necessarily helpful in relating the relationship to Britain's foreign policy as a whole. To conduct a large number of such investigations would not only be extremely costly and time-consuming but, unless they were all clearly related to some general conception of British foreign policy as a whole, they would not be very conducive to its elucidation. Understanding foreign policy in general terms has remained a matter of judgement rather than of measurement: measurement helps us with the detail, but not with the whole.

This study is not conceived as a direct contribution to theory and therefore does not aspire to scientific precision. Rather, it belongs to the 'pre-scientific' approach which aims at the greatest possible clarity of analytical categories but not at premature and probably unattainable 'scientific rigour'. If one wishes to avoid being taken very far from political reality when dealing with a broad subject, one can hardly hope to go very far beyond what Raymond Aron, in his monumental *Peace and War*, calls 'praxeology', an analytical description of reality.

Analyses of foreign policy generally organize all the relevant material into the four following major categories: (1) national capabilities (or power or resources); (2) the international environment (broadly, these two categories can be regarded as the 'reality' encompassing what is relevant for foreign policy at home and abroad); (3) the 'decision-makers'—their organization and frequently also their images of reality; (4) the political will and the determination of objectives. There is no full agreement about the exact delimitation and the exact significance of each category of factors. Most writers centre their discussion on the one category they deem the most important or the most amenable to analysis, and formulate their hypotheses and explanations on the basis of the factors operating within this category.

Britain's post-war foreign policy is frequently discussed in terms of a growing discrepancy between her relatively reduced capabilities and the widespread interests she developed in her 'imperial' past. It is plausible to argue that, with a natural time-lag, the makers of foreign policy have to achieve a degree of balance between the two; the analysis of the impact of Britain's reduced capabilities on the conduct of her foreign policy can be compared with that of the impact of Japan's increased capabilities on the conduct of hers. As it is difficult to adopt a determinist attitude in this matter, political will must be taken into account and is regarded by some as the central factor. Indeed, in the case of Britain, the weakening of political will may be regarded as the main factor determining not only her foreign policy but also her reduced economic strength. It is also possible to centre analysis upon the decision-makers' perceptions of the environment and their effect upon decisions. Each of these foci—capabilities, political will and perceptions—can serve as a reasonable basis for analysis and for partial, though not full, explanations. An attempt is made here to seek a broader basis which incorporates them all.

General hypotheses cannot be expected to supply the basis for a full explanation of a complex social phenomenon. All one can expect from a promising general hypothesis is that it should focus on a sufficiently central characteristic and that its acceptance should not outrage common sense; that it should not preclude refinements, modifications, and qualifications; and that it should be helpful to us in ordering the confused evidence and in asking interesting questions. In all likelihood, we shall never get much beyond my regrettably vague proposal that we regard foreign policy as a dynamic process of interaction between the changing domestic demands and supports and the changing external circumstances. Alternatively and similarly, we can conceive foreign policy as a process of adaptation to changing circumstances at home and abroad.

The starting-point of this analysis is that political processes cannot be directly explained by the underlying socio-economic forces, for these have to be perceived, assimilated, and responded to by the decision-makers. The political culture is the determining factor in how this is done. It is the ideas—the powerful simplifications—which shape social responses; these alter only slowly in the governmental endeavours to meet the major problems of daily life and to satisfy society's major interests. There is an unavoidable time-lag between the problems of the present and anyone's perception of them, a time-lag particularly acute when change is as rapid as that since 1945.

On this basis, the main governmental tasks in foreign policy can be subsumed under two analytical categories: (1) striking a balance between the domestic and the foreign aspects of governmental policies so that these policies are both acceptable at home and feasible abroad; (2) keeping within manageable proportions the time-lag in the adjustment of governmental perceptions of significant changes in the environment.

As the psychologists, social anthropologists, and creative writers have all independently noted, we tend to be governed by ideas fixed in our childhood and/or our tribal past. Hence the main theme of this study is here briefly stated in historical terms, inevitably in a very simplified form. Britain's postwar foreign policy is conceived as the final phase of a long-drawn-out process of adjustment to a position of gradually de-creasing power, which, in the main, consisted of the withdrawal from exposed positions in the world and of the acceptance of interdependence with Western Europe. The beginnings of the first process can be discerned in the gradual retreat from the Western Hemisphere in favour of the United States, culminating early in the present century in the abandon-ment of the British share in the Isthmus Canal and in the withdrawal of the Navy from the Caribbean. The Anglo-Japanese Treaty of 1902 repeated the process in the Far East; the granting of independence to India and Pakistan, the winding-up of the Empire in Africa and in the West Indies, and the withdrawal from east of Suez have nearly com-pleted it. Only a few post-imperial problems still persist and, apart from the intractable issue of Southern Rhodesia, none seems to be very serious.

The second process—that of accepting interdependence with Europe —has been somewhat shorter and less continuous. Already in 1904 Britain responded to her inability to carry on as a relatively detached and independent 'balancer' of the European system by entering the *entente cordiale*. Full involvement began only with the stationing of British troops on the Continent in 1945, first as occupation troops and then as a contribution to NATO; but, until 1954, Britain would not admit that this stationing was permanent and she refused to contemplate entry into the proposed European Defence Community. Commitment to the EEC was slow and, until 1970, not very far-reaching. With the British entry into the EEC, the process will reach its last phase.

The striking difference between this process of adjustment since 1945 and its antecedents lies in its tremendously increased speed and momentum. No other generation has had to accept such a change in scope, nor nearly as fast as we have; we have been forced to compress into one lifespan more adjustment than did several preceding generations put together.

One problem which arises acutely in any analytical study of this kind is how much and in what form historical material should be introduced. Although no attempt is made here to produce a general chronological narrative, several chapters, especially in Part II, include a fair amount of historical background. This is organized in a fairly uniform periodization into: (1) the period of post-war adjustments ending with the Conservative victory in 1951 when the alignment with the United States had been consolidated within NATO; (2) retraction from the world role in 1951–70, sub-divided, wherever appropriate, either by the first application to the EEC or by the Labour victory in 1964; (3) the decisive turn to Europe from the coming to power of the Heath government in 1970.

### The Impact of the International Environment
Although definitions of foreign policy and interpretations of the importance of its various elements greatly differ, both the writers and the practitioners generally agree that foreign policy is an essentially governmental activity which constitutes an interface between the domestic society and the international environment. It is conducted by what may be loosely called the 'foreign policy machine'.[7] The operation of this machine can be conceptualized in terms of systems analysis: on the one hand, it consists of reactions to 'inputs' from abroad and of activities performed abroad which can be regarded as 'outputs' and, on the other, it is also subject to 'inputs' at home where, in addition, it seeks 'supports'

for its activities. In real life the boundaries between the various elements are naturally much less sharp than in this scheme. Not only do domestic and foreign policies confusingly overlap but sometimes it is hard to distinguish clearly between the British policies and the international events that affect them; the state as an actor in world politics is readily confused with the stage itself. For instance, when we discuss Britain's relative loss of power, to what extent do we think about other states overtaking Britain or of Britain positively slipping back? When we analyse British relations with the Soviet Union we cannot meaningfully separate the British side from the relationship as a whole; British moves and actions are intelligible only as part of an interaction and cannot be analysed in isolation from it.

No attempt is made here to discuss all the relevant developments at home and abroad. Some of the major domestic themes are touched upon in chapters 2–4, and the way in which British policy-makers have perceived their country's place in the international system is further discussed in chapter 8. For the international events the reader must be referred to one of the many books on postwar history. This introduction merely aims at assessing in the most general terms the impact of the international environment upon Britain's foreign policy, and the links between domestic and foreign policies. The concluding chapter will consider how far the propositions advanced in this chapter are likely to remain valid in future.

The first and basic proposition is that the impact of the international environment has been exceptionally strong upon Britain. Foreign policy is of course in the main reactive, and even a leading power's conception of its vital national interests seems to be shaped more by the international environment than by domestic forces. This seems to have been true even of the postwar United States. In 1945 it was even more true of Britain, a country not only much less powerful and hence less capable of imposing her will upon others, but also more enmeshed in and dependent upon the international system. As one of the Big Three and as the greatest imperial power, she had as wide a range of interests and responsibilities as the two rising superpowers, in some respects an even wider one; she was also more dependent than other states on world trade.

Second, Britain's long-standing international involvement was accepted unquestioningly by Britain's policy-makers, who, as a matter of course, envisaged her place in the world in terms of her international responsibilities. In the field of economics she played a leading part with the United States in setting up the postwar international trade and financial systems and the Marshall Plan; and she maintained the parity of sterling at a heavy cost to her own economy. In the field of strategy, she took the primary responsibility for organizing the defences of Western Europe and, until 1967, acted as a policeman east of Suez; in Commonwealth affairs, she frequently tried to merge her individual national interests in broader and vaguer Commonwealth policies.

Third, Britain's capabilities were in no way commensurate with the responsibilities she assumed. Not only did she end the war economically exhausted but all the major postwar changes within the international system were working against her: the rise of the superpowers and the shift of the fulcrum of power from Europe; the rise of nationalism outside Europe which resulted in the rejection of imperial rule and in opposition to the exploitation of natural resources by industrialized states; a technological revolution affecting both weapons systems and civilian industry. Britain could not maintain her position alongside the superpowers, or her Empire or even any really meaningful Commonwealth adaptation, or her technological lead. She became fully dependent upon the United States for her defence while her economy, as graphically stated by R. A. Butler, was like the English weather, 'always exposed to changes in the world economic weather, which are, to a large extent, outside our control'.[8] Butler at the same time admitted how much he had been helped by favourable terms of trade during his four years as Chancellor.

Fourth, Britain's power was further weakened by what may be described as her 'eccentric' position within the international system. For some years after the war, her power position remained unique—well behind the two superpowers but well ahead of all others; her participation in the 'grand three circles' (see p. 157), meant that she could not be a really full member of any one of them; her international financial policy based upon the international role of sterling and her investment policy in the Commonwealth, many features of her industrial organization, even her non-metric system and the rule of the road set her apart from other states, especially from her continental neighbours. The divergence was accentuated by fundamentally opposed trends in her power position and in world developments. Although exhausted by the war, Britain started with a power position far ahead of all other states except the United States and the Soviet Union, in some significant respects right in the forefront of technology, with the prestige and psychological satisfactions of victory. Despite her own recovery she has been consistently losing ground not only to the superpowers but also to the several rising middle powers, notably Germany and France, Japan and China. During the postwar period many of the features of her 'eccentric' position which could be deemed sources of strength while her general position was relatively strong, tended increasingly to become elements of weakness as her position deteriorated in comparison with that of other states (see pp. 70ff.).

Finally, a number of converging factors helped to disguise Britain's weakness in 1945: the continuing, though initially reluctant United States military and economic support; the limitations of Soviet power while the Soviet Union lacked nuclear weapons and was preoccupied with her post-war economic and political reorganization; the weakness of the continental states and of China and Japan; the belief that the Empire and the Commonwealth would remain a substantial element of strength; the expectation that Britain would fully recover economically. Later on, right into the late 1960s, the close alignment with the United States and, to a much lesser extent and, although rapidly weakening, the British belief in the Commonwealth as an element of power continued to mask the erosion of her international position.

### The Interaction of Foreign Policy and Domestic Politics

Turning to the interaction between foreign policy and domestic politics, the first and basic proposition to be made is that a fair degree of continuity and congruence exists between the two, that there is a degree of consistency between internal and external political behaviour. One can usefully think about the domestic and the foreign aspects of governmental public policies. Nobody is likely to question the validity of such broad statements as: 'foreign policy consists of a society's attempt at realization on the international plane of what it conceives as good,'[9] or 'the national interest is to maintain, to the extent compatible with preservation of the existing social order, the independence and authority of the nation-state'.[10]

At the lowest level, this congruence can be regarded as the outcome of the common political culture from which stem all policy decisions, whether domestic or foreign, and of the repercussions of actions and outcomes in the one sphere upon the other; Britain's economic weakness undermined the basis of foreign policy and her loss of international power contributed to her economic weakness; successes and failures in the one field affected the national morale and contributed to similar outcomes in the other.

Marxist critics of the foreign-policy behaviour of Britain—as well as of other Western countries—attribute it to the capitalist nature of her society which is enmeshed within the international economic and imperialist systems. This not only greatly oversimplifies the roots of national behaviour but also assumes a complete continuity between domestic politics and foreign policy. It is to ward off such over-simplifications that the second proposition is advanced: although the same governments pursue national interests and formulate policies in both fields, they do so in somewhat different ways. First of all, the parameters of action differ. Limitation of resources acts as a constraint in both but, at home, the government normally has sufficient control over individuals and sub-groups to impose upon them some notion of a general good whereas, abroad, it often comes up against the conflicting and frequently insuperable wills of other states.

Most importantly, the basic objectives of foreign and domestic politics differ. Foreign policy centres on survival and defence. Many of its elements have, of course, an obvious bearing on domestic politics, defence policies and foreign trade, for instance, clearly affect domestic prosperity, but in each context these elements are considered from quite a different angle. Furthermore, whereas it is possible to cast serious doubts upon the existence of a common good in domestic politics, for instance, in the theory of bargaining among sub-groups, it is hard to deny the existential reality of a 'national interest' in foreign policy as this is so frequently invoked; although there is some dispute as to its real existence and certainly much argument about its actual content and substance. Finally, governments, having the monopoly of both diplomacy and defence, the central concerns of foreign policy, play a more exclusive part in its formulation than in domestic politics, where individuals and sub-groups carry more weight.

The third proposition advanced is that when domestic and foreign policy objectives clash, one cannot postulate in general terms which will prevail. If some writers assume that foreign policy is a dependent variable of domestic policy and of the domestic political system, or, *vice versa*, that the latter are the dependent variables of a foreign policy imposed by environmental pressures, they are guided either by a search for excessive methodological purity or by ideological convictions. In fact, the essential minimum in each field from which retreat is impossible is defined within the context of each single situation and not in general terms. Clearly, a government neglecting domestic needs and pressures is bound to lose the next election, whereas one neglecting international needs and pressures may jeopardize the very existence of the nation-state; this was Neville Chamberlain's dilemma over rearmament and appeasement. In the past, continental states, especially Germany, used to recognize necessity and, as a rule, accord primacy to foreign policy; whereas, in her relative isolation, Britain, like the United States, gave priority to domestic politics.

Since 1945 the picture is mixed. On the one hand, the 'necessity' encountered, or rather perceived, in the world environment seems to have been frequently dominant in British politics—thus heavy defence requirements took precedence over pressing domestic-consumption needs in the early postwar period, especially during the Korean crisis; to safeguard sterling, successive governments resorted to wasteful and socially detrimental periods of deflation resulting in the erratic 'stop-go' fluctuations; entry into the EEC was decided upon against a background of popular dislike. On the other hand, the successive governments sometimes found the 'necessity' of domestic pressures equally compelling. Some of these pressures were continuous, for instance, consistent incomes and industrial-relations policies, however economically essential, remained outside the reach of both the Labour and the Conservative governments which, in turn, attempted to introduce them in the 1960s and early 1970s. A specific instance can occasionally be identified: thus the final decision to withdraw from east of Suez in 1967 was partly occasioned by the necessity of making the proposed economies in social services acceptable to the rank and file of the Labour Party.

One can think of the eternally fluctuating domestic and foreign stresses more usefully in terms of the swing of a pendulum between domestic economic priorities and external strategic/political ones than in absolute terms. Such swings of the pendulum governed the alternation between the Whigs and the Tories under Queen Anne: concern with security would lead to military expenditures which eventually grew beyond what was politically acceptable at home and would bring the Whigs into power; the subsequent curtailment of expenditure would lead to military defeats and jeopardize the security of the country, bringing the Tories back. One can find a parallel with the economists' 'cobweb theorem' of the fluctuations in the prices of perishable agricultural commodities with a limited, local market: high prices lead to increased supplies which, in turn, lower prices; eventually lower prices result in shrinking supplies and in a consequent upward swing in prices; the circle then repeats itself.[11] In a somewhat less pronounced form, similar fluctuations can be discerned in British policies in the twentieth century: the colossal military efforts undertaken at a crippling cost during the two world wars were followed, after some lapse of time, by periods in which British governments concentrated upon domestic economics. This line of argument points to the contemporary danger of repeating the errors of excessive disarmament in the 1930s, although, of course, within the international environment today the British defence effort is no longer nearly as decisive.

Whereas the last proposition has been regrettably vague, the subsequent, subsidiary fourth proposition can be stated in the form of a more definite hypothesis: whenever domestic and foreign issues have competed, apart from acute emergencies in either field, postwar governments have tended to devote a large amount of time and energy to the consideration of foreign-policy issues, but to accord priority to domestic needs in the allocation of economic resources. This proposition allows us to explore in general terms one important aspect of the evolution of the concept of Britain's world role which is discussed in chapter 8.

Politicians and even academic writers on politics frequently do not fully realize the implications of the fact that the time and energy of policy-makers constitute a scarce resource. Only a few of the many issues facing the government can receive a thorough rational consideration; all other issues do not receive such consideration in full, and decisions about them are often left to officials to be taken as a matter of routine, or are not taken at all. Routine involves inertia and traditionalism but does not fully preclude change and innovation although, inevitably, the latter are rather slow (see pp. 20, 101).

The choices for consideration at the highest political level have to be governed, not by a clear, rational calculation of the importance of each issue but by what is sometimes termed its 'salience'. 'Salience' is a compound and not clearly defined notion; it can be regarded as roughly equivalent to the immediate, though not long-range importance of an issue but it can also be due to its prominence (through its news value, for instance), to its urgency, or to the intensity of feeling it engenders, none of which need coincide with the issue's intrinsic importance. With her widespread international responsibilities, Britain, after 1945, was in a particularly exposed position. A perusal of the memoirs of the successive prime ministers since 1945, and of the books about them, clearly shows how deeply involved each of them was in many of the foreign-policy issues of the time, some of which now appear to us much less important than the contemporary domestic issues. This was partly due to the urgency of events—best shown by the extreme case of Anguilla's unilateral declaration of independence in 1967–8, which, although bordering on comic opera, took an inordinate amount of the Cabinet's time. To some extent, however, it was due to the preferences of individual prime ministers.

Obviously, in modern times the Prime Minister cannot really concentrate upon much more than one principal issue at a time. Attlee left foreign policy to Bevin and concentrated upon the urgent domestic issues and also upon imperial and defence matters. The first postwar government managed to deal with all the issues on a broad front, but this was not true of its successors. Lord Butler, speaking of Churchill, says that 'the constructive part of his mind always dwelt more naturally on the international scene than on bread-and-butter politics'.[12] Churchill not only concentrated upon foreign affairs but, being justifiably obsessed with the gravity of the international situation in 1953, he determinedly stayed in power despite his advanced senility. Eden, with his life-long experience of foreign policy, was clearly much more interested in this than in domestic affairs.

Macmillan's memoirs are full of spectacular foreign-policy activities and only a small proportion of them deals with the mundane domestic matters. At the same time, he was probably more experienced and interested in the latter than any other postwar Conservative Prime Minister. His comments upon his failure in 1950 to insist in the Cabinet that Britain should take up the Pleven Plan is characteristic:

About Europe, regrets still haunt me. I was so fully occupied with my office [the Ministry of Housing in which he was very successful] which combined the conduct of complicated legislation with the largest administrative job I had ever undertaken, that although I wrote to Churchill to protest, I did not press the issue.[13]

Similarly, as Chancellor of the Exchequer, he was somewhat detached from the Suez expedition of 1956, in which he was merely engaged in working out the cost and assessing the likely American reaction. As Prime Minister, however, he concentrated too much upon such issues as Cyprus and the Congo, or attempts to mediate between the Americans and the Russians, while neglecting the more fundamentally important problems of Britain's economy, although it is hard to avoid the impression that sometimes he deliberately used foreign policy to distract public attention from domestic difficulties. Like Churchill he hankered to stay in office in order to achieve something lasting in foreign policy. In 1963 when he was wavering about retiring, he told Butler that his decision would depend 'on a diagnosis as to whether there is constructive work to be done with the President of the USA and the Kremlin in the field of foreign affairs'.[14]

Sir Alec Douglas-Home, with his expertise in foreign affairs but not in economics, was naturally inclined to take more interest in the former, but Harold Wilson too, with his entirely different expertise, frequently devoted to foreign policy what appears to be an excessive amount of energy, notably in his efforts to mediate on Vietnam; more purposefully, Edward Heath, in the first two years of his government, devoted his main efforts to taking Britain into the EEC, which naturally detracted from his and his Cabinet's attention to the urgent domestic problems of unemployment, economic stagnation, and industrial relations. All in all, although governmental preoccupations with foreign policy arose partly from Britain's position in world affairs, they were to no slight extent responsible for a relative neglect of domestic affairs and served as a smokescreen to obscure their poor state; they also helped to keep in office two Prime Ministers who were well past their prime.

The competition for resources between defence requirements and domestic needs can be conceptualized by the hypothesis that the growing democratization of British society leads to increasing electoral restraints upon governmental expenditures on defence. Governments have to take serious note of the people's preferences, which have come to centre more and more upon higher standards of living and more comprehensive social security. In electoral terms, the domestic demands are 'hard' whereas defence needs are 'soft', and governments are forced to give in to the former at the expense of the latter.[15] The hypothesis does not apply to the beginning of the period, when the people were passively continuing in many of their wartime deprivations and the government could, nevertheless, allocate a much greater proportion of national resources to defence than any other middle power, especially when it engaged in the extensive rearmament following the outbreak of the Korean conflict. It does fully apply, however, to the consumption-oriented society which 'never had it so good' in the 1960s. As domestic demands, especially wage claims, harden, the problem of finding adequate resources for rapidly growing defence needs is aggravated. Thus the hypothesis conceptualizes a major and growing domestic restraint upon the allocation of resources. Domestic consumption demands are, moreover, augmented by urgent needs for domestic investment, which is lower than among Britain's industrial rivals and which is indispensable to provide the required basis for the economic growth necessary both for consumption and for defence needs.

Two subsequent propositions are derived from the American school of 'linkage politics'.[16] Although in 1971 the author of the approach, Professor J. S. Rosenau, himself publicly admitted that his conceptualization had been inadequate as a whole, two points seem particularly relevant to Britain's foreign-policy issues. One is a commonsense and also commonplace proposition that the more a foreign-policy issue encompasses society's resources and relationships, the more it is drawn into the domestic system and the more important and difficult becomes the problem of securing a consensus. Britain has not had the equivalent of a Vietnam but the EEC issue showed some signs of creating such problems, because of the wide range of its domestic repercussions and its association in the minds of its left-wing opponents with what they regard as divisive economic policies at home, especially rising prices and the Industrial Relations Act.

The other proposition is that, like other middle powers, Britain has become a 'penetrated political system', i.e. one in which outsiders have become direct participants. As will be argued in chapter 8 this is true only to a limited extent as far as direct American participation is concerned. Although Britain's dependence upon the United States has been real and American views have had to be taken into account as an important consideration on all major policy issues, Britain acted against American wishes not only, at great cost, in the 1956 Suez intervention, but also, without incurring a penalty, on many other occasions. The proposition is, however, much more cogent when we broaden the concept to the loss of national autonomy caused by any factors, not necessarily the direct influence of other national governments. International economic forces, only partially identifiable in the concrete form of the officials of the IMF or the 'Group of Ten' or the vague 'gnomes of Zurich' played a decisive role in the formation of British economic policies (see chs 3 and 11).

# 2 The Political System

*Continuity and Change*

FOREIGN policy can be reasonably viewed as a dual process—the state responds to 'inputs' from the international environment by endeavouring to change the latter, and/or by adapting its national system. Hence the major aspects of British domestic affairs should be looked into both from the point of view of their impact on the conduct of foreign policy and also from that of the impact of foreign policy and external changes upon them. As both the international system itself and Britain's place in it have fundamentally changed since 1945, the problem of innovation and adaptation is central to this discussion.

All political systems exhibit a contradiction between the forces of continuity and those of change and can be meaningfully classified according to their position in this respect. Undoubtedly the British political system is heavily weighted in favour of continuity—the work of the Cabinet as a committee, departmental fragmentation, the two-party and parliamentary systems, the nature of the political elite—all favour conciliators and manipulators who search for consensus, rather than innovators. The skills acquired in its processes, whether within a party or within the House of Commons, are not particularly useful in the conduct of foreign policy, but continuity in foreign policy is nearly as great as in domestic politics. The British—or perhaps, more precisely, the English—conducted their foreign policies from an island base free from foreign invasions since 1066, as well as from a safe social base which, with the exception of the Celtic fringe, was undisturbed by revolutions or civil wars after 1746 and which was the first to undergo a thorough industrial revolution. The stability of the home base was matched and reinforced by the unique familiarity with the international environment acquired by British explorers, missionaries, traders and, ultimately, imperial administrators. By the twentieth century, not only had one-quarter of the globe fallen under British rule but the remainder was not unfamiliar either. The rebellious Thirteen Colonies had coalesced into a world power based on the same, or at least a very similar language and sharing many aspects of Britain's political culture. The conduct of diplomacy, international law, international institutions, all were shaped largely in the Anglo-Saxon mould.

The stability of the British system was ensured by a number of converging influences such as Britain's geographical position, her deference to tradition, firm patterns of political participation, and habits of collective consultation. Against this background of assured stability, both British society and the British political system managed to be flexible and showed a remarkable aptitude for evolutionary change. Ever since the industrial revolution, the system was adapting itself to the changing circumstances, admittedly with a long time-lag, but in quite a fundamental way. The important feature of this adaptation was its evolutionary, piecemeal character which was not disturbed by any major revolution. The results are neatly illustrated by Clement Attlee's characterization of Churchill: 'There was a layer of seventeenth century, a layer of eighteenth century, a layer of nineteenth century and possibly even a layer of twentieth century. You were never sure which layer would be uppermost.'[1]

The two world wars, especially the second, introduced major discontinuities into British politics. Since 1945 Britain has been subject to great strains in her endeavours to adapt her society and her political system to the needs of democratization and equalization and of industrial modernization at home, and, simultaneously, to adjust her foreign policy to a new, reduced power status. While all these demands for change dramatically converged, the need for stability and for national unity was particularly pronounced and remained the basic overriding objective both in Britain's domestic and foreign policies. Despite some rhetoric to the contrary, the search for stability and for political consensus has dominated the postwar period. It was certainly necessary to preserve them but, judging by some of the untoward results, the emphasis upon them may have been excessive and may have prevented the country from adapting itself sufficiently rapidly to the postwar changes.[2]

Consensus in a society, especially an advanced one, can never be complete and the corrective notion of democratic pluralism healthily counteracts it. Consensus can be defined as solidarity forged around common objects when members of a social group agree with one another about their attitude and relation to them. It is not the only form of solidarity and it raises serious moral issues arising from the symbolic and moral unity which it implies. Especially when the search for consensus is linked with a technocratic political style, it can readily lead to a ritualistic distortion of democratic forms.

In his recent book a severe but generally perceptive American critic of the British political system[3] aptly likened the changes in British politics to swings of the pendulum between two extremes—generally represented by the two main political parties—although occasionally politics moves to a different plateau, as happened after the Liberal reforms early this century or the Labour post-1945 reforms—and as has probably been happening since 1970. Continuity remains very high. The postwar Labour government did not introduce either a full-scale social revolution at home or a 'socialist' foreign policy, as both its ardent supporters and its opponents had expected. It did, however, introduce a welfare state and a degree of nationalization, and it granted India independence, even though Bevin's foreign policy significantly resembled what the Conservatives advocated. The Conservative successors did not go back on these policies. They symbolically stressed their difference by denationalizing steel, but they continued with the welfare state and the other nationalized industries, and with the emancipation of the Empire. Macmillan's concern with industrial relations and with a wages policy and his decision to enter the EEC were continued, although with different emphasis and after some hesitation, by Harold Wilson. By 1973, Edward Heath reverted to several Labour policies which he had previously repudiated.

The two parties represent different outlooks on life and pursue different priorities but, in domestic politics, they both basically accept the major objectives of economic growth and low levels of unemployment, the necessity of improving industrial relations, a degree of governmental control and planning, and a *limited* redistribution of wealth. They divide but do not fundamentally differ about implementation. In foreign policy, the two parties, at least their leaderships, generally accept the results of Britain's inability to influence decisively the international environment, to ensure her security and prosperity, and to protect herself against unwelcome foreign economic penetration. They accept permanent alliances, the possession of nuclear weapons, and the ending of the imperial role. For a while they both accepted the need for Britain's entry into the EEC. Major divisions often cut across the parties rather than between them: Bevin in his foreign policy and Wilson in his attempts to regulate labour relations enjoyed more sympathy among their political opponents than among their left-wing supporters; the Conservative moves in education under Butler and Boyle, or in emancipating African colonies, met with a similar fate.

Consensus and dissent about domestic and foreign policies did not invariably coincide. When the conflicts about the health service and the nationalization of steel were at their height, Bevin's foreign policy met no Conservative and only occasional left-wing opposition. Under the Conservative governments of the 1950s and early 1960s, the fundamental consensus about foreign and domestic policies was only sporadically disturbed; the limited divisions which existed for a short time over nuclear weapons, Suez, and the first application to the EEC did not run parallel with divisions on domestic matters and were overshadowed by the slow, gradual evolution of consensus concerning the diminishing value of the 'special relationship' and the downgrading of the importance of Commonwealth relations.

The basic consensus in British politics was not limited to generalities such as economic growth or peace and prosperity but extended to the methods of seeking them. The idea of moderation, of seeking a compromise, is central to British politics and forms the basis of the competition between the two parties, which vie in their search for the support of the moderate and fluctuating portion of the electorate. At the same time, however, in the British political system it is the business of the opposition to oppose, and the political life of the leaderships of the two parties would often have been easier if they could have truthfully persuaded the more extreme of their followers that there was more substance to the political divisions between the two parties.

As may well be expected, the British evolved a distinct national style of foreign policy engendered by the continuity of both their domestic policy and of their traditional international role. Inevitably, despite the rapid change in circumstances and the professed and (one may assume) genuine desire of the postwar Labour government to adjust policies accordingly, the hard residue of ingrained national habits and deep-seated attitudes continued to determine the conduct of British politics. The national style is thus described by Professor Waltz:[4]

To proceed by a sidling movement rather than to move directly toward an object, to underplay one's hand, to dampen conflicts and depreciate dangers, to balance parties against each other, to compromise rather than fight, to postpone decisions, to obscure issues rather than confront them, to move as it were by elision from one position of policy to another . . .
The movement of policy is customarily steady but slow; governments promote compromise and contrive adjustments between interests in conflict rather than meeting problems head on; ministers calculate carefully even the appearance of leading. Continuity of policy is impressive; coherence has often been confused with it.

This comment on the method and style of British politics, applying both to the domestic and the foreign spheres, helps to explain why it is so difficult to arrive at a clear understanding and appreciation of the actual degree of adaptation and change since 1945. The customary style of the political argument in Britain does not necessarily reflect, and even tends to disguise, actual political activities. In domestic politics political rhetoric was much more extreme than the actual changes. Under the impact of the war, the Attlee Government started with a programme of socialist revolution; a technological revolution and general change became popular in political argument at the end of the 1950s under the impact, one may surmise, of the unsatisfactory results of postwar policies both at home and abroad, brought to public notice by the Suez debacle, the Russian sputnik, slow economic growth and recurrent economic crises. At the same time, the traditional forces continued to operate and the rhetoric of change served to disguise its limitations and its slow pace.

The postwar social revolution did, indeed, introduce a non-selective welfare state and achieve a redistribution of income but the ownership of wealth remained concentrated in few hands—in 1954 1 per cent of the population still owned some 43 per cent of the total wealth—against 34 per cent of it in the United States; capital-gains tax was introduced only in 1965, death duties were often avoided, and a smaller percentage of GNP was taken in income tax in Britain than in Germany. Also the extent of the welfare services was rather restricted—the percentage of the budget spent on social services was high but expenditure on a per capita basis was not (and in comparison with other advanced countries is increasingly less). Harold Wilson's 'technological revolution' was only partially successful in revising the structure of management and failed to reform that of the trade unions and of industrial relations.

In foreign policy, the relation between political rhetoric and actual activities was the very reverse. While political argument continued in terms of Britain's world role, of the 'special relationship' with the United States, and of the leadership of the Commonwealth, actual policy was gradually changing in a fundamental manner. In the first postwar decade Britain abandoned her traditional autonomy in the conduct of her defence policy in favour of a permanent alliance and of the permanent stationing of British troops on the Continent; with the emancipation of the Indian subcontinent in 1945-7 and of Africa in the late 1950s, she gave up her imperial position; throughout the 1960s she was gradually adopting a predominantly regional, Western European orientation and she consummated this slow process by her entry into the EEC in January 1973. Ernest Bevin, Ian Macleod, or Edward Heath are likely to stand out as the great innovators in British foreign policy; even the great traditionalist supporter of Britain's world role, Harold Macmillan, will go down in history as the man who first decided that

Britain should join the EEC.

Actual policies were changing much more rapidly than Britain's national style of foreign policy, which remained consonant with British domestic politics and with the traditional conceptions of her world role. The reassessment and reform of the national habits and deep-seated attitudes which were involved were very slow. They were the subject of continuous arguments among the political elite but were not openly voiced until 1964[5] and consummated in the Duncan Report in 1969. The confused argument about 'renegotiating' the conditions of Britain's entry into the EEC which began in 1973 manifested the strength of the traditional outlook. Even after Britain's actual entry into the EEC the rhetorics of domestic and foreign policies did not become immediately congruent. One can expect that this will happen only with the passage of time when it becomes clear that the opportunities for compensating for domestic setbacks through diverting attention to foreign policy have now largely disappeared and when it becomes easier to weigh the necessary adjustments both of domestic and of foreign policy in a similar way.

The exceptional continuity, extension, and complexity of Britain's foreign policy as well as the traditional political style all stand in the way of a fundamental reconsideration, of a thorough innovation, not only in practice but even in academic thinking about the subject. This may be exemplified by the comparison between two papers on the social factors affecting the making of foreign policy in the recent volume edited by K. Kaiser and R. Morgan on *Britain and West Germany: Changing Societies and the Future of Foreign Policy* (1971). The British contributor, Philip Abrams, analyses social structure and social change, stressing 'the weight of the past' in Britain, whereas the German contributor, Wolf-Dieter Narr, formulates broad general hypotheses about Western Germany. In a way, these hypotheses can also be applied to Britain as well as to other countries, but whereas, within the German context, they are fully meaningful, within the British one they would be hard to apply to empirical material and would be largely academic. One can easily accept Dr Narr's basic hypothesis of a degree of congruity between domestic and foreign policies as being realistic in Britain. His subsequent hypotheses about the congruity between a democratic political system and a democratic foreign policy, the need for legitimacy, the misperceptions of reality and the tendency to preserve the *status quo*, all echo some perennial themes of the radicals in Britain which are discussed in the concluding section but can scarcely serve as a useful basis for analysing the actual policies.

*The Elite and the Consensus*

Though democracy has been established for a relatively long time in Britain, the gradual broadening of the political community to include the working class has only recently been completed. Britain's foreign policy has been traditionally elitist and still remains so. Foreign policy was the last prerogative of the Crown to be ceded to a minister responsible to Parliament. This happened only towards the end of the last century and foreign policy has remained ever since under the control of the Cabinet, with Parliament and the public taking more interest since the end of the first world war but unable to impose their wills. The formulation and execution of Britain's foreign policy is in the hands of a small group which can be called an elite, i.e. a social group defined by and performing a political function. The elite consists of the occupants of top positions within the political, diplomatic, bureaucratic, and military hierarchies, not all of whom, however, necessarily exercise their potential powers and seek to influence others. Besides the occupants of these official positions, there are three clearly identifiable sources of pressure: first, the foreign policy discussion and ginger groups within the parties, both in and outside Parliament; second, the editors, leader writers, columnists, and foreign correspondents of the so-called quality press, a category which can now be usefully extended to include television; and third, the Crown and its advisers, especially the Sovereign's private secretary.[6]

The concept of a British political 'elite' may, however, lay undue emphasis upon the occupants of formal positions. The realities of British political life are probably more faithfully portrayed by the term 'establishment' coined by Henry Fairlie of the *Spectator* in the 1960s, a term which stresses the informal aspects of power in British society as well as the influence these exercise upon its continuity. It denotes a group of powerful men who know each other or at least share each other's assumptions to the point of not needing to articulate them. They wield sufficient power outside the constitutional or political forms to preserve the *status quo*, to block unacceptable policies or the promotion of men whom they deem unreliable. It is a peculiarly English institution, self-recruiting, elitist, more integrated than its equivalent in any other country.

Inevitably our information about the specific roles played by the individual members of the elite in single policy issues since 1945 remains fragmentary, and generalizations about the changes which have undoubtedly taken place since then are bound to be somewhat impressionistic; various observers have plausibly noted such phenomena as the fragmentation of foreign policy among various ministries or the rise of the influence of television.

According to a critical but scholarly observer:

Today, as a hundred years ago, certain institutions, Parliament, Cabinet, the Civil Service, the Judiciary, the Armed Forces, Public Schools and Universities, shape the lives of ordinary people in varying degrees. Others such as landowner- ship, or the Established Church have lost much of their ancient influence and new centres of power have arisen: the Press, the entertainment industry and, above all, the boardrooms of private industry and of the public corporations.[7]

The mainstays of membership of the political elite are money, kinship, and the common educational background of public schools and of the ancient universities. Guttsman traces the decline of oligarchy from early Victorian times and the rise and persistence of the middle class. The remarkably slight class and party antagonism during the 1945–51 Labour government can be justifiably attributed to the large middle-class contin- gents on the Labour front bench, as well as to the reassuring experi- ences of the wartime coalition.[8]

The foreign-policy elite exhibits in a striking manner the character- istics of the general British political elite of which it is part and parcel. Perhaps a foreign commentator is best equipped to perceive and articu- late its intricate and largely informal character and its homogeneity.

They speak a very similar language of ideas, they read the same newspapers, they belong to the same narrow range of clubs, they have been members of the same or equivalent schools, universities and regiments. . . . While the various political, administrative and professional hierarchies are not uniformly and equally represented in this world, none is so much part of it by virtue of social origins and social formation as the Diplomatic Service.[9]

The Empire used to provide the common outlet for the non-conformists who had political ambitions, for the adventurous and ambitious who could aspire to become independent governors and generals. They did not need to disturb the political system at home which bred conformity both among the civil servants and the elected politicians.

Many critics of postwar Britain find fault with the excessive narrow- ness of the British political elite and with its resistance to change. Con- ceivably 'Britain's malaise . . . is . . . a malaise among the few thousand managers of our society who have failed to absorb and communicate new challenges and new ideas.'[10] Some critics concentrate upon the civil service as being largely 'Gladstonian' and on the ritualized national dia- logue based upon traditional moral and intellectual stereotypes. Others pin the blame upon the excessive influence of the City, which has both siphoned off an excessive amount of talent and exercised a conservative influence upon industry.[11] All critics agree that the system curbs innovation by effectively stifling any fundamental criticism. Even so distinguished a civil servant as Lord Strang agrees[12] that the officials are trained for obedience and self-abnegation, which are necessary for the fulfilment of their main duty: that 'public business is expeditiously done'. The pressures of official life are such that, to 'the stronger spirits', the dichotomy between their own views and those of their superiors which they must present and defend, occasionally becomes intolerable; some of them have, indeed, been leaving the service for this reason. The 'weaker spirits' may eventually end with scarcely any views of their own.

The operational strength of this homogeneous and firmly organized bureaucracy provide Britain with an admirable tool for the execution of foreign policy. Its effectiveness is best shown by de Gaulle's description of the concerted assault made by the wartime administration, and quoted with approval by Lord Strang:[13]

To resist the British machine, when it set itself in motion to impose something, was a severe test. Without having experienced it oneself, it is impossible to imagine what a concentration of effort, what a variety of procedures, what insistence, by turns gracious, pressing and threatening, the English are capable of deploying in order to obtain satisfaction. . . . Everyone around us got to work on it, in all ways, at all levels. There were official conversations or informal ones, in which those in the most diverse positions invoked friendship, interest or fear, according to the occasion.

Therefore the American models of 'bureaucratic politics' developed by Professors Allison and Neustadt[14] generally do not apply to British politics. Here co-ordination, although rather informal, is the pattern, and major policy issues are much less frequently affected by a tug-of-war between competing institutions, as in the United States. To take the two major cases of failure since 1945, the Suez action was a non-bureaucratic decision taken politically, against official advice, whereas the prolonged neglect of the Western European integration movement until the end of the 1950s was based upon general bureaucratic agreement.

Bureaucratic efficiency is a great asset and there is a degree of exaggeration in the criticisms advanced that it cramps original thinking by the officials and hence loses the country an important source of innovation. For instance, the officials were slow to become converted to the idea of joining European integration, but realized the need of it before their political leaders; Bevin was greatly helped by his officials in conducting a vigorous foreign policy, admittedly one based on official advice. It is hard to judge whether and, if so, how far and how long, bureaucratic inertia blocked vigorous foreign-policy initiatives imposed from above; probably some of the thwarted initiatives were simply not vigorous enough. The situation is likely to differ significantly from case to case and generalizations would be fruitless.

The relative dearth of innovatory thinking can be traced to a more general central feature of the British political system—the habit of working through committees. The whole governmental structure is based upon a network of committees where consensus and compromise are reached; and a unified governmental policy is determined in a hierarchy of committees, from the Cabinet downwards. They are an excellent democratic expedient for avoiding the excesses of uncontrolled government. They provide also some safeguard against precipitate and potentially disastrous decisions. It is important to note that the major questionable decisions of British foreign policy over the last fifty years all occurred when the Cabinet's attention was engaged too late and its comprehension of the issues at stake was impeded: Chanak, the near-breakdown of relations with the United States in 1927–8, the Hoare-Laval Plan, Munich, the Palestine decision in 1947, Suez in 1956.[15] As it is now increasingly imperative to check foreign-policy decisions against probable domestic repercussions, foreign policy has become more clearly a collective Cabinet responsibility, which is dealt with by a firmly established machinery. It is unthinkable that the pattern of bypassing the Foreign Office and the Cabinet employed by Lloyd George or Chamberlain or, in 1956, by Eden could be repeated. This, however, means frequent ambiguity, evasion, and postponement of decisions. A striking, although perhaps exceptionally pronounced, example is the Labour Cabinet's decision to apply for membership of the EEC in 1967 which meant quite different things to individual ministers, as was clearly divulged during the acrimonious debate which broke out among them in 1971, when Labour's attitude to the EEC was being redefined.

Consensus constitutes an attainable political ideal owing to the great central powers of the Cabinet, within which the major political struggles can be conducted in decent secrecy so that solidarity and form are not compromised. This feature of the British system strongly contrasts with the diffuse American system. To an American, the Cabinet combines the powers of the President with those of Congress along with those of the heads of federal agencies, state governors, and legislatures, mayors of the large cities and even the Supreme Court.[16] Hence, at Cabinet level, the necessity to compromise is extremely high and it is therefore very difficult to change course and to innovate. Harold Wilson's constant concern with not being left in a minority on any foreseeable Cabinet issue[17] is an extreme example of the search for compromise by a Prime Minister in a rather weak position. Others, in stronger positions, still prefer to avoid the disturbance of resignations or Cabinet reshuffles.

Consensus is the ideal, and also generally represents the operational reality within the civil service. Wilson's early attempt to introduce 'creative tension' into the administration of economic affairs by establishing the Department of Economic Affairs as a dynamic counterpart to the conservative Treasury was unsuccessful. Diplomatic memoirs and diplomats still in the service are in fair agreement that, although occasionally differences of opinion arise, in most cases an Office view evolves on major policy issues to which all or nearly all the officials eventually subscribe; a similar consensus seems to have obtained in the Treasury on such major issues as the defence of sterling or the appropriate restrictive measures to combat inflation. Dissidents would be ineffective and, if serious, could scarcely continue in service for any length of time.

For really vigorous political leadership there is little incentive, because conspicuous vigour in office does not pay electorally. As Field-Marshal Montgomery perceptively noted,[18] 'The British people will never follow a dominant personality, or leader, unless they are frightened; at other times they are frightened about where he may lead them. Winston Churchill is a good example.' Against the background of the common political culture of the elite from which the top leaders are recruited and of the committee system it seldom matters very much who reaches the very top, except when the personality is as outstanding as Churchill or perhaps as weak as Eden. The political system tends to bring to the top only people who have been through a prolonged and grinding parliamentary and then front-bench apprenticeship. Their success within the domestic political system, whether within their own party or Parliament, or in elections, is based on conciliatory skills rather than decisiveness. Moreover, they tend to come to power when they are old and usually tired, which not only hampers their own performance but also blocks the advancement of their hopeful successors. The most pronounced example was Churchill during the 1950s, whose illness and senility have been vividly portrayed by his physician, Lord Moran. Churchill resigned only in April 1955 at the age of eighty, after having thoroughly frustrated his heir-apparent, Anthony Eden.

Gradually, however, the consolidated establishment has somewhat weakened. The division lines between the classes have been blurred and skilled and scientific workers have attained incomes and status well above those of the lower middle class, although the slowing down and the temporary halting of economic growth has interrupted this process; the leadership of some major trade unions has become radicalized; the Celtic fringe has become restive; largely owing to international influences, the younger generation has rebelled against conformity. Writers analysing the changes in the composition of the political elite in postwar Britain, such as Rose, Guttsman, or Sampson, note that the historical tradition of a tight integration of the patterns of authority and of close ties between status, wealth, and political leadership, may be disappearing. Although the exercise of political power remains highly centralized, smaller groups have been forming parallel and only partly overlapping elites in industry and finance. No single integrated power elite exists in postwar Britain. On the contrary, possibly the greatest danger lies not in the 'establishment' being too close but in its not being sufficiently integrated as its segments do not seem to communicate freely enough.

The political leaders in the later 1960s, Wilson and Heath, came to office some ten years younger than the average of their predecessors, and introduced new, potentially innovatory elements based upon an efficient, managerial approach to the problems of government. It is, however, rather doubtful whether the forces of continuity have not prevailed. As Lord Wigg bitingly but tellingly comments in his memoirs, and as Wilson's own memoirs confirm, particularly in the period of his slender parliamentary majority of four, Wilson proved to be a master of indecision; his habit of constantly consulting his associates, and his disinclination to arrive at a decision ahead of them, did not equip him to concentrate upon long-term strategies and planning. In his diametrically opposed personal style, Heath banned the word 'consensus' from his political vocabulary and ruthlessly introduced a series of determined policies on social services, industrial relations, aid to industry, and, particularly, a British entry into the EEC, all of which, as the opposition rightly claimed, were 'divisive'. Although mounting economic and social difficulties compelled him to reverse some of his domestic policies, he sufficiently antagonized the working class to enable—or rather allow—Wilson to dissociate himself from several major policies which his Labour government had reluctantly adopted—notably with regard to industrial relations and entry into Europe. The inter-party consensus of the immediate postwar period and of 'Butskellism' became a matter of the past. The Labour programme announced on 6 July 1972 showed accordingly a pronounced swing towards egalitarianism. The 1973 programme returned to the divisive theme of nationalization.

The continuity of the political consensus theme reflects the complexity of an advanced industrial society, the continuation of which depends upon the co-operation of all major sectors. As Heath returned to the idea of consensus in the middle of his term of government in order to secure the co-operation of the trade unions, a Labour successor is likely to return to it to secure the co-operation of the employers. The real question is whether the social system has not become excessively polarized.

## The Political Party System

For all practical purposes, the British political party system consists of two large parties, each of which commands the support of roughly half the electorate. The small Liberal Party has not managed to achieve the political comeback which at one time seemed possible and has merely injected some ideas into the political debates, notably its early support for Britain joining the Western European integration movement. Not being constrained by the customary lines of thinking about British foreign policy by which all the main spokesmen abide in order to appear to be responsible, Liberal spokesmen can occasionally be more outspoken. For instance Lord Gladwyn recalls the adverse, nearly incredulous reaction of both Conservative and Labour politicians to his first speech as a Liberal Peer on 9 April 1965, in which he advocated the complete reversal of British policy east of Suez and an evacuation as soon as possible of all the bases in the area.[19]

There is no radical party with any sizeable following or standing. The electorate are unwilling to accept the exaggerated appraisals and over-simplified solutions of the fringe but they are generally tolerant of them and could be receptive to any appealing new ideas advanced; the temporary success of the Campaign for Nuclear Disarmament is a clear indication.[20]

The party system is geared to domestic politics and foreign policy plays only a minor role in its operation. Characteristically, the two major analyses of the system by Robert Mackenzie and Samuel Beer[21] do not discuss foreign policy or even refer to it in the index. Much of the debate on foreign-policy issues takes place within each party, and it is therefore easy to be misled about its importance in party life. For instance, two American scholars, Robert T. Holt and John E. Turner[22] draw attention to the repeated schisms in the two parties which have resulted in MPs defying the whip. Their conclusion is that foreign-policy issues rock the party system. This is true, but only in a very superficial sense. The parties are, occasionally, disturbed, but the fact that they can tolerate dissent and, indeed, defiance of the whips indicates that the disturbances on foreign issues do not affect their fundamentals and are insufficiently central to their main purposes to exclude the dissenters. The most serious of these rebellions on foreign-policy issues occurred in 1971–2 within the Labour Party. Wilson's tactics in handling the pro-marketeers were based upon his determination to preserve party unity; even if a small proportion of the pro-marketeers been constrained to leave it, they would have ruined its electoral prospects possibly well beyond the next election. Wilson was justified in repeatedly referring to the division over the EEC as serious but temporary. He endeavoured to convince the whole party that the issue should not distract it from the major social and economic objectives on which it was united. If a similarly strong division developed over a central domestic issue, e.g. social services, or industrial relations, or nationalization, it is very doubtful whether persistent dissent within the party could be tolerated.

On the face of it, the British political system carries the risk of discontinuity in foreign policy caused by changes of government. No constitutional conventions exist for consultation between government and opposition; and, in order not to be tied down in its criticisms, the latter generally refuses consultation when offered, except in extreme national emergency. Its spokesmen have full access to the general information in the Foreign Office, but not to the telegrams or to defence costings; moreover, they have not the benefit of the analysis and discussion of the options available prepared by the civil servants. Both parties lack adequate research staff to make up for this deficiency although to some extent the gap has now been filled by improved non-official analysis, especially of defence matters in the Institute of Strategic Studies. The advantages of the opposition are that it has more time for reflection, and therefore is able to pursue longer time-perspectives than the party in office; this is strongly counterbalanced by its lack of responsibility for action and implementation, which breeds a certain air of unreality and makes it receptive to the extremist pressures within the party.

According to Henry Kissinger, major executive foreign-policy decisions in the United States are often taken on a margin of not more than 65 to 35, the Cuban missiles crisis was a case of this uncertainty; one may safely assume that in Britain's straitened circumstances after the war the margin was much higher and that some major decisions seemed nearly inevitable. Moreover, even when fairly even choices were available, the methods of seeking a solution within the Foreign Office and of attaining governmental consensus were identical. When the Labour Party was in opposition, its annual conferences frequently indulged in advocating radical changes on several foreign-policy issues and the leadership often complied, but utopian criticisms soon disappeared once the party had come to power. Not only did the leaderships and majorities of the two main parties appraise Britain's major national interests in fundamentally similar terms, they also held similar views on maintaining her world role. Whichever party had been in power, the general trends of her postwar policy would probably not have been appreciably different; the difference might have lain in the timing of important decisions.

In the urgent postwar tasks, foreign policy was genuinely bipartisan. As has been recorded by his son,[23] the Foreign Secretary's Principal Private Secretary, Pierson Dixon, maintained the closest possible liaison with the shadow Foreign Secretary, Anthony Eden, both apprising him of governmental moves and passing on his views to Bevin. Although much less intimate, co-operation between the two parties remained close on major policy issues in spite of the violent controversies which arose over specific issues such as Katanga, Southern Rhodesia, or the sale of arms to South Africa. The first real division came in 1972 over joining the EEC, but in this case a substantial minority within the Labour Party supported the Conservative government.

Foreign-policy issues have not played an important part in any of the postwar elections, because they have little appeal for the electorate and also because, when they are important, they tend to cut confusingly across both parties. Entry into the EEC is a striking example of this. A difference in the electoral programme on a foreign-policy issue could hardly have affected the evenly balanced electoral contests in 1950 and 1970, when the Conservatives obtained majorities of 17 and 29, or even the Labour majority of 4 in 1964.

Many critics have been struck by a degree of unreality in Britain's postwar political system—the political games and the divisions between the parties became increasingly remote from the fundamental political and economic issues and the feelings of the people; this unreality inescapably extended to the conduct of foreign policy. Hopes were stirred and expectations were aroused on several occasions that the system would be rejuvenated, but every time in vain: when Macmillan included in his government in 1958 a socially more broadly based group of young ministers, or the first Liberal revival, or popular movements like the Campaign for Nuclear Disarmament, or by the rise to leadership of Wilson and Heath, men two generations younger than Churchill and Attlee, or by Wilson's 1963 programme of change. The dynamic action of Wilson's 'first hundred days' in power, based on the Kennedy pattern, soon collapsed; one shrewd observer commented: 'With every week that passes, Mr Harold Wilson reminds one more and more of Mr Harold Macmillan in his last phase. The same reluctance to admit that a mistake has been made, the same forced unconcern'.[24] In 1966 Wilson fought an electoral campaign based on the broad lines of the Conservative foreign policies which he had attacked in 1964: the H-bomb, the pound, the commitments east of Suez; in 1967 he decided to steal their potential electoral asset by renewing the application to the EEC.

Since the Conservative victory in 1970, the system has not changed and the same major domestic problems have recurred in an aggravated form. After some eighteen months in office, Heath had to bow to intractable economic and social forces and to abandon many of his domestic policies, often returning to Labour expedients. On the other hand the changes in Britain's international position have probably made a decisive impact upon her foreign policy, which is now realistically based upon the diminution of her status, upon the acceptance of weakened American and Commonwealth ties, and upon alignment with Europe. Even if the issue of renegotiating the conditions of Britain's entry into the EEC remains firmly enmeshed in inter-party strife and becomes an electoral issue, the outcome is unlikely substantially to alter this new, more realistic basis.

Common concern with the national interest, and the subordinate place of foreign-policy issues in the national political system have thus ensured a high degree of continuity in British foreign policy since 1945; this continuity can be regarded as the extension of the basic consensus sought in domestic affairs. But although both parties can be regarded essentially as combinations aimed at winning elections, whose electoral appeals and programmes are bound to converge, these programmes and subsequent policies sometimes stem from quite different considerations, attitudes, and ideologies. For instance, the Labour Party did not significantly diverge, as many of its followers as well as opponents had expected, from the Conservative attachment to the national symbols of world status, especially the Empire and military strength, or from the traditional appraisal of national interests; nevertheless, their motivations were different. One would expect such attachment in the Conservative Party, which includes many members of a higher social status; one may presume, although scarcely measure, that the many Conservative supporters connected with high military and diplomatic personnel would be particularly reluctant to admit to a lower international status.[25] The Labour leadership, by contrast, was electorally vulnerable to the accusation that their party neglects Britain's defences and was determined to prove its responsible attitude on the issue; a similar argument can be applied to the defence of sterling. A constructive role in the new Commonwealth, in order to expiate the sins of the imperialist generations, was the main motivation of the fundamentalist Labour adherents to the Commonwealth idea, while the Conservatives were more interested in maintaining imperial leadership and economic interests.

Both parties include extremist elements, radical left-wing in the Labour Party and right-wing in the Conservative Party, which represent their divergent ideologies. So long as British politics operated on the basis of a fundamental consensus in domestic affairs, the differences on foreign policy supported by the dissenting extremes rarely assumed a decisive importance. Within the Conservative Party, the Monday Club/Suez Group strongly influenced Middle Eastern policy in the 1950s, and provided the backcloth for the Suez intervention in 1956. On African issues, right-wing influence was unable to prevail against the emancipation of colonies, but played an important part in determining British stands on Katanga, Southern Rhodesia, and South Africa. On Commonwealth immigration and Ulster it also had to be reckoned with. Some right-wingers remain adamantly opposed to membership of the EEC. Sir Alec Douglas-Home, when Commonwealth Secretary and Foreign Secretary, was concerned with the communist threat and tried to shape policies towards South Africa and Southern Rhodesia which the right-wingers favour; neither policy, however, is of central importance.

Dissent in the Labour Party is potentially much more serious. First, the party is ideologically opposed to traditional foreign policy, as Clement Attlee stated in his prewar book:

There is a deep difference of opinion between the Labour Party and the Capitalist parties on foreign as well as home policy, because the two cannot be separated. The foreign policy of a Government is the reflection of its internal policy. . . . It is . . . stupid to suggest as some people do, that a general guide to international politics is to oppose everything that the British Capitalist Government does, but such particular instances of action which can be approved by Socialists do not affect the truth of the general proposition that there is no agreement between a Labour Opposition and a Capitalist Government.[26]

Second, the party constitution allows the dissenters to organize themselves with fair ease and to voice their views at the annual party conferences, the decisions of which need not, admittedly, be accepted by the Parliamentary Party as binding but which constitute an important constraint on the latter.

The four traditional principles of a 'socialist' foreign policy distinguished by Michael Gordon in *Conflict and Consensus in Labour's Foreign Policy* (1967)—internationalism, pacifism, anti-capitalism, and international class solidarity—are mere expressions of aspirations and of certain attitudes rather than a ready basis for an operational foreign policy. The Labour Party has been reiterating its belief in the desirability of such a 'socialist' foreign policy ever since the end of the first world war. The postwar Labour government departed from its programme of seeking close collaboration with the Soviet Union and working through the United Nations, both of which aims proved extremely difficult if not impossible, but Bevin had to use his great personal influence, especially in the trade union movement, to keep the left-wing critics in check. The government violated but did not fully reverse or replace the party's traditional 'socialist' principles. Opposition within the party to the American alignment abated after the Marshall Plan but was strongly revived when the party found itself again in opposition. This led to a new split between the leadership and its radical critics when, in 1953, the annual conference passed a long composite resolution accepting the need for continuing close co-operation with the Americans but simultaneously urging a number of policies scarcely one of which corresponds with those of the United States; the following year the conference carried a resolution against German rearmament with a crushing majority of 6,292,000 to 248,000 votes.

Labour divisions on foreign policy resemble those between the 'fundamentalists' and the 'revisionists' on domestic policy.[27] In fact, the 'revisionists' did not really reject 'socialist' aspirations but merely advocated the rejection of utopianism in their application. As the 'revisionists' argued at the 1954 annual conference, all agreed in disliking the idea of German rearmament; the difference was about the policy to be adopted. While the 'fundamentalists' merely reiterated their aspirations without being able to make realistic policy suggestions, the 'revisionists' preferred to accept pragmatically what appeared to be a necessity and to concentrate upon seeking suitable safeguards. It was therefore relatively easy for the 1958 annual conference to return to the unifying generalizations about the United Nations as a keystone of British foreign policy, the rule of law, and the ending of the arms race.[28]

For a number of reasons the situation in the early 1970s was different. By a deliberate policy decision Heath disrupted the long tradition of a basic national consensus, and Labour opposition on such fundamental domestic issues as industrial relations, prices, and unemployment became inextricably connected with opposition to entry into the EEC. Moreover, left-wing influence over the Labour party greatly increased, owing largely to the radicalization of the leadership of several major trade unions which had been the mainstay of Bevin's moderate, revisionist foreign policy. Although Wilson had been trying hard to preserve the unity and the electoral appeal of his party by mitigating the division over the EEC, if the basic split between the Conservative and the Labour Party persists on domestic issues, it could extend to the fundamental issue of British membership of the EEC. After two prolonged postwar spells in power the Labour Party had, however, firmly become a party of government concerned with its electoral chances and with its responsibilities on assuming office. Its disagreement even on a major foreign-policy issue such as membership of the EEC did not mean that it advocates a really radical foreign policy, dissenting, in A. J. P. Taylor's definition,[29] from the general assumptions and repudiating the aims, methods, and principles of traditional foreign policy.

The four vague traditional principles of Labour foreign policy had been too often set aside since 1945 to remain operationally very meaningful. As an expression of an aspiration maintained, they still retained a certain validity but it seemed likely that they had receded to the limbo of other once radical but now no more than mildly liberal ideas, such as Cobden's harmony of interests and opposition to interventions, Gladstone's bringing to bear of morality, E.D.Morel's ideas of democratic control of foreign policy. Although for a short time the CND sparked off a radical moral fervour, the postwar period proved to be poor soil for encouraging real radicalism in British foreign policy—the United Nations never had the appeal of the League of Nations, the reaction to the Vietnam War did not at all compare with that to the Spanish Civil War. This may be partly because the British had realized their growing powerlessness to exercise a decisive influence upon international affairs. Partly, however, it reflects a similar abatement of radical criticism of domestic affairs: the 'Angry Young Men' offered a very poor substitute for George Orwell's dedicated fervour in combating the 'smelly little orthodoxies' of English life. The tighter party structure and the absence of a challenge equivalent to that of Vietnam in the United States make it unthinkable that anti-establishment discontent in Britain could gather sufficient momentum to bring to power within one of the parties a leadership committed to a really radical reform, especially as a radical change in British foreign policy would have a seriously destabilizing effect upon the security of Western Europe.

All in all, the two-party political system admirably served the purpose of providing competing teams for elections, and a firm basis for continuity of policy. Neither party proved doctrinaire in its policies; in fact, one may argue that, yielding to what appeared to them imperative, each helped to prepare the ground for the electoral victory of the other: Wilson's abolition of controls in 1950 at the Board of Trade logically paved the way for a Conservative electoral victory 'to set the people free'; Selwyn Lloyd's first experiments with indicative planning and pay-and-prices policy prepared the country for the return of Labour in 1964; a similar turnabout of the Heath Government in 1972 may do the same for a future Labour victory. In a way this may be regarded as the best way to serve the national interest—each party being ready to take over when the situation indicates governmental policies closer to its general ideology. In another way it entrenches orthodoxy and eliminates the possibility of real change. Probably 'a country as stodgy as Britain needs an alternative lefter-wing government with a credible and meaningful policy'.[30]

This the Labour Party never provided. It oscillated between ultra-orthodoxy and adventurous leftism; its New Left in the 1970s included various shades of neo-authoritarianism and of left-wing dictatorships abroad. The undemocratic Left united only negatively, in its sharp opposition to the libertarian society with a mixed economy which had developed in the postwar years. In the past, the lack of meaningful alternative domestic policies at home was matched by a parallel lack of real alternatives in foreign policy. At the time of writing, the issue of 're-negotiating' the terms of Britain's entry into the EEC does not appear to be any more real. While attempting to profit by a real public disgruntlement with the British economy and with the immediate results of Britain's entry in 1973, it may not in practice prove to be more than a change of emphasis on the Conservative policies within the EEC.

*Public Opinion*
Appraisals of the impact of public opinion upon the conduct of British foreign policy fall between two extremes. On the one hand, on an analogy with Walter Lippman's analysis of the situation in the United States, public opinion in Britain can be regarded as an important, occasionally decisive restraint, notably in the opposition to rearmament during the 1930s; even if less influential than in the United States, it is clearly more important than, say, in France. On the other hand, one may take the view that British foreign policy is elitist and uncontrolled by public opinion, that the strictures of E. D. Morel and the Union for Democratic Control are still fully valid. Should the pursuit of foreign-policy objectives, which depend largely upon the actions of other states, be left unhampered in the hands of the rulers, or should we be more concerned lest these rulers may determine national interests in terms different from those desired by the people? This is not merely a theoretical problem of the nature and implications of democracy or of evaluating the historical record. It is, for instance, obviously relevant to British entry into the EEC that public opinion played a relatively minor role in the debate on this is characteristic of our confusion about it.

In a political system in which the government of the day faces an election never more than five years ahead, public opinion is obviously a factor. Apart from this practical consideration, many individual politicians are genuinely concerned to operate the system as democratically as possible and to respect public opinion. Nevertheless, Kenneth Younger remarks, apropos of his own experience as Minister of State in the Foreign Office; 'I was somewhat shocked to find out that I could not immediately recollect any occasion when I or my superiors had been greatly affected by public opinion in reaching important decisions.'[31] There is no indication that the verdict of any other politician would be different. 'Vertical' communication with the public appears to be of little importance in the actual conduct of foreign policy when compared with 'horizontal' communication with various expert and interest groups. A good proof is found in foreign policy remaining 'the forgotten issue' in national elections. In 1970, only 38 per cent of the Conservative and 23 per cent of the Labour electoral addresses referred to entry into the EEC. Other foreign-policy areas were mentioned even less—the United Nations by 2 per cent of the Conservative and 18 per cent of the Labour addresses, foreign aid by 5 and 20 per cent respectively.

Studies of public opinion surveyed by Philip Abrams[32] conclusively prove that in the postwar period foreign policy has been an area of low and diminishing salience in British politics. In the election years 1945, 1950, and 1955, 30–40 per cent of the electorate regarded foreign-policy issues as important; in 1959 only 20 per cent expressed themselves as being 'especially concerned' about them; by 1964 the proportion attributing importance to any specific issue of foreign policy sank to 13 per cent, and by the end of 1968, to a mere 2 per cent; up to 23 per cent, however, regarded the general problem of 'raising Britain's standing in the world' among the three most important issues facing the government, admittedly giving it only seventh place among their priorities.

One reason for this phenomenon is a rising concern with domestic problems, another, Britain's diminishing capability to influence the external world. The public cannot see how participation in politics will help to solve the problems which affect them personally—hence the spread of political apathy since the war. This feeling of powerlessness and frustration, this acceptance that decisions must be left to the governors, is particularly pronounced in foreign-affairs matters. A public-opinion poll in October 1971 showed that at that time 50 per cent of the sample opposed the entry into the EEC against 34 per cent who supported it but no fewer than 83 per cent thought that Britain would enter whereas only 7 per cent thought that she would not.[33]

Peter Calvocoressi has developed the view frequently voiced that a poor news service is a major reason for public apathy.[34] Public interest is stimulated erratically and tends to become ill-tempered, as governments, not unnaturally, refuse to take a primary interest in the issues which happen to be taken up by the public. The complementary and more fundamental reason is that, on the whole, foreign-policy issues are neither interesting nor readily intelligible to the general public, whose interests and capacity for understanding are limited to issues directly affecting their daily lives. No external event or foreign-policy move has had serious and lasting domestic repercussions in Britain, with the sole exception of the Suez action.

On the government side, there has been little attempt to instruct and influence public opinion. Although the policy-makers and their opponents do not necessarily articulate this practice even to themselves, it is plausible to assume that it is convenient for them that the public remains ignorant and uninterested. Injecting foreign policy into the complexities of domestic politics would not only seriously hamper the pursuit of national interests; it would also greatly complicate the issues of seeking consensus and the operation of the rules of the game of competition for power between the two parties. Governmental caution is particularly clear in the handling ever since 1960 of the British entry into the EEC. Macmillan was fully aware of the uncertainty engendered by his application within his own party and the possible harm to his electoral prospects; he therefore tried to present Britain's entry in a decidedly low key, as a relatively technical issue. In 1971 and 1972, when the fundamental political importance of the entry had become apparent, the fact that the divisions between the pro- and the anti-marketeers ran across both parties blurred public argument. In this case the government made some effort to pass on information to the public but the issue was too complex, the technicalities too obscure, and the outcome too uncertain for people to understand. As the issue had been dragging on over years, ever since 1960, public attention soon turned to more pressing domestic matters.

While public opinion cannot, therefore, be said to exercise a positive influence upon the general course of British foreign policy, it exercises a negative influence, by imposing restraints, by prescribing the limits beyond which policy should not go. Far from being limited, this negative influence is of fundamental importance. As Kenneth Younger points out, 'public opinion deals very sensibly with broad policy issues', but it does so only as long as the politicians interpret correctly its general, vague wishes. All policy moves may lead to international conflicts and the policy makers must have a rough idea how far the people would back them in their stand; they must avoid moves which can be exploited by the opposition as offending the general wishes of the people; they must avoid the possibility of their influence abroad and standing at home being undermined by a surge of public opinion. Usually the policy-makers are sufficiently attuned to public moods to determine foreign policy within acceptable limits; it is less obvious whether they always exercise what Kenneth Younger calls 'clear and honest leadership'.

Not many occasions can be quoted for a decisive impact of public opinion upon major policy decisions. In the interwar period the pacifist sentiments of the British people which prevented earlier rearmament are the outstanding example; upsurges of public opinion caused the reversal of the Hoare–Laval Agreement and strongly contributed to the ending of intervention in Russia after the Revolution and to the stiffening of British opposition to the occupation of Czechoslovakia in March 1939. After the war, the growing loss of 'the will to govern', and, more specific-ally, the will to become engaged in military actions of indeterminate duration, formed an important element in hastening withdrawal from imperial commitments, decisively so in the decision to terminate the Palestine Mandate. The successive governments had to take note of how far they could safely go in asking the people to pay and to fight. Wilson's interpretation of public opinion as being opposed to the use of force in Southern Rhodesia played a decisive part in his refusal to contemplate military sanctions after the Unilateral Declaration of Independence, quite apart from all the specifically military difficulties of access.

Occasionally, of course, the public mood does not permit moves which appear to be necessary for the national interest; decisions are obstructed and delayed, and the dilatory policy-makers obtain an excuse for their behaviour. This seems to be a reasonable interpretation of Bald-win's refraining from the massive rearmament which he deemed neces-sary in the light of the weakness of the League and the looming danger of war. He rationalized and explained his failure of leadership by the pacifist mood of the country which, as the result of a lost by-election in 1933, he believed to be overwhelmingly strong:

Supposing I had gone to the country [he claimed] and said that Germany was rearming and we must rearm, does anybody think that this pacific democracy would have rallied to that cry at that moment? I cannot think of anything that would have made the loss of the election from my point of view more certain.[35]

Moreover, the policy-makers themselves, sharing as they do the poli-tical culture of the people, share also their moods and sentiments. It is hard to estimate how much the personal inclinations of the policy-maker and the popular moods contribute to a policy. When performing a world role in the service of peace and of the national interest, as they repeatedly declared, both Macmillan and Wilson were also trying to satisfy the British public, and were clearly deriving great satisfaction from their efforts. The relative importance of each of the factors involved in each case is impossible to determine. Wilson, in his memoirs, perhaps surprisingly as he was operating at a later stage when Britain was rapidly losing her influence, seems genuinely convinced of his protestations about the objective value of his moves in world politics; whereas Macmillan sometimes gives the impression of keeping his tongue in his cheek. The desire to satisfy the people and themselves was, however, so closely intermixed that it is hard to discern which was the most important.

Public moods are not always restrictive; on particular issues they can be a positive spur to action. This is in a general way true about all cases when 'the lion's tail was twisted', but especially so in the Suez affair. It is arguable that Britain's graceful withdrawal from the Empire and her shrinking world role had built up resentments among the public which required a spot of adventure, a daring stroke, before settling to a less spectacular foreign policy. This curious mood was aggravated by one of the periodic economic crises following the turn of world prices against Britain by mid-1955, as home prices rose and wage claims swelled. The growing imperial and domestic frustrations, which were later to be voiced so forcibly by the 'angry young men', readily crystallized in the resentment against Nasser who, in the fog of misinformation, readily became the symbol of all Britain's troubles. The public mood was so strong that it affected even Macmillan who, in the words of his biographer,[36] returned to Churchillian rhetoric and wartime moods. It strongly reinforced Eden's own image of Nasser, which was nurtured on the analogies of the situation with appeasement.

As regards the impact of public opinion, Britain's refusal to join the European union in the 1950s may be paralleled in historical perspective, with the rejection of the idea of rearmament in the 1930s. In both cases the leaders' inclinations were similar to those of the people: Chamberlain was generally a 'man of peace', as pacifist by inclination as the general public. The early European enthusiasts, too, were uninfluential; the political leaders fully shared the general public's lack of sentiment in favour of joining the union and were thus reinforced in their negative attitudes. For instance, in 1960 Lord Avon quoted his own words of 1953 about the possibility of Britain's joining a European federation: 'this is something which we know, in our bones, we cannot do!'[37] Had he not been able to speak confidently in the plural, he might have been much more receptive to the European option. However, public opinion, even when coinciding with the personal preferences of the leaders, cannot indefinitely prevail against clear indications of where national interests happen to lie. Macmillan took the political risk of going against public opinion in 1960 largely because he was apprehensive of the political dangers of Britain's staying out of a united Europe; Wilson, fundamentally an anti-European, applied to the EEC because of Britain's precarious economic and political position in 1967, though his major motivation may have been to deprive the Conservatives of the potentially dangerous electoral argument that he had neglected Britain's interests to follow his own and his party's emotional attitudes; Heath, a convinced pro-European, made Britain's entry his major task between 1970 and 1972 despite mounting indications that the public remained opposed to it.

Finally, a few words are required about the ways in which public opinion can be estimated. Frequently it is unclear and divided, and the policy-makers largely depend upon their intuition. The party and parliamentary systems are only of limited assistance in reflecting the opinions of the general public, which, especially on foreign policy, often crystallize only after the event. Any government naturally takes fully into account the strands of public opinion which it ascertains by sounding its followers in Parliament, upon whose immediate support it relies; these in turn must fully consider the views of the grassroots organizers and followers whose support is essential for electoral victory. Pressure groups operate within the parties; the Labour Party, especially, is frequently confronted with strong divisions of opinion at party conferences, but, as long as opinion remains divided, the leadership of the day often ignores or refuses to follow conference resolutions. The opinions reflected in the views of the opposition must also be taken into account in so far as the arguments on which they are based have to be refuted in public debate. Never since 1945 have opinions held by a major section of the public been sufficiently strongly pressed to affect a foreign-policy issue. There has been no repetition of the trade-union pressures for 'hands off Russia' after the first world war or of the accompanying interference with the loading of munitions for use against the Bolsheviks; there has been no parallel with the anti-Vietnam movement among the American students.

The increasingly improving techniques of attitude surveys remain of limited advantage. The questions posed are often too vague; few systematic surveys exist through which significant fluctuations could be traced in answers to identical questions over a long period of time. More fundamentally, as foreign-policy issues are generally of low salience, the strength of conviction and the degree of commitment to an attitude are frequently limited; opinions tend to fluctuate according to recent events. For instance on 7 October 1971, immediately after the expulsion of 105 Russian intelligence agents, The *Evening Standard* recorded the sudden rise of the popularity of Sir Alec Douglas-Home from plus 16 per cent three months earlier, to plus 31 per cent, the highest rating of all the Cabinet members. Welcome as this rise in popularity must have been, a wish to court the public can hardly have been a major consideration in determining the governmental move; and it is hard to imagine that any future decision would be made mainly with an eye to a public reaction which could not be expected to be more than short-lived.

The most heavily polled issue of British foreign policy has been that of entry into the EEC. Only in August 1971, probably owing to the preceding publicity and to the successful ending of the negotiations, did a small lead of one per cent develop in favour of Britain's joining: the support soon sagged and reverted to the previous pattern of fluctuating but persistent opposition. Thus, superficially, the opposition's claim was justified that the government was flouting public opinion by proceeding with the ratification and implementation of the Treaty of Accession. It is, however, extremely dubious whether the opinions expressed were based on any degree of permanent commitment. The majority of the public polled expressed the opinion that entry would take place, and the government was working on the assumption that not only most of the 'don't knows' but also some of the opponents would decide in favour of entry after it had taken place.

The polling of the elite can be more precise, as their opinions are based on better information and are, therefore, firmer. On 1 October 1971 *The Times* reported the results of a study of opinions of a carefully selected sample from people entered in *Who's Who* which, when compared with a similar survey conducted eight years earlier, gave Heath a strongly reassuring picture of a growing support for the EEC. The respondents rated as 'very valuable':

|  | 1971 | 1963 |
|---|---|---|
| Common Market | 62 | 42 |
| NATO | 58 | 63 |
| Commonwealth | 34 | 69 |
| UN | 31 | 44 |
| US 'special relationship' | 30 | 53 |
| EFTA | 23 | 22 |

As the EEC issue became central in the conduct of Britain's foreign policy, the results of the survey revealed a significant divergence between the views of the elite and those of the general public. Moreover, the survey itself, though not the notice in the newspaper, contained significant details about the substantial differences in the evaluation of the various groupings according to the occupation of the respondents. Both in 1963 and in 1971, the Commonwealth had the highest 'very valuable' rating from politicians, the United Nations from politicians and universities, NATO from retired military, the EEC from industry and commerce. The most illuminating item was the dramatic change in EEC support among members of the civil service and of HM forces: in 1963 it amounted to 43 per cent (against 42 per cent average), but in 1971 it rose to 70 per cent (against 62 per cent average) and was higher than that of any other occupational group except industry and commerce, which recorded 71 per cent.

To sum up, public opinion has been and remains a factor which the politicians take into account, although it cannot be clearly ascertained; the significance of opinions increases when they are held by elite groupings and are reflected within the party and parliamentary system and by the policy-makers themselves. In this process it is hard to see how public opinion at large can become a source of innovation. The opposite seems to be true; any new ideas would have to overcome the basic conservatism of the uninformed and the inertia of the political system; small radical protest groups have not obtained a footing within the system. Thus the constant background concern with the public appears to exert an inhibiting force on the politicians' desire to innovate rather than to stimulate them towards innovation.

# 3 Economic and Psychological Factors

*The Economy and the Problem of Growth*

ONE does not need to be a Marxist in order to acknowledge the significance of the national economy for foreign policy. All politicians and writers pay full lip service to the connection between the two but it seems beyond anybody's powers to achieve a satisfactory synthesis. Our theoretical grasp both of foreign policy and of economics is limited and all theories are subject to dispute; clearly the links between the two are even harder to comprehend. It is difficult enough for any one person to become reasonably expert in one of the fields; it is much harder to attain a reasonable understanding of both. The topic is, however, too central to the theme of this book to be omitted or skimped. For the sake of clarity, a brief general explanation of the links is required at the outset, although most of them seem obvious.

First, domestic economy constitutes a major capability. Economic and industrial power is the backbone of a country's capacity to wage and deter war and is essential for such instruments of exercising influence over other countries as aid or technical assistance. It is also the basis of major psychological capabilities: apart from their direct, economic utility, a high Gross National Product and a sustained rate of economic growth are conducive both to international prestige and to a high national morale; if they compare badly with the performance of other comparable states, as in postwar Britain, both prestige and morale suffer.

Second, domestic economy is the major area of competition between external and domestic demands. The problem of how to satisfy both domestic demands and the demands of foreign, especially of defence policy—the aptly named dilemma of rising demands and insufficient resources[1]—is not unique to Britain. Throughout the world governmental activities have been proliferating, independently of the political system and the stage of development of each single country. In postwar Britain the problem was, however, particularly acute, as economic growth was limited, domestic demands rose rapidly and were pressed with vigour while foreign commitments remained widespread and costly.

Competition between domestic and foreign demands is not limited to money but extends also to the time and energy of the decision-makers.

Third, the intimate links between domestic and foreign policies are most clearly seen in economics. Britain's postwar economy was so clearly dependent upon the international system that the evolution of governmental thinking and policies in domestic matters was closely linked with the development of thinking about interdependence. It is significant that Britain accepted the principle of interdependence and the concomitant limitations on national sovereignty in the field of defence through NATO, and in economics through her membership in a series of international organizations.

Finally, given a certain continuity between domestic and foreign policies, the analysis of domestic economic policies may help us to articulate values, attitudes, and assumptions which are relevant to foreign policy but more difficult to discern directly within it. All these may sometimes be more clearly expressed in the area of domestic economy, which is of central electoral interest, and where the political argument ranges more widely and is also, at least in the short run, freer from the constraints imposed upon the conduct of foreign policy by the will of other states. Moreover, psychological attitudes evolved in the one field have an effect upon the other. In general terms, the repeated failures to secure higher and steadier economic growth reinforced the increasing disillusion with Britain's independent world role, and, *vice versa*, the growing discrepancy between the conception of this role and Britain's power position in the 1960s reinforced the gloomy mood at home. More specifically, although it is difficult to discern direct casual relationships, it seems to be significant that the Suez intervention took place between two economic crises and, even more so, that the 1967 decisions to withdraw from east of Suez and to renew the application to the EEC were preceded by the prolonged balance-of-payments crises and followed by the devaluation of the pound.

Britain's economic performance since the last war has been much lower than that of other advanced industrial countries; she entered the period as the second richest country in north-west Europe, surpassed only by Sweden, and ended by 1973 as the third poorest, followed only by Italy and Ireland. Her failure was, however, merely relative; her economic growth in the decades of postwar reconstruction (1951-71) averaged 2·6 per cent per year, an average higher than in past periods, and unemployment was generally kept below 2 per cent. This level of performance was, however, highly unsatisfactory for three related reasons: (1) growth compared unfavourably with that of other industrial countries, especially Japan and Western Europe; (2) her resource-base, which became gradually restricted from the wide-flung Empire to the small home islands, proved insufficient for the growing domestic and foreign-policy demands; (3) the politicians and the public started with the belief that the economy would prove fully manageable with the aid of the tools available to modern economics but were disillusioned.

The notion of a poor economic performance is relative as it depends upon one's expectations. Hence the exaggerated hopes raised by the economists must first be mentioned. Professor Milton Friedman's criticisms addressed to the American Economic Association in December 1971 apply even more pointedly to Britain:

we economists in recent years have done vast harm to society at large and to our profession in particular by claiming more than we can deliver. We have thereby encouraged politicians to make extravagant promises, inculcate unrealistic expectations in the public at large, and promoted discontent with reasonably satisfactory results because they fall short of the economists' promised land.[2]

The precision of economic analysis and the optimism of the professionals that their theories have high predictive powers and offer reliable tools to policy-making made them welcome to the politicians, especially in the bewildering confusion of postwar reconstruction and the transition to a mixed, planned economy. The ground for a reformed economy had already been prepared during the war by the economists and statisticians who were absorbed into the civil service and who permeated the Treasury with Keynesian theories and with the ideas of planning. Under Sir Stafford Cripps a multitude of working parties proliferated; these were to lead to Statutory Development Councils.

The high hopes were soon disappointed. Modern economics is among the most precise, but consequently also one of the most limited, social sciences. It has to work on the basis of clearly stated assumptions which greatly simplify the complexities of real life; consequently all its findings must be understood within the limitations of these assumptions. Therefore an argument precise in itself can readily be a rationalization for social and political decisions the underlying assumptions of which remain hidden. As the economists cannot agree among themselves, with a change of government one set of economic advisers would replace another, a new set of economic priorities would be substituted for the old one. The promises were invariably exaggerated and, looking at the period as a whole, one cannot help gaining the impression that the economy was behaving in a uniformly fitful manner, following the stop-go pattern based upon the Keynesian belief in demand control. Economic advice did, of course, make a lot of difference tactically, especially on whether to pursue an inflationary or a deflationary policy, but it was rarely strategically significant; it merely helped the successive governments to avoid clarifying their social and political objectives, a phenomenon equally pronounced in the domestic and the foreign fields.

Both the Wilson and the Heath Governments were strongly committed to the modernization of British industry as an essential prerequisite for faster economic growth. Wilson propounded the ideal of technological revolution and, rather ironically for a socialist, the amalgamation of smaller units into large combines. The Heath Government set out to restore enterprise and the spirit of confidence in industry by upholding, even more vigorously than its predecessors, the ideal of managerial efficiency. By the 1970s, however, confidence in the validity of economic forecasts and in the utility of economic tools for the analysis of broad social/political purposes had been undermined. Social and political pressures were gradually reducing economics to ascertaining the means and costs of social policies determined by political processes. On several important issues the government withdrew from policies based on limited economic advice, e.g. by ignoring the Roskill Commission's recommendation on a third London airport and by retreating from the 'lame duck' doctrine, notably with respect to Rolls Royce and the Upper Clyde Shipbuilders, and from an economic pricing of the products and services of nationalized industries. Economic advice was also ignored in cases where there were no valid social reasons to consider. Thus the government persisted with costly prestige projects: Concorde—which could be at least marginally justified by the desire to maintain good relations with France—and the third London airport on Maplin Sands and the Channel Tunnel, which lacked even this marginal justification.

Britain's postwar economic problems were shared by other industrial countries. In her case, however, they were aggravated, first, by her exceptionally high dependence upon the international economic system and, second, by a number of domestic restraints on the increase of production. Britain's dependence upon trade was exceptionally high and she also continued to carry exceptionally heavy responsibilities for maintaining the international system. Her defence expenditure was higher than that of her trade rivals except the superpowers, although, in all likelihood, it seriously delayed economic development only in the two years 1951-2 when it cost her a fuller share of the contemporary international trade boom.[3] Much more serious was her continuing and growingly untenable contribution to international financial stability through maintaining sterling at an overvalued parity. Britain's sterling policy is sufficiently central to warrant discussion separately in chapter 11. It is impossible to compute its exact cost to domestic economy.[4]

Britain's socio-economic system was simply not geared to rapid economic growth. In the postwar world of unprecedentedly high growth rates, she was the eccentric advanced state, historically unsuited to keeping up the new pace and burdened with the heritage of having been first in the field. She was suffering the disadvantages of a leading economy being surpassed by others (as, to some extent, was the United States from the 1960s onwards), of losing technological leadership and competitiveness in export markets and of remaining dependent on an enormous range of imports of raw materials and food, with the difficulty, shared only with the United States, that her imports tended to respond to the rise of incomes at home faster than exports responded to their rise abroad.

Instead of being the leading industrial country, she became the lagging one. The United States had reduced her working force in the manufacturing industry to a mere 23 per cent compared with Britain's 37 per cent. From the successful combination in the nineteenth century of migration of unskilled labour, population-sensitive capital formation, and portfolio foreign investment, she moved to a new combination of professional-elite emigration, science-based capital formation and direct foreign investment.[5] Her case might be regarded as the obsolescence of the world's oldest industrial system: inadequate capital formation; inadequate modernization of industrial equipment, industrial relations, and transport; intractable and costly issues of decaying industrial regions, especially Ulster; lingering imperial patterns of investment and trade at a high opportunity cost; only a modest rise in consumption and in the social services, which, though the first to be established, began to lag behind those in other EEC countries.

A graphic contrast to these causes of weakness is presented by the list of social and economic factors contributing to the exceptionally rapid growth of Japan, which appears in the report prepared for the Hudson Institute under the direction of Dr Herman Kahn.[6] (1) high savings and investment rates (about twice those in the United States); (2) superior education and training (i.e. on the American scale and with European quality throughout high school); (3) adequate capitalization; (4) 'risk capital' readily available; (5) technological capabilities competitive with the West; (6) economically and patriotically advancement-oriented, achievement-oriented, work-oriented employees; (7) high morale and commitment to economic growth and to surpassing the West—by government, by management, by labour, and by general public; (8) willingness to make necessary adjustments and/or sacrifices—

relatively mobile capital and labour; (9) excellent management of the economy—by government, by business, and to some extent, by labour— this results in a controlled and to some degree collectivist, but still competitive and market-oriented (but not market-dominated) capitalism; (10) adequate access—on good and perhaps improving terms—to sufficient world resources and markets; (11) relatively few and/or weak pressures to divert excessive resources to 'low economic productivity' uses; (12) current high momentum of growth facilitates further rapid growth. (13) increased emphasis on research and development; (14) availability of skilled labour force in non-communist Pacific Asia; (15) perhaps all future technological, and most cultural and political, developments seem favourable to the continuation of the above advantages. Apart from points 5 and 10, Britain's economy contrasted, often starkly, with that of Japan.

The political system was rendered incapable of dealing with the problems of growth by a combination of Treasury traditionalism and inadequate and frequently ambiguous or conflicting statistical and economic advice. The traditional drain of talent to the City and the City's inability to develop an adequate lead towards the modernization of industry were important additional factors. Although the postwar Labour government was determined to go ahead with planning and, immediately after the war, Britain possessed the most advanced budgetary techniques and was also first in social services, planning was directed to short-range objectives so that the impulse for long-range prediction had to come from industry. Investment policy was repeatedly curtailed during the foreign-exchange crises in 1947, 1949, and 1951, partly because the statistical computation wrongly estimated that investment at home had risen from 14 per cent of GNP in 1938 to 31 per cent in 1947, and that, even after drastic cuts, it was still 22 per cent in 1948. The qualifications, in small print, of these estimates were simply not read and the government was convinced that it was doing so well that a temporary curtailment did not matter.

For a long time, pursuing the technicalities and the limiting assumptions of their analyses, the economists made it rather harder than easier for the politicians to disentangle what was really involved in the balance of payments, in the contribution of defence expenditure to the deficit, and in giving preference to capital investments abroad in low-yield countries in the sterling area. They could offer no clear advice about the likely evolution of world trade and the best use the British economy could make of its opportunities while they lasted. It seems clear in retrospect that the great housing drive conducted by Macmillan as Minister of Housing and Local Government catered for the urgent social need at the cost of subsequent inflation, of neglecting investment in productive capacity, and of losing export opportunities which were not to recur. The politicians, lacking economic expertise, repeatedly refrained from pursuing a policy of greater expansion in order to rectify the chronically ailing balance of payments. Macmillan, in 1961, would have preferred a floating rate for the pound but accepted the view that this was not feasible.[7] Here the politically sound intinct of an economically amateurish Prime Minister was insufficient to overcome traditionalism. Wilson, on the other hand, himself an economist by profession, staunchly continued to defend sterling up to 1967, even when a majority of economists favoured devaluation. (On the possibility of his motives being in part political see pp. 269, 271.) Treasury conservatism and the division among the economists enabled him to support an economically costly decision without much meaningful opposition within the political system.

Macmillan summed up the dilemma of Britain's postwar economics as it confronted the successive governments in the following terms: 'Full employment, stable prices, a favourable trade balance, growth; these form the circle which successive Governments since the war have had to try to square.'[8] Whenever a solution of the major problems seemed within the grasp of the government of the day, invariably one of the elements would go awry and the vicious circle would begin again. Britain's postwar economy was never stabilized for any period of time. As conflicting principles had often to be taken into account, no permanent solution was possible and policy followed the pattern of the swing of a pendulum rather than of linear progress. Although the most fundamental dichotomy was between the principles of governmental control and of the operation of free market forces, and this roughly coincides with the basic socialist and Conservative ideologies, this coincidence and the over-lap with other dichotomies were incomplete. Violent controversies repeatedly arose between the two parties on economic tactics; the favourite, not unjustified, Labour argument lay in accusing the Conservatives of conducting restrictive monetary policies whereas the favourite, and likewise justified, Conservative accusation was that interventionist Labour policies distorted the economic mechanisms. In fact, the basic political consensus extended to economics, because, however much the two parties differed on detail, they both accepted the principle of a mixed, partly planned economy.

The postwar Labour government came into power with the idea of establishing control over the 'commanding heights' of industry, but its nationalization programme was limited and, apart from steel, scarcely controversial, and did not fundamentally alter the method of management. Its Conservative successor's denationalization of much of the steel industry did not make that much difference to its operation. In conformity with their ideology, the Conservatives speeded up the ending of wartime restrictions, which were still lingering, and encouraged consumption. When, however, the consumers' boom was running away at the end of the 1950s, it was Macmillan's Conservative government that tried to curb the free operation of market forces by introducing indicative planning. Wilson favoured government intervention, through the Industrial Re-organization Corporation for instance, but, rather ironically, thus encouraged the growth of more powerful private enterprise and his regional policy was ineffective in preventing a boom in the South-East. Heath decided to scale down government intervention to the minimum but, in view of the ailing economy and rising unemployment, was forced to resume it.

On the central issue of economic growth, successive governmental policies were vacillating and indecisive. Although economic analysis cannot fully account for preconditions of growth, some of them must obviously compete with other social objectives. Thus, after stagnation in the 1930s and prolonged disinvestment during the war, Britain needed massive investment; but this clashed with the Labour Party's principle of equalizing incomes, which to put it simply, means less savings and hence less investment. Investment in industry also competed with other types of expenditure: on social services, on consumption, and on foreign-policy purposes such as defence, aid, and foreign investment. The Labour Party failed to resolve the dilemma between growth and redistribution.

The main dilemma, and the cause of the stop-go fluctuations, was the see-saw between unemployment and inflation, that Scylla and Charybdis of postwar economic policy. Economic policies invariably evolved in vicious circles in which a period of relatively high growth increased inflation, rising prices and wages gradually undermined the competitiveness of industry in the export markets, while increased production and consumption demanded larger imports; the balance-of-payments difficulties created a run on sterling, in the defence of which the government of the day engaged in fierce deflationary policies which reduced growth, induced unemployment, redressed the balance of payments, and saved the parity of sterling. To make matters worse, the spurts of expansion in Britain's economy did not coincide with periods of expansion in world trade so that opportunities for increasing exports were limited. Conservative ideas of substituting 'virtuous circles' of growth did not succeed.

Though, in retrospect, the defence of the parity of sterling is often regarded as the major reason for the deficiencies of the British economy, up to the end of the 1950s preoccupation with unemployment governed the direction of economic policy. Unemployment was the great phobia inherited from the interwar period in Britain, as inflation was in Germany; the postwar British economic orthodoxy became the Keynesian theory, which concentrates upon unemployment and suggests contra-cyclical action to overcome its rise. One of the greatest achievements of the successive postwar governments was to keep down unemployment. Control of inflation was less successful but the rise was moderate until the end of the 1960s.

In the process, economic growth received lower priority. When concern with it did grow towards the end of the 1950s, the country was soon gripped by a catastrophic deterioration in the balance of payments, so that the Wilson Government devoted its main energies to restoring the balance at the cost of deflation which temporarily reduced economic growth to nil. As a result of the belated devaluation in 1967 and of the continuing deflationary policies, the balance of payments was dramatically cured. For the first time since 1882 Britain earned a trade surplus in two consecutive years, reaching £296 million in the second; the current-account surpluses were accordingly high, £602 million in 1969 and £900 million in 1970. By the end of 1971, Britain had managed to repay the short-term debts of some £4,000 million incurred between 1964 and 1969 and to build up official reserves of more than £2,500 million.

Other favourable changes occured in the 1960s. Slowly but fairly steadily the management structure of a large part of industry was modernized, and redundancy payments were introduced which, in conjunction with the existing unemployment benefits, made it less difficult for the management to reduce excessive manpower and to close down inefficient units. This happened on a nation-wide scale under the Heath Government, which, for a while, continued deflationary policies in order to maintain the healthy balance of payments established by its predecessor after devaluation. One of the major inefficiencies of the British economy was thus being gradually remedied.[9] Over the years, nationalized industries, especially coal, had already shown a degree of success in reducing personnel and in improving productivity; in 1970-1 private industry managed to follow suit in a 'shake-out' of some 400,000. In eighteen months the working force in production industries was reduced by $5\frac{1}{2}$ per cent while production rose by 2 per cent, resulting in a solid increase in productivity of some $7\frac{1}{2}$ per cent.

This highly encouraging improvement in productivity was, however, accompanied by the swelling of the numbers of unemployed in the winter of 1971–2 to the politically explosive figure of one million. Fiscal and monetary policies, although applied on a very large scale, proved insufficient to restore economic growth rapidly; and, after a while, it appeared obvious that the unemployed would not be readily absorbed even after the revival had taken place and would require re-orienting and retraining.

By the beginning of 1972 the picture darkened again. The exceptionally severe bout of inflation was an international phenomenon but more severe in Britain than among her competitors. Industrial unrest, inflationary wage claims, trade-union resistance to the new Industrial Relations Act—all impaired the economic prospects on the eve of Britain's entry into the EEC, which could be expected to create additional balance-of-payments problems. In the first months of 1972 the continuous visible trade surplus turned again into deficit, and in June another run on the pound took place, more severe than its predecessors; this time the government decided in favour of floating the pound. During the first months of 1973 a successful prices and incomes policy somewhat curbed inflation, the wave of strikes subsided, and a uniquely high rate of some 5 per cent of economic growth was maintained; in spite of all this, however, simmering labour unrest, the weakening of the pound, and the adverse turn of the terms of trade resulted in a rapid deterioration of the balance of payments, despite greatly increased exports.

*Science and Technology*

The transformation over the same period of time both of Britain's economy at home and of her position within the international system would have been enough in itself to overstrain governmental machinery which had not in the past been geared to large-scale intervention, and was hampered by institutional inadequacies, by recurrent reorganization, and by economic advice that was often contradictory or misleading. On top of all this, the postwar explosion in science and technology introduced new uncertainties, and aggravated the situation still further by its colossal demands on the economy for investment and on governments for decisions on priorities and the direction of policy. If economic advice was unclear and conflicting, scientific advice was unintelligible in its implications. The scale of the social effort required in each major field of advanced technology was of sufficient magnitude seriously to deplete the economy of resources; and on the whole the results were very disappointing.

Quite a close parallel can be traced between British science and foreign policies as both suffered from a similar overcommitment, lack of adequate resources, and lack of criteria by which to choose priorities. The starting-point, too, was similar—in 1945 Britain was a leading scientific and industrial power surpassed only by the United States, and, in a few selected areas, even ahead of her. Had research and development costs remained modest, Britain could have confidently expected to retain and exploit her lead. However, the exponential growth of technology, which could not be fully foreseen in 1945, undermined her efforts to remain in the forefront of science and technology as much as it did her efforts to retain a significant individual world role. In both cases the psychological resistance of the British to giving up their lead was a significant factor in slowing down adjustment to the limited resources they possessed and resulted in great losses. To some extent, scientific and foreign policies overlapped, particularly in the field of defence, which absorbed a large proportion of technological research.

The political implications of technology were as obscure as the economic costs and benefits of development in each separate field. In general terms, the national policy was clear—the successive governments wished to keep Britain in the forefront of modern technology as a basis for successful export industries, advanced weapons systems, and international prestige. This gave little guidance in the choice of priorities; and although it became fully clear only in retrospect, the inability of successive governments to develop a practicable set of priorities in their scientific policies was the dominant feature of the postwar situation.

It would be unfair to blame only the governments of the day; in Britain's long evolution as an industrial power, governments had traditionally played only an indirect role in the growth of industry. The postwar Labour government did indeed start off with ambitious plans for the power industries; it nationalized the railways and thought in terms of integrating the whole transport industry. It did not, however, manage to produce an overall plan, so that the construction of modern motorways and the modernization of railways were greatly delayed and both the power and the transport industries remained uncoordinated. Even at the beginning of the 1970s long-term policy with regard to such basic issues as power and transport remained unresolved after years of discussion.

Prestige, the desire to be in the forefront of advanced technologies, seems to have played an excessive part in the calculations of the military (who wanted the most advanced weapons system), of the successive governments, and also of the individual firms. Huge investments were made, only to be written off because the projects proved to cost more than the country could afford to go on paying. Admittedly, the cancelled projects were not a dead loss as they secured employment and ensured the development of advanced skills; but the arguments in favour of the 'technological spin-off' seem rather exaggerated, and the opportunity cost must have been extremely high although it has not been plausibly calculated. The successive cancelled defence orders amounted to some £1,500 million at least. Britain grossly overinvested in the airspace industry: the scientific triumph of having the Comet, the first jet airliner, on the market as soon as 1953 was spoilt the following year by a spectacular crash which required the temporary withdrawal of the aircraft from service and its modification; another likely winner, the VC10, was produced too late to become a commercial success; the Rolls Royce aero-engine makers who led the world in the evolution of jet engines, despite their technological successes were declared bankrupt in 1971 and were kept in being only by a large government subsidy; the Anglo-French Concorde, flying at twice the speed of sound, had swallowed up by 1973 well over £500 million of British government funds for development which cannot possibly be recovered from sales. In retrospect, it is quite clear that part of Britain's investment, inadequate in its total, was not wisely applied and brought little, and sometimes practically no return.

Particularly obscure were the political implications of the nuclear industry. (On the strategic aspects of nuclear power, see pp. 303ff.) This industry is clearly the hallmark of a first-rate power, but as Professor Blackett[10] observed as early as 1948, it was 'through the artificial separation of the political from the military consequences of atomic energy that Anglo-American policy had gone astray'. The economics of the industry were, however, equally obscure. To start with, Britain built cheaply the gaseous-diffusion plant required, in contrast to France's great difficulties and heavy costs for an equivalent plant; and, with a limited access to United States know-how, she developed nuclear weapons very cheaply too. This skill and luck did not, however, extend to the building of nuclear power stations. Here again Britain led the field, but she backed the wrong technology, the advanced gas-cooled reactor which proved to be much less efficient than the competing American light water-cooled reactors. After an investment of some £1,500 million and no export sales at the end of 1971, the government had, therefore, to consider whether to complete the five reactors under construction in Britain—and end with fairly unsatisfactory results—or buy American ones, despite serious doubts about their safety. The future of the next generation of high-temperature helium reactors was promising, but again it required further heavy investment and the commercial results were uncertain.

Generally speaking, the annual expenditure of some £1,000 million on research and development, higher than that of all the EEC countries combined, did not pay off in terms of commercial returns. Purely scientific research is, by general (though possibly mistaken) agreement, a necessary foundation for applied research; but somehow the commercial exploitation generally lagged and the Heath Government's conclusion that the latter should receive a larger proportion of funds seemed justified.

The technological future remains uncertain, as both the scientific and the commercial forecasts are highly speculative. On the one hand, the argument seems to be valid that it is worth quite a heavy expenditure to keep Britain's skills within an advanced and promising technology both for commercial reasons and to ensure the accruing prestige. For instance, the rather niggardly expenditure of £200 million on space research in the last decade was totally inadequate. On the other hand, Britain by herself obviously cannot find the required capital even for established industries, to modernize the steel industry for instance (estimated early in 1972 at some £3,000 million), or to develop and maintain a full-scale computer industry. The future choices both in defence and in civilian advanced technology lie between buying cheaply in the United States and limiting British industry to selected areas and to subcontracting, or the development of co-operative projects with her EEC partners.

In theory the formation of some form of European technological community, which loomed large in Wilson's European platform, seems to provide the most promising solution and would also be desirable politically, to cement Britain's ties with the EEC (see pp. 172–3, 308–9). The Wilson proposal had not, however, been thought out in any detail and the sporadic attempts at technological co-operation with other EEC members, especially France, have so far given little ground for expecting a ready solution for Britain's technological dilemmas. The future is likely to depend upon both technological and political developments. In technology, it is possible that the advance is now slowing down and approaching a plateau which would make it possible for Britain to maintain relatively large national technologically-advanced industries. In politics, we cannot be certain about the impact of the increasingly more intimate high-level technological contacts within the Community, both military and civilian, of the degree of integration of the Community, and of its relations with the United States and Japan.

### Psychological Factors and Political Will

Psychological factors affecting foreign policy and the element of the political will involved are notoriously hard to assess. Nevertheless, even writers aiming at the most scientific analysis possible cannot escape discussing them if they wish to avoid straying far away from real life.[11] On the one hand, Duncan Sandys's celebrated comment, recorded by Sir Roy Welensky,[12] 'You see, we British have lost the will to govern', can be regarded as describing a central characteristic of Britain's imperial policy; it reflects a state of mind which came to influence the whole of her foreign policy and even her domestic policies. On the other hand, to explain Britain's troubles in terms of a spiritual crisis and to regard her political and economic difficulties as mere surface manifestations[13] appears to be highly exaggerated; it also gives rise to dangerous wishful thinking. As Max Beloff points out,[14] it is no use believing that the will-power could be restored, the tables turned, and Britain's great-power status miraculously revived. A more balanced appreciation can give the psychological factor its due without making it decisive. It seems more probable that psychological, political, and economic factors interact in a circular fashion: changes in each inducing changes in the others. By a similar interaction the impact of domestic experiences affects the international outlook, and conversely.

As viewed from the early 1970s, the psychological impact of Britain's postwar experiences both at home and in her foreign policy was rather discouraging. One only needs, however, to read any of the contemporary accounts, or talk to anyone who took part in public life at that time to realize that, in spite of difficulties at home and perils abroad, the immediate postwar generation was anything but discouraged. The memory of 'their finest hour' was still fully alive. Britain seemed capable of coping with her problems: at home, her economic recovery was remarkably fast and, instead of facing social revolution, she was being peacefully converted into a 'welfare state'; she was still leading in advanced technologies, especially in jet-planes, and she quickly established herself as the third nuclear power. These successes at home were matched by others abroad: the peaceful emancipation of the Indian subcontinent was followed by reasonable stability in the remainder of the Empire; Western defences were consolidated in NATO. Thus in terms not only of her wartime record but also of her postwar performance Britain appeared to be oustanding among other nations—other than the United States. Her position compared very favourably not only with that of the defeated Germans or Japanese but also with that of the French, who were suffering from acute political and social divisions and from the heavy cost of imperial struggles.

In the absence of similarly acute challenges, the British were not called upon to make a comparable economic effort or to undergo a similar psychological adjustment. Both the effort and the adjustment had to be called for after a considerable delay, in much more unpropitious circumstances. The reasons for this delay must be sought in the complex interaction between the political elite and the people. The issue of Britain's world role is discussed in chapter 7; it is relevant to the present theme only in so far as we are concerned with the reasons why, in the immediate postwar years, Britain's leaders did not attempt to correct the British public's image of Britain as a very powerful state.

The Labour government was, of course, painfully aware of the limitations of Britain's power and was conducting appropriate policies to reduce her overcommitment. For several reasons, however, the public were left fairly ignorant of the situation. First, as has been mentioned, owing to a number of ephemeral circumstances, Britain's power remained temporarily unique and the policy-makers themselves were not unjustified in remaining fairly optimistic about its continuation. Second, they were too preoccupied with fulfilling a whole range of international responsibilities vaguely assumed under the umbrella of the 'world role' to think about general long-range developments. Third, the implications of a diminished status were rather unpleasant to think about, and it is the general tendency of man to show reluctance to adopt, retain, or utilize unrewarding alternative ideas. Fourth, the Labour government wished to avoid the odium of acting unpatriotically. Fifth, the general public had sufficient reason to feel depressed about the continuing hardships of daily life at home and the Communist threat abroad, and it seemed gratuitous to add to the gloom by dwelling upon Britain's weakness; on the contrary, it seemed advisable to buttress the belief in her strength. The 'fruits of victory' were slow in materializing for the man in the street, who was still enduring continuing shortages and rationing. Relaxation of mood and liberation of spirit came only with the Festival of Britain in 1951, the subsequent abolition of rationing and the Coronation in 1953; material prosperity and a consumer boom had to await the end of the decade. Possibly a continuing faith in Britain's power and world role helped to tide the people over the initial postwar period. At the same time, however, an opportunity to adjust public opinion to the loss of power was irretrievably lost; if the uneventful emancipation of India is any indication, the mood of the people after the war was resigned and passive and a gloomier international picture might not have hurt so much when people were preoccupied with their daily lives. The conditions for a psychological adjustment were much less propitious in the 1960s when domestic expectations had risen, the majority of the advanced nations were getting over their postwar problems, and a new generation had come upon the scene.

It is hard to judge how far the policy-makers in the first postwar decade were genuinely unaware of the trends or refused to face them or deliberately slowed down public appreciation of them: undoubtedly there were great individual differences among them. The result, however, is unmistakeable—Britain's international status was not seriously questioned until the late 1950s, when doubts converged with a crisis of confidence on the domestic front. Disappointment and a sense of failure both at home and abroad then became cumulative among both the political elite and the general public, though not, one may guess, for identical reasons—the latter, being less interested in foreign-policy issues, was naturally less affected by them.

Quite justifiably, the Suez debacle in 1956 is invariably selected as the turning-point both in Britain's postwar power status and in her psychological outlook. Its impact upon national morale was delayed, this time owing to conscious governmental intention. Macmillan undoubtedly conceived it his primary duty to heal the wounds of Suez not only in British relations with the United States but also in the minds of the British public. An element of unreality gradually crept into British politics. Attempting by political rhetoric to disguise the extent of Britain's loss of power and status, the Prime Minister further delayed the already overdue postwar adjustment. His actions—the application to the EEC and vigorous decolonization in Africa—indicate that he himself was painfully aware of the real power position, both economically and politically. His rhetoric was not therefore the expression of mistaken perceptions but appears to have been a deliberate smokescreen to enable him to engage in reforms. Its growing unreality had, however, two unfortunate results—first, by delaying and muffling public consciousness that British governments were helpless to cope with domestic economy, it encouraged expectations doomed to frustration; second, it helped to widen the divergence between the political elite's appreciation of the situation and that of the general public, which was naturally much more amenable to rhetoric, and it prepared the way for the ending of the postwar consensus on foreign policy.

The prosperity of the late 1950s lacked any solid economic or social foundation. When, in his speech of 15 November 1957, Macmillan repeated his often-quoted theme 'They've never had it so good', he continued in vain with the much less noticed warning: 'The luxuries of the rich have become the necessities of the poor, but people are asking, "what is it all for?".'[15] Macmillan was personally responsible for establishing the 'affluent society', for which he took full electoral credit, but equally so for his inability to get beyond its unsatisfying materialistic objectives and to fill its spiritual void. In his famous phrase he said: 'If the people want a sense of purpose they should get it from their archbishops'.[16] Needless to say the Church could provide it no more than the government.

Moreover, even in the 1950s this material personal prosperity did not appear to be stable. People were bewildered and disillusioned by the succession of ever quickening and deepening foreign-exchange crises and runs upon sterling, each followed by a period of deflation and of economic stringency. Government followed government with new promises and new plans and raised new hopes, but the promises were not fulfilled and the hopes were disappointed. All the repeated changes in economic policy or the attempts to reform attempts of local government, of Parliament, of social services, scarcely made sense when the same basic problems remained unresolved and repeatedly cropped up. The frustration of grandiose economic schemes, starting with the postwar Labour government's Tanganyikan groundnut scheme and repeated in the many cancellations of advanced technological projects after vast sums of public money had been spent upon them.

The uncertainties and discontents exploded in the early 1960s when the rate of growth was reduced and when the last years of Macmillan's premiership were marked by disturbing social scandals. It was understandable in terms of domestic politics, that Macmillan should have endeavoured to retrieve the political fortunes of his declining government by stressing and inflating his foreign-policy successes; but reference to Britain's world role sounded increasingly hollow from a Prime Minister whose political 'credibility' had become eroded. Even those ignorant of foreign affairs could not avoid noting the Russian sputnik, Britain's inability to enter the space programme and failure to develop a missile, or how the Cuban missiles crisis was solved by a direct confrontation between the Americans and the Russians. References to the world role by Harold Wilson sounded even more hollow.

Social discontents were increased by the coming of age of a new generation which no longer shared the wartime experiences of the policy-makers. Britain's youth problems were part of an international phenomenon and the social disturbances in the United Kingdom were much less violent than in other countries. British youth were free from the need to live down the transgressions of the older generation; on the contrary, they could look with some pride upon their country's record. At the same time, born into a generation without a clear challenge, they had little reason to be satisfied with their country's limited postwar achievements. Commenting on his impressions of a recent visit to Germany, Richard Crossman[17] perceptively noted the great contrast between what had by the 1970s become the middle generation in Germany and in Britain. The Germans, who had been born too late to remember the war, remembered enough of the postwar period to realize the colossal struggle for economic and political rehabilitation which they had had to conduct, well knowing that they were a defeated nation and that the world owed them nothing; they intensely enjoyed their success and their high standard of living. The equivalent British generation was bound to feel quite differently and to suffer from a sense of being let down by the world, of having failed to achieve much. The repeated governmental appeals to 'the spirit of Dunkirk' sounded particularly empty to the young who could not remember Dunkirk. In 1961, when in opposition, Wilson justifiably decried the use of this appeal by the Tories as an inadequate answer to Britain's problems; when in power, in December 1964, facing the same problems, he himself appealed to 'the spirit of Dunkirk', with equally disappointing results.

It was noticable that social discontents varied according to social class. After 1945, a large proportion of the surplus income passed for the first time into the hands of the workers and also of the youth of the country. The consumer society ushered in by the Conservative governments of the 1950s did, indeed, lead to a situation in which the working people 'never had it so good'. Real wages continued to climb steeply in the 1960s: between 1963 and 1970 they went up by 126 per cent whereas prices went up by only 74 per cent. Under the Conservative government elected in 1970, the balance swung again in favour of the rich with tax concessions for surtax payers, rapidly rising prices, and the shift to indirect taxation through Value Added Tax. Capital wealth remained heavily concentrated—some 75 per cent in the hands of 10 per cent of the population. Moreover, owing to heavy inflation, real property and all durable assets greatly appreciated, further increasing the great inequalities. Suspicious of the government, hostile to industrial discipline, apprehensive of redundancies through automation, the working people, although still well off, could not be happy about the system.

The hardest hit, however, were members of the middle class, the professionals, who constitute the majority of the political elite. Although they were generally comfortable, their standards of living did not improve in proportion with those of the workers; being dependent on fixed salaries they were unable to profit by capital gains. Thus they lost their position of relative advantage, and many of them resented the inconveniences of the democratically spread social services, such as restricted educational choice and hospital queues from which only the very rich could escape. It is they who coined the term 'the English sickness' for the social malaise which gradually arose. The usual picture they evoked was that of a Britain which had somehow fallen between two stools: the old system which was dying out and the new one which had never been born. Continuity ensured that the old forms persisted but the hope that they would be filled with new contents did not materialize. As quite a large proportion of the middle class, especially those directly connected with the economy of the country, set their hopes on Britain's entry into the EEC as a means of rejuvenation, they were particularly hard hit by de Gaulle's veto. Anthony Sampson reports the recollections of Edward Heath:

I don't think we realized at the time how far de Gaulle's veto in 1963 turned this country in on itself. I didn't realize it fully until October 1964, when I went canvassing in Bexley. It was then that I realized the change from the confidence during the last election in 1959. There used to be a sense of young executives excited and confident at the thought of getting into Europe: but later, after years of lessening profitability, there was much less confidence.[18]

The most plausible explanations attributed Britain's unsatisfactory economic performance not so much to mistaken policies as to structural defects in her social-economic system: in industrial management, especially the handling of exports, in the organization of trade unions, in the inadequacy of governmental institutions, or in some combination of these. All these structural defects were proving intractable to the repeated attempts at reform.

The contrast with Britain's continental neighbours, especially the French, who were, at that time, going from strength to strength, was particularly depressing. With Britain losing in competition with other advanced countries, what had been her traditional insularity showed a tendency to become a narrow parochialism; continuing a world role in these circumstances became increasingly incongruous. There is only a little exaggeration in the way Malcolm Muggeridge, writing in 1963, expressed the malaise which was rapidly spreading among the political elite:

Each time I return to England from abroad the country seems a little more run down than when I went away; its streets a little shabbier, its railway carriages and restaurants a little dingier; the editorial pretensions of its newspapers a little emptier, and the vainglorious rhetoric of its politicians a little more fatuous. On one such occasion I happened to turn on the television, and there on the screen was Harold Macmillan blowing through his moustache to the effect that 'Britain has been great, is great, will be great'.[19]

National pride was being rapidly replaced by a feeling of frustration and the belief that England was going down. This was a compound of genuine economic disappointment and of the feeling that the country was rapidly losing in the pursuit of economic growth, now the generally accepted yardstick of national achievement. 'Knocking Britain' became widespread and even sober comments on the economic failings expressed the malaise and further increased the gloom. For instance, on 9 April 1962 *The Guardian*[20] carried the following characteristically headed item:

### Britain Bottom of the Class

Britain economically came bottom of the class in the annual report published here to-night by the Secretariat of the United Nations Economic Commission for Europe.

Britain has 'the sorry distinction of being the only Western country whose volume of national output was practically unchanged from the previous year' and is 'the one country in which the unemployment situation has seriously deteriorated'.

The economic frustrations were doubly important as social values in Britain were becoming increasingly materialistic.

It is easy to exaggerate the ills of one's own time and place. Some of the various problems and difficulties of contemporary Britain have been matched and surpassed by those in her own past or in the experience of other nations today. The fact, however, remains that their total effect upon the will of the nation and of its policy-makers has been debilitating. The major relevant phenomena are discussed here under the headings of homogeneity, stability, achievement, and purpose.

The confidence of Victorian governments was to a large extent based upon the conviction that they were backed by a homogeneous society at home which, moreover, extended overseas, forming the Empire and founding powerful closely-related new English-speaking communities. Although the Celtic fringe was never fully absorbed and the Irish question remained troublesome, these problems did not detract from the Victorians' confidence. Since 1945, as the overseas outlets have been closed and links weakened, the restriction of economic opportunities has greatly contributed to a revival of nationalism in the Celtic fringe and the re-opening of the Irish problem by the troubles in Ulster. An even more serious challenge to Britain's homogeneity stems from the influx of Commonwealth immigrants from the West Indies, India, Pakistan, and also Africa. The multiracial commonwealth became a disturbing reality on the doorstep of many British citizens which resulted in relatively minor but disturbing racial riots at Notting Hill in 1958. Immigration from the Commonwealth became gradually restricted by legislation, seriously weakening Commonwealth cohesion, but the problems of absorbing the established immigrants, and their British-born children, who by the beginning of the 1960s were rising to some 2 per cent of the total population, have remained unresolved. Instead of Britain spilling over into the world, it is now the world which has spilt back into Britain; instead of being a powerful international link, British nationality has become a source of embarrassment in the case of the East Africa Asians who claimed admission to Britain.

As long as the postwar difficulties could be attributed to transitory problems of adjustment, the social stability generated by wartime requirements and reinforced by the peaceful establishment of the welfare state persisted. By the late 1950s, however, public confidence had been undermined. The postwar changes in the imperial, social, and economic structures had taken place remarkably smoothly and had raised hopes that Britain was endowed with unique powers of adaptation. However, as time went on the adaptations appeared to have been insufficient and her growing inability to maintain a sustained rate of economic growth, an independent world role, and leadership in modern technology overlaid the initial successes. The major economic and social problems proved intractable, and the goal of personal enrichment, stressed since Macmillan had introduced 'the affluent society', merely increased personal frustration, without enabling the successive governments to generate a sense of social purpose. Education, social services, and higher standards of living, which had been confidently expected to improve social stability, all proved to be ineffective in resolving the underlying social problems. From the late 1950s crime and violence increased, and industrial strikes became frequent. Britain's problems in this respect were not, of course, unique. What was unique was the exceptional cumulative sense of lack of achievement and purpose which manifested itself in the 1960s.

At the same time, however, even the most outspoken critics of postwar British society assumed that the postwar turmoil merely overlaid but did not destroy a core of quiet conviction of Britain's innate quality which requires little manifestation. Comparing themselves with others, the British feel they are one of the most successful countries to preserve a feeling of continuous purpose which is indefinable but constitutes a real asset in times of strain. Only the French are comparable. Common sense and a sense of political style can produce sensible solutions; courage and pride in the nation can be called upon, provided the policy-makers manage to mobilize them. Unfortunately none of the postwar governments proved capable of doing so.[21]

The managerial revolution in the later 1960s, the coming to power of a new, younger generation of leaders, did not appreciably change the situation: it improved neither the national economy nor the position of the middle class. The discontented youth of the early 1960s had not become the satisfied middle-aged mainstay of social stability when the youth of the early 1970s became in its turn, discontented. In contrast to Continental Europe settling into its prosperity, the class strife in Britain was becoming exacerbated and, in the early 1970s, disruptive industrial strikes became the major feature of the social scene. Confidence in the basic soundness of the British economy was only temporarily restored following the devaluation of 1967. In June 1972 the pound had to be floated (see pp. 81–2, 274). It lost much of its value in the subsequent year. Heath's programme of managerial efficiency and cost effectiveness proved to have been no more effective than Wilson's talk about a technological revolution.

On the eve of Britain's entry into the EEC the national morale was again low. The majority of the political elite put their confidence in the effects of Britain's joining the EEC, which was expected to stimulate the rate of economic growth and to provide an incentive to remedy the lingering social problems. It seemed at least conceivable that, once Britain had settled within the new context, the EEC could play the useful role of a catalyst in restoring national confidence, although the immediate direct effects of the entry were bound to be disturbing. Moreover, it seemed possible that Britain was well past the worst of her post-war domestic, social and economic adjustments, including some which other industrial countries had not yet made. With the inescapable need to adjust to the EEC and with the improved outlook for doing better in the future both in absolute terms and in comparison with others, it seemed possible that a more stable form of adjustment to the disturbing post-war changes would arise, and that the malaise would pass. Encouraging signs in the first half of 1973 of growth and of attempts to establish a prices and incomes policy were followed, however, by a turn for the worse as regards the balance-of-payments difficulties, inflation, and industrial conflict, aggravated first by a general rise in world commodity prices and, from the late autumn by the Middle Eastern oil crisis, which also had a divisive impact on the EEC.

A rapidly growing interest in the quality of life, in the effects of industrial pollution and of encroachment upon the countryside, concerns common to all industrialized countries, has supplied a segment of the British middle class, especially the young, with an outlet for voicing their frustrations. This could become a useful corrective and adjunct to a renewed period of economic advance. In some circumstances, however, this interest in the quality of life could have negative effects—it might induce the middle class to join the workers in their reluctance to accept modernization; among the youth, it could combine with irresponsible luddite and anarchist attitudes. Again, the EEC framework could prove useful in directing the movement into positive channels; endeavouring to influence the relevant EEC policies could provide a worthwhile, constructive, and also attainable new international role within the regional setting.

# 4 Power, Influence, and Capability

*Power and influence*[1]

EXPLANATIONS of the evolution of Britain's postwar foreign policy frequently centre upon the inadequacy of her resources to continue a policy previously based upon a huge Empire. *Prima facie*, this hypothesis is sufficiently plausible to deserve full exploration. Any hopes of finding precise correlations are, however, bound to be disappointed. The complexity of the nexus is best shown by the confusion obscuring the meaning of the central concept of 'power': it is highly imprecise and has strong emotional overtones. Most modern definitions reject the view frequently advanced before the war that 'power' is an essence, an absolute quantity which can be broken down into meaningful and frequently quantifiable elements such as the size of territory, the numbers of people, of men under arms, of planes and guns. Modern definitions are concerned with the relational nature of power, and agree that it denotes the capacity to produce intended results. Therefore, although in absolute terms during the quarter of a century following the war Britain's economic and military power greatly increased, her relative power greatly decreased; from being third in both respects, she dropped to a much lower place, and her influence diminished more or less accordingly. The difficulties inherent in this situation were enormous; the experience of the United States in the early 1970s showed this again, when, although still in the lead in all significant power respects, she no longer retained an absolute lead and had to adjust herself to an influence accordingly reduced.

Taken by themselves, the quantifiable elements of the state's resources do not explain the nature of its power, as its capacity to use its resources is determined both by the national will and by international circumstances. Imbalances in resources can be redressed by the support of other states, by the constraints arising from the international system, and also by greater determination on the part of a less powerful state, which, in extreme cases, can take the form of a 'suicidal alternative', the determination to perish rather than give in, as shown by the Finns against the Russians or the North Vietnamese against the Americans. The successive British governments repeatedly endeavoured to close 'the power gap' between Britain and the two superpowers by the 'special relationship' and the Atlantic alliance, by the national deterrent, and by Commonwealth support, but were largely unsuccessful. The Suez action not only showed all these to be ineffecive but also demonstrated the nation's lack of resolve.

Defined as the capacity to produce intended results, 'power' comes close to the notion of 'influence'. There is no clear boundary between the two although the distinction is usually based upon the coercive qualities of power. A whole gamut of possible permutations arises in every situation: a fully recognized identity of interests may make all coercion irrelevant: coercion may exist in the background only as an ultimate stimulus or restraint, although no reference is made to it; a threat of its use may be made in a variety of veiled or open ways; ultimately, force may be actually used, ranging from its demonstration or mild application to outright warfare.

In order to take us away from the imprecision, the emotional over-tones, and the limiting coercive connotations of the notion of 'power', modern political scientists often employ the concept of 'capability', which denotes, according to the *Shorter Oxford English Dictionary*, 'power, ability, or faculty, for anything'—in the context of foreign policy—to coerce, to reward, to induce other states to refer to one's ideas, to achieve technical and military superiority, to enforce legal points. Thus 'capability' (the concept of 'capacity' is occasionally used in a partly overlapping manner) is usefully linked with the objectives of foreign policy and stresses its relational nature. For instance, Britain's *Polaris* submarines are hard to analyse as an element in national power in general terms but can be quite precisely analysed in terms of a capability for a set of distinct objectives: in nuclear strategy, as a second-strike deterrent force; in diplomacy, as a means of exercising a degree of influence over the Americans and of securing an international standing as a nuclear power; as a means of obtaining prestige as a technologically advanced nation. Such analysis stresses that it is not only the technical efficiency and the hitting power of the submarines that count, but also their 'credibility', which depends upon a suitable strategy for using the weapons if necessary, both of which must be convincing to others.

If capability prescribes the parameters of what the state can do, political will determines how much it will do with it. The resolve of the policy-makers to pursue their interests is the major determinant of the credibility of their policies—up to a point a weak state can be rendered much stronger by a determined show of will; a powerful state can be debilitated by a display of weakness in the application of its power.

Although we have no means of identifying the exact role of the element of will in political activities, its central importance is generally recognized. For instance, a soldier, Field-Marshal Montgomery, claims that 'the true and ultimate strength of a nation does not lie in its armed forces. It lies in the national character, in its people, in their capacity to work, in their virility.'[2] The historian, Professor W. L. Burn, discusses 'will' at length in his reassessment of the mid-Victorian period,[3] and a contemporary political scientist, Professor D. O. Wilkinson, employs the concept in his analysis of foreign policy.[4] According to the latter, the evolution of Britain's foreign policy since 1945 shows a low incidence of political will. Without attempting to apply his rather abstruse analysis, we shall only examine his conclusion and its implications.

Political will can be regarded as the dynamic element in foreign policy which determines the use of capability; purpose and strength are thus circularly linked. The general trend of Britain's foreign policy since 1945 can be understood both in terms of a reduced capability which gradually weakened the political will but also of a weakened political will which prevented a fuller use of the existing capability. According to Professor Burn, the great contrast between postwar and mid-Victorian Britain lies not only in the latter's greater optimism and energy but even more so in its faith in the power of the human will. Professor Burn draws our attention to the 'simplifying effect' of the philosophical beliefs of the Victorians, who were not attracted by philosophies decrying the possibility of individual rational and responsible choices such as are prevalent in our age.

Britain's solitary stand against Hitler and the subsequent sustained war effort had constituted a supreme exercise of political will which, one may surmise, left the nation and its leadership exhausted. Nevertheless, in the immediate postwar years, British policy-makers showed great determination in coping with the intractable postwar problems, notably by engaging in far-reaching domestic reforms and by contributing to the organization of the defence of Western Europe and to its economic rehabilitation. Only when the urgent postwar problems had been met did the full realization of the loss of Britain's power set in; it was finally precipitated by the Suez action which, in this context, can be regarded as a frustrating attempt to exercise the will. The loss of will and the loss of power were circular. On the one hand, the main reason for the weakening of the political will in contemporary Britain can be sought in the great deterioration of both her domestic and her international circumstances which has been discussed; both were epitomized in the break-up of the Empire. On the other hand, this break-up was hastened by the loss of will illustrated by Duncan Sandys's remarks, already quoted on p. 60.

The multitude of purposes which the *Polaris* submarines can serve illustrates the basic difficulty not only of analysing Britain's foreign policy but also of actually conducting it. Britain entered the postwar period as a world power with extremely widespread interests and commitments; individual capabilities had, therefore, to be related to many frequently divergent purposes. The demands of her role in the central strategic balance or as a leader in modern technology were quite different from those experienced at lower levels of politics and industry. Policy-makers always tended to give precedence to the higher levels—Britain had been traditionally a leading power and the idea of remaining one offered not only strong emotional satisfactions but also greater opportunities. They were fully justified in thinking that, once she dropped out from the forefront of technology, whether military or civilian, she would never be able to catch up. They seem to have based their thinking upon two major assumptions. The first was that the country would have the basic capacity to keep in the forefront—an assumption which was not unreasonable immediately after the end of the war but proved totally wrong when the extent of the technological revolution had become clear.

The second assumption was even less tenable—that the capabilities evolved for major policy objectives would serve minor ones too. There was a basic fallacy in the repeated attempts to develop multipurpose weapons systems with operational demands geared to a variety of purposes; the ultimate product was too complex and costly for limited objectives. To use extreme examples, nuclear weapons were no use in the 'Confrontation' and frigates equipped to deal with submarine threat would not be the most effective means for fisheries' protection, even if they were available in sufficient numbers. Nor did Britain's efforts in several advanced technologies lead to successes in exports. The alleged technological 'spin-off' seems to have been a greatly exaggerated notion; an investment, say, in the car-making industry of only part of the technical skill and capital outlay which were spent on nuclear power stations could have ensured a much greater share of the rapidly growing world markets; the same applies to the £500 million spent on developing Concorde.

Thus one cannot explain foreign policy fully in terms of the state's capability, as the latter covers only the state's potential for action;

action itself depends also on the element of will. Moreover, capability is not only the source of the means of pursuing foreign-policy objectives; if it proves insufficient for these objectives, it is also a source of restraints. It also strongly affects the confidence of the policy-makers and the standing of the country in the eyes of others, which will be discussed in the following section.

## Perceptions of Britain's Power

The rather simple hypothesis that Britain's foreign policy has been largely determined by the limitations of her capability is frequently refined to allow also for the perceptions of her policy-makers, which can be regarded as an intervening variable. To what extent can the evolution of policy be explained in terms of changes in these perceptions, say between 1945 and the aftermath of the 1967 devaluation? This question can be meaningfully answered only if we take fully into account two points: (1) the relative nature of the notion of 'power', (2) that policy was determined by the evaluation not only of the actual situation but also of its dynamics, of the likely trends. If policy in the late 1940s appears to us as overconfident, this was not due to an insufficient appreciation of the limitations of Britain's capability by the Attlee Government, which was fully conscious of the precarious economic and security situation (see pp. 47ff.).

In absolute terms, Britain was, of course, incomparably stronger in 1967 than in 1945; the relative optimism of the late 1940s, when contrasted with the pessimism of the late 1960s, was partly due to her much stronger relative power position immediately after the war, when she was not only miles ahead of all other middle powers but, in some significant fields of technology and of military power, ahead of the Soviet Union and even of the United States; by 1967, the distance from the super-powers had become enormous and other middle powers were rapidly overtaking Britain economically. Another important difference is found in the anticipations of the respective policy-makers. Whereas in 1945 they could expect that, with the assistance of the United States and of the Commonwealth, their country would retain a margin of advantage over the devastated other middle powers and would not fall far behind Russia and America, by 1967, after the Empire had been emancipated and the repeated attempts at achieving a faster economic growth had failed, they could hardly feel confident that the continuous erosion of Britain's power position would be reversed. The two major events which precipitated a revision of the prevalent perceptions of Britain's power were the Suez affair in 1956 and devaluation in 1967;

the final stage of this process stretched well over a whole decade.

Any estimate of Britain's power position is bound to be inaccurate and controversial, especially when both the international environment and the country's own policy objectives and priorities are in a state of flux, and when technology advances so rapidly that existing capabilities become obsolete. Britain's capability is generally compared with those of the two superpowers and of such major Western European states as France and Western Germany. The latter comparison is clearly relevant in evaluating Britain's likely power position within the EEC. Her position should not, however, be determined exclusively on the basis of comparable capabilities. Her overseas connections, which the British themselves now tend to discount in their surge of interest in Europe may prove to be quite a substantial element in her power position within the enlarged Community; they may certainly retain their value in the eyes of some of the overseas partners. Although it would be dangerous to generalize, there may be some substance in the following, admittedly strongly partisan, estimate from Australia:

Land-powers, looking out on a broad territorial expansion have one kind of place in the world. The United Kingdom, as the hub of an oceanic system, has had another. Land-powers may flourish without overseas resources of strength like the Commonwealth and an Anglo-American factor to draw upon. But it is through such overseas connections, economic and political, that Britain's stature is upheld.[5]

Under the circumstances, Britain's policy decisions could not have been based upon any accurate estimates of her capability. On the one hand, overestimates undoubtedly occurred, a particularly serious one in the Suez affair. A miscalculation of Britain's economic capability seems to have been the cause of Wilson's repeated predictions that the Southern Rhodesian rebellion would soon be brought to an end through the application of economic sanctions, although in this case it may have been more a matter of political rhetoric than of serious calculation. On the other hand, the British obviously underestimated, or gave insufficient attention to, or did not find suitable ways for utilizing, the accumulated fund of goodwill which was a considerable but wasting asset, as Britain was not in a position to repeat the favours bestowed and the services rendered to others during and immediately after the war. Her contribution to the maintenance of international peace was reduced, nor could she repeat her generous acts of colonial emancipation, and subsequently she was unable to follow up emancipation with substantial aid. It appears in restrospect that policy-makers at the time were presumably too preoccupied with the central strategic balance and too optimistic in their anticipations to perceive the situation. Thus Britain gradually dissipated the credit she could draw from her stand against Hitler, her struggles for restoring the position of France as a great power, and her early recognition of Communist China; she did not use the opportunities of leading Western Europe in the first postwar decade or of mediating between Japan and South-east Asia in the 1960s; in a somewhat similar way, in the early 1970s, she seemed to be wasting her technological advantages, for example in the air-space and computer industries, in order to allow the French and German industries to build up sufficiently to match the British ones. All these wasted opportunities can only partly be attributed to the absence of suitable clear-cut objectives. The main reason was that Britain's unique, eccentric position in the world hindered the formulation of such objectives.

Although the perceptions of a country's capability held by its own policy-makers greatly affect the shaping of its foreign policy, its power position is ultimately determined through the perceptions of others. A high 'capability rank' is an obviously important ingredient of a strong international strategic position. If the British themselves may have been inhibited in appreciating the full degree of the relative decline in their capability, others were not. On the contrary, if anything, some of them were inclined to exaggerate it. Stalin, antagonized by Britain's adamant stand against his ambitions in the Mediterranean, was bound to repeat the famous question he had asked about the number of divisions available to the Pope. Realism, occasionally accentuated by a degree of *schadenfreude*, coloured many American appraisals. Sir Oliver Franks, for instance, noted with regret that Professor Hans Morgenthau had discounted the value for the United States of Britain's friendship by attributing to her only a slight weight in a conflict with the Russians.[6] Morgenthau's weighting of 100 for the Americans, 70 for the Russians and 10 for the British (which was based upon the nuclear military technology of the early 1950s) was limited and extremely crude but, nevertheless, it meaningfully applied one yardstick of capability for estimating the value of Britain as an ally. In 1969, another American, D. O. Wilkinson, fairly reflected the American view of the impact of Britain's diminishing capability upon her policies:

British policy since the war presents a picture of more or less steady withdrawal of commitments, scaling down and regionalisation of increasingly economic objectives, increasing dependence, and decreasing independent success. All are partly the result of relative or absolute secular declines in economic output and military capabilities and probably also in absolute capacity for collective action. In short, changes in British policy appear to have been very much dependent upon changes in British power.[7]

The concepts of overcommitment and of its adjustment to the capability possessed were fully reflected in the actual conduct of Britain's postwar foreign policy and receive full treatment in the writings on it. One factor, however, seems to have escaped attention—the ambiguous nature of specific capabilities in a power position which is consistently deteriorating. It was more than a disturbance in the balance between economic and strategic political capabilities, which frequently recurs in international politics. Britain's imbalance in favour of the latter was matched by a similar imbalance in the policies of Germany and Japan, which became economically strong while they remained militarily weak. The point about Britain was that she could not redress the imbalance, as her power-base was constantly weakening. Although subject to international and domestic constraints, both Germany and Japan possessed, and are likely to preserve, the capacity to redress the imbalance by building up armed forces; Britain has not only been unable to restore her economic strength but could not afford to develop her military strength in a manner fully commensurate with others. In a gradually deteriorating position of that kind, the value of specific capabilities cannot be taken for granted, as they may serve objectives which have lost their validity; worse than that, what is traditionally regarded as an asset often becomes a liability. Perceptions can be adjusted only gradually and with some delay—it takes time to discover the full cost of continuing the traditional policies. Thus, immediately after the war, both the British and others generally regarded the chain of British overseas bases as real elements of power. As the cost of maintaining them constantly mounted, the successive British governments gradually withdrew from the most exposed positions. It was, however, only in the later 1960s that the conditions for the withdrawal from east of Suez were established by a growing realization that the whole position was untenable and that withdrawal could not be delayed by further piecemeal retreat. Not only were the costs of maintaining a British overseas presence contributing to the balance-of-payments deficits, but the importance of the overseas interests served had been reduced; in Britain, the pro-Europeans in particular were acutely aware of this owing to their pronounced European priorities.

In a residual form, the question of what constitutes an asset or a liability still persists. Is the small British military presence in South-east Asia under the Five Power Security Pact an asset or a liability? The same question can be asked about the partly linked, but much less important or discussed, problem of the CENTO air route by which British personnel can be evacuated from the Far East. The cost of maintaining this route is, of course, negligible when compared with that of the chain of bases in the past. Nevertheless, in the light of the limited interests served, possibly the consistent diplomatic effort required to keep overflight rights and to find contingency alternatives is not really worth while; the route may have become a diplomatic liability much heavier than its limited strategic advantage warrants. One can discern here the possibility that the evolution of British policies regarding the land bases may be repeated on a lesser scale.

Similarly, the international role of sterling, staunchly defended by successive governments until 1967, was abandoned unbemoaned in the agreement for British entry to the EEC in 1972, by which time anybody with even a flimsy understanding of international finance could not but agree that, far from being an asset, sterling had become an extremely grave liability which had undermined the basis of Britain's power position in the 1970s (see pp. 268ff.).

## Britain's capability

Statistics are frequently used in political argument and in political analysis; as has been argued, they are significant both in assessing the means available and in affecting the confidence at home and the standing of the country abroad. Decisions and evaluations are, however, based only on rough magnitudes and not upon refined statistical methods; units in cross-country comparisons may not be strictly comparable and methods of computation may differ. Statistical aggregates may therefore be neither accurate nor comparable. Nevertheless, whenever public attention focuses upon them, they become the stuff of politics. Consequently, no attempt is made here to go into statistical refinements; merely the data that are generally regarded as important are introduced from publications which are widely used and are therefore politically influential. Moreover, due regard is paid to factors which are relevant but not quantifiable.

One may safely presume that policy-makers are governed by some estimate of the general capability of their country but this is often no more than an inarticulate assumption to which they only occasionally refer; moreover, their public references may be mere rationalizations which disguise rather than illuminate their assumptions. Nevertheless, there seems to be little doubt as to which factors are deemed relevant, what are the 'elements of power'. Although individual writers differ in their classifications and emphasis, they generally accept as relevant the commonsense categories of territory, population, economic and military power, governmental organization, social structure, and international position. The classification which has a strong bearing upon diplomatic practice is into 'coercive', especially military power, 'utilitarian', i.e. economic or technological power, and psychological or 'identitive' power.

To start with the geographical/demographic base, Britain is a rather small country, especially when compared with the two superpowers. When compared with the major Western European powers, however, her territory is much smaller than that of France but comparable with that of Western Germany, while her population is comparable with both. The actual figures are as follows:

| Country | Area sq. m. | Population* mid-1969 | Average Population Growth Rate 1960-9 (%) |
|---|---|---|---|
| UK | 89,038 | 55,534 | 0·7 |
| Western Germany | 95,967 | 60,842 | 1·0 |
| France | 212,919 | 50,330 | 1·1 |
| USA | 3,553,888 | 203,213 | 1·3 |
| USSR | 8,650,000 | 240,333 | 1·3 |
| Japan | 142,726 | 102,322 | 1·0 |

* Source: World Bank Atlas, 1971.

Britain clearly cannot aspire to any degree of self-sufficiency comparable to that possible for the Russians or the Americans or even the French. Even if geological exploration proved successful beyond our wildest dreams, the British Isles could not provide more than a small portion of our needs of raw materials; even a colossal expansion of agriculture, which is already very efficient, could not be expected to go very much beyond the 53 per cent of the country's needs which it produces at present. Imperial expansion was one historical answer to Britain's limited territory and resources at home; the idea of interdependence, as stated in Sir Eyre Crowe's classical memorandum of 1 January 1907,[8] was another. Both played a part in determining her policies after 1945. Although one may presume that nobody remained unaware of the slenderness of Britain's resource-base, in the immediate postwar period the perceptions of this base held both at home and abroad were blurred by the lingering memories of the British Empire which had encompassed one-quarter of the area and of the population of the earth; much of it was to remain under British control until the 1960s and it was possible that the Commonwealth would prove to be at least a partial substitute for direct control. The Conservative and Unionist Central Office voiced a widespread view when in a booklet published in 1949 under the title *Imperial Policy* it claimed: 'It is sometimes forgotten that the potential strength of the British Empire and Commonwealth is greater than that of the United States or the USSR.' Similar though less sanguine hopes were expressed about the EEC in the early 1970s. Further-more, although Britain's territory is very small, well down the interna-tional list, her population still ranks tenth, which places her squarely in the same category as other major middle powers. Even more im-portantly, Britain is clearly among the leading powers of the EEC, with the second-largest population and the fourth-largest territory, and this is likely to be the most relevant context for her foreign policy in the 1970s. All in all, even after the loss of the Empire, one cannot regard the limitations of Britain's geographical/demographic base as a serious constraint upon her foreign policy either in the perceptions of the policy-makers or in its actual operation.

It was her relatively low rate of economic growth that constituted the most severe restraint on her foreign policy. She is still, by international standards, a wealthy country, but her national economy has become less and less adequate to maintain and develop advanced modern technolo-gies; even had her performance been better she would still hardly have been able to keep pace with the two Superpowers and with the EEC as a whole. In addition, her rate of economic growth, although higher than ever before in her history, has been substantially below that of other advanced industrialized countries. The average annual rate in Britain in the 1950s and 1960s was around $2\frac{1}{2}$ per cent; in the 1960s it averaged 2·7 per cent against 4·2 per cent in the United States, around 5 per cent in the EEC and as much as 11·2 per cent in Japan.[9] The cumulative effect of this discrepancy was substantial—Britain's GNP gradually dropped well behind those of comparable countries; in 1960 it was surpassed by Germany and in 1965 by France.

In addition, economic performance became subject to recurrent international comparisons and the shibboleth of social success. British per capita income, which is generally accepted as an admittedly very crude yardstick of social satisfactions, also gradually dropped, well below that of Britain's continental neighbours. Owing to the fascination of the statistics of growth, both the British and others became gradually imbued with the idea that Britain is appreciably less successful than other countries.

The relevant statistics of GNP and of economic growth in 1969 are shown in the table on the next page. The deterioration was rapid. Right up to the war, Britain's per capita income was second only to that of the United States; in 1950 she was surpassed by Sweden, by 1970 by eight other Western European countries. In 1960 she was still eighth in the world; in 1969, as in the table, she was thirteenth, and subsequently, by 1971, she became fifteenth.

| Country | GNP Per Capita 1969 | Average Growth 1960-9 |
|---|---|---|
| UK | (13) 1,890 | 1·8 |
| Western Germany | (10) 2,190 | 3·7 |
| France | (5) 2,460 | 4·8 |
| USA | (1) 4,340 | 3·2 |
| USSR | (est. 23) 1,200 | 5·6 |
| Japan | (19) 1,430 | 10·0 |

Source: World Bank Atlas, 1971.

Undoubtedly GNP and economic-growth data are the most prominent factors in determining anybody's perceptions of economic capabilities. There are, of course, many other yardsticks but none compares with this one in prominence and therefore in psychological relevance. For instance, Britain is the second-largest international investor, well behind the United States, but much ahead of any other country. Her investments, which cannot be precisely valued, constitute an appreciable international asset which was rebuilt at the cost of great economic sacrifices after the war, while she was constantly in balance-of-payments difficulties. The profits from the investments were generally slow to materialize and rather low, owing to governmental policies of encouraging them in Commonwealth countries, although returns at home and in developed countries abroad would have been more promising. Nevertheless, by the mid-1960s, the accumulated investments were bringing in substantial returns—in 1962, a net inflow of £620 million after an additional investment abroad of some £500 million.

Not all statistics are very meaningful. After the floating of the pound, for instance, The Times commented editorially on 5 July 1972:

It is worth asking why countries have official reserves at all, if only to dispel the popular notion that they are some kind of ultimate yardstick of national prosperity. They are nothing of the kind. They are merely a technical adjunct of a fixed exchange rate system. If central banks did not wish to intervene in foreign exchange markets to influence the price at which their currency is bought and sold, there would literally be no purpose in holding reserves at all.

This is, of course, perfectly true, but, as Wilson testifies in his memoirs, his government was constantly preoccupied with the level of reserves, and its operations were seriously affected by the sensational importance atttibuted to the monthly statistics. Devaluation had only a temporary effect; the colossal short- and medium-term indebtedness—in actual fact a book-keeping operation—was paid off by 1972, and reserves more than doubled between 1968 and 1972; after twenty months of growth they had risen to over $7,000 million by May 1972. Almost at once, however, in one week of wild speculation between 15 and 22 June 1972, as much as $2,500 million had to be spent defending the parity of sterling, forcing the government to float the pound. Although it is true that the reserves are fundamentally meaningless, until and unless Britain is part of an international economic system sufficiently well organized to be immune from the vagaries of short-term capital movements (either through their efficient control or through allowing a freer play to market forces), they remain of immediate practical importance.

Britain's economic potential may be theoretically considered as enhanced by the exceptional concentration of her wealth. As Professor Karl Deutsch justifiably pointed out, the resources belonging to the top 10 per cent of the population are of special importance as they are more easily mobilizable; the remainder use their resources mainly for consumption. In the case of Britain the proportion may be around three-quarters of the national wealth, but (see above p. 24), this potential has not been fully mobilized for public purposes and her industrial investment is exceptionally low.

Immediately after the war, Britain's *military* capability was far greater than that of any other state except the United States and the Soviet Union, but by the beginning of the 1970s, other middle powers had caught up with her. By 1971 only her nuclear capability remained unique, with the 64 *Polaris* A-3 missiles in four nuclear submarines, although these are very few when compared with the more than 1,700 and nearly 2,000 intercontinental and submarine-launched missiles possessed by the Americans and the Russians respectively. According to expert opinion at home and abroad, Britain's professional forces were of an exceptionally high quality; it is, however, the figures of expenditure and of men under arms which are used to evaluate the respective national military efforts, although, in fact, they are by no means fully indicative of the military value of the capability possessed. *The Military Balance 1971/2* showed clearly that, while carrying a relatively greater burden of defence expenditure than France or Western Germany, Britain could no longer fully keep pace with them from her smaller economic base; the superpowers were ahead quite beyond her reach.

| | | | *As % of GNP* | | | |
|---|---|---|---|---|---|---|
| 1970 | 7·8 | 0·8 | 3·3 | 4·0 | 4·9 | 11 |
| | | *Defence Expenditure ($ million)* | | | | |
| *Year* | *USA* | *Japan* | *W. Germany* | *France* | *UK* | *USSR* |
| 1951 | 33,059 | 86 | — | 1,785 | 2,317 | 27,800 |
| 1960 | 45,380 | 421 | 2,885 | 3,885 | 4,640 | 17,000 |
| 1970 | 76,507 | 1,640 | 6,188 | 5,982 | 5,950 | 53,950 |

*Total Armed Forces (in thousands)*

| Year | USA | Japan | W. Germany | France | UK | USSR |
|------|-----|-------|------------|--------|-----|------|
| 1951 | 3,250 | 74 | — | 610 | 841 | 4,600 |
| 1960 | 2,514 | 206 | 270 | 781 | 520 | 3,623 |
| 1970 | 3,066 | 259 | 466 | 506 | 373 | 3,305 |

Source: ISS, The Military Balance 1971-2.

Britain's traditions are strongly geared to what the modern theorists call *'identitive'* capabilities. As Sir Eyre Crowe conceptualized the diplomatic practice in his 1907 memorandum, even during the heyday of her Empire in the nineteenth century, she based her foreign policy upon peaceful civilian diplomacy, the major principle of which was 'to harmonize with the general desires and ideals common to all mankind' and, specifically, to be 'closely identified with the primary and vital interests of a majority, or as many as possible, of the other nations'. This was the concomitant of her dominant position as the supreme sea power. After this power had waned, Britain was no longer faced with 'the jealousy and fear' of other nations, which Crowe has been concerned to avert.[10] At the same time, however, her diplomatic capability for exercising influence based upon a fund of goodwill[11] was bound to dwindle. Even the goodwill she had earned during the second world war proved a wasting asset, perhaps inevitably, perhaps because she had neglected opportunities of making the most of it (see p. 75).

Several aspects of Britain's successful identification of her interests with those of the United States and of her continental neighbours for the defence and rehabilitation of Western Europe, the less successful identification with the Commonwealth, and the doctrine of the 'three circles' will be discussed in Part Two. As Western anti-communist solidarity weakened, Britain failed to continue a basic community of interests either with the United States, for which other countries had become important as partners, or with Western Europe, which was engrossed in a process of integration in which Britain chose not to participate. The Commonwealth further loosened but, in the eyes of all developing states, Britain remained an imperialist as well as a rich state.

The English language can clearly be considered as a basis of cultural community and hence as an 'identitive' capability. English is the most useful language in international intercourse and therefore many people are willing to learn it, to be introduced to English culture, and to listen to news in English. It is, however, hard to estimate the value of people listening to the BBC Overseas Service, attending courses in English, borrowing books from libraries, or coming to study in Britain. Judging by the strenuous efforts of the French to maintain their language in international use, the English language should be an important asset; the successive governments, however, have not been able to develop a coherent cultural policy or to evolve and finance ambitious cultural strategies.

The degree of a state's influence depends not only upon its actual capabilities but also (and perhaps even more) on its *international standing*, prestige, recognition of status; as Britain's economic, military and technological leadership was dissipated, these diminished accordingly as a source of prestige. The various ills of Britain's postwar social life should not, however, obscure the fact that in the eyes of many foreigners Britain remains a sane, democratic, and reasonably tolerant although economically not very purposeful society. In communist countries the only standing that Britain enjoys, and it is by no means insubstantial, is based upon the belief that British citizens enjoy an exceptional amount of personal freedom. This rather important prestige element was, however, threatened by the recent deterioration of the social fabric in Britain accentuated by the habit of 'knocking Britain' and by the issues arising from citizenship rights of Commonwealth immigrants and prospective immigrants.

*Choice and Use of Capabilities*
In the past the British sought diplomatic influence based upon the harmonizing of interests; this was supported by naval power as a background threat which was occasionally used for a definite limited purpose. After 1945 the harmonizing of interests proved more and more difficult. It was successful immediately after the war, when, on the basis of common defences against a communist threat, Britain established the 'special relationship' and NATO; she participated in European economic rehabilitation, and co-operated with the independence movements within the Empire. The community of purpose did not, however, last for long. Britain did not identify herself with the European integration movement in the 1950s; the community of Western defence interests was somewhat weakened by the detente; commonwealth relations after independence were by no means smooth and became affected by the Rhodesian issue; the successful EFTA organization was too limited to counteract Britain's growing isolation both from the superpowers and from Western Europe. One of the major advantages of becoming a member of the enlarged Community is that it will provide a suitable framework for a new co-operative start.

The military end of the pattern was even more adversely affected, as the international conditions for the traditional limited use of British naval power had disappeared. First, much of Britain's military effort was directed towards new defence tasks, the permanent peacetime stationing of a large contingent on the continent and the evolution of a nuclear deterrent. Second, even within the Empire and the Commonwealth, the opportunities for decisive small-scale military efforts which could support diplomacy rapidly disappeared. Britain effectively intervened on a number of minor occasions, but the successful interventions in the Emergency in Malaya and in the Confrontation between Malaya and Indonesia, and the prolonged action in Cyprus were all on a much greater scale and of much longer duration than the traditional limited uses of force.[12]

A number of political and military factors contributed to this state of affairs: the strength of nationalism was aided by the sophistication of guerrilla warfare techniques and of the weapons which even very small states or dissident movements could acquire from communist sympathizers—even a very large gunboat is vulnerable to missiles; and the international climate of public opinion was strongly opposed to Western intervention. Gradually it became more and more unlikely that British military forces could be used for the traditional limited purposes. Neither could the British deterrent be effectively employed to close the power gap.

The withdrawal from the Canal Zone base and the 1956 Suez intervention demonstrated not only the difficulties confronted by the British forces and the limitations of the forces themselves, but also the intellectual confusion about their possible use. When the position of the forces in the Base had become untenable owing to Egyptian hostility, the 1954 House of Commons debate about withdrawal was conducted under the shadow of the Russian menace and the vulnerability of the base to a nuclear attack: it was left to Jo Grimond to point out that, under the current doctrine of 'massive retaliation', the likelihood of local, non-nuclear wars was higher rather than lower. When Eden decided on intervention in 1956, he did not dispute the validity of the 1954 arguments for withdrawal; moreover, instead of defending a position based upon a legal treaty, he had now to attack, contravening international law and without having harmonized Britain's interests with those of her major allies, especially the United States; finally, Britain lacked sufficient numbers of paratroops to mount a swift, decisive action. The military intervention was slow and massive—it involved 80,000 troops, 150 warships including seven aircraft-carriers and 40 submarines, 80 merchant ships carrying stores and 20,000 vehicles. the French doubted whether this massive scale was warranted—it is hard to say how far it was due to an overestimate of the fighting power of the British-trained Egyptian army, the memories of Arnhem, or the vague hope that the intimidating size of the force would help to counteract all the other disadvantages.

The lessons of the unsuccessful Suez intervention were reinforced by those of the successful Confrontation, at the peak of which as many as 55,000 British troops were employed. A major military overseas operation became unthinkable, not only in a politically unpropitious situation but also because of the crippling cost, even when conditions were promising. The opportunity arising through the ending of the Confrontation was the major factor in hastening the timing of the British decision to withdraw from east of Suez—the danger of another involvement of this kind ever arising in the future had to be strenuously avoided.

In the immediate future, while her contribution to NATO remains a steady commitment and while the military involvement in Ulster lasts, Britain will simply have no spare capability to undertake any military action elsewhere. It is plausible to assume that, during the deadlock in the negotiations over the rent for the Malta base in March 1972, Heath decided to withdraw rather than risk another Confrontation which would have strained the Armed Forces beyond their capacity.[13]

Although the economic and the political strands of Britain's external relations have traditionally been kept fairly separate, Britain's position as a great trading nation is regarded by many as an important capability. The Labour Party has been traditionally inclined to endeavour to substitute economic for military instruments. Even in Britain's greatly weakened position in 1947, the party's pamphlet, *Keep Left* (p. 40), developed the argument that she was in a strong bargaining position as a debtor country because she was also the biggest importer in the world—provided she did not get further into debt. The strength of Britain's commercial position for harmonizing her foreign policy with those of others was eloquently repeated by the then Foreign Secretary, Michael Stewart, in a BBC interview on 12 January 1969:

We are a great trading nation. It matters far more to us that, on the whole, the world should be at peace than that we should get 100 per cent of our own way in any one part of it. That means we are increasingly accepted as a country that has not got a special axe of its own to grind other than the axe all mankind has to grind of making the world more civilised and more prosperous. I think that is why so often when I go abroad as Foreign Secretary I am faced with the situation of country after country saying, 'We want your help.'[14]

Trade and investment, and membership of the sterling bloc were substantial links reinforcing the existence of the Commonwealth, although the British did not evolve clear policies of how to derive political benefits through bestowing economic ones. There was no equivalent of the French policies of granting 'political' loans to allies or of securing administrative control over loan recipients. As Britain lost her leading position in international economics, what had been legitimately regarded as assets in the past, now turned into liabilities. Despite her diminishing share of world trade, she remained the dominant trading partner for some Commonwealth countries, especially New Zealand and the West Indies, which constituted a serious liability in the negotiations for entry into the EEC at a time when both the economic and the political benefits of the Commonwealth had greatly decreased. Britain's indebtedness could not be turned to political advantage as the *Keep Left* pamphlet had proposed in 1947. She was kept solvent during the attacks on sterling by the Group of Ten concerned with maintaining the international monetary system but this did not secure influence for her; on the contrary, it subjected her economy to restrictive deflationary directives; in 1956 the run on the pound and the American refusal to authorize the £300 million the British had requested from the International Monetary Fund was the decisive reason why the Suez intervention had to be halted.

Despite the high prestige of the British culture, in contrast to the French, the British did not evolve any deliberate policy of using cultural instruments for the purposes of foreign policy in any coherent way. The general value of British cultural activities abroad, the success and the cost-effectiveness of the limited activities undertaken were, nevertheless, recognized. Thus, in 1954, the Drogheda Report[15] recommended a strictly non-political cultural policy in the expectation of considerable political and commercial benefits, although only after a number of years. The Duncan Report of 1968[16] praised the work of the British Council as cost-effective and only recommended a reorientation towards Europe and a greater stress upon culture instead of the previous stress upon the teaching of English, libraries, and the development of professional contacts and of educational facilities. *The Annual Report of the British Council 1969/70*, commenting on the implementation of the Duncan Report, explained the major political considerations in choosing priorities for cultural activities: 'will it open a door, or keep a foot in one, provide the setting for a special occasion, cultivate or compliment the receiving country, encourage trade?'[17]

# 5 Perceptions and Sources of Behaviour

*Basic Assumptions*

IT is a commonplace but also commonsense notion that foreign policy is built upon estimates of the trends in the international environment and that a resonable foundation for it can be found only in correct estimates. Individual events cannot, of course, be foreseen but trends, tendencies, and dispositions can. Many historical blunders can be explained by avoidable failures of foresight due to mistaken estimates, stupidity or wishful thinking. In 1909 Balfour neatly stated the problem in these words: . . . people who look forward and grasp the essential facts which will govern the future grouping of nations may be able to exert a profound influence on the political future of the world.[1]

A proper understanding of the world is particularly important for Britain, a country whose power is relatively limited when compared with the range of her interests: she can neither restrict herself to a foreign policy narrow in its scope like many small powers, nor afford as many mistakes as a country with a relatively much greater power potential for its foreign-policy purposes. Perceptions of reality are in fact so important that many writers focus their analysis upon them. This has, however, the drawback that we have to depend mainly upon the policy-makers' own statements, which are never fully reliable. To start with, it is difficult to disentangle the underlying perceptions from sheer political rhetoric. How far, for instance, did Macmillan and Wilson express their actual perceptions and beliefs when they were grandiloquently referring to Britain's world role? One cannot do more than resort to an impressionistic interpretation that whereas Macmillan was generally more sceptical, Wilson was more inclined to believe in his own rhetoric.

Moreover, the statements are the products and not the sources of policy decisions and, within their different timing and setting, they do not reproduce the occasions on which the actual decisions were made and the alternatives considered and discarded. In a country as complex as Britain, where the number of issues, institutions, and personalities involved is very large, an analysis of recent years cannot but be extremely tentative. It would, for instance, be very hard, if at all possible, to re-construct 'the attitudinal prism' of the policy-makers,[2] the lens through which the setting is filtered and which governs their perceptions, al-though many of the elements of such a presumed lens are discussed in the latter part of this chapter and in the subsequent one. Only a few less precise notions are employed here, in the way in which they often occur in political argument and are defined in dictionaries: politicians often accuse one another of acting on 'wrong assumptions' and of holding faulty 'images' or 'perceptions'. In theory, these two terms are fundamentally different. According to their relevant dictionary meanings, an assumption refers to taking things for granted, whereas an image refers to the percep-tion and evaluation of reality; assumptions are generally unspoken and refer to beliefs which are fundamental and upon which one's reasoning rests, whereas images have a much closer link with ones' consciousness and with real life. In fact, both are based upon the political culture and lifetime experiences of the individuals and the line between them is sometimes quite hard to draw. One can, for instance, speak of Bevin's 'assumption' of a Soviet threat in 1945 or of his 'perception' of it. Both would stem from the British political tradition of distrusting the Soviet Union as well as from Bevin's personal negative experiences with the communists both in the British trade-union movement and inter-nationally. 'Assumption' in this connection conveys that he adopted his attitude unquestioningly, 'image' that he took into account the over-whelming Soviet power contained only by the uncertain nuclear deterrent, the ideological attractions of communism to the French and the Italians, and, most dangerously, to the Germans, and the expansionist Soviet behaviour in Eastern Europe, the Mediterranean, and the Far East.

If, on the one hand, assumptions merge into perceptions, on the other, they can merge into values and aspirations. It is one of the re-current themes of political argument that politicians not only perceive what they wish to perceive, but that they hide their preferences in seemingly objective and generally unarticulated assumptions, either through ignorance, or in order to deceive others, or to spare themselves the trouble and often the pain or shock of a more realistic appraisal.

It is a fairly arbitrary task to choose for analysis the assumptions which are most relevant. In foreign policy, as in all other areas of social behaviour, the assumptions are legion; most of them remain hidden not only from those who analyse behaviour from the outside but also from the people directly involved. The human tendency is to remain consistent in one's thinking, to restrict adjustment to the minimum; this works for continuity and tradition and frequently blinds us to such evidence as disturbs the balance of our image. Only when discrepancies have become really blatant, and policy outcomes highly unsatisfactory and disturbing, are our assumptions fundamentally re-examined.

In a simplified form, the historical roots of the basic assumptions of Britain's postwar foreign policy derive from three major periods. First, most strongly established, were the traditions of a dominant imperial power which reached its apogee in Victorian times; the assumptions concerning Britain's central role within the international system are firmly rooted there. Second, her interwar experiences, particularly appeasement but also the spread of communism after 1919, the American withdrawal into isolationism, and the failure of the League of Nations were frequently noted. Somehow policy-makers did not seem to note with equal clarity the lessons of Germany's rapid recovery after the first world war or the fact that the failure of British co-operation with France had been the crucial reason for the collapse of the interwar system. Third, her recent wartime experience confirmed her central position as one of the Big Three and led the policy-makers to assume that the Americans could be managed, the Commonwealth would co-operate, and the Russians would create difficulties. Thus the 'lessons of history' partly reinforced and partly contradicted one another.

Max Beloff[3] identifies as the central assumption upon which British foreign policy has been based, 'that the United Kingdom is a political unit whose motive force is provided by the collective desires of its citizens and that it is the business of the government to pursue these as far as lies within its power'. In this cautious formulation, the assumption does not detract from the facts of reality—it corresponds with the constitutional practices of the country but acknowledges the facts of interdependence by stipulating that the frequently overwhelming international forces must be taken into account.

This assumption has not been universally accepted without question. Immediately after the war, in particular, some, especially on the extreme Left, were expressing the view that national states belonged to the order of the past and that Britain should, therefore, endeavour to merge herself in the United Nations. This was neither a very popular nor a well-thought-out view; it expressed a preference for using the United Nations as an instrument of foreign policy but gave no guidance as to substance of policy; as it would clearly have been unrealistic simply to assume that Britain would leave decisions about her vital problems to United Nations majorities. Another, more influential Commonwealth school believed that Britain should not pursue a policy of her own but one of the broader Commonwealth system, which would be governed not by British national interests alone but by those of all its members. The former alternative looked into the uncertain future, whereas the latter was based upon the interpretation of the past and of its consequences in the present. Both were unrealistic and both collapsed under the impact of postwar developments—the growing frustrations, especially with the anti-colonial majorities in the United Nations and the ineffectiveness of the Commonwealth as a political organization.

The central assumption was accompanied by another: that Britain's domestic arrangements, the international system, and Britain's role within it would all return to some approximation of prewar 'normalcy'. It stands to reason, and all contemporary evidence confirms this, that not only the Prime Minister and the Foreign Secretary but the whole political elite were acutely aware of the fundamentally changed international circumstances and of Britain's weakness in 1945. These facts were clearly perceived and sometimes voiced by the Russians, by many Americans (notably by Admiral Leahy at Potsdam) and by many Australians. Unlike these foreign observers, however, the British persisted in regarding this state of affairs as merely temporary.

Several reasons can be adduced for the lingering belief that Britain would fully recover and retain some central place within the international system. First, the convergent pressing security and economic problems demanded full attention and left no spare capacity or time for fundamental reappraisals in a country exhausted by five years of total war. Second, confidence in Britain's traditions had not been undermined, as on the continent, by defeat and failure; on the contrary, she emerged from the war in the glory and with the prestige of being one of the Big Three; she expected and received recognition for her war effort. Third, the tradition of pragmatic thinking was reinforced by the revulsion against the ideological thinking of the interwar period which had led to the excesses of both Marxism and fascism. Fourth, the central elements of the situation, e.g. the strategic role of nuclear weapons, or the alignment of world currencies, or the technological revolution, could not be fully understood or foreseen. Fifth, a number of converging factors helped temporarily to disguise the extent of Britain's weakness and to promise a fairly full and speedy recovery: the continuing, though at first somewhat reluctant American support; the belief in the Commonwealth as a source of strength; Britain's relatively strong position when compared with the continental states of China or Japan, whether in military power, in the strength of the socio-economic structure, or in prestige. Finally, as any revision would fairly obviously have amounted to a diminution of Britain's standing, there was an underlying psychological reluctance to engage in it. It is therefore scarcely surprising that, despite a realistic perception of Britain's weaknesses, the expectations of full economic recovery and the attachment to a world role were long-lived.

The confused though important arguments about British sovereignty employed in the 1972 debate about the EEC refer to the increasingly questionable validity of the central assumption of British foreign policy. The argument can be thus restructured. The assumption that Britain would continue as a political unit whose main motive force comes from the inside has been weakened by the erosion of the accompanying assumption that, once the postwar world had got over the war disturbance and settled into some form of a stabler order, Britain would have sufficient capabilities to satisfy the wishes of her citizens and to continue playing a significant individual world role. It no longer lies within the powers of the government to pursue effectively the desires of its citizens; joining the EEC would probably make it more effective in this respect. This, of course, would amount to a major modification of the basic assumption of British foreign policy, and the anti-marketeers oppose it on these grounds. The major difference between 1945 and the early 1970s is that whereas in the former period the questioners were in a minority, this time it is the government itself which has revised the assumption.

Bearing in mind that 'assumptions' carry not only unquestioned fundamental beliefs but also elements of contemporary perceptions of the major features of the international environment and of expectations for the future, the policy-makers' basic assumptions in the immediate postwar years can be summed up as follows: (1) the Soviet Union and international communism constitute the major threat; (2) the United States is the only possible provider of security and of economic support—but not a very reliable one; (3) the Commonwealth and the remaining Empire can constitute an element of power for Britain; (4) Western Europe is capable of economic and political recovery but not of effective integration; (5) the United Nations has a doubtful future as a major instrument of foreign policy. All these assumptions were closely interconnected, as all referred to Britain's position within the international system, her world role, and her world interests. The policies in the major fields emanating from them will be discussed in some detail in chapters 8–11. Here it suffices to note that, by the early 1970s, these assumptions, too, had been eroded by the flow of events. Only the negative and relatively unimportant assumption regarding the United Nations still holds good; the others have had to be heavily modified or discarded outright: the 1945 views about Western Europe and the Commonwealth are obviously untenable and the validity of those about the Soviet Union and the United States has, to say the least, substantially diminished.

Returning to Balfour's statement, it is arguable that the failure in 1945 to grasp the essential facts which 'govern the future grouping of nations' was an important element in limiting Britain's 'influence on the political future of the world'. When the specific policies are examined the question will be asked how far, in view of Britain's central power position in 1945, the assumptions held by the British amounted to self-fulfilling prophecies—especially in provoking the hostility of the Russians, in helping to paralyse the United Nations, and in obstructing the integration of Europe, and how effectively these assumptions were questioned by their critics. First, however, some questions regarding the forces shaping the assumptions should be looked into in a general way.

### Perceptions and Myths
How far were the assumptions based upon a realistic perception of the world? Extensive knowledge of the world by individual Britons is an important contributory element of an official image which is likely often to be better informed than those of other nations not enjoying similar international contacts. In 1963 the American Professor Bruce M. Russett quoted as still relevant the following opinion by another American, Nicholas Roosevelt, expressed in the 1930s:

Thanks to the existence of a large body of persons in England whose business has been almost entirely dependent on foreign trade and who have, in consequence, had to inform themselves thoroughly about international conditions... a constant watch on world affairs is maintained by influential persons in England with the result that the interdependence of the various parts of the modern world is better understood there than anywhere else.[4]

Thus the Foreign Office had a propitious background for establishing its own expertise and for drawing upon supplementary outside sources. The fund of knowledge and understanding was consolidated by the expertise of the Overseas Services of the BBC and of its Monitoring Service.

The ways in which a well established civil service operates are inevitably traditionalist. Images carefully built up by observation are relegated to files which, after a short time within the operational department, end in the central research department. They are, of course, occasionally referred to, but generally only the inherited agreed attitude determines the continuing image. The bureaucratic inconvenience of going back to the origins of the prevalent perceptions and of questioning conventional wisdom is, by necessity, great; traditionalism seems to be inevitably proportional to the operational efficiency of the bureaucracy—in Britain it is, therefore, very pronounced. The priorities are, likewise, traditional. It was institutionally difficult to incorporate the European integration movement in other official perceptions of the post-war political realities of Western Europe for the simple reasons that there was no special department or official to be responsible for them. There was thus nobody to press for an appraisal of the situation or a decision and it was partly because of this that the governments of the 1950s delayed any final decision, in the expectation that the integration attempts would not succeed but, should they succeed, that Britain would still have an opportunity to join later on. This was a reasonable appraisal in 1950 and in 1954, but not in 1957.

Obviously not all information can be expected to be full and correct and not all appraisals to be realistic. Even in Britain's intimate relations with the United States many avoidable misperceptions occurred. Professor Richard E. Neustadt[5] convincingly analyses the British (and American) failures, in the Suez and Skybolt affairs, to comprehend the subtleties of each other's domestic political system. Churchill, Bevin, Macmillan, and Wilson obviously all went to great trouble in forming a realistic perception of American intentions and policies, although Wilson and, to a lesser extent, Macmillan seem to have overestimated British influence upon the United States. Sir Anthony Eden, by contrast, treated the Americans rather cavalierly, especially during the Geneva Conference in 1954 and over the Middle East, notably in the Suez affair.[6] It is important to note that Sir Anthony was the only postwar policymaker who seems seriously to have departed from the perceptions of the officials in this respect.

In relations with Russia, the British appear to have been more realistic and flexible than the Americans or the French in perceiving Soviet intentions and in interpreting Soviet policies. They were the first to perceive both the dangers inherent in Soviet capabilities and possible intentions after 1945 and the possibilities of a detente in the early 1950s. In the 1960s, however, when the French and, considerably later, also the Americans had become actively engaged in a detente, the British attitudes remained conservative (see pp. 193ff.). Only long-range historical perspective will enable us to tell to what extent this was due to prudent realism or to loss of flexibility.

Two major factors affected other perceptions. First colonial and Commonwealth affairs were institutionally separated until their final integration in the Foreign and Commonwealth Office in 1970. The perceptions and evaluations of the Colonial and Commonwealth Offices on the crucial problem of nationalism and emancipation did not coincide and they clashed strongly over the issue of the Central African Federation. As these issues played a central part in British United Nations policies, the co-ordination of British views on this important forum created a problem.

Second, the continuing governmental preoccupation with Britain's world role lent salience and importance to the policies and intentions of the two superpowers and to Commonwealth policies. Other, less salient, relationships accordingly received less attention at the top. This is particularly clear in the case of relations with France, which, throughout the war and right up to the end of the 1960s, were consistently subordinated to those with the United States. Churchill's priorities were determined by the situation during the war—he did his best to secure a great power status for postwar France but clearly had to give precedence to his efforts to maintain Anglo-American co-operation. His priorities and his relative neglect of the relations with de Gaulle were fully justified and were not based on any misperceptions or blurred perceptions of de Gaulle's policies.

The Foreign Office files can hardly have been incorrect in their appreciation of French foreign-policy aims in the postwar years but the successive governments simply did not pay very much regard to them, remaining preoccupied with other, more pressing matters. Thus, despite the fruitful co-operation over the Marshall Plan, Britain was not forthcoming about the French problems with regard to German rearmament and Indochina, and abruptly severed her brief co-operation with the French in the Suez affair. In *Pointing the Way*, Macmillan elaborates upon the care which he lavished upon appreciating Kennedy correctly and establishing his relations with him, whereas in his relations with de Gaulle, though these were crucial for the application to enter the EEC which was being negotiated, he seems to have relied fully upon his wartime recollections, at that time some twenty years old. By the beginning of 1969, after the British perceptions of de Gaulle's intentions had been shaped by his two vetoes, the Foreign Office was completely unreceptive to proposals for bilateral talks which he made to the British Ambassador in Paris, and prevailed upon Wilson[7] to divulge these to the German Chancellor, breaking confidence and greatly increasing tension with the French. The French archives may eventually confirm that this was not a justified act of prudence but a loss of opportunity due to a well established image of the President as being hostile to Britain.[8]

In the case of Britain's relations with the European Free Trade

Association, no such doubt or ambiguity existed in her perceptions of the attitudes to her imposing a surcharge upon imports in the 1964 crisis or to her applications to join the EEC. In this, as in other sets of relations with smaller states, it was not a question of misperceiving their attitudes and wrongly anticipating their reactions but merely one of ignoring them in order to pursue what the governments of the day regarded as more important British interests. There is no indication in Britain's postwar record that perceptions in individual cases were strongly affected by any broad objectives or principles of foreign policy. The central place of the 'special relationship' does not seem to have affected the outcomes to any great extent; it is even more doubtful whether it ever affected the underlying perceptions (see pp. 203ff.). One is left with the impression of a pragmatic, case-to-case policy in which evaluations were based upon quite a realistic perception of each individual situation. If policies were unsuccessful, this was due more to confusion about the nature and the implications of the complex British interests involved rather than to serious misinterpretations of reality. The only signal exception can be found in Britain's refusal to take full part in the Messina talks in 1955, which was based upon the mistaken anticipation that they were bound to fail, and that therefore the inevitable clash between the British opposition to full-scale integration and the continental views about its desirability should be avoided. This crucial failure to anticipate correctly deprived Britain of the last opportunity to help to mould the political shape of Europe. Until a fuller history can be reconstructed, in general terms one can attribute the failure largely to preoccupation with Britain's world role and the Commonwealth, compared with which European affairs were much less salient.

To take the important issue-area of colonial emancipation, when compared with the records of other imperial powers, the successive British governments can be credited with a realistic perception of the strength of nationalist movements in the dependencies, although, in some cases, events naturally moved faster than had been anticipated. The record of adjustments was, nevertheless, somewhat mixed. Britain was liberal in her grants of independence—except where she came up against the intractable settlers' problem in Southern Rhodesia. On the whole, she also quite readily adjusted her economic interests from a footing of political superiority to one of co-operation based upon common economic interests, although not as readily in the Middle East regarding oil as the Americans did; she was much slower in adjusting her chain of bases.

The Heath Government has inaugurated an era which, for several converging reasons, may lead to a fundamental revision of British perceptions. First, the focus of attention has shifted decisively to Western Europe. Not only is the general governmental directive to the officials to 'think European', but, with the passage of time, the images of the non-European world are likely to become blurred. Second, ever since the beginning of the Nixon Administration in 1968, co-operation between Britain and the United States has gradually become less unique and intimate, both the Americans and the British turning more to their own national interests. The policies of the two countries have not necessarily clashed but they have coincided less and less, as the United States has concentrated on cultivating bilateral relations with the communist powers, and as Britain has upon her relations with the EEC. It seems likely that, in the longer run, despite the continuing ease of Anglo-American communications, the mutual perceptions will become less full. Third, with the weakening of the post-independence links and the repatriation of the majority of British experts from the developing world, a major source of British expertise on it has been rapidly diminishing; characteristically, both in academic analysis and in the books written for the general public, the Empire and the period of British rule have received much more attention than the post-independence period. Lastly, within the Western European context, the growing interdependence which had been recognized as inevitable not only in defence but also in major economic issues, has made it imperative to co-ordinate British policies with those of her partners to a much greater extent than hitherto. This inevitably will require an increasing degree of co-ordination of the national images upon which these policies will be based. Although this is an aspect of the British entry into the EEC which has not received public attention so far, it is undoubtedly one of fundamental importance. The evolution of Community policies has been obstructed not only by differing national conceptions of individual national interests but also by differing perceptions of international realities—progress towards greater co-ordination of foreign policies, which is the avowed British objective, will require greater co-ordination at both levels.

Perceptions are based upon information but as this cannot be complete or fully reliable, they also include an element of 'belief', by which we loosely refer to confidence that something exists or will exist. If such beliefs prove false but linger despite accumulating evidence, they are often referred to as 'myths'. There is, of course, no demarcation line between the two; it can be drawn only in retrospect and, even then, without much precision. A belief is based not upon certainty but upon probability or plausibility; it is impossible to determine the point at which belief is converted into myth.

For instance, the two major postwar British beliefs, in the lasting importance of 'the special relationship' with the United States, and in the importance of the Commonwealth as an element of Britain's power, both gradually weakened, but, whereas the United States link retained substance throughout the period, the Commonwealth links became much more rapidly attenuated; far from being a source of support, the Commonwealth became rather one of weakness, of numerous military and economic responsibilities, not compensated for by trade, which remained substantial but was diminishing in its importance, or by any meaningful political support. Thus, in the late 1960s, it became customary to speak about the Commonwealth myth (or, similarly, of the myth of sterling) but not about the myth of the 'special relationship'. The confusion between the terms is such that some of the more exaggerated expectations of the benefits of Britain's joining the EEC can be referred to as a nascent myth—the EEC is unlikely to prove a panacea for all of Britain's ills, as some of its supporters hope, and in historical perspective it may appear to be as misleading as the imperial and Commonwealth ideas were in their last phases.

A time-lag in the revision of the existing beliefs was inevitable, considering the extensive scope of Britain's adjustment to postwar circumstances. With considerable exaggeration and with some irritation, but not without some justification, one outspoken American critic speaks of 'myths, slogans, clichés and catchwords', among which he includes the strength of sterling, Commonwealth ties, colonial responsibilities, outward-looking, Atlantic Community, special relationship, international co-operation without federation, and sovereignty of Parliament.[9] The remaining sections of this chapter look into a few major sources of British foreign policy with a view to determining some causes of the time-lag in the adjustment of the policy-makers' perceptions.

*Rationality*

In many ways, references in political argument to 'rationality' are quite similar to references to 'national interest": both serve as the basis for praise and opprobrium and are accepted as ways of arguing about our likes and dislikes. Both, therefore, constitute political data which deserve analysis and clarification as far as possible. In this analysis 'rationality' is equated with being reasonable, being governed by some general rules of orderly thinking rather than by other, non-rational elements, such as sentiments or traditions. The concept follows common usage and therefore remains imprecise.

References to the 'rationality' of foreign-policy decisions are perhaps not as explicit as those to their relevance for the pursuit of 'national interest', but they are implicitly present in most political arguments. It can be taken for granted that the proponents of a move in foreign policy, unless they are consciously governed by a 'non-rational' consideration, such as deeply felt sentiments or imperious demands of the domestic system, invariably assume, though do not necessarily argue, that this move is rational; their opponents frequently assume and argue the opposite. Any controversial decision in postwar British foreign policy can be, and actually has been, argued about in terms of its rationality, from the emancipation of India and Pakistan in 1947 to entry into the EEC in 1973.

While the scope of application of the term 'rational' in political argument is extremely wide, it is much narrower in application to actual policy behaviour and to the political analysis of the latter. To start with, only the salient sectors of reality are subject to full rational scrutiny—the less important ones are often dealt with largely on the basis of their relevance to the salient sectors. Moreover, salient issues are also generally urgent, which limits the time available to the policy-makers for rational assessments in depth. Lastly, as will be discussed later, the concept of 'rationality' does not readily apply to all the elements of decision-making.

Presumably the most promising way of searching for non-rational or irrational behaviour would be by looking at a few instances with unfavourable outcomes. It becomes immediately obvious that no clear rational principles can be discovered to apply to value choices. From the perspective of the 1970s, Britain's prolonged pursuit of a world role, discussed in Chapter 7, can be regarded as 'irrational', although only in its last stages. It did not, however, appear so to the British elite or public in the 1950s, and to argue conclusively about the rationality of continuing it even later would be futile, especially as the value of international prestige is hard to calculate, and that of electoral gains is an ever-present and 'rational' consideration for the government of the day.

Doubts, however, arise as to how 'rational' was the behaviour of Macmillan's and, particularly, of Wilson's governments when they continued to play a world role in the 1960s. The prestige accruing through their activities diminished as Britain's efforts became increasingly less promising and less successful, and Wilson's initiative as the Co-Chairman of the Geneva Conference may be justifiably regarded as having reduced rather than enhanced it. Both governments have been accused of having expended much energy on foreign-policy issues at the cost of domestic ones. However, it is misleading to judge choices of priorities in politics, and one may suspect also in large areas of economics, by such a simple 'opportunity cost' analysis. Admittedly both Prime Ministers used their world-role performances to distract public discontents from the unsatisfactory state of the domestic economy but would a greater expenditure of their energies upon the economy necessarily have produced more positive results? Wilson, and possibly even Macmillan, devoted as much attention to Britain's economy as they were capable of doing; in the absence of suitable expedients to improve its performance, additional efforts might have been as counter-productive as many of those that were actually made.

As regards the formation of assumptions and images, the concept of 'rationality' is likewise of limited use. The basic assumption that Britain would somehow recover her power position within the international system may appear unreasonable to us in the 1970s but did not appear so to the British decision-makers immediately after the war. If their assumption of Soviet expansionism was wrong, as some 'revisionists' today claim, how could the decision-makers of the day discover this without taking unacceptable risks? This assumption was revised by the Conservative governments in the 1950s only against the background of relative security provided by NATO; the assumption of Britain's future recovery sufficient to play an independent world role was gradually revised and was finally abandoned only with the coming of the Heath Government. If the analysis of 'rationality' can be applied to the choices of values and the formation of assumptions at all, it refers only to procedures. In general terms, it seems unreasonable to carry on with the same policies starting from similar assumptions within a rapidly changing international environment without periodical revision, although we must, of course, allow for the limited capacity of governments for undertaking such revisions. The argument about rationality thus turns to one about tradition (see below, pp. 101ff.); behaviour is irrational which delays rational rethinking of values and assumptions for too long, after the policies pursued have clearly proved to be unsuccessful.

The most appropriate area in which an analysis of rationality can be used is that of ends–means calculations. In the words of the leading sociological theoretician, Talcott Parsons:

Action is rational in so far as it pursues ends possible within the conditions of the situation, and by means which, among those available to the actor, are intrinsically best adopted to the end of reasons understandable and verifiable by positive empirical science.[10]

Superficially, this definition appears to be precise, although it does not offer a very firm base for a clear-cut analysis. If, for instance, we take the Suez expedition of 1956 as a *prima facie* irrational decision, arguably, in the short run, Eden could have expected to attain the several ends he pursued—keeping the Canal open, restoring Britain's authority, and toppling Nasser—through a fast military action and the occupation of the Canal Zone by paratroops. The only clearly irrational element of his action was the slow-moving military intervention which could not secure these ends: as, however, he had no means for a more effective, faster intervention, the ends were unattainable and hence their choice irrational, too. In fact, additional longer-term elements must be added to this analysis. Supposing a fast military intervention had been possible and had secured Eden full military control of the Canal Zone—how on earth would the forces have been able to retain this control, as only two years earlier they had proved incapable of doing so? Antagonizing the whole Arab world, the United States, and the United Nations all added up to a cost so high that the rationality of Eden's actions must be questioned even on the assumption of its possible immediate success.

Quantification in monetary terms of costs and benefits is only a subsidiary method of reasoning in foreign-policy issues. Obviously the government's inability to meet the immediate costs has repeatedly narrowed the parameters of its action—e.g. of such decisions as whether to maintain a separate zone in Germany or responsibility for Greece and Turkey in 1947, to build another aircraft carrier in the mid-1960s, or to maintain an effective east of Suez role. As soon, however, as we go beyond the immediate future, estimates become uncertain. Is the turn from east of Suez to Europe justified in terms of the growing trade with Europe and of the diminishing prospects in the Third World in the past or, on the contrary, is the next round of economic growth likely to be prominent in the latter? Nobody could reliably forecast the short-term costs of entry into the EEC as agricultural prices were rapidly changing and the Community's Common Agricultural Policy was vulnerable to many pressures; the long-term opportunities for growth could be estimated only in quite impressionistic terms.

*Tradition and other Obstacles to Rationality*
An important alternative to rational thinking is found in what is variously called prescription, tradition, conservatism, inertia, &c. What all these refer to is policies which cannot be attributed to conscious, deliberate choice, but are based rather upon confirmed habit, practice, and lack of rational consideration, and are characterized by continuity and inertia,

by legitimation of historical tradition, and by durability of routine.

Tradition often plays a more important part in politics than it is given credit for; in restrospect, historians often discover continuities which survive real revolutions, such as medieval traditions after the Renaissance (Karl Becker), British traditions in the United States, *ancien régime* traditions in post-revolutionary France (Georges Sorel), nationalist traditions in Communist Russia and China. British political culture is much more directly steeped in history than that of her continental neighbours. Having industrialized early and having been free for a long time from the upheavals of a social revolution or of a defeat in war, Britain has enjoyed, and, as some would put it now, has also been the victim of, exceptional continuity. The undisturbed and successful past is an obvious point of reference for thinking about the present which is felt to be continuous with it. Britain's 'political culture' can best be characterized as a particular and peculiar mixture which merits the ambiguous description of 'traditionally modern'.[11]

Tradition is so strong and the past is such a salient feature of Britain's culture, that forms have a tendency to survive their substance. This applied even to British postwar literature until the 1960s. All were aware of the passing of the pre-war civilization but many of the books written continued to express the sentiments of the interwar period; instead of trying to comprehend the new world, they asked how much of the old world had survived.[12] This characteristic is even more pronounced in politics, in which, as Walter Bagehot has noted, the elements of the constitution which stop being 'effective' are retained within the system for merely ceremonial purposes; in the initial stages, few notice the changes in the distribution of power. Professor Waltz,[13] for instance, was struck by the fact that successive adaptations to Britain's reduced capabilities ever since the beginning of the century were not clearly explained to the public: the military alignment with France and Russia was disguised under the ambiguously loose name of *entente*; the Phillimore Report of 1918 represented the League of Nations as a renewed Concert of Europe and hence the Covenant did not command much debate in the House of Commons; in the earlier parliamentary debates, British entry into the EEC was represented as a predominantly economic issue. 'A hard residuum of national habits and deep-seated attitudes has remained' even after the individual world role has dwindled.

The concomitant is that the changes proposed often fell short of what should have been aspired to under the circumstances. Neither the *entente cordiale* nor the League of Nations fully met the needs of the day; and, regarding the continent, until faced with a *fait accompli*, the successive governments were merely trying to prevent and obstruct a fuller union instead of endeavouring to exercise at least a degree of control over the integration movement.

The first reason for the power of conservatism lies in the physiological limitations of the human brain. So many matters require attention in foreign policy that all of them simply cannot be rationally considered. The situation was particularly acute after 1945 when the Labour government was faced with a uniquely wide range of foreign and domestic policy issues; it was not really remedied while the successive governments were pursuing foreign policy within its traditional wide scope.

Institutionally, the continuity of British foreign policy was ensured by the strength and cohesion of the civil service and the skills historically evolved by the diplomatic service, although the latter was somewhat diluted by its amalgamation with other external services. This tradition played a crucial part as the successive Prime Ministers did not seriously question it, either because they partook of it or otherwise because they were unable to formulate rational alternatives. Once the climate of official opinion has crystallized into a defined attitude or policy-position, the policies stemming from it assume, within the political system, an aura of near-inevitability. A forceful Foreign Secretary can command full co-operation for his initiatives as long as his own views are in basic agreement with those prevalent among the officials, as was the case of Ernest Bevin. George Brown, however, soon fell out with his officials and could not prevail against them. Arthur Henderson's experience in the interwar period showed how arduous, perhaps impossible, is the task of trying to prevail. He insisted on Britain signing the Optional Clause of the Statute of the World Court against the views of the legal advisers, but the latter managed to insist on reservations which rendered the signature a fairly meaningless gesture. The Prime Minister can, however, occasionally bypass the Office, as did Chamberlain over appeasement and Sir Anthony Eden over Suez, in both cases with costly results.

Other obstacles to rationality can be found in the structure of Britain's defence: its intricate bureaucratic processes, the commitment required by modern technology of vast resources to new weapons systems, often a whole decade before they can become operational. Britain maintained the costliest and technologically most ambitious defence programmes of all the middle powers, and even when the latter began to catch up, the rigidities of her system remained unique. The economic and social obstacles to a rational policy of change and its implementation—industrial obsolescence, the insistence on full employment at all costs, the commitment to welfare expenditure, electoral considerations, and so on have already been discussed (see above pp. 47ff.).

These institutional and administrative factors are strongly reinforced by an economic one. Once policies are fully established, they involve an investment of resources which would be greatly reduced in value through any change and may be deprived of value altogether if the change is fundamental. This seems to be at least a reasonable contributory explanation for continuing to maintain overseas bases and commitments, or the nuclear deterrent; it was sometimes easier to retain them beyond their utility, not only because their reappreciation was difficult but because they represented potential assets of foreign policy which would be reduced or even scrapped in the process of revision; in some cases cancellations and withdrawals threatened to cost as much or more as staying put.

Some important obstacles to change are psychological—stubbornness, pride, refusal to admit oneself in the wrong, often, indeed, mere wishful thinking. Most important of all may have been the British reluctance to consider revision and change when these were obviously likely to be to the detriment of Britain's status. It seemed preferable to continue traditions as far as possible in the hope that adaptations would be minimal; each successive government hopefully started with new recipes for economic revival so that nobody seemed to realize the danger that continuing delays in a fundamental readjustment could increase the scope of the adaptations necessary as Britain's position was weakening rather than getting stronger.

Finally, a number of widespread British interests were involved in the maintenance of the *status quo* or rather a return as far as was possible, to an approximation of the pre-war *status quo*. As long as it seemed possible, it was in Britain's interest to continue rather than to innovate.

By the beginning of the 1970s the impact of the factors working for continuity had greatly weakened: post-imperial interests had been drastically reduced; the more limited scope of British foreign policy, now primarily regionally-oriented, allowed an opportunity for its more intensive reconsiderations; with the lapse of years, a return to an approximation of the old *status quo* had become unthinkable; the conservatism of the civil service had either diminished or had been overcome by the politicians, following the unsatisfactory outcomes of many traditional policies, notably the defence of sterling; the successive setbacks to Britain's national pride had made the nation and its political elite more receptive to change; indeed, some segments of it were positively eager to depart from tradition and to adopt a foreign policy adapted to the reduced status. The stage was set for the drastic changes introduced by Heath.

He ended not only the consensus in domestic politics but, parallel with it, fundamentally revised the traditional close ties both with the United States and the Commonwealth. It can be said that Heath attempted to apply a rational cost-effective reasoning to the conduct of Britain's foreign policy, as neither the 'special relationship' nor the Commonwealth bonds remained paying propositions. This did not, however, necessarily amount to a swing from tradition to rationality. One need not be an anti-marketeer to conceive the possibility that one orthodoxy may merely be superseded by another one, that one tradition may be replaced by another, new one.

Although we cannot thus be sure to what extent Britain's entry into the EEC will enable policy-makers to apply rational calculation to major foreign-policy issues, as it is applied to the specific ones within the EEC, it will certainly help to bring an end to some well-established traditions. First, it will shift the focus of attention from relations with the superpowers and from the various issues and changes within the global system with which Britain cannot effectively cope as an individual nation-state, to the more manageable regional system within and through which she will have to operate in the future. Characteristically, the major issues of Britain's diplomacy in the first half of 1973 were how to shape Community relations with the United States and her position on the future international financial system and the European Security and Co-operation Conference: Britain clearly had no scope and consequently made no attempts to develop individual national policies on any of these.

Second, as was partly noticeable already during the 1971 negotiations, the need to consider individual policies in respect to their bearings upon Britain's central EEC policy imposes a rational scrutiny with a fairly clear criterion of evaluation on practically the whole range of Britain's foreign policy. Undoubtedly, as has been argued, continuity will not be fully broken; indeed, changes are unlikely to go nearly as far as those following major political revolutions in other countries. One may, however, hopefully assume that the new awareness due to 'thinking European', the rational scrutiny made necessary by the entry into the EEC, will at least create an opportunity for a far-reaching revision of traditions; how far the actual revision will go will depend on the circumstances and, to a large extent, upon the political will brought to bear both in defence of traditions and in favour of innovation.

*Paradigms*

Another non-rational guide to foreign policy behaviour is often found in the behaviour of other states which are chosen as paradigms; states which seem to be in a basically similar situation and are doing reasonably well, and the most powerful and successful states of the period tend to be widely imitated. In a way, following examples is similar to following one's own tradition as in both cases imitation of precedents deemed appropriate offers an easy substitute for laborious reasoning afresh. States which lack their own tradition make extensive use of paradigms. Many new states, for instance, started their foreign policies on the basis of those of their ex-metropolitan states and substituted the experiences of the latter for their own. With her rich tradition, Britain had no need to follow any paradigms in the past; indeed, she had been the leader and innovator in many domestic and foreign domains. When her power position was seriously weakening at the beginning of this century, British traditions remained, nevertheless, fully relevant, being to some extent also followed by the Americans and by the Dominions. This feeling that the Anglo-American tradition remained relevant was strongly reinforced by the wartime and postwar partnership. Some of Britain's postwar difficulties can be traced to the ensuing Anglo-American tangle. Although the gap in resources between the partners was becoming colossal, for a while it was rather hard to realize just how asymmetrical the partnership was becoming, so that in many respects the pursuit of common traditions and objectives became transformed into following the United States paradigm, a paradigm which was highly unsuitable for Britain owing to the great discrepancy in power. The discovery of the hard realities of the situation was impeded by the natural psychological reluctance to admit the extent to which Britain had lost power and had become dependent.

Inevitably the British followed advanced American technology, both military and civilian. They were unable to maintain their lead in a few areas, e.g. jet engines or nuclear generating stations, and became dependent upon the Americans for military and economic co-operation. Until the American domestic and Vietnam crises in the late 1960s, the United States became also the paradigm of a successful dynamic mass society; Kennedy personalized the dynamism of change for the British public at large, and, even more importantly, for Harold Wilson, who copied some of his behaviour, e.g. the image of the dynamic first 'hundred days'.

British leaders could not readily find an example elsewhere, and rightly regarded their country as being in a unique position, much more powerful than that of others except the superpowers. Hence British domestic and foreign policies remained largely unique. In the area of

East–West relations, Britain was not merely following the United States but inaugurated both the cold war and the detente; she pursued a highly individual policy of building a welfare state at home, of emancipating her Empire and of leading in the rehabilitation of Western Europe. When all these individual policies lost momentum and Britain's resources were being gradually surpassed by those of other middle powers, it was in the policies of the latter, especially of France, that new paradigms were occasionally sought. This was a slow, difficult, and very confused process which can be best explained by examples.

Economic growth was an area in which Britain at first behaved idiosyncratically. Aided by the favourable trends in world trade as well as by generous American assistance, the post-war Labour government managed to reach ambitious export targets despite the expenditure of resources on the welfare state and the disturbance through nationalization. Only in the late 1950s did Macmillan realize the danger of Britain falling behind not only the superpowers but also the middle powers in her resource-base and decide to pursue economic growth as a major social objective. His failure can partly be attributed to his choice of the wrong paradigm—that of efficient business management on the American pattern in order to produce a higher rate of return. The social climate of Britain, however, in contrast to that of the United States, precludes ruthless competitive behaviour; people are just not sacked, unemployment on anything approaching the American scale is unacceptable to the people, and Macmillan himself would have been utterly opposed to such a thing.

Rather ironically for a Conservative prime minister, he then turned to the French paradigm of indicative planning and to its institution the *Commissariat du Plan*, which were, perhaps rather naively, credited with the upsurge of French economy, although the German economy was doing even better on a non-planned basis. Again, the political culture in Britain proved to be too different to allow of a successful transplant, largely because Britain lacks the necessary casy links between civil servants and industrialists based upon a common educational background, which exist in France. 'Neddy', the equivalent of the *Comissariat* which was established in 1961/2, failed, and the nine little 'Neddies', which followed the French pattern of the *Commissions de modernisation* were only partly successful.

In foreign policy, Britain's world role as a close associate of the United States made it inevitable that she should in some respects follow the paradigm of her much more powerful partner. The successive British governments were not denied the opportunity to exercise a degree of initiative, and to pursue their own views when at variance with the United States, even in the crucial area of East–West relations. Certainly within the Commonwealth and in the Middle East, Britain continued to develop quite individual policies (see pp. 113ff.). The most important influence of the United States lay not so much in the impact of its example upon individual policies as upon Britain's attributing a primary import- ance to the East–West relationship in which she could play only a rela- tively small, and rapidly diminishing role. The traditional British idea of playing a world role was thus assisted by the United States paradigm to the detriment of attention paid to other levels of foreign policy. Signally in Europe, where Britain was intimately involved, the British tradition of staying aloof from peacetime alignments was reinforced by the role played there by the United States. Despite their defence involve- ment and their generous economic assistance, the Americans could only be regarded as, to some extent, outsiders. This buttressed the incli- nation of the British to regard themselves in the same light, although the Americans themselves strongly and persistently encouraged them to jon the movement towards a political European union.

The strategy governing British relations with the United States was to exercise influence through accommodation; similar strategies were pur- sued also by Western Germany and by Japan, from much weaker starting-points. The French under de Gaulle developed the opposite strategy of trying to exert influence through self-assertion and later through direct challenge. With the gradual loosening of the 'special relationship' and with Britain's entry into Europe, one cannot exclude the possibility that in the future a much amended and liberalized version of Gaullism may serve as the paradigm for her relations with the United States rather than her own past policy. Likewise in Community politics to which Britain is a newcomer, she is bound to find herself studying the patterns of behaviour of the other established members. Again, French policies are likely to serve as a paradigm although, in view of the different national styles, one which may be only partly acceptable. All in all, in her new situation as a middle power with a strong regional focus, Britain's own traditions require a drastic adaptation, and here other middle powers rather than the United States are more useful as suitable paradigms.

Likewise, the future of Britain's defence effort may be governed less by what the Americans and the Russians do, than by the defence policies of other middle powers. As one of the somewhat simplified contributory explanations of the relative lack of success of Britain's economy is the contrast between her heavy defence expenditure and the freedom from similar burdens long enjoyed by Germany and Japan, it is relevant to note that German expenditure has been rapidly catching up and now surpasses that of Britain in absolute terms although it still constitutes a lower percentage of her GNP. This does not, of course, mean that Britain is likely simply to imitate what these middle powers are doing, but their policies and modes of behaviour can serve as yardsticks of comparison for their British equivalents. The Duncan Report has already intimated that the appropriate size for British diplomatic missions may be gauged by comparing them with the missions of other middle powers. Similar examples of what other middle powers are doing are likely to play quite an increasingly important part in the adaptation of British traditions.

*Chance*

Rational processes, traditions, examples of others, or a combination of these, encompass the origins of foreign policy which are discussed in political argument; they do not encompass all the origins in real life. Whether following their reasoning or some tradition or example, statesmen are assumed to make deliberate, conscious choices and generally endeavour to give the appearance of doing so. In fact, in many situations, no decisions in the real sense of the word are taken, things just happen, although the statesmen involved do not like to admit it and, if asked, tend to deny most strenuously the imputation that they have allowed things to lapse or that policy moves are due to mere chance. The convention of political life is that politicians are purposeful, that they pursue definite objectives, that they can defend their choices by reference to some legitimate principles. The real facts of life are, however, different. A state decision is frequently a 'casual unreasoning action by ordinary men in positions of extraordinary power'.[14] In an often-quoted passage H. A. L. Fisher stresses

the immense part played by the accidental and fortuitous in human affairs. The influence exercised upon day to day transactions by such forgotten and unavowed causes, personal friction or friendship, momentary impulse or bouts of ill-health, or the chance alternations of hours of energy with hours of lassitude.[15]

To apply these categories to the post-war record, who could deny the great significance of the friction between Sir Anthony Eden and John Foster Dulles or of Eden's and Churchill's ill-health when they were Prime Ministers, or of the personal relations between Macmillan and Eisenhower and Kennedy, or of Macmillan's tiredness in the last stages of his government?

The extensive scope of Britain's foreign policy and the multitude of her commitments arising both from the post-war situation and from her imperial past reduced the proportion of issues which could possibly be thoroughly deliberated or referred to precedents of tradition or to paradigms, especially as the pressure of events was great. On the one hand, the top decision-makers were engrossed in issues of extreme urgency, such as the threats of economic disaster, the organization of Western Europe against communist expansionism, and imperial issues such as the emancipation of the Indian subcontinent or the struggle in Palestine. On the other hand, at low levels of the bureaucratic machinery, policies simply continued. As Britain was involved in so many issues, there was no way of questioning the exact purpose of each single involvement and the appropriateness of each single policy pursued.

All the postwar governments, starting with Attlee's, were aware of Britain's overcommitment and were consistently trying to reduce it, to make foreign policy more commensurate with Britain's power base; Eden's Suez expedition was the only important exception. The process lasted a quarter of a century which, in view of the immensity of the task, cannot be regarded as very long. As the process did not follow a blueprint but consisted of pragmatically determined moves and changes, the decision-makers inevitably not only attended to the obviously urgent and important tasks but were frequently preoccupied by others which, though ephemeral, were salient. Thus postwar and post-imperial commitments and bases inevitably received much attention although they were soon to be abandoned. Wartime commitment was the only reason why the largest military operation—involving up to 100,000 troops, including the Indian Army—should have been conducted in the Dutch East Indies, a country in which Britain had only extremely limited interests; involvement in the 'Confrontation' with Indonesia was equally fortuitous, as the offence given to Indonesia by the federation of Malaysia was not really serious; its size, up to 55,000 troops, was grossly disproportionate to the nature of the quarrel.

The memoirs of statesmen, especially of Macmillan and Wilson, clearly illustrate how erratic their preoccupations appear even from our short time-perspective. Most bizarre of the fortuitous way in which issues become prominent was the affair of Anguilla in 1968; what cannot but be regarded as an extremely trivial matter took up much of the time and energy of the Foreign Office and the Cabinet, largely because its significance had been blown up by the mass media and had preoccupied public opinion.

If in some instances, the treatment of such complex issues, stretching over a long time, as Palestine, Egypt, Southern Rhodesia or Ulster can be attributed to a lack of clear policy and sheer muddleheadedness, it can, also, to some extent be explained by the intractable nature of these problems which made undecided and vaccilating policies appear preferable to clear but inflexible ones, although this could be regarded as giving hostages to fortune. In retrospect, three major identifiable mistakes can easily be discerned among these lasting issues: the defence of an overvalued sterling, an undue prolongation of the world role, and the rejection of the invitation to join the European integration movement. The handling of sterling may be attributed to traditionalism coupled with ignorance of the policy's implications, an ignorance shared by foreign politicians and experts. Retraction from the world role was really fast, though not quite fast enough. The Foreign Office guesses in 1950 and 1954 that Britain would have another chance to join the European integration movement if it succeeded, were fully justified. The refusal to participate in the Messina talks in 1955 which led to the Treaty of Rome can be attributed largely to misconceptions. In all three cases events evolved rather erratically and the ultimate outcomes were determined by a narrow margin rather than by overwhelming preponderances of conflicting forces; in all, chance played an extensive role; signally, the Messina talks could easily have failed, in which case the evolution of British European policy and hence foreign policy in general would have taken an entirely different shape.

# 6 The National Style

*Pragmatism*

IT is generally accepted that pragmatism is an all-pervading characteristic of Britain's political life, including her foreign policy. Its effects are paradoxical; it is justifiably regarded both as an element of strength and of weakness; it ensures flexibility but, at the same time, it does not prevent an exceptional continuity. Perhaps its basic implications are best disentangled by differentiating between its effects in times of emergency when the basic priorities of foreign policy are clear and pragmatism helps to meet them, and times of lesser stress when it seems to obstruct the determination of priorities.

The meaning of pragmatism is most easily explained by contrasting it with continental traditions of attachment to principle. The Duke of Wellington, for instance, used to say that the French ran their armies on a splendid harness but, if one part gave way, the whole harness was lost. The British by contrast, used an old rope; if one part gave way they made a knot in it. More recently, Harold Macmillan, when explaining, at the Strasbourg Assembly on 16 August 1950, the differences between British and Continental approaches to the Schuman Plan, thus summed up the generally held image of the meaning of 'pragmatism':

The difference is temperamental and intellectual. It is based on a long divergence of two states of mind and methods of argumentation. The continental tradition likes to reason *a priori* from the top downwards, from the general principles to the practical application. It is the tradition of St Thomas of Aquinas, of the Schoolmen, and of the great continental scholars and thinkers. The Anglo-Saxon likes to argue *a posteriori* from the bottom upwards, from practical experience. It is the tradition of Bacon and Newton.' He added that the Scots are closer to continental habits.[1]

Macmillan's analysis comes close to the definition in the Oxford dictionary of the concept as a doctrine that 'the conception of an object is no more than the conception of its possible results'. It describes the pronounced tendency of the British policy-makers to eschew ideology and to concentrate upon the concrete details of their environment.

This pragmatism is the natural, perhaps the inevitable, reflection of the traditionally wide scope of British foreign policy. For instance Lord Strang commented[2] 'within the Foreign Office the events of international life are seen as very compelling'. Similarly, Lord George-Brown, recalling his days as Secretary of State for Foreign Affairs, stated that he was 'not only impressed, but almost oppressed, with the sense of how many questions we were faced with and had to handle at the same time'.[3] He referred to the fantastic tempo at which the Foreign Secretary had to live and to the crushing weight of problems with which he had himself to deal. On the other hand, the interconnection between all the issues must be constantly borne in mind.

And part of the conflict between what the Foreign Office is doing about this or that issue, and what other people in Parliament or out of it think it should be doing, arises from this quite natural misunderstanding of the degree to which one issue conditions the responses to be made on others. Each problem has its own inherent merits, virtues and difficulties. But Europe relates to the Middle East, the Middle East relates to the Far East, the Far East relates to relations with America, as does Europe, as does the Middle East. They all relate to relations with Russia, and relations with either Russia or America involve relations with China. Wherever one turns, the issue of one's attitude and ambitions about the future of the United Nations arises.[4]

On the other hand, there is no time or opportunity to deliberate and decide clearly about priorities. The many conflicting and competing calls have to be treated on their individual merits and cannot be related to a general conception of national interest or foreign policy as a whole except in a fairly perfunctory manner, by considering the impact of the various courses of action available upon Britain's major relationships and a few general principles. This calls for essentially pragmatic thinking, the tradition of which, in a circular way, strongly affects the determination of Britain's international behaviour.

In the late 1960s, an increasing number of observers became critical of the impact of pragmatism upon British politics and the conduct of British foreign policy.[5] Pragmatism is not necessarily, however, a wrong basis for foreign policy as might be implied from these comments; otherwise it would be impossible to account for Britain's successes in the past. Pragmatism helps policy-makers to preserve the maximum flexibility possible, to avoid excesses due to ideological commitments, to concentrate diplomatic efforts upon specific interests, to recognize hard facts. Only in exceptional conditions do all these virtues turn to vices. It is not an accident that the criticisms of British pragmatism began to mount in the later 1960s when the implications of Britain's waning power position had become clear. As the military bases abroad turned from assets into liabilities, so the essentially advantageous pragmatic traditions of the past became increasingly detrimental to sound policies in a rapidly deteriorating power position which made clarity of purpose and definition of priorities more and more imperative.

The traditional style of policy served the country well immediately after the war when a number of extremely urgent economic, security, and imperial problems had to be dealt with without delay and when the overriding priorities of security and of economic recovery, coupled with Bevin's vigorous leadership, lent foreign policy a unity of purpose. It served the country badly in subsequent years when the capability for the traditional leading world role was rapidly diminishing and when Britain was faced with the necessity of making fundamental choices of priorities, especially between Europe and the traditional oceanic outlook.

In general terms, recent critics of British pragmatism note that British decision-makers prefer to concentrate upon specific tasks and are sceptical about forecasting, planning, generalizing, and theorizing, all of them laborious, costly, and energy-consuming, and, also, the suspicion lingers, not very 'practical'. Hence what Andrew Shonfield terms 'the cult of the implicit', a tendency to avoid harsh and precise formulations; hence the inclination to meet difficulties not by immediate action but by postponing unpleasant decisions, to blur grand choices, to avoid dilemmas, to be reactive rather than active. Even in the eyes of a severe American critic, Professor Waltz,[6] the resulting style was consonant both with domestic politics and with Britain's traditional international role.

Pragmatism has however the drawback of inhibiting the formulation of a coherent policy. The thinking of the policy-makers tends to be dominated by external facts, e.g. actions by other governments, rather than by a conception of their own objectives. Whereas the former take on a hard, fixed quality, the latter tend to be fluid. Policy becomes purely reactive; it aims primarily at an adequate response to events and not at specific objectives. Only great pressures produce the sense of purpose which makes all the difference to foreign policy; this is shown by the impact of Churchill's taking over from Chamberlain in 1940. The historical accretion of policies inevitably leads to an accumulation of dichotomies and inconsistencies. The natural reaction of the pragmatic policy-makers is to retain as much flexibility of policy as possible, to keep the options open. Sometimes this is reasonably successful. For instance in the ostensibly insoluble choice between white and black Africa, the successive British governments have come under strong criticism at home and abroad on the issue of Southern Rhodesia. From the British point of view, sitting on the fence has proved to be difficult but possible, and economically reasonably advantageous. Thanks to the indecisive economic sanctions, Britain incurred the antagonism of the White Rhodesians but warded off a complete Commonwealth rupture. She lost her trade with Rhodesia but managed to preserve the much more important trade with South Africa without disrupting that with Commonwealth Africa, exports to which have now surpassed those to South Africa. In other cases, however, reconciliation of policies proved impossible—e.g. the mistaken assumption that membership of the 'three circles' would prove possible was a major cause of later policy failures (see pp. 157ff.).

Pragmatism also encourages a divorce between thinking on general lines and political action. As Keynes had noted about economics, social action is never divorced from theories; those who claim to be exclusively pragmatic simply follow misleading conventional wisdom and pursue antiquated theories. Frequently pragmatism defeats itself by allowing policy-makers to go on using traditional vague concepts and images long after circumstances have drastically changed. Thus, even if one makes full allowance for political rhetoric, the British leaders continued to pursue an independent world role into the 1960s (pp. 160ff.) and some of them clung to an outworn image of Western Europe as aiming at federal integration, after the European integrationists had reluctantly accepted the constraints upon the integration process imposed by President de Gaulle. As compared with economics, the situation in politics is aggravated by the fact that political argument invariably involves principles, but, unless these are systematically clarified, only a tenuous link exists between political rhetoric and real life. On the one hand, policy tends to be described as reasonable or practical on the basis of mere conventional rules of diplomatic behaviour which are given a status approaching that of indisputable facts; on the other, although policy-makers are only too happy to invoke general principles in order to explain and rationalize their 'pragmatically', i.e. traditionally or impressionistically, determined decisions, these principles do not in fact directly affect their aspirations and operations. Through making it easy to rationalize governmental actions by broad and vague principles which are not operationally specific, pragmatism thus encourages and protects uncoordinated foreign-policy activities.

Closely linked is the impact of pragmatism upon indecision; this is particularly noted by independent-minded and energetic, although not necessarily practical participants and observers. Thus, for instance, C. P.

Scott vigorously denounced the conduct of the first world war in the *Manchester Guardian*: 'Nothing is foreseen, every decision is postponed. The War is not really directed—it directs itself'. And Lord Strang thus comments on the interwar period:

no clear policy was framed. The new problems of a changed and changing world tended to be interpreted in terms of old conceptions. Our position in the world had altered for the worse and we did not seem to recognize this in our actions. . . . We behaved as though we could play an effective part in international affairs as a sort of umpire or mediator without providing ourselves with the necessary arms and without entering into firm commitments.[7]

During the last war, Churchill frequently pressed impetuously for decisive—though often impractical—actions. Sir Pierson Dixon recorded that, to his mind inconsequentially, Churchill complained both of the Foreign Office always wanting to do something, contravening Talleyrand's principle '*surtout pas trop de zèle*', and of its presenting the arguments inconclusively so that the pros and cons cancel each other out.[8] A turmoil of activities characterized the Wilson Government but, behind them, Wilson was a master of avoiding difficult decisions and of postponing them as long as possible. Wilson's obsession was consensus and this provided an excuse for indecision. Lord Wigg probably hit the nail on the head when he pointed out that 'pragmatism, if you are constantly below deck having a chat with the crew, is dangerous in rocky seas— the more so if you are disinclined to act before the crew have taken a decision'.[9] Naturally enough the greater the unpleasantness, the greater the reluctance to make a decision—as was shown by Wilson over devaluation.

Finally, 'pragmatism' with its stress upon the case-to-case approach inhibits the acceptance of planning. Planning is only a recent fashion in the West; in a way it was a reaction to the planning in totalitarian states which set out to alter things and thus could predict the future which they were out to control. Although Britain led in the realm of social planning in the West when she embarked upon the welfare state in 1945, her conversion to planning in foreign policy came somewhat later than in the United States, following the example of other states and the evolution of techniques of prediction and of military planning. Forward planning in foreign policy was introduced as an unpleasant and unreliable but unavoidable expedient, in the words of Charles Burton Marshall 'not because the future is predictable but because it is not.'[10]

Because of its dependence upon the actions of other states, foreign policy cannot, of course, be really planned. All that planning can contribute to is a more rigorous analysis of perceived trends, a less facile projection of these trends into the future. Thus the absence of a planning department in the Foreign Office—as well as the great immediate pressure—no doubt facilitated the persistence of a basic conception of Britain's independent world role and of an inclination to base official anticipations upon a degree of wishful thinking. The notion of returning to business as usual after the War, the expectation that the constitutional and defence arrangements connected with the emancipation of British territories or the oil concessions would prove lasting and the Commonwealth links strong were perhaps not unreasonable, however far-fetched many of them seem in retrospect; planning may have hastened the revision of these views. It is more difficult to think that Wilson really believed that the economic sanctions against the Smith regime in Southern Rhodesia would prevail within a short time, as he claimed, or that de Gaulle would refrain from vetoing a renewed British application to enter the EEC in 1967; in both cases, however, Wilson's behaviour may be more plausibly attributed to a desire to meet domestic pressures, and his confident declarations of expected success to political rhetoric rather than to genuine expectations.

Closely connected with pragmatism is the pronounced characteristic of continuity in British foreign policy. In the course of its recent history the United Kingdom has been less disrupted by either internal or external events than any other state. With their sense of tradition, the British evolved a number of flexible, pragmatic principles for conducting foreign policy. As has been mentioned, these mainly practical rules help to obstruct the formulation of an integrated policy at any given time; they also ensure that individual policies preserve a degree of continuity even though the principles themselves are highly flexible.

*The Geographical Factor*
Geography obviously greatly influences foreign policy, though it does not determine it, as Napoleon and many others have claimed. Its impact is particularly ambiguous in the case of Britain—although close to and partly in Europe, she is not fully of it; the Channel which forms a barrier between the two, is scarcely twenty miles wide at its narrowest point. Despite its ambiguity, the image of Britain as an offshore island has exercised a powerful influence upon British foreign policy. Its classical formulation by Sir Eyre Crowe in his memorandum of 1 January 1907 warrants repetition:

The general character of England's foreign policy is determined by the immutable conditions of her geographical situation on the ocean flank of Europe as an island State with vast oversea colonies and dependencies, whose existence and survival as an independent community are inseparably bound up with the possession of preponderant sea power.[11]

These sentiments lingered after the second world war. In the great speech on 18 November 1946 in which he answered his left-wing critics' demands for a Third Force, Attlee elevated geography to a major principle of foreign policy which precluded such an alignment.[12]

When explaining Britain's refusal to join the EEC, in a lecture at Columbia University on 11 January 1952, Eden emotionally declared:

This is something which we know, in our bones, we cannot do.

We know that if we were to attempt it, we should relax the springs of our action in the Western democratic cause and in the Atlantic association which is the expression of that cause. For Britain's story and her interests lie far beyond the continent of Europe. . . . That is our life: without it we should be no more than some millions of people living on an island off the coast of Europe, in which nobody wants to take a particular interest.[13]

Such oceanic determinism is no longer accepted today even by the staunchest anti-Europeans. The oceanic links remain powerful but gone are the colonies and dependencies, and the Channel could soon be tunnelled under. In fact, even in the past, the oceanic orientation was incomplete. In the field of strategy, the British traditionally distinguished between their maritime strategy, based upon a full command of the seas, and their continental strategy, based upon the balance of power; both had to be complementary. In foreign policy proper, the division was equally real but was not clearly articulated. The oceanic orientation appeared, nevertheless, to be the most important. Britain's objectives in Europe were negative—merely to prevent a concentration of power which could threaten her, especially hegemony by one state. Hence her intermittent interventions against the successive 'rogue' states of the period—the Habsburgs, the French under Louis XIV and Napoleon, the Germans under Wilhelm II and Hitler. Since the beginning of this century, however, Britain's preoccupation with Europe has become overwhelming and constant, while the maintenance of her imperial and other overseas interests has become increasingly more difficult. After 1945 the latter rapidly receded as the dependencies were gradually emancipated and the economic importance of the Commonwealth countries gradually diminished both as trade partners and as areas of profitable investment. Sir Eyre Crowe's formulation continued to exercise a fascination. The image of Britain's island position underpinned the doctrine of the 'three circles' (see p. 157), and imbued her repeated refusals to join the European integration movement with an aura of near-inevitability.

Although geography is clearly a major physical factor in foreign policy, its influence is hard to assess with any degree of clarity; it is frequently invoked as a determining cause but the invocations appear to be more in the nature of rationalizations than of reliable statements of motives. Britain's turn to Europe is, of course, likely to undermine, and perhaps, ultimately destroy, the lingering remnants of the traditional oceanic orientation but not necessarily the inclination to argue in geographical terms which lend the argument a matter-of-fact, down-to-earth air. Once Britain is established within the enlarged Community, especially if and when the tunnel is built, the interpretation of her geographical position is likely to be reversed. Her close proximity to the continent could loom increasingly large as a reason for participating in its economic and political organization as her offshore position loomed large in the preceding 'three circles' policy and oceanic orientation.

## Traditions of International Co-operation

The outstanding characteristic of British foreign policy and diplomacy is found in what Sir Harold Nicolson called its 'civilian' character. It was the policy of a satisfied and prosperous state with no military influence upon its domestic politics. Co-operation instead of conflict, profitable trade and cheap diplomacy instead of costly and wasteful warfare, peace rather than war, became the guiding principles of British foreign policy. Britain, as it has been put, had 'the moral opportunity' to develop a peaceful foreign policy; she took this opportunity. Thus her interests happily merged with those of others; her policy was based upon self-interest but was also happily in conformity with moral dictates and humanitarian aspirations. It was possible to assume, as Sir Eyre Crowe did, that what was good for the world was good for Britain, which amounted in fact to saying also that what was good for Britain was good for the world. Thus the tradition of co-operation was clearly rooted not only in Britain's lack of self-sufficiency but also in her central and dominant position within the international system.

The general nature of British diplomacy is thus summed up by Sir Harold Nicolson:

As opposed to the warrior conception of diplomacy, there stands the commercial, the mercantile or the shop-keeper conception. This civilian theory of negotiation is based upon the assumption that a compromise between rivalries is generally more profitable than the complete destruction of the rival. That negotiation is not a mere phase in a death-struggle, but an attempt by mutual concession to reach some durable understanding. That 'national honour' must be interpreted as 'national honesty', and that questions of prestige should not be allowed to interfere unduly with a sound business deal. That there is probably some middle point between the two negotiators which, if discovered, should reconcile their conflicting interests. And that, to find this middle point, all that is required is a frank discussion, the placing of cards upon the table, and the usual processes of human reason, confidence and fair-dealing.[14]

According to Sir Eyre Crowe, the major principle conducive to this peaceful civilian diplomacy was 'to harmonize with the general desires and ideals common to all mankind' and, specifically, to be 'closely identified with the primary and vital interests of a majority, or as many as possible, of the other nations'. He saw their 'primary and vital interests' in the maintenance of their independence, but as the conception of common interests changed through the ages, Britain managed to identify herself with them. The principle of harmonization was meaningful, although it favoured British interests; it did not amount to a mere disguise for British dominance. As her power position was based on very slender resources at home, Britain had really no choice but to harmonize her policies—otherwise 'the universal jealousy and fear' inspired by her supreme sea power exposed her to the grave danger of becoming isolated and confronted by a hostile combination,[15] a danger which she only narrowly avoided following the Boer War. To use twentieth-century expressions, Britain was in no position to develop a 'myth of omnipotence'; 'going it alone' was obviously extremely precarious for her.

This explains why the concepts of 'civilian diplomacy' and of 'harmonization' did not lose their relevance even after the eclipse of the British Empire. They had evolved while Britain played a central role within the international system, but they were not rooted in a dominant power position which Britain had never possessed. The postwar conceptions of Britain's 'world role' were the natural developments of the traditional 'harmonization' idea. A Central Office of Information pamphlet published in 1961 could refer to British support for the United Nations, the Organisation for European Economic Cooperation, the Colombo Plan, NATO, disarmament, and detente. Even the Suez action was only a partial exception. The pamphlet described it as undertaken because Britain and France regarded it as the only practical measure for safeguarding a common interest in the international waterway.[16] This may be regarded as a mistake in judgement—the common interest in keeping the waterway open did not amount to agreement on armed intervention and the expedition was doomed from its inception owing to the lack of harmonization of British policy in this respect with the majority of other states, especially the United States. Faced, however, with the isolation resulting from this faulty harmonization, Britain immediately reversed her policy to restore it, although the French were not inclined to do so.

Harmonization was further articulated as support for the *status quo*, international stability, and law and order; as the principle of 'free trade' in economics, and as that of 'balance of power' in the political/strategic field.

Once the Empire had been firmly established, Britain became a staunch advocate of the *status quo*. It is important to bear in mind her rather negative interest in Europe, as her major interests were spread throughout the world: all she needed in Europe was a degree of stability so that her security would not be threatened, but she was not particularly interested in the details as these did not directly affect her. Hence the tradition of British European policy became one of support for the existing structures in order to maintain strategic stability but with a realistic acceptance of the *faits accomplis*. This pattern underlies Britain's championship of Turkish control of the Straits, her support for the integrity of the Austro–Hungarian Empire in the last stages of the first world war, and her acceptance of the Soviet sphere of influence in Eastern Europe in the last stages of the second world war and in the postwar period. The conception of stability was dynamic—Britain would not pledge herself to an unconditional support of the existing order, especially in Eastern Europe as was demanded by France in 1919, in the belief that stability cannot be achieved without allowing for the possibility of change. Nor would she intervene in the domestic affairs of other states, even in revolutions and civil wars, until and unless these actually threatened the balance of power: as soon as a new state or government had achieved a degree of stability it would be recognized.

All these principles evolved within the European context but were fully applied after the war to the independence movements and to the emancipated units of the Empire. A basic support for the *status quo* was modified by Britain's realistic readiness to accept change and to recognize the facts of power; the jailed leaders of rebels were readily released to become leaders of new states. Britain pursued the principle of non-intervention whenever the new units departed from agreed constitutions and treaties.

International law is a sufficiently important factor in Britain's foreign policy to warrant a separate section, alongside the one on morality, at the end of this chapter (pp. 142–50). It is discussed here only briefly, conceived as a buttress of the existing international order and as one of the major aspects of 'harmonization'. The support the British gave to international law, especially in verbal diplomacy, was fully in line with their general preference for co-operation to conflict: they supported the development of a body of international rules of behaviour which stabilized the world and helped them to peacefully pursue their interests. On the whole, they were quite realistic in appreciating the limitations of international law and the unreliable nature of its protection, but occasionally they seemed to strive for any form of agreement, however unrealistic and unreliable. Thus Sir Pierson Dixon criticized the British tendency to settle, however badly, when discussing the 1954 treaty with Egypt; regarding the inconclusive Council of Foreign Ministers in May 1946, he expressed his strong conviction that it is better to disagree than to give in, despite the resulting disappointment of public opinion at home.[17]

It is well worth while distinguishing two separate aspects of such 'unrealistic' agreements. On the one hand, they amount to accepting the facts and purchasing time—this was a justification of the Munich Agreement in 1938 as much as of the 1954 Anglo-Egyptian Treaty. There is, moreover, a real virtue in getting an agreement even as ambiguous as Resolution 242 of the Security Council on the Israeli–Arab conflict, which Britain was instrumental in proposing, as it established at least a common starting-point for all subsequent attempts at negotiations. On the other hand, such agreements become politically dangerous by encouraging policy-makers to put excessive trust in empty formulae and to shun reality. Statesmen have, of course, to express trust in the agreements they conclude, but their pronouncements often amount to no more than political rhetoric. Nevertheless, Eden probably did genuinely believe that both the 1936 and the 1954 agreements with Egypt were workable. During the debate on the latter in the House of Commons on 29 July 1954[18] when speaking about the prospects of reactivating the base, he went so far as to present the treaty as a gain in strategic mobility. 'There is no vacuum', he said 'because as a result of these arrangements, we shall be able to redeploy our forces and make them mobile to an extent that they have not been hitherto.' This unrealistic trust in the agreement played an important part in blocking advance in military planning; Eden did not establish a strategic reserve or procure means of rapid transport, the lack of which crippled British military capability in the area when the treaty broke down only two years later.

'Free trade' was an idea extremely advantageous to Britain, as the country which was the first to industrialize and hence the one to profit most from it; for a commercially-minded nation, it assumed an overwhelming importance. This was particularly true of the radicals; anticipating the ideas of the modern functionalist school, Cobden was a great believer in free trade as an alternative to war and as the easiest path to peace. 'Commerce is a great panacea', he said, and he advocated 'as little intercourse as possible betwixt the *Governments*, as much connection as possible betwixt *nations* of the world'.[19] Although the British went to great lengths in their belief in the autonomous operation of economic forces divorced from power politics, Sir Eyre Crowe, for one, fully appreciated the important connections. Confidently and justifiably he asserted that free trade strengthened interested friendship and, at the very least, made others less apprehensive of British naval supremacy than they would have been had she been a predominantly protectionist Power. Her policy of free trade was an important attraction to other maritime Powers who preferred her supremacy to a naval balance of power depending upon the protectionist Germans, as envisaged in the German naval challenge early in the century.

The principle of 'free trade' was never fully accepted by other nations as the basis of international economics but, although unilaterally applied, it served Britain well as long as she was a powerful imperial state—it ensured her cheap food supplies and enabled her to maintain a substantial, though diminishing, proportion of world trade. During the Great Depression the policy became untenable in face of mounting protectionist walls. In the Ottawa Agreements of 1932, Britain abandoned the principle of free trade in favour of imperial preferences. She has been economically too weak since 1945 to play a decisive role in re-establishing free trade, and, although she fully participated in the successive attempts to liberalize international trade, she herself has maintained a fairly protectionist regime. The debate in 1971 about her proposed entry into the EEC showed that the principle had been eroded not only operationally but even as an aspiration. Although entry amounted to joining a bloc, pronouncedly protectionist in agricultural produce, the anti-marketeers somehow did not repeat the ringing arguments of the Corn Law debates. Nevertheless, free trade would, on the whole, suit Britain's interests when she is in the EEC more than those of the other partners, both in order to retain as much as possible of her existing overseas trade and to ensure cheaper food supplies. She will probably, therefore, continue to favour it in her new historical role, as a principle of harmonizing the interests of the enlarged community with those of the other trading blocs and of the developing countries.

As Britain's main dealings were with other great powers, harmonization at this level created a strong preference within the diplomatic service for 'secret' diplomacy (i.e. private negotiations) as a method of doing business. Characteristically, the only chapter on diplomatic practice in Lord Strang's book on *The Foreign Office* is all devoted to a criticism of 'open diplomacy' and of 'diplomacy by Conference', and in the Central Office of Information publication, *Britain and the United Nations* (1964), the brief section on United Nations diplomacy consists mainly of Sir Pierson Dixon's account of the advantages of secret over open diplomacy.

Britain's weakening power position vis-à-vis the United States, however, made the advantages of multilateralism obvious as the asymmetry of the relationship can be at least partly balanced by bringing into play other middle and small powers. The general trend of British postwar diplomacy has, indeed, been in favour of multilateralism—as Christopher Mayhew rightly points out, Britain's bilateral treaties have been generally replaced by regional ones, like NATO, SEATO or CENTO, or otherwise have lapsed. NATO has been a particularly advantageous organization as it has enabled Britain both to maintain her 'special relationship' with the United States and to play a leading role in organizing Western European defences; SEATO and CENTO, however, did not develop into parallel fully-fledged defence organizations.[20] The situation has been much more difficult in the United Nations where, lacking the full support of any group of members, Britain has found herself subjected to mounting criticisms as a colonial power and, until and unless the Southern Rhodesian issue fades out, her position is bound to remain difficult.

The traditions of harmonization provide a good foundation for Britain's policies within the EEC and her relations with its other members. Despite their great attachment to autonomy and to national sovereignty, the British are traditionally adept in two basic modes of accommodation which, according to the 'neo-functionalist' theoreticians of the EEC, are important in the integrative processes of the Community: first, in finding, whenever possible, a common denominator and, second, in splitting the difference. They are better equipped than any other major EEC member, certainly better than the French, to proceed to the third, most clearly integrative mode of upgrading the common interest, through stressing what the partners have in common and postponing the settlement of disagreements.

*Balance of Power and Power Vacuum*

With the principle of balance of power, we move to the very fringes of co-operative behaviour. It was the expression of harmonization in the political/strategic field by marshalling the support of like-minded states opposed to the domination of any single state or group of states. Simultaneously, however, it aimed at organizing coercion in case the co-operative methods failed. British continental strategies evolved around the notion of equilibrium. In the words of Sir Eyre Crowe: 'It has become almost an historical truism to identify England's secular policy with the maintenance of this balance by throwing her weight now in this scale and now in that, but ever on the side opposed to the political dictatorship of the strongest single State or group at a given time.'[21] The balance principle did not apply to Britain's overseas policy, in which her objective was to retain naval supremacy, but only to Europe, a theatre in which the limitations of her capability were obvious. Here, even at the pinnacle of her power Britain could not act alone. Even Palmerston, at his most exuberant, could not contemplate a fully independent action. All he did was to alter the famous doctrine of Henry VIII, *cui adhaero praeest*, to the even more confident one: 'with such support as I choose, I get the upper hand', meaning that the equilibrium would be always in Britain's favour but Britain would still depend upon its maintenance.[22]

The principle of 'balance of power' presented some difficulties even within the limitations of the European context. It did not really square with Crowe's more general formulation of the principle of harmonization, as it meant joining the weaker side—a minority rather than a majority. The two formulations can, however, be reconciled by postulating that, having grasped the principle of international order which is based on a balance, the British had identified a 'primary and vital' interest of the majority and were acting on its behalf even if others foolishly ignored it. Such reasoning would have been fully in conformity with Victorian ideas although Crowe did not articulate it. Inevitably, too, the principle became eroded in the twentieth century when Britain became incapable of playing her historical role of a balancer, because her power, even joined to that of France and Russia, was insufficient to prevail against the Central Powers; the balance in the first world war had to be restored by the Americans. When neither the isolationist Americans nor the communist Russians were readily available to redress the balance against a remilitarized Germany in the 1930s, Chamberlain departed from it altogether in favour of appeasement, which can be construed as the opposite principle, that of composition, based upon the notion that the interests of states are ultimately reconcilable. The situation was saved only at the last moment by a return to the balance principle and the formation of an anti-Nazi coalition.

Moreover, Britain's changing conceptions of the contemporary balance caused violent oscillations in her relations with the individual powers which were bewildering to others and made her an unreliable ally. Thus, at the Versailles Peace Conference, the British shifted from an intense anti-Germanism to supporting Germany against France and her allies; to the appeasers in the 1930s, Hitler's moves appeared to be no more than a redress from the objectionable provisions of the Treaty of Versailles, but by the end of 1940 Britain was dedicated to the destruction of Nazism; the Russians were welcome to help to redress the balance against Hitler in 1941 but, already towards the end of the war, Churchill was busy trying to erect a balance against them.

The balance of power became an even more important guide to action after 1945 when the lessons of appeasement loomed large and the British were painfully aware of the dangers of attempting conciliation so long that it might become too late to form a coalition against the likely adversary, should this become necessary. Churchill strongly opposed the partition of Germany, which would have destroyed any chances of establishing a postwar balance in Europe, He reiterated the validity of the principle: 'to oppose the strongest, most aggressive, most domineering power . . . and thus defeat and frustrate the military tyrant whoever he was. I know of nothing which has occurred to weaken . . . the wisdom upon which our ancestors acted.'[23] Similarly, Bevin, determined to prevent Russia dominating Europe, pursued the policy of balance as the most promising expedient, although this did not deter him from undertaking the unpromising attempts to establish a concert between the Big Three with their associates.[24]

Britain acted squarely within this line of tradition when her foreign policy was finally anchored on NATO, the main instrument for restoring the balance in the cold war. In a weakened power position in which she could no longer play the decisive role of the balancer and was permanently tied down to one side, the principle no longer commanded much popular appeal and was not frequently referred to. Sir Alec Douglas-Home remained its most outspoken proponent at high levels. Being strongly convinced of the dangers of communism, he firmly rejected the possibilities of neutrality and provocatively analysed the dangers of non-alignment when visiting New Delhi in October 1955. At the same time he equally firmly rejected appeasement, reminding his audience that three times in half a century Britain had been rebuffed in her efforts at conciliation—by the Kaiser, by Hitler, and by Stalin—'and the lessons we and our friends in Europe have learnt in a bitter school is that weakness invites aggression and that neutrality has no meaning in the context of totalitarian ambitions'. In his 'political testament', dictated in December 1963, Sir Alec returned to the concept of a balance—Britain becoming part of Europe within an Atlantic context so that the Western and the Eastern blocs would be in balance.[25]

Since the last war, the main balance has shifted decisively from

Europe to the global context, centring upon the nuclear equilibrium between the Russians and the Americans, the meaning of which is very remote from the traditional notions of balance, based, as it is, upon deterrence. Britain's influence upon this central balance is very limited and her attention is now directed mainly to Europe. Here the notion of balance may not be as frequently referred to as it was in the interwar period but it clearly retains its value in helping to analyse the relations between western and eastern Europe, especially in the eventuality of an American withdrawal, and is bound to play a significant role in British relations with the other members of the EEC in the context of Community politics until and unless a fuller community is established.

The principle of 'balance of power' thus remains the dominant traditional category of thinking about strategy but, in the light of Britain's diminished power and narrowed range of options, it can no longer serve as a basis for a flexible foreign policy for her. Her postwar alignment with the United States, within NATO, has been stable, and, once she weathers the initial difficulties in joining the EEC, her alignment within Western Europe is also likely to remain so. Both alignments are indicated by the desire to balance the Soviet bloc; and, until and unless the balance-of-power principle can be replaced by another one, both seem indispensable.

The principle of balance of power determined not only the partners whom Britain sought to enlist but also the adversary who was to be opposed. Her opposition to Russia under Stalin fell into this line of tradition; in essence, it was not based upon a conflict of ideologies or upon direct national competition but was due to his threat to the European balance of power. Stalin was in the line of the great arch-enemies, Philip II of Spain, Louis XIV, Napoleon, Wilhelm II or Hitler—all of whom exercised despotic power and attempted to dominate the continent of Europe by force; the only difference this time was that the attempt at domination extended to the whole globe and that the United States and not Britain was the main balancer (see pp. 294-5).

The concept of the disturbed equilibrium was frequently linked with that of a 'power vacuum'. The underlying image was that of an expansionist communist Russia seeking outlets and advancing wherever and whenever she did not meet with adequate opposition. The spectre of a power vacuum in central Europe underlay Churchill's adamant opposition to the division of Germany; the Dunkirk and Brussels Treaties aimed at buttressing weak regimes in France and Italy so that a power vacuum would not arise there. No British outpost overseas was abandoned without a consideration of the resulting power vacuum and of how this was likely to be filled; this pattern of behaviour had already been established early this century when Britain avoided creating a vacuum in the Caribbean and the Far East by passing the responsibilities for the defence of these two regions to friendly powers—the United States and Japan respectively.

British reasons for establishing post-imperial regimes were by no means exclusively power-political; they included concern for the welfare of the people and for the protection of British interests. The unattainable aspiration lay in the establishment of a strong and stable, preferably representative government, friendly to Britain and buttressed by a regional defence organization which would include Britain, in order to maintain her influence, and also the United States, to provide the ultimate military support. The actual policy patterns differed from area to area. In Australasia the problem was taken care of by the Americans in the framework of the ANZUS Pact which regrettably excluded Britain. The power-vacuum apprehension did not extend to the British possessions in Africa, as the communist menace here seemed much smaller than elsewhere, although Britain reacted strongly to the Russian's attempts to extend their influence into the Congo. Macmillan, for instance, on Sir Pierson Dixon's recommendations, reluctantly supported the Security Council resolution on Katanga of August 1960, solely because its failure would have meant an even less acceptable Russian-sponsored resolution which would also fail. This would have led to the withdrawal of United Nations authority and troops, leaving the field open for the Russians.[26]

The British concern with a power vacuum had strong and not altogether advantageous effects in South-east Asia and the Middle East, where two regional defence organizations had been established, SEATO and the Baghdad Pact (later renamed CENTO), neither of which was militarily effective, or popular among the regional peoples. Even more serious was the impact of the vacuum doctrine upon the British resolve to maintain unpopular and ultimately tottering regimes, especially monarchies and sheikhdoms in the Middle East. Here Soviet expansionism was clearly in evidence and the radical nationalist alternatives seemed unpromising, not only for this reason but also because they seemed to threaten British economic interests and not to be in the interests of the people concerned, as we interpret them. Fear of the power vacuum may however have played a central part in inhibiting the readiness of the British to give in to nationalist demands here as elsewhere in the Empire. Bevin, for instance, told the House of Commons on 24 May 1946: 'There must not be a vacuum. If the Egyptian Government try to force a situation in which there is a vacuum—meaning that we have gone and that there is nothing there for security instead, regional defence or other organization—to that I can never agree.'[27]

This fear greatly contributed to the strengthening of British efforts to buttress the regime of Nuri-as-Said in Iraq, and to oppose that of Nasser in Egypt, efforts which were doomed to failure. In both cases, apprehensions of the Russians filling the vacuum were only partly justified. Russian influence was not firmly established in the Middle East until the Arabs became fully dependent upon the Soviet Union for military and diplomatic support against Israel. Had the British been less governed by the strategic vacuum concept, they might have found it somewhat easier to accommodate the forces of Arab nationalism and to abandon traditional regimes declining in popularity. One must, however, bear in mind the generally unpromising international situation in which all 'progressive' nationalist movements tended to be anti-imperialist and pro-communist, as well as the fact that in no case did British support for a declining regime go anywhere near the lengths of the American support for South Vietnam.

'Vacuum' is not, of course, a very precise notion; its ambiguity was shown by the debate over the governmental decision to withdraw from the Suez Canal base, implemented in the 1954 agreement with Egypt, when the traditionally power- and hence power-vacuum-minded Conservatives then in office took the decision while the Labour opposition quite effectively used the concept in opposing it. Parallel with the reduction in the scope of Britain's foreign policy in the 1960s, the importance of the vacuum principle also has been reduced. The withdrawal from east of Suez, which meant that Britain could no longer accept the responsibility for the filling of the vacuum, was happily mitigated by the rapidly increasing momentum of detente between the great communist powers and the United States, but was accentuated when the Soviet Navy appeared in the Indian Ocean and the Persian Gulf. The operational implications for Britain, were, however, limited. Whether one accepted at their face-value governmental declarations about the Five-Power Security Pact in South-east Asia or the intention to resume the sale of arms to South Africa in support of the Simonstown Agreement in the early 1970s, in the belief that they were due to concern with the power vacuum which had arisen; or whether one attributed them to internal pressures within the Conservative Party, to Mr Heath's electoral promises, or to Sir Alec's idiosyncratic personal views, the importance of these moves was extremely limited.

The vacuum principle reflects the realities of power politics too faithfully to be altogether abandoned as a basic category of thinking. For instance, in the crucially important Persian Gulf area, British diplomatic efforts after the announcement of withdrawal clearly fell within the pattern of endeavouring to fill a vacuum. The contrast between the post-withdrawal arrangements in Greece and Turkey in 1947 and those from the Gulf in the early 1970s is not due to a diminution of British concern with the vacuum left behind; there was simply no longer any chance of persuading the Americans to take over—in fact, from the American point of view, the announcement of the decision to withdraw could not have been worse timed. Political arrangements within the area posed formidable problems—the United Arab Emirates organization was established with great difficulty at the end of 1971, but, even with the token American naval presence in Bahrain and a token British presence in Oman, its military potential remained extremely limited. Difficulties were created among the Arabs when the British, together with the Americans, decided to support the Iranian military build-up.

The vacuum principle still clearly applies to the peripheries of the central strategic area in Europe, for instance, if governmental instability or popular unrest became serious in Greece or Turkey, but this would not be the responsibility of Britain alone as it would involve the whole of NATO.

## The Threat and the Use of Force
Thus British foreign policy shows two main strands: civilian diplomacy with a commercial background and a military strand centring upon the concept of 'balance of power'. While the blood-bath of the two world wars and the tremendous military costs and the shadow of a nuclear war have all reinforced Britain's concern with peace, the lessons of appeasement have shown how essential military preparedness is for security. The resulting British defence policies are discussed in chapter 12; the present section deals only with the employment of force as an adjunct of diplomacy.

The British did not confuse military power with influence. They realized that they could not maintain their vast Empire with their slender military forces without at least the passive support of the native population. Attlee acted firmly within this tradition by deciding after the war that India was untenable, and thus saved the country from the possibility of facing predicaments similar to the French calamities in Indochina and Algeria, or of the American one in Vietnam. Nevertheless, a natural concern with the military/strategic appreciation of international events could not but reinforce the well-established British tradition of using threats of force and limited force for specific foreign-policy purposes; despite the Suez debacle, the tradition lingered well into the later 1960s. The fact that Britain was more active in this way than other states is substantiated by statistics covering the fifty years between 1919 and 1969.[28] Among the cases identified, Britain participated in the following proportion:

|  | Britain | | Total Number of |
| --- | --- | --- | --- |
|  | Victim | Assailant | Identified Cases |
| 1919–29 | 1 | 22 | 36 |
| 1930–9 | 3 | 11 | 27 |
| War period | — | 4 | 9 |
| 1945–55 | 3 | 11 | 34 |
| 1956–65 | 3 | 5 | 36 |
| 1966–9 | 1 | 6 | 15 |

It seems that, after a relative lull between 1956 and 1965, Britain has regained prominence among the states involved in gunboat diplomacy. The record looks, however, much less militaristic if we bear in mind that all these actions consisted of concentrations of ships but did not lead to actual fighting. Moreover, only three actions were undertaken on behalf of British interests alone—against Argentina in 1966 concerning the Falkland Islands, against Egypt concerning the closure of the Straits of Tiran in 1967, and against South Yemen to ensure the evacuation of civilians at the end of the same year; the other three were undertaken on behalf of the United Nations against Southern Rhodesia.

One may readily agree with David Vital that only the greatest and the smallest powers remain comparatively uninhibited in their use of force,[29] and that the constraints upon Britain, which is neither, are great. Moreover, the British Navy is now so greatly reduced that it is unlikely to command sufficient force for individual 'definitive' actions promptly enough to make them readily effective or to prevail upon the foreign governments to comply. She may, however, as in the recent cases referred to, continue to use her limited forces for what James Cable calls 'expressive' purposes, as a support for diplomacy, which falls short of the capability to secure the desired ends by military means but goes somewhat beyond a mere 'showing of the flag'. Only one of these six latest cases was clearly unsuccessful—that against the closure of the Straits of Tiran—and it would hardly have made much difference had Britain had much larger forces available than HMS Victorious and the few other ships held 'in readiness against any eventuality in the Eastern Mediterranean'. For the mainly expressive purposes of the other actions, the limited British resources were adequate.

This, of course, was not true of what Cable calls the 'definitive' or 'catalytic' use of force, the requirements for which are much greater. In fact, already in the nineteenth century British forces had occasionally been inadequate for such actions. For example, although the Foreign Secretary described the American naval bombardment of the Mosquito Protectorate in 1853 as an outrage 'without a parallel in the annals of modern times', the British government could do nothing owing to the vulnerability of Canada.[30] This, however, did not prevent the flourishing of British gunboat diplomacy in other, less inhibited circumstances.

Britain has used substantial force on several occasions since 1945, mostly arising from postwar occupation problems and from the winding up of the Empire. The evolution of policy is best demonstrated by a brief account of a few outstanding cases of the use or of the contemplated use of force, especially of the well-documented Suez expedition. There is little need to dwell upon the Korean conflict, in which the British participated largely in order to ensure American participation in the defences of Europe, or on the Malayan Emergency and the Confrontation, in which imperial and post-imperial responsibilities combined with a large economic stake in Malaya. Much more telling is the case of the non-use of violence after Iran had nationalized the Anglo-Iranian Oil Company and seized the giant refinery at Abadan. On 26 June 1951 the British government sent to Abadan the cruiser Mauritius, which was later reinforced by destroyers. The flotilla was dispatched for the limited objective of evacuating British civilians, which it completed on 3 October but it also clearly served as a general warning to Iran. Herbert Morrison, who was at the time Secretary of State for Foreign Affairs, records[31] that he himself was in favour of 'sharp and forceful action', a reaction which he regarded as representative of the average non-radical Englishman. The Cabinet, however, was left in little doubt that the mounting of an efficient attacking force would have required much time and thought and that the intervention might therefore have been a failure. In the end, they had to abandon any military projects. The striking features of this story are: first, that Morrison regarded it as a fairly natural inclination to use force on sufficient provocation; second that the Cabinet as a whole presumably devoted quite a lot of attention to this idea; third, that its rejection was due to military and not to political constraints. By Morrison's account, had a more adequate force been readily available, the Cabinet would probably have authorized its use. Ultimately, of course, the economic pressures against Iran proved effective and Britain obtained a satisfactory settlement.

The pattern of the politicians contemplating the use of force and the military advisers being opposed to it was repeated on all subsequent occasions, notably in the Suez affair, when the Chiefs of Staff were clearly procrastinating hoping against hope that no military action would take place. This case warrants most attention as it is the major instance of Britain's using force after 1945 and it has been the subject of extensive analysis.[32]

To start with, one must stress the curious psychological mood in which the expedition was rooted. 1956 was a year in which the accumulated exasperation with life in postwar Britain and with the lion's tail being repeatedly twisted, was aggravated by the recurrence of an economic crisis caused by the turn of world prices against Britain in mid-1955 which resulted in a rise in prices and in a swelling of wage claims at home. Hugh Thomas plausibly suggests that the graceful withdrawal from the Empire and the shrinking world role had built up resentments among the British who required a spot of adventure before settling to a less spectacular foreign policy. Macmillan was affected and returned to Churchillian wartime rhetoric and Eden was particularly vulnerable as, together with Selwyn Lloyd, he had negotiated what Churchill had called the 'scuttle' from Egypt in 1954 and had assured his party that Nasser was trustworthy; both were smarting from recent setbacks in the Middle East—the Czech arms deals, the sacking of Glubb Pasha just when Selwyn Lloyd was holding talks with Nasser, and the strife in Cyprus. To Eden, Nasser readily became another Hitler.

A fog of misinformation and of faulty images of Egypt was prevalent in Britain: the inability of the Egyptians to run the Canal, Nasser's perilous position and the assurance of his speedy replacement, the Russian plots, the efficiency of the Egyptian air force. Moreover, the government misinterpreted American attitudes, largely owing to the authoritative opinions of Macmillan, who remembered his wartime and immediate postwar successes and had got on well during his recent visit to Washington; it also misinterpreted the attitudes prevalent in the United Nations, by confusing the idea that they were vindicating the principle of free traffic for the common good with the conviction that this would lead others to condone Britain's using force. For different reasons and in somewhat different ways, the Conservative and Labour Parties were both unrealistic. Labour, according to its traditions, advocated resort to the United Nations; as Britain clearly lacked adequate capability for a swift action, some spokesmen both for the Conservative and the Labour Parties went to the length of suggesting the setting up of a base in Haifa in order to bring troops closer to the Canal Zone.

Even against this confused background, it did not seem unreasonable to threaten Nasser with force; the accumulation of troops and transport closer to Egyptian shores was in the best traditions of gunboat diplomacy, and the Menzies Mission commissioned by the Conference of Maritime Powers added the threat that this force would be actually used if Nasser failed to accept the compromise proposed by the Conference in the form of an international board including the Maritime Powers and Egypt. Unfortunately, this threat became quite ineffective when, as Menzies later complained, President Eisenhower pulled the rug clear out from under his feet by announcing that he would go to any lengths to secure a peaceful settlement, i.e. that he would not condone the use of force.

In retrospect, it seems clear that a rational evaluation of the interests involved and of the best means of securing them would not have permitted actual military action. The direct interests involved could have been better secured without it—the loss of the 45 per cent profits from the Suez Canal shares during the remaining twelve years of the concession could have been adequately compensated by the confiscation of Egypttian assets in London; the passage of British ships through the Canal could scarcely have been jeopardized (except in the very short run), as Egypt herself and the Middle Eastern oil producers were interested as much as Britain was in its efficient operation. The possible repercussions of its nationalization, declared in deliberate defiance of British influence, through encouraging the Arab countries to nationalize British interests, were greatly exaggerated, as the precedent had already been set in Iran and the continuation of British investments depended on their commercial utility to the producers and not upon their military protection. British action was thus not based upon a rational calculation that it was suitable for securing the British interests involved.

British gunboat diplomacy was not based on any clear doctrine, and its basic principles can probably be reduced to those of using force only in the last resort and effectively. Failing a more elaborate national doctrine, it seems worth-while to subject the Suez action to the mixed, prudential and ethical, criteria proposed by St. Thomas Aquinas for a 'just war', which with remarkable realism combine ethical and common-sense criteria: a just cause; a just intention; a reasonable chance of success; if successful, the action should offer a better situation than the one that would have prevailed without it; the force used should be proportionate to the object. Clearly the Suez action was doubtful on all scores. It can be largely explained in terms of the psychological predispositions, the misperceptions and absence of a clear rational calculation of the best means of securing the interests involved—or rather of the failure to apply such an analysis which had undoubtedly been undertaken by the Foreign Office. The crucial element, however, remains to be discussed—that of the principle of the Thomist 'just cause' which sanctions the use of force. It is relevant not only to this case but also to the formulation of later British attitudes to the use of force, which were greatly affected by the Suez experience.

The Charter of the United Nations clearly condemns the threat or the use of force in international relations, with the sole exception of self-defence against an armed attack. Although the Suez action led some British and Commonwealth lawyers to argue that the Charter does not bar necessary force to protect vital interests against injustice or against violations of international law, there is little doubt that the legal advisers of the Foreign Office in 1956 knew that this was not the generally accepted view, or the view that would probably prevail in the case.[33] Ultimately, the questions boiled down to the old principle of 'harmonization'—had Britain been able to persuade the majority of the United Nations, or at least the United States, that the use of force was justified, her action would not have been quite so strongly condemned. The root of her difficulty lies in the historical nexus between Britain's imperialism and her world role as a policeman. Historically, domination over others carried with it notions of international order but, not unnaturally, these two linked aspects had a very different impact on the British and on other nations; the former thought in terms of their world role, the latter in terms of imperialism.

Both Eden and Gaitskell represented the image of the English liberals, so ill-attuned to the postwar world—they both spoke of 'law' and 'theft' and of Hitler, and seemed to be quite genuine in seeking not only the preservation of a British asset but also a suitable way of contributing to world order. There was no dissent in Parliament from Eden's statement that Britain could not accept a settlement 'leaving the Canal in the unfettered control of a single power', although this, in a way, was precisely what he had done in 1954, admittedly in favour of Neguib and not of Nasser. The Labour Party fully concurred with the idea of bringing the Canal under international control, although it was favoured by the United Nations, whereas the Conservatives were thinking about 'Maritime Nations'. Outside Britain, however, and particularly in the new states, the British action appeared to be clearly imperialist, especially as it was linked with the Israeli action.

Major importance can be attributed to the traditional acceptance of the use of force as an instrument of foreign policy. It was not rejected in principle by any sizeable portion of the public in Britain; Aneurin Bevan got little support for his argument that the use of force was quite unthinkable owing to the dangers of escalation, as this would have given *carte blanche* to any aggressor. Even the Americans did not completely demur at the ultimate use of force, although they were rather ambiguous about the conditions for its justification; for instance, as Eden records,[34] Dulles demanded a prior 'world opinion so adverse to Nasser that he would be isolated'. Gaitskell appeared to be less demanding, stipulating merely that force should not be used except under circumstances 'consistent with our belief in, and our pledges to the Charter of the United Nations'. The conditions for attaining universal support, a majority, or even sizeable support in the United Nations simply did not exist, and hence, had the government been realistic, it would have discarded the possibility both of American and of Labour support. All this argument does not dismiss the possibility that a swift and successful occupation of the Canal would have secured the acquiescence, if not the full support, of the Americans (see pp. 218–20); although the British government did not possess the adequate military capability, a swifter action was physically possible and only the uncertainty about the military and political risks involved inevitably precluded the essential speed and determination.

The costs of the intervention were high. Sir Pierson Dixon, who was in a good position to judge its extent, discusses the revelation of Britain's weakness and indecisiveness and the throwing away of her moral position on which her world status had largely depended, depriving her especially of a standing to speak up against the use of force by the Russians.[35] The impact of the lessons of Suez upon British attitudes to the use of force was fundamental but not immediate. This was to no small extent due to the fact that, following her compliant withdrawal of troops, Britain soon managed to mend her fences with the United States, and also, although more slowly and less completely, those with the United Nations and the Arab states. The expedition made it abundantly clear how strongly the climate of international public opinion was opposed to armed interventions in pursuit of individual national interests, and how such interventions strengthened the social support for the attacked regime and thus enhanced its determination to resist. It also demonstrated the limitations of British capabilities, which was later greatly increased by the growing vulnerability of ships to guided missiles. Finally, it destroyed what had remained of Britain's reputation for the determination and resolution which are essential for success. The parameters within which force could be employed greatly narrowed.

The next major issue involving the use of force was that of Southern

Rhodesia. Diplomatic pressures upon the Southern Rhodesians, arguments, appeals to loyalty to the Crown, and threats were all ineffective, and Wilson came under the crosscurrents of domestic and international pressures. As he describes in his memoirs,[36] he thought of these pressures as being organized in four 'constituencies': the Labour and the Conservative Parties at home with public opinion behind them, and the Commonwealth and the United Nations abroad. The two latter were pressing for strong action and the General Assembly passed a non-binding recommendation that Britain should employ force to remove the rebellious regime. Wilson, however, was governed by the domestic political situation, which was delicate. The Conservatives were strongly opposed to the use of force. While a minority within the Labour Party urged it, there was a danger of a breakaway on the right which would have meant a defeat for the government, whose majority had been reduced to one on the day of the Unilateral Declaration of Independence. Wilson states that he took the line against the use of force because he believed it was right, and that it was, in fact, the one that his party would support; perhaps it would be more appropriate to think in the reverse order—that his line was determined by the imperious restraints of party management but that he also considered this policy to be right. In any case, he rejected the possibility of using force, and, when pressed, allowed only for the unrealistic exception 'to preserve law and order and to avert a tragic action, subversion, murder, and so on' at the request of the Governor. One may leave aside the rather complex problem of adequate capability—a very limited quick military intervention at an early stage might well have toppled the regime on the basis of its appeal to the South Rhodesians' loyalty to the Crown. It seems clear that the occasion to use force in an action which was internationally demanded was abandoned owing to domestic pressures.

Nonetheless, the idea of organizing a major international action in defence of Britain's vital interests reappeared in 1967, when the Egyptians closed the Straits of Tiran, provoking an Israeli armed attack and thus jeopardizing Britain's Middle East oil supplies. It is on public record that the Prime Minister stated that the British government would join with other interested governments to assert the right of passage for vessels of all nations through the Straits of Tiran, and that the Admiralty announced that *Victorious* and other warships were held 'in readiness against any eventuality' in the Mediterranean. Although the concert of Maritime Powers had not worked in 1956, Lord George-Brown[37] confirms that he hoped that this time, with American participation, these Powers would declare that they would not suffer the closure of an international waterway and that, if necessary, they would assemble an international naval force and escort convoys through the Straits. According to the second, 1972, edition of Patrick Gordon Walker's *The Cabinet*, both Wilson and Brown advocated the use of force and were overruled only after three Cabinet meetings.[38] Apparently, a crucial factor was the decision of the Defence Secretary, Denis Healey, to oppose the action, following the advice of his experts. The caution against the employment of ships in the narrow waters was well justified, as in October of the same year the Israeli destroyer *Eilat* was destroyed at a range of at least ten miles by an Egyptian boat which used only four missiles.

Modern technology, which has put sophisticated weapons into the hands of many small states, has thus severely limited Britain's capability for a substantive naval action, and seems to have decisively reinforced the other pressures against Britain's using force. Public opinion at home seems to be increasingly opposed to the use of force in general, and to support the postwar British practice of keeping diplomatic relations open, whatever the provocation; the United Nations constitutes an increasingly weighty external restraint against any action directed against a new state. It seems likely that the use of limited force by Britain, acting alone or in concert with a few associates, has now become unthinkable in any substantial fashion; British participation in an international enforcement force, despite the abortive initiative of Wilson, seems unlikely in the foreseeable future, as both the international and the domestic situation do not seem to favour it.

*Morality*
It is not a matter of ethnocentric exaggeration to contend that Britain is more concerned with the problems of morality and of international law than most other states. There seem to be two reasons for this. First, she has been involved in a foreign policy of an exceptionally wide scope which was governed by broad conceptions of a world role; second, moral issues have played an important part in the political argument at home, e.g. regarding nuclear weapons, or Southern Rhodesia, or the sale of arms to South Africa, or support for the American bombing of North Vietnam. Being involved means taking a stand and generally expressing it in moral or legal terms; thus a powerful constraint is formed on future policy decisions. Lord Trevelyan, for example,[39] has justifiably expressed his personal doubts as to whether it was advisable in principle for the British to make statements in support of the actions of another state for which they were not responsible, however much they agreed with these actions, and despite the pressures for support engendered

through our alliance. This applies with particular force to Britain's support for the American bombing of North Vietnam. The British government having declared itself in favour of this, was forced to declare its objections when it withdrew its support. Moreover, waves of public indignation frequently lead to parliamentary debates on issues of foreign policy, debates which are couched in strong moral terms and force the government of the day to take a stand in such terms. This can be particularly embarrassing when the issue concerns a state with which Britain generally maintains friendly and close relations, such as South Africa, Spain, Greece, or Portugal.

The gradual limitation of the scope of British foreign policy and the subsequent redefinition of her world role, combined with the growing domestic economic preoccupations, enabled her to take a somewhat more detached attitude to the more remote conflicts in the early 1970s. The studied non-partisan attitude of the British to the Indo-Pakistani conflict in 1971 strongly contrasts with Britain's strong involvements in 1965 and, even more so, with the Nigerian–Biafran problem. The diplomatic correspondent of *The Times* (20 December 1971) reported plausibly that the British diplomats were quietly congratulating themselves on the successful outcome of this detached policy, as Britain found herself in a much more advantageous position than the United States, the Soviet Union, or China, all of whom took up rigid positions early in the conflict.

It is difficult to draw a clear distinction between moral and legal rules, particularly in an international system as fluid as that since 1945. Both can be regarded as part of the whole gamut of social norms governing the behaviour of states. As in domestic systems, the scope and nature of these norms are determined by the ways in which social needs are perceived and consensus is achieved; according to the social importance of the rule and the degree of consensus attainable, sanctions are provided to reinforce it, ranging through various degrees of social opprobrium and moral condemnation to actual, though rather ineffectual, enforcement measures. The blurring of distinctions between legal and other norms of behaviour is the dominant note of modern sociological interpretations of international law. It is also noticeable in the actual practice of states; Grant Hugo reflects it when discussing the Suez action in terms of international morality, whereas it could be discussed in much the same way in terms of international law—as a breach of the prevailing norms of behaviour.

The condemnation of 'utopian' foreign policy expressed by E. H. Carr in 1939 fully explains both the initial postwar attitudes to international rules of behaviour adopted in Britain and their gradual transformation.

Theories of international morality are . . . the product of dominant nations or groups of nations. For the past hundred years, and more especially since 1918, the English-speaking peoples have formed the dominant group in the world; and current theories of international morality have been designed and expressed in the idiom peculiar to them . . . Both the view that the English-speaking peoples are monopolists of international morality and the view that they are consummate international hypocrites may be reduced to the plain fact that the current canons of international virtue have, by a natural and inevitable process, been mainly created by them.[40]

Thus Britain's support for the rules largely of her own making did not merely favour the international order but was clearly beneficial to her own interests. This does not in any way detract from the fact that this order was in many ways also beneficial to others, although, of course, the subject peoples could not be expected to appreciate the benefits of the *pax Britannica*, or the undeveloped nations the benefits of free trade in the way the British themselves did.

Britain's international reputation for hypocrisy, epitomized by the phrase 'perfidious Albion', may be attributed not to national insincerity but rather to a national distaste for logic and planning. As the British prefer to deal with situations after they have arisen rather than to prepare for them, they show a pronounced tendency to violent fluctuations between idealism and realism, between humanitarianism and self-interest.[41] The temptation to actual hypocrisy arises most strongly when British statesmen defend vital national interests while claiming to defend some abstract idea. For instance, the memorandum circulated by Sir Arthur Hardinge, the Under-Secretary of State in 1908, said that whether Britain would vindicate the neutrality of Belgium would depend upon British policy and the circumstances, but the official explanation of Britain's entry into the first world war stressed that her moral position involved, as a matter of honour, keeping the solemn engagement to Belgium 'otherwise our moral position would be such as to have lost all respect'. This may appear to be a mere convenient rationalization, but there is an obvious danger in confusing virtues and interests. As was pithily put by Lord Beaconsfield on 17 January 1878, in an age in which the moral principle had not yet become firmly established:

We know very well when we talk of 'British interests' we mean British material interests—interests of that character which are sources of wealth or securities for strength of the country. We do not want to be informed that the cardinal virtues are British interests. We possess and endeavour to exercise them, but they have not their [*sic*] peculiar character which the British interests that we refer to possess.[42]

From his personal political experience C. M. Woodhouse[43] convincingly argues that the question 'which policy is morally right?' ranks with 'which policy is likely to preserve peace and which to lead to war?' and 'which policy can the country's economy afford?', as an issue on which divisions between and within the parties occur. The need to explain and to defend governmental policies in moral terms constitutes an important constraint, as it has to be taken into account in calculating the costs of proposed political actions. It is, however, impossible to attribute to it a far-reaching importance.

The Labour Party in particular is subject to strong pressures from its Left, but pacifism and strong moral opposition within the party did not prevent Labour governments from developing and maintaining Britain's nuclear weapons. A Labour government, at the time of its most outspoken criticism of South Africa, allowed a deal between Rio Tinto Zinc and the South African government on uranium mining which virtually gave the latter a nuclear capability.[44] George Brown explains in his memoirs why, as Foreign Secretary, he favoured the sale of Buccaneers and of naval equipment to the Union, although he loathed apartheid. First, exports were urgently needed to help limit the cuts in governmental expenditure prepared for the deflationary package in March 1968; second, refusal could lead to further losses of the South African markets; third, the equipment was strategically useful but could not be used for internal oppression.[45] Economic needs came first and prevailed over moral rhetoric, but the latter helped to perpetuate illusions about the Commonwealth and the United Nations.

British moral argumentation abroad was equally confusing. In condemning the colonial policies of other powers, Britain antagonized them, but the new states still thought she did not go nearly far enough. The rhetoric was added to the difficulties of explaining and defending British actions. Maurice Challe[46] records the exasperation of the French at British behaviour in the Suez affair. Besides noting 'the strange destiny of this old solid people, of this old commercial people which hoped by yielding, to keep their markets', he also complained that Sir Anthony's main preoccupation, to avoid appearing to be an aggressor, led to 'all-pervading hypocrisy' which made the allies prepare 'more or less murky pretexts'. The moral cloak also proved predictably threadbare in the United Nations and in the eyes of the Americans. Eden completely confused international support for keeping the Canal open with support for Britain's using force. The explanation that the action aimed at preserving international order was not convincing, especially after it had led to the actual closure of the Canal.

In the perennial tug of war between order and justice, the *status quo* and revisionism, the stability of legal rules against the flexibility of moral ones, Britain was firmly tied by her traditions and interests on the side favouring the *status quo* but insufficiently flexible to accept irresistible change. She was much less stubborn in the defence of her imperial interests than other imperial powers. The Attlee Government set remarkable and exceptional standards in meeting independence claims within the Empire, but the British were much less compliant when pressed within the General Assembly. Their resistance to departing from a stand in favour of the *status quo* and of its standards was reinforced by the smarting effect of the 'dual standards' applied by the developing countries and the United Nations. India's non-alignment implied that she did not demand or expect the same standards from the West and from the Russians; her own behaviour in Kashmir and her occupation of Goa made her moralistic stand against wars and aggression seem hypocritical. Lord Home (as he then was) during his 1955 visit to New Delhi found it hard to accept Nehru's preachings that the military pacts of the West were immoral. Particularly galling was the stand adopted by the United Nations in 1956 on Suez, when the Russians got off much more lightly over Hungary, or, on a much less important issue, when the United Nations supported Spain in her claims to Gibraltar.

The confused judgements on the Suez affair demonstrate how hard it is to evaluate the impact of moral restraints upon British foreign policy. This was Britain's most flagrant departure from her professed moral standards, but it was, at the same time, an equally flagrant departure from political expediency. Is it possible to segregate the two strands of evaluation? Denis Healey, for instance, quoted the following reasons:

Firstly, it was totally immoral—inconsistent with any attempt to get order in world affairs; second, totally dishonest, because it was based on deceiving all our friends and allies except the French; third, it was bound to fail because we wouldn't get away with it and fourth, it coincided with Hungary, which made it shaming beyond belief. On top of everything, it undermined the rest of our foreign policy, based upon Anglo-American alliance. [47]

If pressed, Healey would perhaps agree that the force of the individual arguments was by no means reflected in the order in which they were listed.

## International Law

Our understanding of the role international law plays in international affairs has been considerably developed and refined since the last war, and the debates of the interwar period, which concentrated upon the question why people and nations obey law, sound today somewhat abstruse. On the one hand, we can now more readily differentiate between legal rules and divide them into categories about which more meaningful generalizations can be made than about international law as a whole.[48] On the other hand, we have moved towards a fairly general consensus that rules of law constitute one category within the spectrum of rules of social behaviour and that the notion of 'law' must therefore be broadly understood. Few would dissent from the following summary of the relationship between law and order:[49]

[International order depends upon] 'an infrastructure' of agreed assumptions, practices, commitments. . . . These too are international law, and they are reflected in all that governments do (p. 16).

Law reflected in the assumptions, concepts, institutions, and procedures of international society is not the kind of international law one commonly thinks about because it does not, on its face, direct governments how to behave. But in fact, all law is intimately related to national behavior. Even that 'submerged' law molds the policies of governments (pp. 21–2).
[quoting from Myres S. McDougall:]
That nations are the actors, the legislators, the executives, the judges of international law has led some international lawyers to see law not in terms of norms, standards, and obligations, but as a 'policy-oriented', 'comprehensive process of authorative decisions' made largely by the nations themselves' (p. 35).

On law and policy Henkin comments:

The two are often contrasted, suggesting that law is obligatory while policy is voluntary. In fact law and policy are not in a meaningful contrast, and their relation is not simple, whether in domestic or in international society.

Law is generally not designed to keep individuals from doing what they are eager to do. Much of law, and the most successful part, is a codification of existing mores, of how people behave and feel they ought to behave.

The traditional British attitudes to international law are parallel to those to international morality and closely connected with them. Both arose from the close concern with the international system and from the principle of harmonization, discussed above. The general line of policy can be described as pragmatic, concerned with the reconciliation of support for the existing order with a flexible acceptance of revisionist claims when supported by sufficient force and based upon acceptable moral principles. That was why, after 1945, the British accepted (although with considerable reluctance) the anti-colonial claims which eroded the province of domestic jurisdiction of the colonial powers. This was not different in principle from the acceptance of the claims for national self-determination at the end of the first world war; the differences lay only in the wider application of the revisionist claims and in the fact that, this time, they directly affected Britain's own interests.

The question of the fundamental British attitudes to international law is of considerable importance in the initial period of her membership of the EEC. Some politicians regard the divergent British and continental outlooks on law as a potential major root of misunderstandings and mistrusts. The Common Law tradition indicates that treaties and agreements should be solemnly undertaken with the full intention of abiding by them, whereas, in British eyes, to the continentals they are often no more than programmes which may be much more easily deviated from. Not unnaturally, each side tends to regard itself as the more reliable and trustworthy partner in any legal relationship and this egocentric view is, naturally, not shared by the other one. In fact, the traditional British respect for international law was based upon the country's close identification with the international legal system in the nineteenth century, a system which had been shaped by Britain and fashioned largely to protect her own interests.[50] In the postwar world Britain is no longer able to play such a central role in the rapid transformation of the international legal order, which is influenced more decisively by others, the developing states and the superpowers. The changes are frequently adverse, notably in the successive infringements upon the open-seas doctrine, epitomized in the exasperating conflict with the Icelanders over their fisheries' limits. If the argument that Britain's attitudes to international law are more positive than those of her continental partners has probably a degree of validity today, this may not remain so for very long. The maintenance of the rules of law is, of course, an interest which is pursued by every single state, owing both to a general interest in the international order and in the state's individual reputation. It is, however, an interest which is pursued in competition with other interests. Clashes need not necessarily occur but, when they do, in order to abide by law, the state must regard observance of law to be more advantageous than its violation. Even today, to some extent this may remain truer for Britain with her traditional involvement in the world order than for other nations. Resort to the law favours the protection of her interests, enshrined in the *status quo*, but respect for legal norms, which advocate changes frequently adverse to British interests, is not binding. Britain is certainly well aware of international law.

The constant stream of legal advice from the Law Officers of the Crown, which has been collected by Lord McNair,[51] includes numerous instances of advice that the government either could not take a proposed action or had no grievance against the action of another government. Regrettably, the collection does not include an analysis of the effects of the opinions upon governmental action. It is hard to assume that the opinions were invariably followed, and we know that in the admittedly exceptional case of the Suez action the legal advisers' warnings were disregarded on the highest political orders. Sometimes invocation of international law serves merely to rationalize policy. The Heath Government, for instance, did not ask the Law Officers whether international law would justify discontinuing supplies of arms to South Africa, which would have been indicated by resolutions of the Security Council and by South African support for the illegal regime in Southern Rhodesia. It asked the very narrow question whether it was under an obligation to continue supplies under the existing contracts, and, although Law Officers' opinions are normally kept confidential, it published their affirmative opinion early in 1971.

By the nature of things, reference to specific rules and treaties is part of the routine of the various departments of the Foreign and Commonwealth Office. The Science and Technology Section, for instance, must constantly refer in its activities regarding nuclear technology to the provisions of the Non-Proliferation Treaty. Moreover, domestic public opinion is generally in favour of international law—Britain has not been subject to unequal or oppressive treaties, and pressures to violate international norms or temptations to maltreat aliens rarely arise; on the contrary, violations of international law carry the stigma of guilt and can scarcely be expected to be disguised in an open political system. This is by no means decisive on politically sensitive issues; the legal argument that the government was in breach of Britain's obligation under the UN Convention on Refugees when refusing entry to certain Ugandan refugees, was scarcely noted in the press.

Only occasionally does respect for international law lead to distortions of argument and of judgement, as the vaguer moral rules frequently do. Sir Pierson Dixon was, however, justified in noting a propensity on the part of British governments to seek legal agreements as cosy pseudo-solutions instead of squarely facing the differences of views and of interests, notably in the case of Sir Anthony Eden, who really believed that both the 1936 and the 1954 treaties with Egypt were workable. It was again, characteristically, Eden who, after the event, produced a legal rationalization of the Suez action saying that Britain was constrained to maintain her treaty rights as otherwise 'no reliance could be placed on any international agreement and the whole structure and basis of international relations would cease to exist'.

On the whole, the British view of the place of law in the international system has traditionally been realistic—it is based upon a perception of the world in which no international consensus obtains on major issues and in which military balances and legal structures uneasily combine to maintain a degree of order and stability. Although, as has been argued, Britain did not shrink from using force in 1956, and has occasionally resorted to its implied threat, her preference is for legal processes. This does not mean that subtleties of legal or quasi-legal rules are followed when the chips are really down. Britain recognizes necessity like any other nation and the fact that she has traditionally been opposed to the weakening of the stability of international treaties, by refusing to accept the validity of the doctrine of *clausula rebus sic stantibus*, can be attributed not only to her desire to maintain the rule of law but also to her having been, on the whole, a satisfied nation whose interests have required the protection of law and not its change.

In fact, in real emergency, for instance when sterling was in jeopardy, governments did not abide by binding agreements—Wilson imposed a temporary surcharge upon imports and Heath floated the pound. In both cases, however, it was more a question of principle than of rigid legal rules, and the breach consisted largely in failing to consult or advise in advance. Inevitably, in the process of gradual retrenchment in the scope of Britain's foreign policy, she was forced to abandon existing commitments but this was a political and not a legal process. The most serious cases in the interwar period were those of Spain and Czechoslovakia. Britain has abandoned many commitments since 1945; when possible, she substituted other arrangements, for instance, American protection in Greece and Turkey in 1947, the Five-Power Agreement for the defence of Malaysia, and various federal schemes. On the whole, in the process of shedding her commitments, she was less ruthless than either France or the United States.

The British invoked no general principles but, as all the withdrawals were due to their diminishing capabilities, one may regard them as being based on the implied invocation of necessity. The retreat from the declared commitment about the Straits of Tiran can serve as a clear example. On 4 March 1957 the British delegate to the UN General Assembly declared:

The Straits of Tiran must be regarded as an international waterway, through which the vessels of all nations have a right of passage. Her Majesty's Government will assert this right on behalf of all British shipping and they are prepared to join with others to secure general recognition of this right.[52]

This was a political declaration but, as it was made with the clear intent of reassuring the Israelis, arguably this amounted to a situation of an estoppel, with the legal implications that a unilateral renunciation by Britain would be illegal. Ten years later the principle was reaffirmed in the House of Commons—both by the government and the opposition on 31 May 1967. As stated above, the Cabinet was actually contemplating the use of force and Sir Alec Douglas-Home declared on behalf of the opposition that it would not be reasonable to press the government on the means it intended to employ.[53] In the event, Britain's power to act alone was insufficient, and the other states, especially the United States, were not willing to join.

The exceptional British departure from the tenets of international law in the Suez affair warrants some detail. Nasser was very careful to stay well within the rule of law governing nationalization. The British protest was therefore couched in terms of

the arbitrary and unilateral seizure by one nation of an international agency which has the responsibility to maintain and to operate the Suez Canal so that all the beneficiaries of the Treaty of 1888 can effectively enjoy the use of an international waterway upon which the economy, commerce and security of much of the world depends.[54]

Lawyers could not agree whether Nasser's move involved any violation of international law and, if so, how serious this violation was.[55] This lack of legal certainty and the United Nations Charter's prohibitions against using force may be regarded as an additional restraint upon an immediate British military reaction, which was also, of course, blocked by more central military and political difficulties. Without the excuse provided by Israel's attack, a later use of force would have been so blatantly illegal that one cannot dismiss the possibility that even Eden's resolve to act might have been curbed.

Israel's action was not clearly illegal in terms of the Charter, because her excuse of self-defence was at least not implausible in law. The Anglo-French argument was much feebler—that they were acting as policemen to separate Israeli and United Arab Republic forces and to keep the Canal open. Even if this had been a *bona fide* explanation, which it patently was not, and although the case was so exceptional that it created no precedent which could easily be extended to permit the use of force to protect any interests a state considered vital, Britain could not expect the majority of the nations to accept this interpretation. One can subscribe to the view[56] that the balance of advantages might have appeared different had the law been clearer; it was sufficiently ambiguous to permit a guess that a successful action described as temporary would not be regarded as a serious breach of law, and that meanwhile Nasser would be overthrown. But the British and Australian attempts to develop a doctrine which would legalize the Anglo-French action soon wilted in the face of universal disagreement in other countries. The mounting criticism of the legal aspects of the British action was forcibly expressed by Lord Attlee on 12 November 1956, when he came rather close to accusing the government of having committed aggression.

In many official announcements, successive British governments have declared their support for international law in general terms. Sometimes this is done as a mere statement of a scarcely attainable aspiration, sometimes in a highly realistic fashion. For instance, the official commentary on the Covenant of the League of Nations expressed the opinion that 'ultimately, and in the long run, the only alternative to war is law', and that the Covenant could never be entirely satisfactory because of its bias towards the political rather than the judicial settlement of disputes. By contrast, the official commentary on the UN Charter stated that 'no enforcement action by the Organization can be taken against a Great Power itself without a major war. If such a situation arises, the United Nations will have failed in its purpose. . . . The creation of the United Nations is designed to prevent such a situation from arising by free acceptance by the Great Powers of restraints upon themselves.'[57]

The British have traditionally been sceptical of a 'normative' role of international law and were particularly wary of extending the scope of the United Nations, especially of the erosion of the domestic jurisdiction clause. For instance, Bevin clearly stated the important British interests at stake when discussing the Security Council's seizure of the Indonesian issue: 'in view of our responsibilities to so many territories in the world, I feel I must take precautions to see that in a slipshod manner the Security Council shall not go outside its proper jurisdiction'.[58] Likewise, British adhesion to the optional clause of the Statute of the World Court carried for a while a broad reservation excluding the Court's jurisdiction in respect to 'any question which, in the opinion of the Government of the U.K., affects the national security of the United Kingdom or of any of the dependent territories'.

The World Court has rarely dealt with really important British legal interests. On the few occasions when Britain did resort to it, international law proved a poor protection for British interests. In the earliest case, that of the Corfu Channel, the Court condemned not only the Albanian but also the British action—moreover, the Albanians refused to pay the compensation awarded to Britain. In the Anglo-Iranian case, despite the important stake, the government relied throughout the dispute on peaceful means of settlement, although the constraints upon the use of force were pragmatic rather than legal. One of the British moves was to turn to the World Court. The Court's Interim Order of 5 July 1951 held that, pending the settlement of the dispute, the operations of the company should be allowed to continue without aggravation as before the beginning of the dispute, but the Iranian Government refused to abide by the Order. In the Anglo-Norwegian Fisheries case, the Court accepted the Norwegian claim for an unorthodox demarcation of the line of territorial waters.

In many disputes in which Britain was defending her traditional, legally established interests against claims by other states based upon non-legal principles, she tried in vain to persuade the other side to accept the jurisdiction of the World Court: Argentina with regard to the Falkland Islands and Spain with regard to Gibraltar, were adamant in their refusals. Although Iceland accepted the jurisdiction of the Court in the 1961 Fisheries Agreement, she refused to abide by this undertaking in the 1970s. Despite occasional minor successes either in the World Court or in other international arbitral tribunals, all in all, international law and the World Court have failed to protect British interests threatened by various revisionist claims. In a period of change this could scarcely be otherwise and Britain had to rely on political and diplomatic rather than legal processes to deal with the pressures.

While of little use to Britain in defence of her traditional interests, international law may serve her better in the 'lower profile' world role which she has been adopting in world affairs. In special political contexts for nations reluctant to take sides, invocation of international law affords some protection from pressure by either side.[59] Britain's mediation efforts in the Middle Eastern conflict in 1967 and her studied neutrality in the Bangladesh conflict in 1972 point to a possibility that she may profit from international law in this way in the future. Her traditional doctrine of recognizing governments in actual control of their countries is helpful here, as for instance her acceptance of the change of government in Chile in 1973.

British support for international law has always been stronger on the declaratory level than in actual policies. This is even more true of her support of its development which is sometimes given (with regard to aspects of the law of treaties, for example) in the knowledge that the actual agreements are unlikely to be ratified or even signed. As a country with a well-established interest in the international legal order and with a wealth of legal expertise, Britain is likely to retain a lively concern in the evolution of international law, although Lord McNair may have been justified in thinking that she has not been 'pulling her weight' sufficiently in the past. As a maritime nation, she has certainly been active where her interests were directly affected, although here the traditional national root in prize law has now, naturally, dried up. She has been fighting losing battles to preserve the regime of the open seas from excessive encroachments by littoral states upon traditional British fishing interests; after the wreck of the Torrey Canyon, she initiated a study of the relevant issues of maritime law and practice; she has also taken a leading part in the movement to control the use of the oceans for the dumping of toxic wastes.

# 7 World Role and National Interest

*The World Role for a Middle Power*

BRITAIN'S wartime record ensured for her a position perpetuating her traditional claim to be represented at the exclusive top-level councils dealing with global politics: she was one of the Occupying Powers in Germany and a Permanent Member of the Security Council endowed with the power of veto; she expected and demanded a 'seat at the table' whenever major questions affecting the international system as a whole were discussed. Much of Britain's postwar foreign policy was directed towards the central, global balance. Some of it, to be discussed (ch. 9), related directly to relations with the United States and the Soviet Union, but much of it can be subsumed under the concept of a 'world role' which is discussed here.

'Role' is a mere intellectual construct; decision-makers determine their policies in the more specific terms of 'interests' or 'functions'. The concept has, however, played an important part in the public debates about Britain's postwar foreign policy and hence can serve as a convenient focus for its analysis. Unfortunately, its interpretations differ widely and are often emotionally charged. On the other hand, it is possible to regard the successive conceptions of Britain's world role as something nearly inevitable and politically useful, as, at first, they correlated with the actual function Britain had within the international system and, in later stages, they served as a useful device to accustom public opinion at home to the loss of status. On the other hand, concern with a world role, which was prolonged beyond Britain's waning capabilities, can be blamed for a relative neglect of the integration movement in Western Europe and for reinforcing Britain's determination to maintain the international exchange role of sterling. In more general terms, the lingering idea that Britain had an independent central role to play has come under criticism for its lack of realism and for the wrong priorities it implied. Indeed, ever since Dean Acheson in his West Point speech in December 1962 coined the phrase: 'Great Britain has lost an Empire and has not yet found a role', much political argument has been conducted in Britain in an endeavour to define such a role or find 'a place in the world'.

International theory is only partly useful, as the concept of the 'role' is well articulated only in sociology and less so in political analysis.[1] The sociologists generally agree that the term 'role' refers to behaviour-decisions and actions, and represents the dynamic aspect of the individual's position or status. Role theory generally focuses on the interaction between the role conception and performance by the individual involved and role prescription by others. This analysis does not, however, readily apply to the behaviour of states as, except within the limited context of international organizations, their position within the international system is much more vaguely determined, and their status and, even more so, its implications are often uncertain. In the case of Britain there were no clear objective criteria to determine whether she was still enjoying a great power status in the 1960s, or (whichever status was attributed to her) the appropriate extent of her peace-keeping responsibilities east of Suez. The actual specific decisions taken by the Wilson Government, notably to refrain from intervening in Southern Rhodesia but to intervene in North Borneo, to withdraw from Aden and then from east of Suez altogether, were all primarily guided by the assessment of the specific interests directly involved, of the domestic needs and demands, and of the trends of events abroad. Remembering that the conceptions of 'role' are fundamentally mere mental constructs, we can, nevertheless, surmise that these general conceptions played an important background part in the process. One can regard them as being in a circular relationship with the specific decisions—while the assumed world role meant that, *prima facie*, Britain should continue her traditional peace-keeping responsibilities, the cumulative inability to maintain her individual responsibilities eventually eroded the 'world role' and led to its redefinition and to the withdrawal from east of Suez.

Thus role conception is not only an intellectual construct describing in shorthand certain basic psychological attitudes but has operational implications which require analysis. The successive governments had, of course, to operate within the parameters prescribed by their limited resources as well as by the expectations of other governments and by internationally determined norms of behaviour whether based upon law, treaty, or custom. Nevertheless, they themselves were ultimately responsible for the decisions taken and the current role conceptions were relevant in shaping the latter. It was in keeping with the firm conception of Britain's world role in 1947 that the Attlee Government diverted some grain ships to alleviate the famine in South-east Asia at the cost of having to introduce bread-rationing at home; it was in keeping with its weakened conception that the Wilson Government decided to withdraw from east of Suez. The contrast between the floating of the pound in June 1972 and its stubborn defence in 1967 can be largely attributed to the revision, the scaling-down, of the conception of Britain's role within the international financial system during the intervening five years.

If we accept the validity of this argument, the general lines of the evolution of Britain's postwar foreign policy can be subsumed under, and even partly explained by, the evolution of the successive conceptions of her world role. Analysis requires a distinction between these conceptions, Britain's actual position in the world, and the roles prescribed for her by others. The British conception was quite realistic immediately after the war. The Attlee Government was well aware that Britain's resources were stretched to the utmost and that commitments must be reduced but Britain was still an imperial power with widespread possessions, and a victor state in occupation of parts of ex-enemy territories, with the second largest navy and the most advanced bombers, well ahead of all states except the two superpowers. Until the later 1950s, Britain's world-wide imperial and post-imperial responsibilities were still real, and she was still a major factor in the East–West context.

In a way, performing a world role is another expression for exercising influence within the international system. This is an obvious major foreign-policy objective for all states with any political weight, especially for a state which depends for its trade on the stability of this system as much as Britain does. Britain's record, when compared with those of other middle powers, does not appear to be at all unusual. The closest comparison lies with France under de Gaulle, who, after the ending of the Algerian crisis, was temporarily quite successful in playing a world role founded upon a strong home base which could boast of sustained economic growth, of political maturity and of reasonable economic and social stability; upon a strong influence over the other members of the EEC, especially the Federal Republic of Germany, over the French ex-colonies, and, more dubiously, upon an independent nuclear deterrent. Ultimately, these capabilities for playing a world role faded out following the 1968 disorders. The French strategy of playing off the two superpowers one against the other was no more successful than the British one of trying to influence one of them, but France could retract from her search for a world role to the Western European regional setting within which she had an established leading place. She also benefited from a much better balanced economic base than Britain, having enjoyed a much higher and more sustained rate of economic growth and having completed her adjustment to operating within the EEC.

The Federal Republic of Germany and Japan started from the fundamentally different position of being defeated powers. It was inherent in their situations that, after attaining control of their foreign policies, they had to accept their loss of world power status. They started with foreign policies of very limited scope, and adopted pacific, non-military behaviour which saved them expenditure on defence and enabled them to develop their economies by leaps and bounds and to seek their main roles in economic foreign policies. Only in the second half of the 1960s did the Germans discover, in Herr Willy Brandt's words, that they were 'an economic giant but a political pigmy' and gradually develop a political/strategic role more commensurate with their strength; after rather slow beginnings, the Japanese followed suit fully only after the series of 'Nixon shocks' in 1971. In both cases, the reasons lay not only in their consciousness of recovered strength but also in the realization that their respective national interests could best be pursued by their own efforts. Apparently, assuming a world role is a natural thing for the larger middle powers, all of whom are alike desirous of preserving a degree of independence in the pursuit of their national interests; a continuing world role for Britain can thus be regarded as something rational and customary. Communist China is possibly an exception, although the interpretation of her foreign policy remains controversial. She seems to show a predominantly regional, Asian orientation, making forays into broader spheres of international politics only as an extension of her regional policies, and making them only sporadically and selectively. Such detachment has the advantage of enabling her to select the issue and the time and method of involvement, and to avoid unwanted involvements outside her immediate region. Will China now lose much of this freedom once she is compelled to declare herself, like all other members, on the issues of the day in the United Nations?

In the 1960s, criticisms of the British world role began to mount at home and abroad, often referring to its current concepts as dangerous myths, to the illusions of independence, and to the over-ambitious scope of British policies. It was becoming increasingly clear that Britain's resource-base was inadequate for her widespread commitments. Moreover, the British governments did not define their country's role in the way her partners wished them to do, which, in terms of the theoretical analysis sketched out, can be regarded as a growing discrepancy between the role definition by the British governments and the role prescription by others. Thus the British did not see their role in the 'special relationship' in the same way as the Americans, who preferred to see Britain join

Europe, nor their role in Europe in the same way as the Europeans, whether the integrationists or de Gaulle, nor their role within the Commonwealth in the same way as its new African members; Britain's role in the Middle East was disputed by the local nationalists, by the Americans and by the French.

Lord Gladwyn records[2] that the debate over Britain's postwar role began inside the Foreign Office as early as 1942–3, with a division of opinion roughly corresponding with seniority and age. The senior officials tended to favour a great power arrangement in which Britain would play a full part; the junior ones generally maintained that this would be beyond her power and that she should hand the torch over to the Americans and the Russians. Ultimately, however, a consensus was reached for reasons which remained valid after the war. It was thought that 'if we did not fulfil our world-wide mission Britain would sink to the level of a second-class power and become either a European Soviet state or a penurious outpost of American pluto-democracy, or a German *Gau*, as the forces might dictate'.

The conviction that Britain could exercise influence upon the shape of world politics only by continuing to play a central role in them further delayed the adjustment of British perceptions and policies to postwar events. There were, however, additional factors which slowed down this adjustment. In the first instance, it was impossible to evaluate the positive and the negative aspects of Britain's power position in 1945, especially as this involved the intangible considerations of prestige. The adjustment of the broad world-role conception to Britain's diminished power base meant not only shedding commitments but also abandoning bases of power and influence. For instance, the chain of overseas bases constituted both, and their credit and debit sides remained in doubt until the later 1960s. As no government can be expected to give up its assets voluntarily, adjustment was inevitably piecemeal, in response to specific pressures, and not general. At least a partial reversal of fortune seemed possible and only during the 1960s did it become gradually clear that Britain had lost her relative power position in the world for good.

Moreover, the British political system militated against a public admission that Britain's status had been reduced, either by the government of the day or by the Opposition, although some of their members may have held and privately expressed much more sceptical views than those in public announcements. First, it was a question of public morale. The loss of the Empire and of power, in spite of victory in the War, gained at a very high cost, could have deprived the nation of all confidence had not the successive governments dwelt upon Britain's continuing world role. This was important during the time of shortages immediately after the war, even more so, perhaps, under Macmillan whose material goals did not fully satisfy national pride which had been grievously hurt during the Suez crisis. Belief in a world role helped to preserve a sense of importance and self-respect, although it was proving an increasingly misleading guide to policy. Macmillan was masterly in stressing Britain's power and status, her deterrent, and her close relations with the United States. In a period when all these were becoming increasingly unreal, he used them to good account to enable him to continue the rapid winding up of the remnants of the Empire without splitting the Conservative Party and without depriving the people of all confidence. Second, it was a question of electoral advantage and of the personal standing of the leader; Macmillan and Wilson used their foreign initiatives partly, occasionally perhaps mainly, for this purpose.

The political and economic assumptions underlying the traditional conceptions of Britain's world role were not challenged outside the governmental machinery, whether on the Left (e.g. by Crosland or Strachey), or on the Right (by the Bow Group) or in the universities. Radical dissent could offer no reasonable alternatives and its only strong manifestation, in the Campaign for Nuclear Disarmament, soon died out. In the 1960s, however, the rhetoric of the world role gradually yielded to the changing perceptions among the political elite of the implications of Britain's power position. According to the 1969 study of European elites by the Massachusetts Institute of Technology, as late as 1959, 72 per cent of the British elite were classing Britain as the third most powerful nation in the world, but the proportion rapidly dwindled in the following decade, to 51 per cent by 1961 and to 39 per cent by 1965; in the last year, only 8 per cent believed that Britain would remain the third most powerful nation by the year 2,000 and only 57 per cent that she would remain among the world's first five nations.[3]

The customary political style of the leadership was adjusted to this changing appraisal of the European issue by the elite, although with some delay. By 1964 British frontiers were clearly no longer in the Himalayas, but Harold Wilson went so far as to say at the Lord Mayor's Banquet at Guildhall on 16 November: 'We are a world power and a world influence, or we are nothing.' However, at the turning-point of Britain's proposed entry to the EEC and of her becoming a predominantly regional power, the White Paper of 8 July 1971 more soberly referred to a continuing world role, no longer to be played independently, but within the new EEC setting: 'our country will be more secure, *our ability to maintain peace and promote development in the world greater*, our economy stronger, *and our industries and people more prosperous*' (author's italics).

## The 'Three Circles' and the Resource Base

All the successive attempts after 1945 to play a world role were based upon the assumption that Britain had some such part to play along with the superpowers, although she could not hope to match their capabilities. This deficiency in capabilities was not simply glossed over; it was expected to be at least partly compensated for by Britain's widespread global interests expressed by the paradigm of 'the three circles', by her being the hub of the Commonwealth, by some attributes allowing her to exercise moral leadership, by her nuclear weapons, by the excellence of her diplomacy, or by some combination of these. Before proceeding with the actual role definitions, one should summarize how these compensating factors were perceived.

The 'three circles' concept stemmed from Churchill, who expressed it as follows:

I feel the existence of three great circles among the free nations and democracies. . . . The first circle for us is naturally the British Commonwealth and Empire, with all that that comprises. Then there is also the English-speaking world in which we, Canada and the other British Dominions, and the United States play so important a part. And finally, there is United Europe. These three majestic circles are co-existent and if they are linked together there is no force or combination which could overthrow them or even challenge them. Now if you think of the three inter-linked circles you will see that we are the only country which has a great part in every one of them. We stand in fact at the very point of junction and here is this island at the very centre of the seaways and perhaps of the airways also; we have the opportunity of joining them all together.[4]

When Churchill came to power in 1951, the concept became a major foundation of Britain's foreign policy to the point of the government instructing diplomatic missions to use it in their publicity. It was a pronouncedly egocentric conception, the effect of which can be likened to that of geographical projections focusing upon one's country: by the sheer method of presentation, the country becomes the centre of the Earth. Undoubtedly, being accustomed to having the map-grids concentrating upon Greenwich helped the British to accept the validity of the conception: although not nearly as powerful as either the United States or the Soviet Union, Britain alone belonged to all the three concentric circles and hence was perceived to play a central role in the international system. Her standing in each circle was understood to be strongly reinforced by her participation in the other two, which no other member of the given circle shared. Thus the British position in Western

Europe was greatly strengthened by her 'special relationship' with the United States; and, *vice versa*, being in Europe but not of it added to Britain's special stature in her relations with the United States, setting her apart from the continental powers. The Commonwealth link could be similarly employed; Attlee, in particular, was fond of using Britain's close relations with India to gain leverage in Washington or as a convenient excuse for pursuing a line of policy not favoured by the Americans; he also used the 'special relationship' as a leverage point in New Delhi. Heading the Commonwealth was thought to increase Britain's weight in Europe as well as to excuse her from entering into any form of close political union there.

The conduct of foreign policy on this basis gave great scope to British diplomacy, enabling Britain to act as a bridge between the individual circles and as a spokesman of one within another. The concept of the three circles was fundamental to the evolution of British ideas regarding other, more specific factors which were thought to allow the country to continue as a world power.

The *Commonwealth* was regarded in the first instance as a source of physical supports—its wartime record, the rapid and friendly withdrawal from India and India's successful incorporation in the Commonwealth, the subsequent stabilization of the Empire for a whole decade until the emancipation of Ghana and Malaya began the final phase of its dissolution, all contributed to confidence in its stability. Protected markets and military bases appeared as important elements of Britain's power.

The Commonwealth was also regarded as a major source of moral leadership. The British record was in shining contrast to the desperate last-ditch struggles of other colonial powers, the Dutch in the East Indies or the French in Indochina. No wonder that much of British public opinion, especially among the elite, persisted in regarding the Commonwealth links as 'very valuable' right into the 1960s; this regard diminished only at the end of the decade; Britain could be justifiably proud of her record as a model reformed imperial power, the only one which had managed to decolonize smoothly. The extreme leftists in the Labour Party were particularly enthusiastic for the New Commonwealth. They felt a moral obligation to repay the ex-colonial peoples for having ruled and exploited them within the Empire; they approved of the Third World strivings for non-alignment and they expected that Britain could exercise the role of a leader of the non-aligned bloc provided she pursued a policy of genuine neutrality and gave generous aid.

Britain's 'moral leadership' as an element of her world role was also sought by some in other areas of her policies. In the late 1950s, the Campaign for Nuclear Disarmament (CND) sought virtue in unilateral nuclear disarmament. It was based upon the idea that Britain, as one of the three first nuclear powers, should renounce her weapons unilaterally and thus prevent the further spread of nuclear weapons and persuade the superpowers to follow suit. While there were only three nuclear powers, the idea did not lack a certain persuasive force—conceivably a non-proliferation treaty and a limitation of the nuclear armoury of the superpowers might have been attainable in 1957 or 1958. The idea was, however, too contrary to the power-political realities to have the slightest chance of commending itself to the Conservative government of the day, and was also rejected by the leadership of the Labour Party, not only by the moderate leader, Hugh Gaitskell, but even by the previous leader of the left wing, Aneurin Bevan, who, as the opposition spokesman for defence, dramatically announced that we would not care to enter 'naked' into a conference room, having stripped the country of its nuclear weapons. Unilateralism was never incorporated in the mainstream of public opinion.

Another, much vaguer, socialist conception of the world role was based upon the establishment of the welfare state—Britain becoming a world-wide example of a socialized but tolerant and peaceful country, a paradigm both for the capitalist states oppressed by the spirit of competitiveness and by the fear of communism, and for the new states striving both for economic growth and for social equality. As this idea did not indicate a special line of policy, it did not lead to any organized movement, like the CND. It petered out as Britain's economic growth lagged and as socialism became tarnished in the new states and less influential in Western Europe. In the 1960s it became gradually clear that setting an example to other nations was unlikely to be fruitful as the latter would follow the British lead only when it suited their own interests, and also because Britain had not so much to offer them as other states, and had no ideas that might appear persuasive either to the superpowers, engaged in a direct dialogue, or to the West Europeans, engaged in integration movements, or to the new states, concerned with their economic development.

Some politicians thought that Britain's weakness was compensated for by her possessing capabilities not possessed by others, namely *nuclear weapons*, shared only by the superpowers, and an exceptionally experienced and skilful diplomacy. At first, there was some justification for this view of nuclear capability; while there were only three nuclear powers Britain was in a category of her own, separate from the other middle powers. The actual deterrence value of her limited weapons was small, but by no means negligible until the superpowers had evolved new and more complex weapons and had abandoned the strategy of massive retaliation. Then, and even more so when France and China had become nuclear powers and several other states had reached the technological capacity to follow suit, Britain's nuclear capacity became much less important and certainly could not be regarded as compensating for her economic weakness.

In all role conceptions, great store was set by the use of British diplomacy. At first this was, indeed, a great asset. Besides the unique advantage of her traditional negotiating skills, Britain also enjoyed intimate links with the United States and with the new Commonwealth countries, many of which continued to depend upon London for information and for diplomatic and/or military assistance. Despite the continuing success of NATO, the British links with the United States gradually became less uniquely intimate as other American allies grew in importance; the new Commonwealth countries fully emancipated themselves; Britain found herself ill at ease with the multilateral diplomacy which developed in the United Nations, and was excluded from the EEC. Diplomacy became increasingly more difficult in a situation in which Britain was rapidly losing influence within all the three circles and yet maintaining the ambition to play an individual role in East–West relations.

Last but not least, the historical basis for Britain's claims to be recognized as a world power must once more be stressed, especially her contributions to maintaining international order during the heyday of the Empire, her major role in the two world wars, and her place as a leading commercial power and as a banker for the sterling area. All these factors were particularly significant in the immediate postwar period and their relevance decreased only gradually.

### The Changing Conceptions of Britain's World Role

The evolution of the prevalent conceptions of Britain's world role from the end of the war to her entry into the EEC can be briefly described in terms of a process of transition from an aspiration to maintain her position of a third, though smaller, superpower to one of being a powerful state of second rank, which was accompanied by a shift of emphasis in British foreign policy from the global to the regional context. The evolution has been steady but the Suez action in 1956 and events in 1967 can serve as convenient landmarks to divide it into three periods. Within each period the prevalent official conceptions of Britain's world role are briefly analysed with special regard to their relation to her capabilities and to the views of other states.

Already during the war Churchill had some misgivings about the chances of Britain's continuing as one of the Big Three powers, and the Foreign Office seriously considered whether it would be possible or, indeed, desirable (see pp. 175ff.). Nevertheless, the official policy throughout the war was to continue Britain's efforts to remain in the front rank, otherwise, it was thought, she would risk becoming a helpless second-rank power. Although the United States and the Soviet Union carried more weight, Churchill managed to preserve a significant role for Britain and to exercise considerable influence upon the joint decisions. He employed a mixture of three strategies—influence upon Roosevelt, with whom he maintained intimate relations, a mediating role between the Americans and the Russians, and direct negotiations with the Russians. Even during the war, especially towards its end, the mixture of these strategies did not prove fully successful. The Churchillian combination was clearly untenable after the war and each of his three strategies had its advocates in Britain. The Labour Left favoured accommodation with Russia, and, when this proved impossible, supported the role of an 'honest broker' between the Americans and the Russians. The government soon adopted the strategy of close co-operation with the Americans in relations with Russia, while preserving the maximum possible individual role for Britain within the Commonwealth and the Middle East, maintaining order there by her own efforts; in Western Europe Britain acted as the main organizer from the outside and as the link between the region and the United States. This foreign policy as well as the underlying concept of the 'three circles' was also supported by the Conservatives and was continued by them when they came into power in 1951. It was based upon the combined notions of the defence of vital British interests and of a deeply felt British responsibility for the world system, notably demonstrated in the massive rearmament programme in 1951 and by the near-permanent commitment of British troops to the Western European Union in 1954, both moves being strongly opposed to the traditions of keeping armaments down in peacetime and avoiding permanent entanglements on the continent.

Britain's capabilities were stretched but her economic recovery was remarkably fast; with the support of the Commonwealth and the aid of the atomic weapons which she was rapidly developing, she could expect to keep her place in the world. Others were not so optimistic and preferred Britain to limit her role. The growing discrepancy between the American and the British views was forcibly expressed by Sir Oliver

Franks in his Reith lectures of 1954, in which he decried the American sceptics and critics:

There are some who suggest that the future of Britain lies in making a break with the past and giving up the traditions of greatness. The thing to do is to withdraw from world affairs and lead a quiet life in our island, democratic, contented and reasonably industrious. This is impossible. Geography and history forbid us. For us there is no middle way. Nor do most of us think there is, except in the world of make-believe. We expect to have a say about our destiny and we are not prepared to leave it to be decided by others. We assume we have influence and power among nations.[5]

The doubts about Britain's world-role conceptions were augmented after 1950 when the Western European states began their move towards integration in which Britain refused to participate, despite European and American urgings. Britain's main diplomatic interest remained in the central power balance. Although Eden played an important part in helping to settle the issues of the German military contribution to NATO and of the French withdrawal in Indochina, he tried, mainly, to achieve a detente with the Soviet Union, the conditions for which seemed much more promising after Stalin's death. Dulles was very sceptical about Eden's policies, and, together with Adenauer, strongly opposed the Eden Plan for reducing tension in central Europe. He also disliked the British initiatives for a summit meeting and regarding Indochina.

The Suez affair destroyed Britain's independent world role in the Middle East. It completely undermined her power position by demonstrating her lack of capacity to act independently and her lack of resolve and it also undermined the credibility of the two main pillars of her world role—the support of the United States and of the Commonwealth. The national disaster had, however, the effect of reinforcing rather than weakening Britain's determination to continue with her world role. The dominant note, especially among the Conservative leadership, was to salve the national pride wounded by this humiliating defeat. In his first broadcast, on 17 January 1957, the new Prime Minister, Harold Macmillan, said:

Every now and again since the war I have heard people say: 'Isn't Britain only a second- or a third-class power now? Isn't she on the way out?' What nonsense. This is a great country, and do not let us be ashamed to say so. . . . Twice in our life-time I have heard the same old tale about our being a second-rate power, and I have lived to see the answer.[6]

Both parties agreed that it was Britain's role to maintain peace, law, and stability in the world, with special responsibility east of Suez.

For Macmillan, the mainstay of the post-Suez world role was renewed co-operation with the United States, choosing to regard the Suez episode as a temporary aberration. He apparently retained the belief that he had expressed before Suez, when he was Foreign Secretary in Eden's government, that, thanks to her diplomatic skills and political stability, Britain could 'establish for herself in the nuclear age a position of authority as the chief source of moral inspiration for the whole world'.[7] Helped by his Anglo-American family background and his close relations with Eisenhower and Dulles, he expected successes comparable to those he had achieved during the war, as the British Minister Resident to Allied Forces Headquarters, first at Algiers and then in Italy. Although he was then operating without any resources to back him up or even a legal standing, he had managed to wield strong influence over the American theatre commanders. It was there that he had formulated his philosophy of the British–American relationship about which he talked to Richard Crossman during his visit to Algiers:

We, my dear Crossman, are Greeks in this American Empire. You will find the Americans much as the Greeks found the Romans—great big, vulgar, bustling people, more vigorous than we are and also more idle, with more unspoilt virtues but also more corrupt. We must run the AFHQ as the Greek slaves ran the operations of the Emperor Claudius.[8]

The successfully restored American co-operation extended into the nuclear field and helped Britain to consolidate her own success in developing the thermonuclear bomb—from 1955 the nuclear deterrent could be elevated into the central element of British defence policy. American support—which meant, at the same time, a degree of dependence—and nuclear strategy then became the mainstays of Britain's world role and helped to disguise weaknesses in other respects; after the recovery from the post-Suez crisis, Britain's economy failed to register a sustained growth and the support of the Commonwealth became even more dubious after the spate of grants of independence in the late 1950s and early 1960s and the withdrawal of South Africa. Moreover, much to Macmillan's alarm, the Six managed to establish the EEC while the sputnik and the evolution of nuclear technology increased the gap between Britain and the superpowers.

Macmillan, for one, was now fully aware of Britain's rapidly deteriorating position. While he was conducting summit diplomacy in a flurry of publicity, he was realistically endeavouring to join the EEC and was emancipating Africa. In his memoirs he clearly expresses his view that, already at the beginning of the 1960s, like any other middle power, Britain could no longer decisively influence world affairs although through skilful diplomacy, as in the case of the Congo, she could sometimes avoid the worst possible outcome. He explains his arduous diplomatic efforts to secure the abortive summit conference of May 1960 in the following way: first to avoid the risk of a serious catastrophe; second, to avoid a serious diplomatic defeat for the West; and third, to satisfy public opinion. One may question whether the order of priorities in Macmillan's mind was not the reverse, public opinion coming first, and whether 'Britain and he personally' should not be read for 'the West'. It is true, however, as Macmillan divulged only in the last volume of his memoirs, that he was continuously consulted by Kennedy throughout the Cuban missiles crisis.[9]

Macmillan's efforts to act as a middleman between the Americans and the Russians were successful as regards the Partial Nuclear Test Ban Treaty which, as Kennedy later acknowledged, was made possible by Macmillan's steadfastness of purpose and determined perseverance. Britain's role east of Suez was also a reality, as was demonstrated for instance in the successful 1964 intervention in East Africa to quell military rebellions at the request of local governments. In his article in the *Spectator* of 23 April 1965, Ian Macleod still clearly reflected the traditional view of Britain's world role:

Alone among America's allies Britain is a member of all the three collective security alliances: NATO, SEATO and CENTO. Beyond these, we fulfil widespread defence obligations inside and outside the Commonwealth. By ourselves in Malaya, and with America's preponderant forces in Korea, we have fought Communist aggression and beaten it back. When India was attacked by Communist China, Britain reacted at once with military aid. Malaysia, the New Commonwealth bastion against Communism in South East Asia, has for months been the scene of British defence operations on a substantial scale. Meanwhile, in the entire sea area east of Suez across the Indian Ocean, the Royal Navy plays the leading role in safeguarding the free world's commerce and security.[10]

The Labour government which came into power in October 1964 was determined to carry on with Britain's world role despite the precarious economic situation. In his Guildhall speech the following month, Harold Wilson proudly expressed the sentiment that Britain was a world influence and a world power or she was nothing. It was not a mere rhetorical flourish; he determinedly continued Macmillan's foreign policies and ultimately abandoned them owing only to a combination of increasingly less propitious international circumstances and the government's inability to right the economy which culminated in the devaluation of sterling in 1967.

Wilson's major efforts—and greatest failure—lay in the economic performance at home, due largely to his determination to maintain the parity of sterling. In foreign policy he resolutely pursued Macmillan's two strategies of acting as an *interlocuteur valable* between the Americans and the Russians and as a policeman east of Suez. He recalls the former in proud detail in his memoirs without giving much attention to the major reason why his efforts failed, which was realistically summed up by Lord George-Brown; the mediation attempts 'petered out, partly perhaps, because we were too anxious to be intermediaries and didn't check with the Americans beforehand'. Wilson's last and most sustained effort, involving repeated communications with Washington, was made during Kosygin's visit to London in February 1967. It proved disastrous to Wilson's—and Britain's—standing, especially in the eyes of the Russians and, to say the least, was unhelpful for Soviet–American relations. When Wilson returned to the Vietnam issue during his visit to Moscow in January 1968 he was in no position to make any initiatives and his intervention amounted to no more than an expression of concern and an exchange of views.[11]

The east of Suez strand of Britain's independent world role also came to an end in 1967. Already the Commonwealth had been offering increasingly less scope. In the Indo-Pakistani conflict Wilson successfully mediated in the Rann of Kutch dispute in June 1965 but was unable to do so in the more serious fighting in Kashmir which broke out in September and which was finally settled through the good offices of the Russians. He was unable to alleviate the civil war in Nigeria or to solve the problem of the British subjects of Indian and Pakistani origin who were being expelled from East Africa. By 1966 the government decided to leave Aden and to cancel the order for a new aircraft-carrier. The 1966 *Defence Review* announced in unmistakable terms the end of an individual east of Suez role:

First, Britain will not undertake major operations of war except in co-operation with allies. Secondly, we will not accept an obligation to provide another country with military assistance unless it is prepared to provide us with the facilities we need to make such assistance effective in time. Finally, there will be no attempt to maintain defence facilities in an independent country against its wishes.[12]

The ground was prepared to withdraw British troops from east of Suez once the confrontation with Indonesia had ended. The economic crisis in 1967 was only the occasion, not the cause, of the decision to withdraw which was announced in July—the immediate foreign-exchange savings were minute.

Wilson's turn to Europe which preceded this decision did not amount to a deliberate rational restriction of Britain's world role to a regional contest. It was rather a resigned acceptance of Britain's growing inability to act in the traditional manner owing to the continuing decline of her economy. In a speech at Swansea on 25 January 1964, Wilson had thus commented upon the last stages of the Macmillan Government: 'never had our influence been weaker than when a conservative government, bankrupt of ideas about regenerating our economy, looked to the Common Market to solve all our economic problems'. Wilson's political opponents could have applied these words with even greater justification to the situation at the end of 1966.

The negative reasons for Britain's renewing her attempt to enter the EEC were clear enough: the lagging of her economic performance far behind that of the EEC, her waning influence, and the rapid reduction of the two main traditional strands of her world role with the withdrawal from east of Suez and the development of bilateral relations between the Americans and Russians. Her main diplomatic task was no longer to act as an intermediary between the two superpowers to prevent a dangerous confrontation but, rather, to avert a precipitate American withdrawal from Europe or a collusion between the two superpowers at the cost of Britain and of Western Europe. Some steps towards establishing the new Western European front were taken in 1969 on the initiative of Denis Healey, by attempting to revive the Western European Union and by establishing the informal Eurogroup within NATO, but the proposed entry to the EEC became confusingly mixed up with lingering notions of Britain's world role and with parochial 'Little England' sentiments. The anti-Europeans could combine in their arguments these parochial sentiments with the traditional British devotion to the oceanic outlook and the world role, in combinations best suited to their individual outlooks. Already in 1954, Eden, an ardent anti-European, combined these parochial and oceanic sentiments when contemplating 'the formidable step' of indefinitely committing British troops to Europe. 'We are still island people,' he said, 'in thought and tradition, whatever the modern facts of weapons and strategy may compel.' By the end of the 1960s, the parochial sentiments were becoming stronger. George Brown, although a committed pro-European, records in his memoirs his disquiet at the speed with which Britain was withdrawing from east of Suez and his disagreement with those favouring this withdrawal, whom he suspected either of wishing to retreat into a narrowly conceived 'Fortress Europe' or of reverting to some 'Little England' idea.[13] His conception of a new, European role for Britain represents the expectations of many pro-Europeans and therefore warrants quoting:

It is our business to provide political leadership, to provide the stability that for so long has eluded the democracies of the mainland of Europe. I have as much arrogant patriotism in me as anybody else and I don't want to see Britain becoming just one of the small European States. That is why I feel we must support the idea of a united Europe, play our full part in bringing it about, and offer leadership wherever we can.... So I am convinced that Britain's role is in Europe, that it is a powerful role . . . and one which will pay us great dividends in every way.[14]

Although still appealing to some anti-Europeans, by the early 1970s Britain's individual world role had effectively ended; it would have died a natural death even without her entry into the EEC, as she became less able to contribute substantially to the security and prosperity of the members of the Commonwealth and counted for less in the East–West relationship and as an ally and trading partner of the United States, for whom the Germans and the Japanese had become increasingly important. Even the widespread notion that Britain was more 'outward-looking' than the Community was no longer fully valid—it still applied to her defence, which, however, was rapidly contracting towards Europe; her importance as an exporter and importer and aid-donor to developing states was now less than that of the combined EEC.

Nevertheless, her national interests still extend more widely into the outside world than those of her new continental partners; specifically, she remains vitally interested in preserving as much of her overseas trade, especially cheap food supplies and markets, as may prove possible now that she is a member of the EEC; whereas German interests tend to focus on Eastern Europe and French interests on international finance, Britain's world involvement both with the United States and with the developing world is likely to remain greater. It is, of course, true that Britain could have pursued her existing outside ties and interests without becoming a member of the EEC, but it is clear that she would have found it increasingly difficult to play a significant role in world affairs and hence to protect her interests. Despite the limitations which it imposes on her freedom of manoeuvre, membership of the EEC should free Britain from two fundamental constraints upon her preceding efforts to play a significant world role: her insufficient capabilities and her inability to persuade other major states to agree to her own role definitions. Britain possesses adequate capabilities to play a full part within the EEC and her own conception of her world role to be played through it has, at last, coincided with the role prescriptions which both her EEC partners and the United States have been advancing for many years. What still remains to be seen is how far the British will generate the necessary dynamism to impel the enlarged Community to play a meaningful world role; this will be obstructed by the traditional inability of the EEC to reach internal agreements, which is likely to increase in the transitional period.

### National Aspirations and National Interests[15]

Edward Heath entered office in 1970 with the well articulated objective of reforming national life both at home and in its foreign relations. He repeatedly referred to the need to apply the yardstick of the 'national interest' both to Britain's domestic arrangements and to her foreign policy, and to his determination to do so. His article on 'Realism in British Foreign Policy' published shortly before his electoral victory[16] started with two quotations from Palmerston, one of which runs: 'we have no eternal allies and no eternal enemies. Our interests are eternal and perpetual and those interests it is our duty to follow'. At the Lord Mayor's Banquet soon after his election he stated: 'The time has come to establish clearly and unmistakably that British foreign policies are determined by British interests.' His underlying assumption was that the clarification of her actual interests would save Britain from the confusion of the traditional vague ideas and empty formulae, that realism should become the key-note of policy. Within two years references to 'national interest' became less frequent and, although a new style had been introduced both in her domestic and her foreign policies centring on economic growth and a European orientation, Britain was facing continuing formidable economic and social problems, and suffering from insufficient capabilities and a weakened political will.

The concept of 'national interest' or 'interests', which is so frequently invoked in political argument, sounds persuasively simple and appealing when compared with that of 'role', which stems from political analysis and has no popular appeal. It certainly shifts the emphasis of foreign policy from Britain's environment to herself, it emphasizes that the objectives of foreign policy refer primarily to the nation's own needs and wants, it helps to complete the transformation of Britain's place in the world. There is, of course, nothing fundamentally new in the recent emphasis upon Britain's national interests—she, like all other nations, has always pursued them in the past. The notion of 'national interest' is, nevertheless, a convenient focus for reflecting upon major obstacles in Britain's postwar adjustment, especially the confusion between her two basic aspirations: to ensure an international order, and to secure the most advantageous place for herself within this order. The historical role of Britain was that of a leading power and hence her natural tendency was to preserve the old order within which her status had been assured. Her place within the postwar order had now changed. Her identification with the international order could not remain as full as in the past; the Commonwealth, in particular, was no substitute for the Empire.

The concern with Britain's 'national interest' which recurs in Heath's pronouncements can be regarded as a sensible expression of the change of emphasis in British foreign policy. But 'national interest' is by no means a clear concept; on closer examination it proves to be extremely complex and confused. In broad terms, we all understand what it means; few would argue with the terse definition advanced by the Brookings Institution as 'the general and continuing ends for which a nation acts'.[17] Even fewer, however, would agree on a more precise, operational definition of these ends: can we speak of one, general 'interest' or are we in fact faced with a congeries of individual 'interests'? If there is one national interest, is it objectively identifiable so that policy objectives can be logically deduced from it, or is it a mere subjective statement of preferences and guesses? If it is accorded objective existence, an interest easily becomes an abstraction which is not very different from any conception of 'role'; if denied it, it is no more than an expression of personal preference; one national interest is too vague, a multitude of national interests is uncoordinated. In fact, the main dichotomy in British foreign policy is not between pursuing a world role and national interest, both of which postulate a degree of purpose. More fundamental is the dichotomy between both of these and a purely pragmatic, case-to-case behaviour, dispensing with any broader frame of reference.

The difficulty of clarifying the meaning of 'national interest' is shown by the occasional distinction made between our 'aspirations', or what we want, and our 'interests', or what we need. According to one recent analysis,[18] aspirations are, by their very nature, vague, and based upon broad ethical or sentimental arguments, such as 'justice, honour, obligation, gratitude, the principles of democracy, the interests of humanity, the natural instincts of repugnance or esteem', and often lack relevance for actual foreign policy. Interests are concerned with 'the likelihood of early and material advantage to the British people'. Discussion of the national interest does not, however, lead to a clearer definition than: 'the international interest is to maintain, to the extent compatible with the preservation of the existing social order, the independence and the authority of the nation-state'.

Operationally, this is not more relevant as a guide to policy discussions than aspirations are; the distinction appears, therefore, to be inconclusive. The inevitable confusion about ends-means relationships obstructs a neat ordering of values. Attlee's declaration of support for international organization as the basis for British foreign policy can thus be dismissed as irrelevant aspiration, but it can also be interpreted as the most promising means of preserving Britain's independence and authority, although, of course, in this case Attlee's expectations were frustrated.[19] To say that British entry into the EEC is in Britain's interests but contrary to her aspirations is not the most illuminating way of explaining why three successive governments have been trying to achieve it, although at least one of them did not really want it. The issue is much more meaningfully analysed in terms of the EEC being a promising, perhaps the only promising, instrument for maintaining Britain's independence and authority, although one the British do not particularly fancy. The greatest shortcoming of the sharp distinction between aspirations and interests is that, in political argument, the term 'national interest' confusingly refers to both of them.

Common usage is not fundamentally wrong in its logic since, in a way, if we need something we naturally tend to aspire to it, and, *vice versa*, if we aspire to a thing it really becomes a need. What we require is an analytical distinction which would help us to understand the links between our needs and wants which are clearly crucial to political action. This perhaps is better sought not in a dichotomy but rather in a spectrum, at the one end of which we place ostensibly unattainable aspirations and at the other mundane low-level interests; we can divide this spectrum somewhere in the middle and speak about two levels of national interest, the aspirational and the operational; we must, however, bear in mind that issues constantly shift within the spectrum. Even what to some appears as an 'irrelevant aspiration'—Attlee's idea of using the United Nations as a mainstay of British foreign policy—could become an operational interest if, which is admittedly unlikely, organizational changes took place; *vice versa*, the traditional interest in securing the fullest possible United States strategic and economic co-operation could become a fairly 'irrelevant aspiration' if the enlarged Community and the United States happened to be permanently at loggerheads.

In fact, this synoptic way of looking at foreign policy enables us to assess more soberly the changes contemplated by the Heath Government. New governments tend to claim to be more realistic than their predecessors and to introduce fundamental changes which, in perspective, often appear to have been rather insignificant. Even if one accepts the argument that the excessively slow revision of the scope of Britain's world role in the 1960s was detrimental to her specific national interests, especially to an orderly economic growth, Heath's intention to shift the emphasis to the 'national interest' does not *ipso facto* mean that British foreign policy will become thoroughly revised. The tradition of continuity, the inevitable bureaucratic inertia are likely to preserve it in much the same way as in the past, although with a changed focus. The priority accorded to the EEC, first to the entry and then to the country's adjustment to membership and to endeavours to develop the institution on the desired lines are, however, likely to lend a general coherence and consistency to British foreign policy. Quite independently of how beneficial or otherwise this membership may prove in other respects, this general sense of direction is likely to prove very useful.

The advantage of distinguishing between the aspirational and operational aspects of foreign policy may be considerable in clarifying what precisely Britain will try to achieve within the new context, and in drawing a clear-cut distinction between British national and Western European aspirations, thus avoiding some repetition of the dangerous blurring between individual national and broad systemic goals which has taken place in the past. As an increasing range of areas require internationalization, it seems essential to explore as fully as possible the nature of the national interests involved in order to find a guideline to what can be retained within full national control, what requires only a degree of international regulation and what can be best met by a full merger with others. Entry into the EEC was only the first step towards internationalization within the Western European context, and far-reaching decisions will have to be made within it during the next few years on a number of issues vitally affecting Britain's national life. The avowed aim of the Government is to help to establish a strong Community which will wield influence in world affairs, on the assumption that this will serve British interests. As the Opposition constantly stresses, the price of entry has been fixed very high, but one could accept the government's contention that it was the lowest negotiable one. How far will 'national interest' provide a guide to determine policies in the future, when Britain's own, immediate interests clash with those of fostering the strengthening of the Community? It is clear how the government would act in a real emergency, as when it decided to float the pound in June 1972 in spite of the recently accepted Community agreement on a narrow margin of exchange rates—the Wilson Government behaved in a similar way when it imposed a surcharge on imports in 1964.

Stress upon Britain's national interests does not, however, clearly determine how the government would proceed in a situation which does not constitute a real emergency. It seems clear that it intends to protect Britain's specific interests—for instance, it insisted that her ailing paper industry should enjoy a higher though not very adequate temporary tariff protection against the imports of paper from her EFTA partners who were not joining the EEC. There is little guidance, however, in the notion of 'national interest' on how to proceed where long-term interests have to be reconciled. As Britain has joined the Community after the initial adjustments between its original members have been completed, her position is bound to be eccentric and therefore initially somewhat uncomfortable. The main difficulty will inevitably arise over the Common Agricultural Policy (CAP) and the high food prices involved in it, which is likely to give rise not only to a Labour attempt to 'renegotiate' the accession agreement but also to a determined Conservative effort to reform or abolish the policy.

Another important issue has already arisen in the field of advanced technologies. By what criteria is the position of Britain's air-space industry to be determined? As the industrialists have been justifiably remonstrating, an aspiration to participate in a joint Western European programme is not, by itself, a sufficient operational programme to secure the maximum possible national advantage for Britain. The general pattern likely to be acceptable to the prospective Continental partners would be one of rough equality with the French and German industries, with smaller Italian and Dutch components. This would involve a much faster growth for the Continental industries and possibly a run-down for the British air-frame industry to compensate for British air-engine predominance; in addition, French ambitions may be larger and may not be fully satisfied with one-third. In other words, we are in a typical complex bargaining situation in which the British negotiating position will be largely determined by the force of the pressures and arguments brought to bear by the three components of the domestic air-space-industry—air-frames, engines, and electronics—and by the governmental estimates of what is most desirable and at the same time most feasible.

Using the yardstick of 'national interest' cannot add much to the usual ways of determining priorities although it may help to clarify them to a limited extent. It may assist in assessing and comparing more systematically the bargaining positions of the major partners and, even more importantly, it may help to prevent a solution through uncoordinated moves which are likely to lead to an outcome unsatisfactory to British interests. Although all the Western European partners accept the same need for co-operation, their individual national interests are still in strong competition. Piecemeal arrangements around individual projects and between individual firms are unlikely to result in a distribution of the industry between the individual countries in a way which would prove

satisfactory to Britain. An agreement on principles between the participant governments seems an essential prerequisite but this cannot be
achieved without a clear articulation and reconciliation of the national
aspirations of all the partners as a basis for a working agreement. The
longer this is postponed, the more Britain is bound to lose, as her air-space
industry is larger than that of her prospective partners and she cannot
retain the technological lead in the fields in which she still possesses it.

All in all, Britain's participation in the EEC will require a careful
assessment not only of the many particular interests which will have to
be adjusted but also of her general aspirations. The Heath Government
is on record as aspiring to the evolution of a closely-knit community
with a common currency and a common economic policy which would
exercise real influence upon the international system. Even many staunch
anti-Europeans would readily agree that this aspiration may warrant a
compromise on Britain's particular interests, provided her vital interests
are not affected; even the staunchest pro-Europeans would set some limit
to the concessions Britain should make in the process.

In retrospect, one of the fundamental difficulties of British foreign
policy while it centred upon the performance of a world role appears to
have lain in a dispersion of interests, in the lack of a Clausewitzian 'centre
of gravity', which is the prerequisite of a rational strategy. In several
respects this policy has become more concentrated and hence, at least
potentially, more manageable. The 'three circles' and the diffuse global
policy have been replaced by a regional, Western European orientation;
economic growth and social welfare rather than self-preservation have
become the major national aspirations which, for British diplomacy,
has meant a shift away from high politics, from situational interests to
commercial ones, as finally voiced in the Duncan Report. The swing of
the pendulum has probably not been completed. It seems unlikely that
in the near future Britain will continue to pursue vague, global aspirations
to the neglect of her immediate interests, as in the past; she will rather
pursue narrowly conceived immediate interests to the neglect of global
policies.

# Part Two
# Major Policy Areas
# 8 The Setting in 1945

*Wartime Origins of Britain's Alignments*

IN different periods and to different people, the priorities attached to relations, friendly or hostile, with other states or groups of states seem 'natural' and warranted by historical traditions. In the 1950s the oceanic outlook was dominant, and close relations with the United States and the Commonwealth seemed 'natural' to the predominant majority of the British; the only exceptions were a few rather uninfluential members of the political elite. But by 1964 Kenneth Younger could convincingly state the thesis for Britain's turning to the continent in *The Changing Perspectives of British Foreign Policy*.[1] Interpretations of her historical record and even of her more remote tribal memories changed similarly, although more slowly. In 1972 Roy Jenkins could maintain that:

Britain always has been primarily a European rather than an imperial power . . . we have never been away from Europe. Even at the height of our world dominion a great part of our endeavours and interests and conflicts were bound up with Europe and not with our transoceanic empire. Our culture was strongly European, and so to a large extent were the everyday details of life. Most of our diplomatic effort was devoted to trying to maintain our interests amongst European dangers, and when these peaceful efforts failed it was European wars which engaged our full national effort, inflicted major national damage, and burnt themselves into our popular consciousness. . . .

At times we thought we could detach ourselves, but it never worked. The phrase 'splendid isolation' was first used in 1896. Within eighteen years we were more deeply and disagreeably involved in Europe than at any time before or since.[2]

One can only wonder whether such an interpretation, which today must appear as special pleading to the many British sceptics on the subject of Europe, will not be accepted as orthodox a decade or so after Britain's joining the Community. If one compares this interpretation with the many statements about the primacy of the oceanic outlook and of the affinity with other 'English-speaking' people in the immediate past, it becomes obvious that remote historical perspectives do not determine the country's foreign policy any more than does its geographical location.

Clearly there is no convincing way of establishing the strands of historical continuity in a manner which could not be contradicted by the next generation. Policies are, of course, continuous, and Britain in 1945 was not starting with a *tabula rasa* in a new, postwar world; the main continuities are, however, more profitably sought in the immediately preceding period, in wartime diplomacy. A convenient starting-point is 1942, when Britain first became engaged in planning for the postwar period. Among the memoirs and studies which supplement Sir Llewellyn Woodward's official history,[3] we are fortunate in having available an account by Lord Gladwyn, based upon his role in the Economic and Reconstruction Department of the Foreign Office from the time of its establishment in that year. Lord Gladwyn's memoirs[4] are exceptionally revealing in that they refer in much greater detail than has hitherto been customary to the debates within the Office and the memoranda circulated there; and also because at that time the Office was forced into consistent thinking about postwar arrangements by the fact that the Americans were already engaged in it, and by the long-range implications of American relief activities and political proposals.

Despite the leading place of Britain in the early stages of the war effort, a long and frank discussion developed in the Foreign Office as to whether she could and should also fulfil her 'world-wide mission' after the war; some younger officials in particular thought that this would be undesirable and beyond her power and that she should therefore 'hand over the torch' to the Americans and the Russians. On the whole, however, the alternative status of a second-class power was unacceptable, as, in the long run, it was deemed to carry with it the grim prospects of coming under Soviet, American or German domination.[5] It was obvious that Britain could not play a decisive part in determining the postwar settlement, whatever its details might become but that she could best secure her interests by playing an initiating and mediating one. This was the rational basis for a continuing world role.

The disposal of Germany was clearly the central issue which could bring the Allies together or drive them apart. Ominously, the Foreign Office itself was deeply divided on the issue. Germany was, however, to be the object of disposal and not a partner; the independent variable was the behaviour of the United States. The starting-point of the planning was a memorandum by Gladwyn Jebb, distributed early in August 1942, in which he discussed 'Relief Machinery, the Political Background', looking for a suitable British response to American policy, which at that time was clearly aiming at a kind of *Pax Americana*. Should Britain accept subordination or try to whittle it down with the aid of her Western

European allies and with the Russians—to ensure more autonomy for Western Europe under British leadership and for Eastern Europe under Soviet; should the maintenance of the Empire and Commonwealth be her primary objective; and would it be desirable to ensure the survival of Germany and the rehabilitation of France as great powers. He focused the discussion on an American proposal for a small, probably four-power, 'Policy Committee' to direct the United Nations; this became the basis of the Foreign Office document 'The Four-Power Plan', which can justly be regarded as the foundation of postwar policies.

The 'Four-Power Plan', the product of long discussion, incorporating many divergent ideas, was extremely flexible. It started with an assumption that the Big Three would all take account of their world-wide responsibilities and would be both able and willing to enter into appropriate world-wide commitments to prevent any nation from troubling the peace again. Many doubted whether the assumption applied to Russia, and suspected Soviet intentions in the Near East, in Eastern Europe, and regarding Germany. In a forceful later comment Professor Lionel (later Lord) Robbins convincingly argued that, as any economic arrangement with a totalitarian state was unlikely to prove possible, co-operation would be limited to security and would result in a very precarious balance. The second assumption was that the real objective of the Four-Power concert would be to keep Germany and Japan down; failing that, the whole conception would lapse. A number of doubts were stated and the problems of applying the policy were analysed, but the policy conclusion was to pursue the Four-Power idea if it could be put into operation, though not until and unless the Americans had been committed. The United States was recognized as the fulcrum of a viable global policy. The grand strategy suggested, should difficulties arise, was to hint to the Americans that too stiff terms might push the British into a close working alliance with the Russians, and to the Russians that they might provoke close Anglo-American co-operation and thus become isolated.[6]

Britain's major partners were forced upon her by circumstances; and she was only free to choose the most promising and flexible strategy to cope with them. At first American designs seemed most alarming but, by the end of 1945, when it was generally accepted that the United States would not retain her forces in Europe for more than a year or so after the Armistice, the major concern turned to securing American participation in Europe's defences. In 1942 and 1943 the Russians could be theoretically considered as possible partners in moderating American designs, but, although even at the end of 1945 their policies could be interpreted as 'defensive-offensive' (see p. 194), fruitful co-operation with them could scarcely be counted upon. The French under de Gaulle were determined to press on with their demands in Western Germany in conformity with their age-old objective of a Rhine frontier, which could not be considered by the British owing to the formidable American opposition.[7] Thus, ultimately, the major assumption of 'The Four-Power Plan' as to the willingness of the four powers to cooperate proved to be unwarranted. Britain was thrown upon an alternative policy—that of securing American support and, eventually, of restoring Germany and collaborating with her—an alternative envisaged in the Plan but not the most promising one for safeguarding British interests.

The mere fact of the institutional separation of imperial and Commonwealth matters, which were the domain of the Colonial Office, prevented the Foreign Office from considering in any depth the value to be attached and the primacy to be accorded to imperial links. Britain's wartime European allies represented in London could be confidently counted upon for support but little weight could, at that stage, be accorded to it. Thus, in terms of a power-political image of the world, Britain's primary relations lay with the United States and Russia, the nascent superpowers; France was a weak and also an unwilling partner at the time. The most promising strategy was to draw a clear boundary between Eastern Europe, where Russia would, inevitably, have the dominant influence, and Western Europe, led by Britain, and, with the assistance of the Americans, to maintain a balance between the two.

Much to their exasperation, the officials were also subjected to broader, more visionary ideas. On the one hand, there was Churchill with his grand ideas of strengthening British links with the other 'English-speaking people', as well as of establishing a Council for Europe, somewhat on the lines of the proposals advocated by Coudenhove-Kalergi in the 1920s; embarrassingly, during a visit to Turkey in February 1943, he made the Turks privy to the latter idea. Gladwyn Jebb was sufficiently roused to compose, as a joke, a document on Churchillian lines, but admits that his exasperated version of a Churchillian future came closer to the reality of 1948 than the 'realistic' Anglo-American official plans of 1942. Churchill's sweeping ideas were power-political, too, and merely happened to assess future power-political developments more adequately. On the other hand the Foreign Office was also confronted with the radical idea of a world government presented by Arnold Toynbee, Director of its Research Department, whose ideas were, in principle, supported by Attlee. Jebb[8] thought that these ideas had no chance for two reasons. First, an academic historian could scarcely be effective in a world of 'struggling politicians, overworked bureaucrats, and fierce military men whose idea was "to get on with the war".' Second, the idea was attractive but 'did not in itself qualify a man to draw up plans for what should immediately be done in the chaotic situation that would follow the end of hostilities'.

Nevertheless, towards the end of 1945, both the government and the opposition became favourable to the idea of strengthening the United Nations, which, at that time, had not yet started its operations. Jebb, its Provisional Secretary-General, wrote privately to Sir Alexander Cadogan, the then Permanent Under Secretary, and summed up the proposed reforms as follows: to use the Organization for the settlement of important and urgent political issues, to abolish the veto and to take, at an early stage, some preliminary steps towards the constitution of a world state. Apparently this was a serious political initiative which had support within the Foreign Office. Jebb attributed its impetus to the theoretical cast of mind of the new Legal Adviser, Eric Beckett. His own view was that the proposals were cogent in logic and equity, but that the necessary amendment of the Charter was impossible, and that it was preferable to save an imperfect organization rather than to cripple it from the start by reform attempts doomed to failure. When one bears in mind the enormous difficulties of reaching the compromises of the Charter at the San Francisco Conference, it seems reasonably probable that a greater degree of agreement could not possibly have been found after the postwar disagreements had further crystallized and the atomic bombs had been exploded. Even the most idealistic supporters of the idea of world government could not reasonably claim that it was the British bureaucrats who obstructed a real possibility of an initiative to reform the international system.

The episode is interesting as an illustration of the flexible frame of mind of Britain's policy-makers which enabled them seriously to consider quite a radical alternative to traditional diplomacy. Although the traditional power-political ways of thinking about foreign policy undoubtedly obstructed the adoption of this alternative, even an idealist could not but see the basic difficulty that a British initiative would not have been decisive, especially in view of the uncooperative Russian policies, and that a move in this direction would probably have been interpreted as a manifestation of Britain's loss of power and of her desire to opt out.

The central and influential role Britain occupied in the conduct of the war meant that the Americans and the Russians would be her main diplomatic partners, but the postwar American alignment was by no means clearly foreseeable; the American plans were suspect and, even towards the end of the war, the difficulties arising in relations with the Russians did not really involve Britain's vital interests. It took some time for the diplomatic fronts of the cold war to harden, but the stage in 1945 was firmly set for Britain's main diplomatic and defence efforts to be directed to the problems of Germany and of Western security, and hence to the central power balance; the inevitable consequence of this concentration was that relations with other, smaller, and less powerful states were subordinated to the mainstream of British policy. This concentration of diplomatic interest and effort upon the central power balance persisted long after many British interests could have been more effectively pursued at lower political levels. Later on it seems to have become a major contributory factor in the neglect of the European integration movement at its early stages.

*The Domestic and Economic Issues in 1945*
During the war, domestic politics were subordinated to the necessities of the war effort and domestic needs and demands were satisfied only at basic levels. The ending of the war did not spell the end of this situation: the British people were used to wartime restrictions and could be expected to continue accepting them without a major rebellion, as indeed they did. The relief of having got rid of the war amounted to a relative contentment despite the continuing rationing of goods and the general drabness of daily life. Bevin commented on the people's 'poverty of desire'. Moreover, the government's political position was extremely strong—it obtained an overwhelming majority in the House of Commons following the unexpected electoral victory based upon 47·8 per cent of the total vote against a mere 39·8 per cent for the Conservatives. It had a clear mandate for the social change to which it was committed by its electoral manifesto, and, even to the staunchest Conservatives, some change in the economic and social structures seemed imperative after the prolonged and sustained war-effort. Thus, despite the overwhelming nature of its many problems and its paucity of resources, the postwar Labour government was in a strong position to control and marshal domestic forces, and was under only slight domestic restraints in initiating and conducting its policies at home and abroad. The British economy could be rehabilitated only through a gigantic surge in exports and the government had no option but to leave consumption needs at extremely low levels of satisfaction and to reduce as rapidly as possible Britain's external commitments. One can scarcely discern here any clash of priorities as both consumption and defence were deliberately reduced to minimal levels.

The essential congruence between the government's domestic and foreign policies is somewhat more difficult to grasp; for while it successfully engaged in the construction of the 'welfare state' at home a 'socialist' foreign policy remained outside its grasp. The record clearly indicates that both policies stemmed from the same background of a cautious, moderate approach to governmental problems which pragmatically set its sights upon what seemed to be attainable rather than upon utopian aspirations. Although both its supporters and its opponents expected the government to introduce really radical reforms, it shrunk from doing so. The respective weight and impact of all the factors that contributed to this caution are hard to evaluate. First, the experience gained by its senior members who had served in the Coalition Government had made them acutely aware of the problems of governing. Second, it was a predominantly middle-class government; only 6 of the 20 Cabinet Ministers, 6 senior and 13 junior members of the government were trade-union sponsored.[9] Third, the government was strongly committed to the social reforms proposed during the war by the political centre, especially in the Beveridge Report, but less so to the collectivist ideas about the economy sponsored by the Left—it tended to prefer the conventional patterns favoured by the civil servants and the economists to far-reaching social and economic controls. Fourth, and probably most importantly, it was dealing with an economy in a desperate state urgently requiring immediate remedies. This, rather than the encouragement of uncertain, however ingenious and imaginative experiments, was the government's primary task. Fifth, Britain's recovery depended upon assistance from the arch-capitalist United States which could not be expected to favour anything strongly socialist. This did not amount to Britain's becoming a 'penetrated system' which forfeited full autonomy of decision, but it constituted a powerful restraint. Finally, no doubt, the government wished to serve the nation in its difficult situation as best it could and to prove itself worthy of re-election. All in all, continuity, moderate reform, and compromise rather than fundamental change and innovation were the hallmarks of Labour's domestic policies.

Perhaps such a policy was inevitable in the absence not only of an ideological commitment to fundamental change but also of clear ideas of how it could be achieved except by going towards the unacceptable extreme Russian collectivist pattern. The management of the national economy and of industrial relations remains even now much more of an art than a science; it was infinitely less sophisticated in 1945 and consequently the government left intact many of the entrenched structural inefficiencies of the British industrial system, especially the antiquated wage structure which was later to constantly bedevil the British economy; attempts at economic planning were soon abandoned; the established economic interests were preserved and encouraged by the Keynesian cheap-money policy with a 2 per cent bank rate which engendered inflationary pressures.

Nationalization, which was one of Labour's major electoral planks, did not amount to the establishment of full control over 'the commanding heights' of industry—in the case of the Bank of England it added little to the already existing controls while the public corporations established in the fields of civil aviation, electricity, gas, coal, and land transport, changed ownership but not methods of management; neither the power nor the transport industry was integrated. Concern for established interests delayed the only really controversial nationalization, that of steel, until 1950 and was demonstrated by the extremely generous —and costly—compensation to the owners of the unprofitable coal-mines. Finally, although highly differential income-tax rates were retained, no wealth or capital-gains taxes were introduced. All in all, the government failed to make full use of the unique opportunity for modernizing Britain's economy which existed in 1945, and this was to become one of the major reasons why Britain later found it so difficult to compete with her industrial rivals who had been forced to rebuild and renovate as they had suffered greater damage, or with the much wealthier and more dynamic United States.

Even the 'welfare state' was not as fundamental an innovation as it appeared at the time. Many benefits were tied to contributions and, with the exception of the universal health service introduced in its far-reaching form only owing to the determination of Aneurin Bevan, it amounted to little more than an amalgamation and tidying up of historically established social-welfare measures. Little advance was made with housing and the educational system was only partly reformed.

This is not to say that the government was not kept extremely busy or that, in the short run, it was not highly successful. Its moderate programme commanded general social support, as the working class obtained sufficient reforms to be reasonably satisfied while the other classes, having become aware of the 'black spots' in Britain's social life during the social mixing forced by the wartime evacuation programmes, were not haunted by the spectre of a revolution and were receptive to some measure of reform. Political consensus followed this social agreement. In 1947 the Conservative Party annual conference accepted into the party programme its hitherto marginal tradition of 'Tory Democracy', strongly manifested between the wars by the concern for the 'condition of the people' shown by such politicians as Macmillan. The report of the conference's Industrial Policy Committee, entitled *Industrial Charter*, acquiesced in most of the welfare state and, implicity, in the high taxation involved, and also in the principle of a managed economy. Subsequent fierce parliamentary battles over the establishment of the health service and the nationalisation of steel appear in retrospect to have been largely symbolic. Although socially highly desirable, this basic consensus resulted in a relative immobility of Britain's social structures so that the needs for a more radical reform had to be met in the much less propitious circumstanes of the later 1960s and early 1970s. Moreover, it deprived British political life of dynamism. Successive governments, independently of their political hue, did the same things in much the same way, although with different emphasis and under different labels.

This lack of dynamism due to consensus applied in equal force to foreign policy. Before turning to the latter it is necessary to analyse the major international aspects of Britain's economic weakness, which constituted the major restraint on her freedom of manoeuvre both at home and abroad.

The unexpectedly sudden cancellation of Lend-Lease supplies on 21 August 1945 dispelled any illusions as to the magnitude and urgency of the economic tasks awaiting the government. Over one-quarter of the nation's wealth had been expended on the war effort; Britain emerged burdened with nearly £3,500 million of debts, mainly within the sterling area, and unable to pay out of her current earnings for much more than one-third of her imports of food and raw materials, which were running at some £2,000 million a year. The government was deeply conscious of the debilitating effect upon British foreign policy; Bevin, in particular, repeatedly emphasized what a difference it would have made 'if I could export so many million tons of coal a year'.[10]

The main immediate governmental effort was to secure temporary assistance to tide Britain over her difficulties in the hope or expectation that, given time and an opportunity to recover, she would regain her economic strength and much of her power. The only possible solution of the immediate problem lay in United States assistance which was secured by the Loan Agreement providing $3,750 million credits with an additional sum to cover British liabilities under Lend-Lease; an additional credit amounting to one-third of the American one was also secured from Canada. Britain's plight was temporarily and unsatisfactorily resolved, showing in embryo all the economic/political difficulties which were to beset her over the subsequent years. First, she could get no assistance from the Commonwealth; Hugh Dalton recalls how the

Cabinet's hopes for a voluntary writing off of one-half of the sterling debt, entertained in the latter part of 1945, were disappointed when the creditors, with the partial exception of Australia and New Zealand, refused to scale down the debts, while a tough Anglo-American line on the issue was politically precluded as this would have jeopardized the political settlement with India, which received the highest priority.[11] Second, Britain had no possible alternative to American assistance, but this was given only after hard bargaining, on stiff conditions, and with the humiliatingly short time of a mere twenty-five days, including the Christmas recess, for parliamentary ratification. Third, the loan episode showed the incomplete grasp of international economics by the majority of the experts in the field. Keynes, for one, foresaw how untenable was the undertaking insisted on by the Americans to make sterling fully convertible within twelve months after the Loan Agreement had come into force, as indeed it proved to be; but he was unable to persuade the American economists. The rate fixed for sterling at $4·03 seems, in retrospect, too high, but this was not apparently realized on either side; were the British governed partly by the consideration of keeping sterling 'heavy', as a symbol of power? When, after a period of increasing weakness in 1949, Sir Stafford Cripps was forced to devalue, he decided in favour of a 'once-for-all' cut of $2·80 which was so low that the boost for exports was offset by their excessively reduced price and by the increased costs of imports.[12]

Despite all that, and despite the shortage of capital for the necessary investment and modernization and the critical fuel situation, especially in the winter of 1946–7, Britain made rapid headway in industrial production, notably in such modern technologies as machine tools, chemicals, electronics, aircraft, and synthetic fibres. Having lost most of her foreign investments and other sources of invisible income, she engaged in an export drive aiming at a 75 per cent increase over her prewar figure in order to pay for her imports. This she achieved by 1950. There was no repetition of the post-1918 malfunctioning economy with high unemployment. This was largely due to continued spartan standards of consumption at home allied with a favourable international environment. International trade was booming, Britain had no serious competitor except the United States, which, having established a common front in the incipient cold war, behaved co-operatively in economics; the imaginative and generous European Recovery Programme of 1948, which pumped $16,000 million into Europe of which Britain received $2,400 million, strongly contrasted with the harshness of the 1946 loan. Thus a combination of American generosity, absence of international competition, and restricted domestic demands helped to engender optimism about the basic soundness of Britain's economy. Engrossed in their immediate pressing tasks, policy-makers did not accord sufficient urgency to the fundamental tasks of modernizing and undertaking fundamental structural changes in British industry, especially by eliminating inefficient units, running down unpromisingly uncompetitive industries and reforming labour relations.

## Foreign Policy Issues

In Lord Strang's authoritative recollections, the four main questions of Britain's foreign policy in 1945 related to: (1) the continuation of United States involvement; (2) the degree of moderation employed by the Soviet Union in the use of her new power; (3) the defence posture of the free people (especially in Western Europe); (4) the appropriate policy to be pursued by Britain in relation to her foreign commitments in 'her changed position in the hierarchy of forces'.[13]

The future behaviour of the two superpowers was clearly the independent variable on which future British policies would mainly depend. Already during the war Britain could not match them in production facilities and in numbers of men under arms, but, largely owing to the force of his personality and the power of his ideas, Churchill played an important part in the councils of the Big Three. This did not apply to the Far East where Britain's role had only been a minor one ever since the Fall of Singapore—she participated only marginally in the Pacific campaign and Churchill did not take part in the crucial Yalta talks on the Far East. Although Churchill's relations with Roosevelt were intimate, the latter disapproved of his efforts to draw a clear dividing line between the Soviet and the British spheres of influence in Europe. Towards the end of the war Roosevelt, and, even more, Truman, were determined to avoid the suspicion of 'ganging up' with the British against Stalin. Despite Churchill's misgivings, the Americans adopted a conciliatory attitude on Eastern Europe at Yalta and decided to adhere to a previously agreed demarcation line for the advance of troops, depriving themselves of an important potential bargaining asset; this left the West in a politically and strategically disadvantageous position without securing Stalin's goodwill.

At the end of hostilities the British position in Europe was therefore dangerously exposed. While the Russians appeared to be expansionist, the withdrawal of American troops from Europe was proceeding apace and could be expected to be completed within a short time. Five million British men were under arms and required the ancillary services of four million civilians. British troops were in occupation in Germany, Austria, and Venezia Giulia, and were engaged in severe fighting in Greece. Outside Europe they had to keep India at peace until its independence was achieved, were expected to accept the Japanese surrender in Southeast Asia and to participate, though only in token size, in the occupation of Japan; moreover, they had to maintain internal security throughout the Empire. It was essential for Britain's economic recovery to cut back the military effort immediately, and the targets were ambitiously set at reducing manpower by 80 per cent by the end of 1946 and defence costs correspondingly. Although Churchill exerted great efforts to restore France to a great power position, de Gaulle harboured hard feelings against the 'Anglo-Saxons' and, moreover, the French were militarily weak and were preoccupied with keeping Germany down, so that, initially, their political line in Europe was closer to the Russian than to the British one.

The Labour government's foreign policy was influenced by three major factors. The first of these was the continuity from the wartime Coalition Cabinet in which both the Prime Minister and the Foreign Secretary had been prominent members. Indeed, in the first foreign-affairs debate in the House of Commons after the election, both Ernest Bevin and Anthony Eden testified that there had been no serious differences of opinion on foreign policy between the Conservative and the Labour leaders during the war.[14] The second and very much less significant factor was the party's commitment to a 'socialist' foreign policy. The Labour electoral manifesto adopted at the 1945 Annual Conference confined itself to generalities:

to take the greatest notice to apply Socialist analysis to the world situation; to oppose the crystallisation of power politics into a so-called League of Nations of victorious Powers; and to struggle for the establishment of the United States of Europe as being the only means of ensuring a just and lasting peace.[15]

As is argued in some detail in the next chapter, the major policy line arising from these sentiments, a close alignment with the Soviet Union, soon proved impossible.

A third and much more important factor is found in Ernest Bevin's personality and views. Although acutely aware of Britain's economic weakness, Bevin was determined to use opportunities and to take initiatives in the fluid postwar situation. He was in a uniquely powerful and unobstructed position at home. He consulted closely with Attlee but commanded his full and unquestioning support. Attlee believed that 'foreign affairs are the province of the Foreign Secretary. It is in my view a mistake for the P.M. to intervent personally except in exceptional circumstances'.[16] One must bear in mind that Bevin developed a foreign policy which was a Cabinet policy; within the Cabinet imperial matters were not his domain and Attlee remained in general charge of defence and of nuclear matters. Within the Cabinet, however, Bevin was a dominant figure. With massive trade union support he could always safely stand up to his left-wing critics, who, at one time, amounted to some one-third of the party. Moreover, although not a particularly good parliamentary performer, he had no trouble in the House of Commons, as his policy commanded the support of the opposition; and he felt perfectly at home in the Foreign Office. Lord Strang bears witness that Bevin, although lacking formal education, had such a powerful and incisive mind and so sound a conception of and experience in international relations and in bargaining techniques from his trade-union experience, that he readily commanded the full loyalty and support of his officials. Although Bevin's left-wing critics frequently accused him of adopting the official perceptions and views, it seems more justified to claim that his and the officials' views closely coincided. It is, however, true that Bevin pursued his strong and orthodox views without checking them against any opposed and broader ideas. Characteristically, he was always suspicious of Labour intellectuals and had decisively broken with G. D. H. Cole, the only one who had profoundly influenced him and who was actually holding different views on foreign policy.[17]

Although Bevin's views and policies reflected such overwhelming necessities of international life that it is difficult to conceive of any other Foreign Secretary behaving very differently, undoubtedly his powerful personality strongly contributed to the final shape of Britain's postwar foreign policy, both in its stress upon relations with the superpowers and in its relative neglect of other relationships.

Concerning the former, it is impossible to answer with any degree of certainty whether the involvement of the Americans or the containment of the Russians was dominant; both were clearly of primary importance. The merging of these two main objectives of British foreign policy into the cold war raises the question whether the advantageous event was fortuitous or was deliberately aimed at by Bevin. In view of Britain's major problems in 1945, alignment with the United States seemed 'natural', no substitute being available for a number of reasons. First, the United States was the only potential supplier of essential and urgently needed economic and defence assistance. Second, despite the difficulties recently encountered—especially in connection with the termination of Lend-Lease, the loan and the nuclear exchanges—the relationship was hopefully manageable, being facilitated by the record of wartime co-operation and by the continuing personal links on both sides at many levels. Third, the leaders of the two main parties were agreed upon the desirability of such an alignment and Bevin successfully kept his left-wing critics under control. Finally, against the background of postwar events, such proposed alternatives as a close understanding with the Soviet Union, dependence upon the United Nations or the Commonwealth, or the establishment of a viable 'Third Force' in Europe became increasingly utopian.

As, in the immediate postwar period, the Americans were pursuing a policy much more accommodating to the Russians than the British regarded as wise, and were contemplating an early withdrawal from Europe, it was obviously necessary for Bevin to persuade them to the British way of thinking; the political conflict in Europe had to be defined in military terms to secure the acceptance of military aid by Congress.[18] Bevin's skilfully timed communication to the State Department of 24 February 1947 which led to the Truman Doctrine, and his Western Union speech of 22 January 1948 in the House of Commons which helped the Administration to get the European co-operation Act passed by a large Senate majority of 69 to 17, could be interpreted by some 'revisionist' historians of the cold war as a deliberate British attempt to ensure an American involvement. Such Machiavellian cunning does not, however, seem to have been in Bevin's character. He was concerned with Britain's weakness and urgent needs and beyond that, equally strongly, both with the Soviet and the American strands of foreign policy. Even if the cold war link appears to have been due to circumstances rather than to a deliberate British design, it nevertheless determined the future direction of British foreign policy in which relations with the two super-powers were inextricably mixed.

Bevin's preoccupation with these two main strands of foreign policy, though fully justified by the circumstances, could not but affect his drive for European unity. His health, too, was failing. To quote Hugh Dalton's remarks about his indecision over Palestine:

Bevin's great gift, as it once was, of seeing apparently separate problems as part of a wider whole, has now degenerated, with weariness and ill-health and ill-success, into the opposite vice of not being able to keep separate things separate, or to settle, or make up his mind, on one problem at a time.[19]

After his House of Commons speech on 22 January 1948, an initiative with regard to Europe was expected both by the Americans and in Europe, and also in Britain, although Churchill was aiming at a unification of Western Europe along a final ideological division of Europe whereas the Labour Party, part of which still believed in the possibility of a Third Force, refused to support Churchill's initiatives. As contemporary newspapers commented, although Bevin began by expressing the need for precision, his proposals were highly ambiguous. Briefly to summarize these he asked for closer unity with France excluding, however, formal union; security arrangements among 'kindred souls' in the West such as the Russians had organized in the East, but not directed against any country; mobilization of the 'moral and material' forces; the economic build-up of Europe; and a 'spiritual union'. He did not limit the Union to Europe and did not exclude its possible extension to the colonies. Although he mentioned that the 'resources' of the United States would be needed, in deference to the susceptibilities of the Senate he did not actually propose a multilateral treaty, let alone a multilateral defence organization.[20]

It is hard to decide how firm Bevin's thoughts about a future defence organization were at this stage. The possible military aspects of the proposed Union were only hinted at by his reference to the Treaty of Dunkirk concluded between Britain and France in 1947. The Western Union speech prepared the ground for the American participation which was eventually institutionalized in NATO, but even the two official histories of that organization differ as to what he may have had in mind. The earlier one (1959) speaks of defensive alliance but the later (1962) only of economic and social consultations. Bevin may have been thinking of such consultations in Europe, even, ultimately, of a British/French integration or some kind of 'Third Force'; the obscurity may have been deliberate, to keep open as many options as possible and to avoid gratuitously antagonizing anybody; his poor parliamentary performance on that day may have been further impaired by acute ill-health. Nevertheless, his preoccupation with the central American/Soviet balance appears to have been an additional reason for his attaching less importance to the details of European organization. This original ambiguity contributed in no small measure to the untidiness of later arrangements which eventually clashed: Britain was instrumental in completing the separate arrangements under the OEEC for European/American economic co-operation and similar ones for the NATO defence organization, but failed to participate in the European political integration moves which dominated the 1950s.

# 9 Britain's Major Relationships I: The Superpowers

IT is not the purpose of this book to discuss even in the most general outline all Britain's major relationships with other countries. The few presented here have been selected partly owing to their intrinsic importance but partly also in order to provide some historical background for the themes previously developed. British–Soviet relations are discussed at the outset and in greatest detail because, being largely confined to the central balance of power, they serve to illustrate British attitudes to this much more clearly than the far more ramified British–American relations; the only angle of the latter discussed here is the 'special relationship' and its impact upon other issues of British foreign policy. The subsequent chapter is devoted to three areas of foreign policy more loosely connected with the central power balance: the Commonwealth, Western Europe, and the United Nations.

## The Issues between Britain and the Soviet Union

Relations with the Soviet Union played a central part in Britain's postwar foreign policy; one may argue that they determined its general direction towards an Atlantic alignment focusing on the 'cold war'. And yet the amount of business now conducted with Moscow is only a fraction of that conducted with Washington. The reasons for this apparent contradiction are not far to seek: major issues of British–Soviet relations relate to world order and global strategy which are generally dealt with on the multilateral level, or with (and lately often exclusively through) the United States. Immediately after the war, however, Britain had to deal directly with the Soviet Union on a large number of issues; these were connected mainly with her extensive world role and with communist threats to the Empire, and have either disappeared or greatly dwindled in importance. Whereas the fear that a war could break out over Berlin, the Congo, or Cuba played a central role in Macmillan's diplomacy,[1] the Soviet naval expansion in the early 1970s not only seemed much less menacing against the background of the general detente but clearly could not be Britain's primary responsibility.

The assessment of Soviet policies remains one of the major tasks of British diplomacy: the gravest possible threats to the country's security could arise from Soviet nuclear missiles and submarines, and its vital economic interests in Middle Eastern oil could be jeopardized by Soviet moves. These issues are, however, part of Western or NATO interests and Britain has no major specific national interests directly involving Russia as the Germans have. Mutual trade remains fairly small and unbalanced—between 1962 and 1970 Soviet imports to Britain rose from £94 to £220 million and British exports to Russia from £58 million to £102 million. Between 1969 and 1972, in contrast to the rapid increase in Western trade with Russia and British trade with Eastern Europe, British exports to Russia actually dropped by some 7·2 per cent. There was every reason to think that this was caused by a deliberate Russian policy of discrimination, following the expulsion in 1970 of the 105 Soviet representatives implicated in espionage, a policy which was renounced by the Russians only in 1973.[2] Nor may it be easy for Britain to hold her own against her European rivals now that, as from 1 January 1973, the EEC is operating a common commercial policy towards Russia. The problems of nationals on both sides are frequently troublesome, despite their severely limited numbers, but are not of great importance.

Although in the early stages of the common struggle against Hitler, Britain and the Soviet Union were treating each other as equals, the discrepancy between their respective powers made the relationship increasingly asymmetrical. After the war the British were keenly aware of Russia's economic weakness when compared with the United States. Although some Labour adherents expected a great upsurge in the Soviet economy owing to its centralized management, Russia's deficient capabilities were stressed, for instance, by Aneurin Bevan as an argument against the possibility of Russian aggression: 'I do not believe that a nation, however large its manpower, coldly contemplates launching 25 million tons of steel *per annum* against the combination of 140 million.[3] However, the unexpectedly swift development of Soviet nuclear weapons greatly impressed the British, as the launching of the sputnik was to do in 1957. Inevitably, Soviet capabilities had to be balanced by American ones, and thus Britain's relations with the Soviet Union became an important factor in her relations with the United States, the determinant factor, one may argue, in persuading the Attlee Government to seek a military alignment with the latter. As time went on, in a circular way, the momentum of this American alignment became a major factor in British relations with the Soviet Union.

In the eyes of the Russians, the mutual relationship was always largely a function of the relations between the two countries and the United States. Already during the war, Churchill's friendship with Roosevelt and his ability to exercise influence over the latter were his major assets in the eyes of Stalin. After the war, being power realists, the Russians were more sceptical than others about Britain's ability to continue as a world power, but as Lord Trevelyan[4] records, even in the early 1960s they did not write the British off—they retained the respect born of past common experience in German wars and, much more importantly, they regarded the British as the only people capable of exercising influence upon the Americans. Both sources of influence have since waned. During Wilson's Vietnam initiatives the Russians finally discovered that British influence upon the Americans was limited and, once they engaged in close bilateral negotiations with the latter, especially in the SALT talks, they no longer needed an intermediary. In another way, the degree to which the American factor dominated Soviet attitudes to Britain was expressed in the continuous Soviet efforts to drive a wedge between Britain and the United States and thus to weaken the solidarity of the Western alliance; the Russians regarded British politics as being dependent upon American ones and attributed unfriendliness and the limitations of trade to this dependence. It would, indeed, be no exaggeration to say that, throughout the period, British relations with the Soviet Union were practical rather than friendly and that they oscillated between correct coolness and outright hostility, even though declarations of friendship were exchanged on several occasions. The standard leftist explanation, that Britain was subservient to the United States,[5] is, however, clearly inadequate, as on many significant issues British policy seriously deviated from American. The historical record must be examined to discover also other determinants of British attitudes and policies, especially the reactions to Russian actions, whether the latter affected Britain directly or pertained to the global balance, or were even restricted to the communist bloc and Russia herself.

Before analysing this record, it is necessary to glance briefly at the issue of ideological antipathy. If, for the Russians, the British were the arch-imperialists and arch-capitalists, until later replaced by the Americans, for the British, Russia was a source of dangerous ideological subversion; her co-operation in the war had been forced by circumstances and had been strained and uneasy. The British dislike of communism was reinforced by a general revulsion against ideologies and dictatorships and, in the case of the Conservatives, also by their dislike of state management of the economy, the expropriation of foreign investments, and the confiscation of private wealth. Apart from the few ultra-leftist publications, public media are generally, though perhaps sometimes subconsciously, unfriendly. They still follow some of the pejorative terminology of the cold war which makes it natural to differentiate between western 'governments' and communist 'regimes' or western 'police' and communist 'security forces'.[6]

Public opinion in Britain occasionally wells up against the Soviet Union to the point of circumscribing the possibility of improvement in Anglo-Soviet relations; such was notably the reaction to the two Soviet interventions in Czechoslovakia, in 1948 and 1968. The waves of indignation are, however, temporary and the lingering unfriendliness or even aversion of the general public cannot be regarded as a conclusive or even a very significant factor. Immediately after the war, before the memories of the alliance had been overlaid by subsequent disagreements, the Labour Party was in a state of euphoria about the possibility of continuing a friendly co-operation with 'socialist' countries. Left was expected to speak to Left. Even the traditional Labour hostility to the British Communist Party was temporarily overcome to the point that a resolution calling for 'progressive unity' between it and the Labour Party failed at the 1945 annual conference by a mere 95,000 votes. Bevin had to overcome strong opposition within the party when governmental policy turned against Russia and only the expansionist Soviet moves abroad and the restrictive Soviet policies in the Eastern bloc, especially the persecution of the Social Democratic leaders, estranged many of the original sympathizers.

The traditional pragmatic outlook of British foreign policy meant that co-operation with Russia would be governed by the estimation of national interests and not by ideological antipathy. Despite his exceptionally pronounced anti-communism, Churchill did not hestitate to offer Stalin an alliance; even when the pressures of the war had somewhat slackened, Britain decided to support Tito and then maintained generally friendly relations with communist Yugoslavia. It is plausible to assume that the Foreign Office and Bevin, whose views generally corresponded with those of his officials, would not have been closed, for purely ideological reasons, to the possibilities of co-operation with Russia. The philosophy of the British as well as the American attitudes (which is most clearly articulated in the writings of George Kennan) can be summed up as follows: Whereas many people in the Western Governments came to hate the Soviet leaders for what they *did*, Communists seemed to hate the Western Governments for what they *were*, regardless of what they did. It is therefore to the actions of the Russians that we must turn.

The shadows of imperial rivalries and of the Russian threat to the North-West Frontier of India were far in the past, although occasionally Soviet expansionism revived memories of them, but the more important recent experiences encouraged scepticism about the chances of co-operation. The 'Popular Front' in the 1930s and an alignment to oppose Nazism before the Molotov-Ribbentrop Pact had not perhaps been given a fair chance, partly owing to the understandable mistrust on the part of the West, but the Russians seemed fully responsible for the extreme difficulties of wartime. It seemed imprudent to attribute more importance to postwar co-operation plans and to the later Russian proposals for 'peaceful co-existence' than the Russians themselves appeared to do. Repeated Russian pronouncements referred to 'peaceful co-existence' as mere periods of temporary detente during which the inexorable march of history would tilt the balance of power in favour of communism as nothing less than a higher form of class-struggle between the two opposing systems. The practical question seemed limited to the degree to which the Russians would, meanwhile, feel inhibited in actively aiding this march, whenever an opportunity arose. Hence, inevitably, Soviet actions which appeared unfriendly would affect relations with Britain much more than unfriendly actions by states with a nationalist rather than a communist orientation, not only because Russia was more powerful but also because her avowed intentions were unfriendly.

*The Evolution of British–Soviet Relations*
The immediate postwar situation was ineviably dominated by the grave military imbalance in Europe created by the rapid diminution of American forces which were expected to be completely withdrawn in 1947, while the deterrent value of the new automatic weapons was uncertain and the major Western European powers still prostrate. Nevertheless, despite the warnings about Soviet intentions by some experts, notably George Kennan, with an optimism which may seem to us remarkable after the intervening spell of the cold war, the British, American, and French diplomatic experts as well as politicians seemed hopeful that a *modus vivendi* might be found, though they were clear that the Soviet Union remained ideologically fully committed to communism, and fully aware of the aggravating effects of Stalin's personality. The Western attitudes were epitomized in George Kennan's dictum that we cannot be friends but need not be enemies.[7]

In March–April 1945, the British representative in Moscow soberly assessed the situation as follows. Although Soviet policy was clearly entering a boisterous phase, it could be regarded as 'offensive-defensive'. The Russians would, in violation of previous agreements, ensure changes in the social structures in the Balkans in harmony with the Soviet system, but they would refrain from interfering in Greece. At the same time, they had not given up the intention of collaborating with the Western powers and would continue the meetings. Although this violated the British interpretation of the notion of 'free elections' which had been agreed upon, it amounted to a policy of limited objectives none of which endangered a major British interest. By 'co-operation' the Russians understood 'something like a division of the world into spheres of interest and a tacit agreement that no one of the partners would hamper or indeed criticize the activities of the other in its own sphere'. Therefore Britain's quarrels with the Russians should be confined to issues on which she was prepared to stand her ground—where her important interests were involved, as in Greece, Iran or Turkey—but it was useless to quarrel over Rumania or Bulgaria. Britain should avoid the extremes either of confusing the Russians with the Nazis, as there was no essential conflict of vital interests between Britain and the Soviet Union, or of thinking that they would soon 'settle down' and that the adverse experiences after Yalta should be forgotten. Britain's task was to show strength and determination to defend her interests, to make it clear that there was a limit beyond which the Russians could not safely go, and to guide the Western world to resist Soviet pressures and infiltration. [8]

The three major points of the British representatives' assessment can thus be summed up as follows: first, the Russians are, on the whole, unfriendly and extremely difficult to deal with; second, limited agreements with them are, nevertheless, possible; third, Britain should realistically recognize Russia's vital interests, but be prepared and show herself prepared to defend her own, although her means are limited. British policy towards Russia showed a continuity on all these points. For instance, already in August 1940 Sir Alexander Cadogan had noted in his *Diaries*: 'Russian policy will change exactly when and if they think it will suit them. If they *do* think that, it won't matter whether we've kicked Maisky in the stomach. Contrariwise, we could give Maisky the Garter and it wouldn't make a penn'orth of difference'. [9]

During his nineteen months in the European Advisory Commission Lord Strang found the Russians extremely difficult negotiators, who, however, might eventually give in when subject to sustained and well thought-out Western attitudes. [10] Sir Alec Douglas-Home thought much the same in the late 1960s. When speaking about the last British success at the superpower level, the Partial Nuclear Test Ban Treaty, he commented: 'the only way you can ever get anything done with the Russians on a limited front on a particular issue at a particular time that happens to suit them'.[11]

British policies were clearly based upon a full awareness of the Russians' vital interests: in view of their wartime experiences they could be expected to insist on extending their control over Eastern Europe and to be sensitive to any possibility of Germany becoming rehabilitated and conciliated; they desperately needed economic means for rehabilitation; they were naturally apprehensive of the American monopoly of nuclear weapons. The British could not, however, develop a coherent friendly policy towards Russia without persuading the Americans and without meeting a reasonable Russian response. American policy was not essentially harder but merely inconsistent. On the one hand, they insisted on strong protests about Soviet actions in Eastern Europe which the West could not stop; on the other, they were not ready to draw a firm line elsewhere, and, as soon as hostilities were over, were withdrawing their troops before a final agreement and demarcation had been reached.

Russian behaviour was gratuitously offensive and menacing. Although Britain was ready for concessions on Poland, in April 1945 the Soviet government concluded an agreement with the puppet Provisional Government of that country, making such concessions impossible without a complete loss of face on the part of the Western Powers. It rebutted friendly British overtures asking for a Russian contingent for the victory celebrations in London and for cultural exchanges; it tightened domestic policies, criticized British policies, and tried to drive a wedge between the Americans and the British; even more serious was the Soviet encouragement of the communist fronts in France and Italy which threatened to upset the balance of power in Europe. By the time hostilities in Europe were over, it was difficult to attribute the behaviour of the Russians merely to their sensitiveness or clumsiness, as it gave the impression of a deliberate policy; whether it was merely a tactical design aiming at gaining as much advantage as possible before the West had built up resistance or a long-term expansionist design, the only reasonable response for Britain seemed to *be* strong and to *appear* strong. Despite the lingering fears of American domination and the dilemma that a close alignment with the United States would further jeopardize British relations with Russia, such an alignment was becoming increasingly more desirable for Britain.

Particularly menacing was the direct clash of interests arising from Russia's challenge to Britain's position in the Mediterranean, which was one of dominance now that her French and Italian rivals had been weakened. At the London meeting of the Council of Foreign Ministers in the autumn of 1945 Bevin explicitly postulated that he expected the Russians to respect British strategic interests there, but the Russians continued to press hard into the area especially through Persia, through staking a claim to participate in the trusteeship over Tripolitania, and also through Greece, although they refrained from direct support for the Greek communists.

Until the beginning of 1947, hopes of an arrangement with the Soviet Union did not fully disappear. The British were willing to consider any possibilities of agreements and to maintain the closest possible official and personal contacts with the Russians, but at the same time to treat the whole relationship like one co-ordinated strategic operation in which unilateral concessions would not be granted and reciprocity would be required. This policy operated under an important domestic constraint, as public opinion in Britain was polarized between extreme partiality to the Soviet Union, based upon the wartime alliance and fed by Soviet propaganda, and some traditional anti-communist prejudices. Even some political leaders and officials continued to explain away Soviet actions and to advocate further gestures of friendship in the hope that accommodation might thus be secured. Although gradually Britain aligned herself against all major Soviet policies, be it the division of Germany or the extraction of heavy reparations from current production or the tightening of Soviet control over Eastern Europe, all these policies could be attributed to the Russians' wartime experience and to their vital strategic interests. Russia's refusal to participate in the Baruch and Marshall Plans could be plausibly explained by her legitimate fear of American domination.[12] Hugh Dalton[13] asked himself whether it was right to refuse the Russians German reparations from current production; together with several other members of the government, he thought that the only hope for allaying Russian suspicions lay in divulging the nuclear secrets to them. Although the Russian attitudes at the Council of Foreign Ministers remained hostile and unyielding until the councils ground themselves to a halt, even at the beginning of 1947 the Foreign Office was divided between those who blamed the Russians entirely and others who were concerned with avoiding provocation by the West and were hopeful that a settlement was still possible.[14]

Here again, Bevin's dominant personality played an important part in the immediate postwar period; he repeatedly returned to the notion of three possible patterns of international order—a balance of power, a hegemony by one power, and a Concert of the Big Three. He strongly preferred a Concert and he made repeated personal attempts to reduce friction with the Russians to the minimum. Several times he offered to extend the 1942 treaty of friendship; he took great care to avoid gratuitous offence, for instance, at the Labour Party's Annual Conference in July 1946, he declared that he would not press unduly for an alliance with France because he wished to avoid the division of Europe, and the next month he urged Morgan Phillips to be friendly in reporting on his good-will mission to Russia in the *Daily Herald*; According to Francis Williams[15] he insisted that the Russians be invited to participate in the Marshall Plan not for the sake of appearances alone; in his conversations with John Strachey he repeatedly expressed the hope that 'perhaps they will play after all'; he urged the Board of Trade to start negotiations with Russia after the deadlock over Germany in the spring of 1947 in order to keep some lines of communication open.

In all these dealings Bevin so staunchly and outspokenly defended British interests and so vigorously rebutted Soviet accusations that his radical critics accused him of insincerity in his friendly approaches. The accusation seems to be unwarranted but Bevin's policy was, indeed, dual. He was adamantly opposed to a Soviet hegemony and was determined to prevent it and, while supporting a Concert, he was simultaneously working hard for the less desirable but much more promising alternative of a balance of power with American participation. Bevin was essentially a practical man, governed to a great extent by his personal experiences which had been negative both with the communists in the British trade union movement and with the Russians during the war. On the basis of these experiences, he can hardly have believed in the validity of the traditional socialist idea inherited from classical liberalism that all conflicts are unnecessary, as they are based upon misunderstandings and misperceptions. Moreover, the historical lessons of appeasement loomed large. He may well, therefore, have thought a balance had better chances of success, and therefore have worked harder for this than for a Concert. Nevertheless, he gives all the appearance of having tried to reach some understanding with the Russians. With his strong standing within the party he did not really need to cover himself against the accusations that he was pursuing anti-communist policies—he did not generally take much notice of his critics and it is highly implausible and out of character to assume that his conciliatory moves were not genuine but were merely a smokescreen to reassure the left wing.

The alignment with the United States which ultimately decided the fundamental transformation of British policies towards Russia was somewhat fortuitous; it provided an answer to Britain's security problem but only at the cost of hardening the East–West conflict into the cold war. The Fulton speech, of which Bevin was not apprised in advance, was unwelcome to those still concerned with seeking an agreement with the Russians, as was also the American tendency to assume that whenever the Russians were in a minority they were also wrong.[16] According to Dalton, the British communication to the State Department of 24 February 1947 which precipitated the Truman Doctrine (see above, p. 187) was not really meant to force the hand of the Americans; although Truman's strong reaction was welcome, it was by no means expected.[17] The Truman Doctrine brought into the open the argument of the Soviet menace which, as Dalton notes, had previously been used in the American political debate only privately and discreetly. Moreover, the announcement of the Doctrine coincided with the beginning of the Moscow session of the Council of Foreign Ministers and therefore appeared to the Russians as an attempt to torpedo the conference.

Despite the aggravation of East–West relations through the Communist coup in Czechoslovakia and the initiation of the Berlin blockade, in 1948 Soviet policy changed with the announcement of a five-year plan, which put the stress upon economic development. Soviet military strength was not reduced but Russian pressures against the Middle East abated. The new line of Soviet offensive indicated by the establishment of the Cominform was not rigorously pursued after Zhdanov and Voznesensky were removed from leadership. By that time, however, the pattern of hostile East–West relations had become firmly established. At the Labour Party annual conference in 1950 Bevin claimed: 'With the support of every member of the Cabinet I tried from the moment I took office until 1947 to be friends with the Russians . . . What did I get? Nothing but aggression or threat of aggression'.[18] Towards the end of the Labour government, in a speech delivered on 7 April 1951, the Minister of State, Kenneth Younger, fully and authoritatively evaluated the current British interpretation of Soviet behaviour. Russia did not want war, as she was internally too weak, but neither did she ever intend to co-operate in postwar reconstruction, as was shown by her abstention from the economic and social activities of the United Nations and the Marshall Plan, and by her behaviour in Austria and in Berlin, and by her persistent and vicious propaganda. The Russians hated all the socialists who refused to accept their doctrine, did not abide by the results of free elections, and apparently had no objection to the use of force as had been witnessed in North Persia in 1946, in Berlin in 1948, and in the supply of arms to

North Korea; they maintained armed forces much larger than was necessary for mere garrison purposes. If allowed heavy preponderance, the Russians would use their strength ruthlessly, and the only way to influence them was through being strong enough and ready enough to persuade them that co-operation would pay better. The stage was set for Britain reluctantly to accept the rehabilitation and limited and controlled rearmament of Germany, a policy which had been theoretically considered in the first Foreign Office memorandum on postwar planning[19] as an unwelcome alternative if great power co-operation failed.

Although some communist critics of Western policies explain the cold war by 'the mirror effect' of hostile Western moves which the Russians merely reciprocated, it is hard to assume that the detente attempts in the early 1950s came to an end mainly owing to the Western decision to rearm Germany. Certainly the British were busy in asking for renewed negotiations. Impressed by the explosion of the first Soviet A-bomb on 24 September 1949, in 1950 Churchill noted the new situation and asked for fresh Western diplomatic approaches, without abandoning the military one: 'Let us therefore labour for peace, not only by gathering our defensive strength but also by making sure that no door is closed upon any hopes of reaching settlement'.[20] Dalton[21] reports that Georges Bidault was struck by the inconsistency of the tentative and vague British approach, as Churchill was proposing a summit one week, and next week the rearmament of Germany, to which the Russians were dead opposed; undoubtedly, the Russians were even more struck by this inconsistency. Nevertheless, already in 1952, before Stalin's death, they on their side made a few tentative overtures for economic conferences. After his death, the British cautiously waited for the clarification of the foreign policy of the new leadership, expecting it to continue Stalin's policy for the time being but keeping a fairly open mind about future developments. By then, with the future of NATO clearly dependent upon the United States, the British had to take American reactions fully into account. The obvious danger was that the Americans, then in the throes of McCarthyism, would over-react themselves, and either become over-optimistic and decide to withdraw from Europe or try to use the opportuntity for making moves which could be regarded by the Russians as offensive and would make the latter close their ranks. Helpfully, by then NATO had become a well-established forum where the alliance partners could frankly exchange their national views of Soviet moves and, although agreement was by no means complete, could also reach a common evaluation of their significance and of the most rational counter-strategies.

At first, the changes in Soviet foreign policy were very slight, a change of tone and emphasis rather than in substance; no scope appeared to be given during 1953 for an immediate new attempt at searching for a *modus vivendi*. Towards the end of the year, however, the situation began to appear both urgent and more promising. First, it was becoming clear that Britain could not possibly keep up in the nuclear race; second, the slow conciliatory moves of the Russians encouraged the exploration of some worthwhile agreements, especially progress towards the Korean Armistice and the Austrian State Agreement. Third, Soviet internal politics showed signs of liberalization, to culminate later in Khruschchev's secret speech at the Party Congress in 1956. Finally, the West could now negotiate from a position of reasonably adequate strength secured by NATO.

Eden became concerned with the possibility that, once the nuclear race had reached saturation point, both the reactive strength and the political cohesion of the Western Alliance would decline. He was also keen on exploring promising avenues for Britain to play a world role and for himself personally to exercise his diplomatic skills. He deliberately shifted the emphasis of British foreign policy from a military to a diplomatic focus:

Our main weapons of resistance to Soviet encroachment have hitherto been military. But do they meet the needs of the present time? I do not believe that the Russians have any plans at present for military aggression in the West. On the other hand are we prepared with other weapons to meet the new challenge?[22]

Eden was instrumental in reactivating East–West exchanges at top level. Although in those days it was extremely difficult for the American president to leave the United States, as he had to carry with him all his security paraphernalia, Eisenhower was persuaded to participate in the Geneva summit in July 1955; Bulganin and Khrushchev were invited to and visited London in April of the following year. Eden also provided the substantive proposals for the detente known as the Eden Plan. His first plan was put forward as the basis for Western proposals at the preceding Conference of Foreign Ministers in January 1954 and then at the Geneva summit itself; it provided for German reunification to be followed by the establishment of a demilitarized zone in Central Europe and for a European Security Pact. At the Geneva Conference itself, Eden went further. In line with Eisenhower's 'open skies' proposals, he put forward an additional plan for the establishment of a joint inspection of the forces actually confronting each other in Central Europe. This, he suggested, could enter into operation independently of the main plan.

In other words, the additional plan involved a proposal for a *modus vivendi* in Central Europe which could come into operation without awaiting the resolution of the issue of German reunification, a shibboleth which was only to be abandoned in the late 1960s. Understandably, the Germans, who were supported by other NATO partners, strongly opposed the plan and Eden had to drop it; for the same reason the Russians found the plan positive.[23]

British–Soviet relations were gravely disrupted in 1956. Bulganin's letter threatening to use rockets over the Suez affair was a hostile gesture; although Eden was apparently unimpressed by it to the point of omitting to mention it when he telephoned to Sir Pierson Dixon, the British representative at the United Nations. Furthermore, the Soviet invasion of Hungary caused great indignation in Britain. By 1958, however, largely for domestic reasons, Macmillan returned to the temporarily suspended diplomatic initiatives for a detente. These culminated in his visit to Moscow in February 1959, during which he associated himself with Khrushchev in a declaration of common interest in the study of the limitation of arms and forces in agreed areas in Europe, the original Eden Plan, which had meanwhile been refurbished by the Polish Foreign Minister, Rapacki. The two statesmen also declared that 'differences between nations should be resolved by negotiation and not by force' and prepared the way for progress towards the abortive summit meeting in Paris in May 1960 and towards the Partial Nuclear Test Ban Treaty of 1963. Agreement on modest trade and cultural exchanges followed.

Undoubtedly this was the peak of British–Soviet relations. Later initiatives in East–West relations were taken by others, first by de Gaulle, who set himself to lead the West and to be the spokesman for Germany, and did not shrink from declaring his recognition of the Oder–Neisse frontier, whereas the British government sufficiently heeded German wishes to refuse to go so far. More importantly, direct communication between the Americans and the Russians, which had begun with the Camp David talks between Eisenhower and Khrushchev and was then encouraged by Kennedy, gradually became the pattern. The British continued in their endeavours to play a role in this central relationship; although they were less and less in a position to do so effectively, for some time their role remained by no means insignificant. Indeed, early in 1965, Kosygin suggested the revival of the meetings of the co-Chairmen of the Geneva Conference of 1954, which had been suspended by Khrushchev, and then went along with Wilson's initiatives to end the Vietnam conflict despite the latter's unswerving diplomatic support for the Americans. The British attempts petered out in 1967 and 1968, largely because the

Russians were unable to exercise control over the North Vietnamese, whose moves, especially the Tet offensive, made the Americans unreceptive to the British proposals.

The Labour victory of 1964 initiated a propitious amendment of the strategic doctrine: from 1965 the White Papers on Defence openly stated that a deliberate Soviet aggression in Europe was unlikely, even on a limited scale, and the Sandys doctrine of 'massive retaliation' was dropped; Britain took a leading part in the early non-proliferation talks and in revising NATO's strategy at the end of 1967. Nevertheless, relations between the two countries took a turn for the worse, in all likelihood because by 1967 the Russians fully realized that, despite Wilson's initiative, he was unable—and possibly unwilling—to exercise effective influence over American policies in Vietnam. At the end of the 1960s, the major initiatives passed decisively to the Americans and the Russians, who had by then firmly established direct communication, and also to Western Germany under the leadership of Willy Brandt. The adverse effects of the Soviet invasion of Czechoslovakia in 1968 upon public opinion in Britain was more severe and lasting than upon that of any other Western country and British/Soviet relations deteriorated accordingly. Hence, although Wilson's Minister of Technology, Anthony Wedgwood Benn, made several visits to Moscow to encourage trade, the political conditions for a substantial growth of such trade did not exist.

The Conservative government elected in 1970 had no major direct bilateral dealings with the Russians on issues of world order. The pronouncements of Sir Alec Douglas-Home, both before and after the election, expressed a deep-seated apprehension of communist expansion, increased by the deployment of the Soviet Navy in the Mediterranean and later also east of Suez. The British government was spurred to attempt to revitalize NATO and was given a reason, or at least a convenient rationalization, for a decision to allow the resumption of sales of arms to South Africa. Whereas British governments used to lead during the previous attempts at an East–West detente, ever since 1968, they had begun to lag behind their partners. By the early 1970s the Heath Government, influenced both by political caution and by military scepticism, was less than enthusiastic about the various levels of East–West negotiations, be it Herr Brandt's Ostpolitik, the European Security and Co-operation Conference, or the Mutual Balanced Force Reduction (MBFR). In 1971 the government decided to reduce the ranks of Soviet diplomatic and consular staff officials in London which had been swollen by large numbers of individuals apparently engaged in intelligence operations. The expulsion of the 105 Soviet representatives, which could be fully justified in terms of Britain's national security, manifested, nevertheless, the ebb of relations between the two countries and led, in turn, to their further deterioration: its adverse effects upon mutual trade and cultural relations lasted into 1973.

Until the end of the 1960s Britain perceived her major strategic interests in relations with the Soviet Union to be in closer correspondence with the United States than with her continental neighbours. In the early 1970s, despite a continuing idiosyncratic French foreign policy, her perceived interests came closer to those of her continental neighbours, in respect to such crucial issues as the increasingly intimate bilateral American–Soviet strategic talks, the imminent danger of the reduction of American troops stationed in Europe, a full Soviet acceptance of Western European integration, or the Russians' exercising restraint in their relations with China and with the Third World. For a number of years all the consultations regarding Western relations with the Soviet Union had taken place within the context of NATO, and the national British decisions were made within this context. The major change lay in Britain's abandonment of the fairly individual world role which she had been performing in close alignment with the United States and in her acceptance of the primacy of the Western European alignment. Instead of exercising initiative, Britain was now showing somewhat more caution and scepticism than either the Americans, the Germans or the French; this seemed to be more the result of a somewhat different appreciation of Soviet intentions than of a difference in the actual objectives pursued.

Another avenue of collective relations with the Soviet Union opened in January 1973 when the enlarged Community assumed powers to conduct commercial policy with the Eastern bloc on behalf of its members. This removed from full national control an area of Soviet-British relations of particular importance at a time when the Soviet Union was rapidly increasing her international trade. Moreover, it seemed possible, although, at least in the short run, very unlikely, that the Community might also become a focus for the co-ordination of Western European defences.

### The 'Special Relationship' with the United States

The British Embassy in Washington, which is unique in its size and in its replication of the major Whitehall structures, can be taken as a rough yardstick of the exceptional amount of business conducted between the two countries. Ever since 1945 the association with the United States has undoubtedly been Britain's most important and comprehensive relationship. Its uniquely intimate nature is not disputed by anyone but its precise significance and its effects frequently are. Its critics emphasize, Britain's excessive reliance upon American military assistance, particularly after the Nassau Agreement of 1962, and its crippling effect upon her relations with Europe, especially with France; second, sterling's dependence upon the dollar and the equally crippling effect of this upon Wilson's self-confidence and his freedom to manage the British economy. Others are more struck by the generosity of the Americans and their tolerance of Britain's continuing to pursue many policies with which they disagreed; the Americans did not use Britain's dependence upon United States military and economic assistance to demand compliance but generally only adopted attitudes described by Roy Jenkins as 'sympathetic and admonitory'. Neither interpretation is fully convincing.

'Special relationship' aptly describes an association of exceptional intimacy, based upon close and continuous international co-operation. In a sense Britain's relations with Australia and Canada came within this category, although these were much more limited in scope and were not so called. 'Special relationship' is not a clear-cut, well defined concept. It meant something quite different for the British, for whom it represented a central element of their foreign policy, and for the Americans, for whom it was much less important. Characteristically, only the British were in the habit of referring to the concept; of all the postwar American presidents, only Johnson and Nixon actually used the term, in a period when the relationship had lost much of its reality.

The essence of a 'special relationship' seems to lie in consultation and understanding rather than in agreement and influence. It can be analysed at three distinct levels: of the political leadership, of the officials, and of the public. Most spectacular was the top political level, exemplified by Churchill's close relations with Roosevelt and Truman, and Macmillan's with Eisenhower and Kennedy. These two British leaders, however, were the exception rather than the rule, both in their family connections with the United States and in their exceptional warmth towards the Americans. Eden, with his remote, somewhat patronizing attitude, represented more truly the tradition of Britain's interwar foreign policy; under Wilson and Heath the intimate pattern was again disrupted. The most effective and important layer was the official one, the habit of the military, intelligence, and civilian personnel, not exclusively of the highest rank, of engaging in a constant interchange of information and views on all issues of common interest, with the normal barriers of secrecy, both about security and technology, being, on the whole, fairly drastically reduced. This habit, which was based on wartime memories and friendships, throve against the background of the common outlook and feeling of the British and American elites and peoples throughout the first postwar decade. Issues of common interest were constantly discussed through the various stages of the formulation of national policies, before these had crystalized; and hence national policies miminized conflicts between the two states. Consultation and understanding did not necessarily amount to agreement but, in most cases, they resulted at least in an agreement to disagree, so that major open conflicts at higher levels were avoided. Indeed, as long as relations were normal, i.e. as long as the Foreign Office and the State Department were in full control, a serious conflict between the two countries was inconceivable. Characteristically, the two major cases of a breakdown—regarding Suez and Skybolt— were rooted in the political bypassing of official routines.

The 'special relationship' was limited in its application both geographically and functionally. It referred primarily to the central strategic balance and to Western European security, and its impact upon the handling of other issues was roughly proportionate to their distance from these central areas. It is not at all clear how far its effects extended from the strategic/diplomatic domain in which it was developed to the handling of economic issues. The linkages between economics and politics were somewhat unclear even during the war, when elements of commercial competition occasionally intruded upon the basic common objective of strengthening the war effort; Bevin was certainly aware of them when handling the issues of American involvement in the defence and economic rehabilitation of Western Europe and so was Macmillan during the Suez crisis; but their exact nature is fairly obscure. The only clear case of such linkages can be found between the sterling crisis and the issue of British support for American actions in Vietnam during the Wilson period. Johnson used the sterling issue to bring pressure upon Britain about Vietnam and the Labour government certainly felt constrained by its financial dependence upon Washington, although, conceivably, this was mainly a convenient argument for Wilson to damp down criticism within the Labour Party.

The three important characteristics of the 'special relationship' were first, its asymmetry, second, the different conceptualizations of it by the British and the Americans, and third, the misunderstandings between the two sides.

As regards the first point, the relationship was never one between equals. In the nineteenth century, Britain was a fully dominant factor in American foreign policy, whereas the United States played a relatively minor part in Britain's perceptions of the world. The rather peripheral importance of the Western Hemisphere issues—except Canada—to the British helps to explain why they so readily yielded to successive American demands. The roles became reversed in the first world war. In the interwar period the British were always eager to draw the Americans into world politics but nevertheless frequently acted as if the latter did not exist at all. The second world war again demonstrated how decisively Britain's very survival depended upon the United States.

The reversal in mutual significance was largely due to the reversal in the power of the two states. Although the first world war had already shown the United States to be more powerful, her subsequent withdrawal into isolation and her low levels of armaments disguised the growing discrepancy of power. On the eve of the second world war, in 1938, out of a population slightly over one-third of that of the United States Britain maintained some 428,000 men under arms as compared with a mere 328,000 Americans; her GNP was still about one-third that of the United States and her per capita income only slightly lower. Only Britain's exhaustion by her total war effort and the simultaneous upsurge of American industry put her into a different category of power. Although some Americans immediately noted Britain's weakness, this did not, at first, seriously affect her great power status. Although strategically and economically dependent on the United States, for several years she remained the only possible major ally, much more reliable and powerful than any other. With the passage of years, Britain was left far behind the superpowers in her strategic strength and behind other middle powers in her economic growth. While, for her, the American association retained its central importance, her own importance to the United States constantly diminished.

The difference in conceptualization stemmed from the growing disparity in resources: the relationship was, in fact, 'special' only for the British. This became clear already in the immediate postwar period when the Americans appeared to be the only possible partners for Britain in maintaining an international order within which Britain could enjoy a degree of strategic security, assistance for economic rehabilitation, and conditions for a gradual and orderly withdrawal from the Empire. Although the Labour Left cherished the idea of an association with the Soviet Union, such an association would have been unpromising in these vital respects even had the Russians been willing to consider it. The Americans, however, clearly showed that, on all major issues, they had no serious intention of adjusting their foreign and defence policies to accommodate British interests: they abruptly ended Lend-Lease, attached the convertibility clause to the loan, and proposed to withdraw their troops from Europe without awaiting some agreement with the Russians. Only the cold war, which made their vital strategic interests converge with those of the British, made them really concerned with Britain.

In retrospect, the heyday of the 'special relationship' can be aptly conceptualized in terms of a learning process in which the United States was assuming British responsibilities and was learning from British experience, one might say absorbing the imperial ethos. The learning process is highlighted in the personal relations between Truman and Churchill and Kennedy and Macmillan. In the process, the Americans gradually moved from their wartime opposition to British imperialism towards the established British view. This is shown by the case of Greece, in the contrast between Truman's agreement in 1947 to take over the British role and Admiral King's refusal to ship British troops there in 1944. To use Macmillan's well-known metaphor (see above, p. 163), in the late 1940s and early 1950s, the British were acting to the Americans as the Greeks had to the Romans. In the course of the learning process, however, as the Americans gained confidence, the nature of the relationship gradually changed, and they came to expect United Kingdom support rather than advice. The conceptualizations of the relationship on both sides of the Atlantic began to diverge again. After the initial period, United States 'deference' to British views became more and more limited. To some extent it continued in the central area of relations with Russia: although the Americans did not support British attempts at a detente, American and British experts continued to co-operate closely, including the drafting of telegrams to Moscow. It persisted for a while in the Eastern Mediterranean, somewhat longer in the Middle East, and even longer in the Persian Gulf and in Southern Asia. The Americans, however, held their own views and did not defer to the British in the areas of international economic policy, and deferred very little to them in their German and Western European policies immediately after the war.

The third major characteristic of the special relationship can be found in the nature of social communications between the two countries. Many writers and politicians spoke of an 'Atlantic community' with a common language and close cultural ties, and other similarities. Attention and communication were available for the development of mutual sympathies, trust, consideration, and for treating each other's requests sympathetically. In fact, misunderstandings easily arose when the correspondingly high expectations of each side were not fulfilled. Mutual responsiveness sometimes failed, the common language and culture were the basis not only of easy communications but also of easy misperceptions: as both countries were outspoken in their domestic debates, each other's moods and views were easily misunderstood. The most glaring example can be found in the Suez case in 1956 (see pp. 133ff.).

Turning to the historical evolution of Anglo-American relations, we can discern in them 'persistent, even steady, progress from mistrust to cordiality', ever since the later eighteenth century or at least since the Monroe Doctrine.[24] Some historians talk about 'an unavowed alliance', once the remaining conflicts between the two countries in the Western Hemisphere had been resolved early in the twentieth century. In fact, the historical record is much more ambiguous. The two nations saw eye to eye only over short periods and only over areas of common interests. The 'unavowed alliance' related only to the Western Hemisphere, which the United States wished to convert into its exclusive sphere of influence while Britain was happy to leave the responsibility for it in friendly hands. Co-operation in the first world war came late, was incomplete, and did not apply to Britain's postwar problems; interwar relations were remote and at times unfriendly. Thus the integration of the two countries in the common enterprise to defeat Hitler, which was aptly named 'special relationship', was a new event in British–American relations. Co-operation in the second world war was full, including consultation both at the official and the political level, the pooling of resources and the operation of common boards and commands and a common atomic-bomb programme. It must, however, be noted that American assistance was granted only after British resources had become depleted and that the Americans joined the war late and only after having been forced to do so by the Japanese attack. They retained full responsibility over the Pacific theatre, and major differences arose over a variety of important issues, such as the future of the Empire, the division of Europe into spheres of influence as proposed by Churchill and Stalin, the handling of the Russians, and the French problem and de Gaulle. Characteristically for British thinking, the first wartime plans for the postwar order considered by the Foreign Office in 1942 were evoked by American proposals which the British felt might be tantamount to the imposition of a *pax Americana* (see pp. 175ff.). Russia was at the time too weak to constitute a menace, and was even, theoretically, considered as a possible associate for Britain in organizing Europe, divided into two spheres of influence, in order to prevent the likelihood of American domination.

The last stages of wartime diplomacy were marked by a deterioration in the diplomatic co-operation between the two countries; Roosevelt was determined to deal directly with Stalin and differed sharply from Churchill on such crucial issues as the delimitation of postwar Europe, the disposition of Germany, the status of France, and the future of the British Empire. Moreover the intimate personal relations between Roosevelt and Churchill ceased with the death of the former and the electoral defeat of the latter. A series of shocks ensued: as Keynes had warned, the Americans were interested in the future and not in the past—'the old soldier showing his medals' would not be a persuasive advocate.[25] They continued their opposition to British imperial positions; they treated Britain harshly in her economic straits; they were rapidly dismantling their military strength in Europe without paying sufficient regard to the necessity of finding a prior agreement with the Russians. The 'special relationship' was re-established in 1947 on the basis of a common perception of a communist threat, but even this fundamental perception was not fully identical, except during the short period between the Truman Doctrine and the beginnings of the detente movement some time in the mid-1950s, specially during the crucial first 'fifteen weeks' in 1947. Although, at first, the British had to persuade the Americans of the seriousness of the Soviet danger, from 1947 they both became fully committed to their anti-communist alliance. Otherwise, British and American interests did not coincide and often directly clashed—over tariffs, nuclear weapons, the Middle East, and the nature of the security arrangements. Britain participated in the Korean conflict of 1950–1 but even here differences arose, especially over Communist China.

In the early 1950s, the relationship changed and became much less 'special': in the first instance, Britain became much less important for the United States in the latter's central strategic balance with the Soviet Union; Britain's nuclear programme was far behind whereas the Russians exploded their first H-bomb in 1952, only nine months after the Americans. Moreover, West Germany was becoming increasingly important: her economic recovery was rapidly restoring her as a major power, and she was both the only possible source of additional manpower for NATO and a potential strategic threat, should she decide to turn neutral. Second, the limitations of Britain's own power were becoming obvious as her economic recovery was slow and the Commonwealth did not fulfil expectations of its becoming a source of strength. Third, British-American differences in the Middle East, exacerbated by the personal antipathy between Eden and Dulles, flared up to the point of a direct confrontation over the Suez intervention. Simultaneously, the respective perceptions of the threats of communism, the very foundation of the alliance, also began to differ, too. Eden was much more strongly aware than the Americans of the possible scope for new initiatives which was opened up by Stalin's death. He was eager to exercise his diplomatic skills and to find a new, more independent place for Britain in East–West relations. He opposed Dulles's idea of a joint military intervention in Vietnam, and, despite the latter's misgivings, was instrumental in concluding the Geneva Agreements of 1954; in Europe itself, Eden launched the Plan named after him (see above, p. 200), which constituted the first Western effort to reach a detente in Europe.

Suez signified a breakdown of the 'special relationship' both at the official and political levels. Eden's bypassing of the Foreign Office broke the established pattern of official communications, both at higher and at lower levels, and engendered suspicion in the United States Administration. (The CIA, however, was not ignorant of the British plans.) At the political level, not only were the mistrust and dislike between Eden and Dulles further accentuated, but Eisenhower, a staunch friend of Britain, was filled with a sense of moral outrage at what he saw as an old-fashioned imperialist aggression.

Macmillan conceived the rebuilding of a close relationship with the United States as his main task. This proved easy at his initial meeting with President Eisenhower at Bermuda in March 1957, to a fair extent owing to the changed nature of nuclear technology. Following the Russian lead in rockets, the Americans became vitally interested in a forward base for their guided missiles and obtained it in Britain. In return, the British attained a degree of nuclear protection and influence through the 'two key' system by which the missiles were controlled. Moreover, at a further meeting with the President, in October, Macmillan secured an almost complete restoration of the nuclear collaboration which had preceded the restrictive MacMahon Act which had itself already been somewhat relaxed before Suez. Britain again became fully associated with the United States and secured a cheap development of her nuclear weapons, although at the cost of depending on the United States for the next generation of guided missiles.

Rather incongruously, this restored strategic association did not coincide with an identical reappraisal of the political aspects of relations with the Soviet Union. On the contrary, American and British views began increasingly to diverge, since Macmillan remained determined to work for a detente and to continue playing an individual work role as a mediator between the United States and the Soviet Union, whereas the Americans were becoming increasingly sceptical about his initiatives. The divergence crystallized around the issue of summit meetings, which the British advocated but the Americans distrusted. Macmillan decided on his own on his dramatic visit to Moscow in February 1959. The visit in itself did not succeed in achieving an East–West detente and strained the special relationship, but it helped to improve British–Soviet relations and to precipitate the gradual breaking of diplomatic ice between the United States and the Soviet Union. Although the summit eventually convened in Paris in May 1960 was abortive, the setback was not decisive. Macmillan's diplomatic initiatives served the useful purpose of holding together the whole Western alliance in the confusion following Dulles's death, the beginnings of Gaullist pressures, and Khrushchev's disorienting initiatives. Two years later, in 1962, the Cuban missile crisis was the last case of really close top-level consultation between Britain and the United States on a major East–West problem (see p. 164). It decisively inaugurated an era of increasing direct contacts between the two superpowers, without a British intermediary or any British participation, symbolized in the 'hot line'; but Macmillan's last successful independent initiative, for the Partial Test Ban Treaty negotiations, proved important in hastening the detente.

In the course of the British–American rapprochement, memories of Suez had to be obliterated and an attempt was made to reconcile the interests of the two countries in the Middle East. The United States retreated from the unilateral approach to the area embodied in 'the Eisenhower Doctrine', and agreed to participate in the Military Committee of the Baghdad Pact; in stark contrast to previous differences, the two countries concerted their interventions in Jordan and the Lebanon in 1958, on the eve of which Macmillan was said to have commented that sometimes it is better 'to do wrong together than to do the right things alone'.[26] The major negative result of revived British–American co-operation was upon relations with de Gaulle's France and with Western Europe as a whole.

Already in the early 1960s, however, the evolution of Intercontinental Ballistic Missiles (ICBM) began to undermine the major strategic basis of the nuclear special relationship. Moreover, Britain could no longer rely on a full coincidence of American and British strategic interests in Europe, as de Gaulle had previously noted: in the Cuban missiles crisis, although the British were closely consulted, the decisions were made by the Americans alone; it became clear that their new strategy of 'graduated deterrence' could lead to differences in Europe, and that, in this crucial security area, Britain's interests might coincide more closely with those of her continental allies, even though the ultimate United States deterrent continued to keep the nuclear balance. At the same time, the Americans became increasingly unwilling to accept continued British attempts to play the role of an intermediary with the Russians. President Johnson quite ruthlessly destroyed Wilson's last major attempt to do so during Kosygin's visit to London in February 1967, by insisting on a last-minute change in the wording of the negotiated agreement.[27] The issue of the increasing American involvement in Vietnam, which was the occasion of Wilson's attempt estranged the two countries for other, more important reasons: Wilson adamantly refused even a token British military contingent; and a large sector of British public opinion became strongly critical of the Americans and did not even approve of Britain's positive diplomatic support. Differences also arose over United States aid continuing to Indonesia during the Confrontation.

Wilson's abortive application to join the EEC and then Denis Healey's successful initiative to form the Eurogroup within NATO were the hallmarks of the growing distance between Britain and the United States. The Americans, who had been favouring European integration all the time, supported these moves. For them, after her withdrawal from east of Suez, Britain was rapidly becoming one of their European partners, traditionally friendly but not necessarily the most important one.

Heath opened a new era in British/American relations. He came to power with a firm continental orientation and without any personal links with the United States. His overriding foreign-policy objective was to secure Britain's entry into the EEC; and when the negotiations to this effect had been successfully concluded, the end of the 'special relationship' was formally declared in the communique issued after the Nixon–Heath meeting in Bermuda in December 1971; this had been preceded by a number of shocks and surprises in American foreign policy, in a way resembling American moves in 1945—the abrupt change in policy towards China, the lack of any advice about the drastic economic measures announced in August 1971, and the strong American support for Pakistan in the Indo–Pakistan War. The term 'special relationship' was now relegated to history—it was turned into a 'natural relationship'.

It seemed unlikely that in her new, European role, Britain could, as readily as some optimists had previously thought, cast herself in a new individual world role as a bridge between the enlarged community and the United States. The close personal relations between many British and American officials and the well-established habit of co-operation between the two countries were indeed bound to prove useful in establishing the machinery for consultation which was badly needed between the EEC and the United States; they were at least fully familiar with each others' views on all substantive issues and, on many of them, they did not widely diverge. Heath repeatedly declared himself in favour of establishing closer relations between the EEC and the United States but he showed no intention of acting as a mediator and interlocutor; it would not have been commensurate with Britain's waning economic power and would also have obstructed his efforts to find a suitable role within the Community, especially in the delicate early stages of British membership.

The common basic Anglo-American objective of Western European security persisted, although in a greatly changed form. The logical extension of the historical partnership in this respect could be expected to merge further into a broader European–American partnership which could be based on NATO or the enlarged Community, although neither institution was ideally suited for the purpose. The ultimate shape of the relationship depended upon the outcome of East–West negotiations, proceeding at their various levels—directly between the two superpowers, between the two Germanies and, on a broad alliance basis, in the European Security and Co-operation Conference. Britain participated only in the latter.

*Alliance Politics*

The wide and open discussion of foreign affairs in the United States and the central place of Anglo–American relations in British foreign policy combine to offer some general insights as to how the latter was operating. Although allowance must, of course, be made for the uniquely intimate nature of Anglo-American relations, some analogies may prove valid for the EEC context, and certainly some light is thrown on the interrelationship between central and less central issues.

The most striking phenomenon is the limited impact of the central relationship upon other policies conducted by the two allies. The basic common interest in containing communism in Europe—strongly reinforced by the traditional historical and wartime ties—resulted in a firm and close peacetime alliance, without precedent in the past of either nation. Combined with the established pattern of consultation, logically this should have led to co-ordination, or at least accommodation, of other, less important national interests of the two countries. This did not fully happen. Four general reasons for this suggest themselves. First, the foreign policies of world powers, as the two partners were throughout the period, include such a variety of issues and interests that full co-ordination, even within each country on its own, is an unattainable end. Second, the relationship was not equal but asymmetrical. In the central relationship, Britain undertook some initiatives on her own but, in the last resort, had to take her cue from the United States. Had her other policies been co-ordinated, this would inevitably have exercised an enormous restraint on her foreign policy as a whole, and would have put her in a position fully subordinate to the United States. Naturally, successive British governments determinedly asserted their independence on interests not falling squarely within the alliance; for their part, the Americans diplomatically preferred not to press their views and thus offend their important partner. Third, world interests did not fully overlap in scope and intensity; in the early part of the period, while Britain was the dominant power in the Middle East and in South-east Asia, American responsibilities and interests in these two areas were limited; towards its end, when American interests had greatly increased, Britain was retreating into Europe. Fourth, as both countries are democracies, the constraints imposed by the electorates on the conduct of foreign policy were occasionally significant. Nevertheless, Britain managed, on the whole, to conduct her relations with the United States smoothly. There were several serious disturbances, notably over the Suez and Skybolt affairs and about Palestine, but, with the exception of a temporary break after Suez, the continuity of the central alliance was not seriously disrupted.

How did the two partners fare in asserting their individual interests? Each disagreement could have ended in various ways—either with one side prevailing, or with both finding a mutually acceptable compromise somewhere in between their respective positions or by agreeing to disagree. The historical record includes many instances in which the great disparity in power forced Britain to abandon those of her interests opposed to or even merely unsupported by the United States. There was not much reality in Churchill's idea that the Old Dominions, which he included with the United States in one of the 'three circles', would somehow reinforce Britain's position within it *vis-à-vis* the latter. Wartime traditions and the respect in which the Americans generally held their most important postwar ally, were of much greater significance in enabling Britain to pursue her interests as she saw them and to try to persuade the Americans to support them. As many of the issues at stake were important in themselves, they warrant mentioning in some detail, especially the Suez affair.

In the context of Western Europe (see pp. 233ff.) the successive British governments withstood the continuous American pressures on them to join the European integration movement. Macmillan eventually became converted to the idea in 1960 because he had become convinced that the cost of exclusion was too high and the promise of membership and possible leadership attractive. By that time British and American policies coincided, especially as the willingness of the Kennedy Administration to proceed with the liberalization of world trade improved the prospect for Britain's continuing her overseas trade when within the Market. Previously, however, the British had only reluctantly accepted American initiatives for the rapid political rehabilitation and the rearmament of Western Germany; they stood firm against the threat of an 'agonizing reappraisal' and rejected the American-supported plans for the European Defence Community, but exercised their initiative to resolve the subsequent impasse. The basic strategy of NATO was inevitably based upon American ideas but, nevertheless, Britain effectively stalled the American proposals for an integrated NATO nuclear force which was to include her own deterrent. Thus dependence upon the United States for defence imposed restraints and pressures on Britain's European policy but did not prevent her from pursuing her interests even when these were opposed by the Americans.

While Europe was the primary concern of the British, they fully appreciated that the Americans have a Pacific coast. Although the British defended their own interests and differed from the Americans on several major issues, they accepted that the latter had their own legitimate order of priorities, and merely tried to moderate their behaviour. The sole instance of a really full co-operation in the Far East was the Korean conflict. Britain only contributed some 12,000 troops as compared with the 160,000 to 200,000 sent by the Americans, but had the valid excuse of conducting a parallel anti-communist action in Malaya on her own and also of being faced with an increased danger in Europe. The lack of sufficient consultation channels did, however, create awkwardness, especially in view of General MacArthur's initiatives; the weekly meetings within the United Nations Committee of Sixteen were inadequate. The British were extremely anxious that the conflict should not be extended without prior consultation, but were unable to exert any influence. Attlee's flight to Washington in an attempt to dissuade Truman from resorting to the use of the A-bomb was apparently unnecessary, as the President had already decided against this. In this case, Britain's lack of influence was not put to the test, but she was helpless in preventing the involvement of China.

A whole range of disagreements over the treatment of Communist China ended with a reluctant agreement to disagree. Britain's early recognition of the Central People's Government in Peking was in line with her habitual doctrine of recognizing governments in *de facto* control whereas non-recognition by the Americans was equally in line with their traditional doctrine that recognition is a political act which can be made conditional. One can safely assume that consultations on the subject were prolonged and acrimonious, but ultimately the Americans accepted the logic of Britain's being concerned with Hong Kong, her investments and trade, and the reactions of India. A similar agreement to disagree was reached about Britain's continuing her small trade with China through Hong Kong, with Hong Kong continuously informing the American government of its details. The two governments often voted differently on the issues of China's representation in the United Nations. The divergent recognition policies had, however, to be reconciled when negotiating the peace treaty with Japan in 1951—the compromise reached was to exclude both China and Taiwan from the peace conference.

The outcome of other disagreements was less happy. Although the Americans accepted, on Britain's insistence, a clause in the peace treaty that Japan should be free to choose to recognize either China, they, in fact, forced the Japanese to recognize Taiwan by making it abundantly clear that the Senate would otherwise refuse to ratify the treaty. Britain was most mortified, however, by the Americans firmly insisting that she should be excluded from the ANZUS Pact. This treaty merely recognized the fact that Australia and New Zealand had passed under United States protection, which had happened after the fall of Singapore, and no British interest was directly affected, but sentiments were deeply wounded. The incident is hard to explain, except by the Americans' lack of appreciation of the depth of British sentiments; the alleged reasons were insufficiently convincing to the British. Finally, in the 1950s, the Americans became more involved in the defence of Taiwan than the British thought prudent; in 1971, however, they suddenly reversed this policy of support in order to restore relations with Communist China. This was highly embarrassing to the British government, which had no opportunity to retreat from the compromise formula it had been supporting that the future of Taiwan was subject to determination by the peace treaty, an issue which was blocking an agreement to raise British–Chinese diplomatic missions to full ambassadorial level.

All in all, in the Far East, an area in which the United States was preponderant but where Britain had an important interest in Hong Kong and also in trade with China, the United States did not alter any line of policy in response to British influence. Throughout the period, Britain was not an important factor in American Far Eastern policies. In recognition of her special interests, the Americans accepted that Britain would pursue her own policy towards China. By 1971, however, the 'special relationship' had been so eroded that the Americans failed to communicate to the British the impending change in their China policy.

It was much more painful to both sides to agree to disagree about the 1954 Geneva Conference on Indochina, which to Eden represented a statesmanlike method of extricating the French from their involvement, whereas to Dulles it meant the distasteful prospect of sitting at the same table with Communist Chinese representatives and agreeing to communist rule over some 12 million people in North Vietnam. The violent disagreement continued over the subsequent American involvement in Indochina—Britain's influence helped to persuade the Americans to withdraw their support from a right-wing government brought into power in Laos by a CIA-supported coup, but it was ineffective in the course of the deepening American involvement in Vietnam. Here a compromise was achieved—the British did not send the token military contribution which the Americans desired but gave them their full diplomatic support, however reluctantly. On their part, the Americans did not support British operations in Malaya and did not seriously restrain Indonesia during the Confrontation. Thus, the record in South-east Asia indicates that the alliance did not result in coordination of policies, despite the common objective of containing communism in the region. Both a reason and a mitigating factor can be found in the lack of a substantial overlap in the two countries' interests: Britain was primarily interested in Malaya, the United States in Indochina, and the American involvement began only about the time of the French withdrawal from Indochina, when Malaya was on the road to independence. The Western attempt to establish a common institutional setting on the NATO pattern produced only a weak and ineffective imitation in SEATO.

Its strategic location and its oil made the Middle East much more directly relevant to the central alliance. There was, indeed, no doubt about both partners being equally concerned with the exclusion of the Russians from the southern flank of NATO, but they could not reach agreement about the strategic arrangements for the region. The British, being the traditionally dominant Power in the Middle East, were unable to induce the Americans to underwrite their policies, which aimed at maintaining their own influence. While the British were acutely aware of the importance of their Middle Eastern strategic and commercial interests and were also deeply attached to their lingering imperial position, especially as regards the Suez Canal, the Americans failed fully to appreciate either the importance of these interests or the intensity of these sentiments. It was extremely hard for the two countries to reach agreement about basic strategies. The British were reluctant to redefine their policies and accused the Americans of unwillingness to help them in their difficulties and of occasional irresponsible meddling; the Americans tended to dismiss British concerns as 'imperialism'.

Against the background of this basic disagreement, many specific conflicts arose: for instance over the lack of American support for British policies in Iran in 1946; and over the Middle Eastern Security Organization which eventually took the shape of the Baghdad (later CENTO) Pact, which the Americans refused to join. The problem of Palestine became the subject of continuous acrimonious disagreements. The British were unable to persuade their partners to take joint responsibility for a solution and were greatly hampered in extricating themselves from an untenable position by American pressures and tergiversations. The subsequent immediate recognition of Israel by President Truman and the lavish economic aid bestowed upon the new state increased the difficulties inherent in the British position in the Arab world. Besides this, the oil interests of the two countries had traditionally been in competition, and Britain obtained no support in her dispute with Iran which began in 1951. Within two years, however, the United States government came to recognize a basic identity of interests on the issue—to maintain the flow of oil from the Middle East. This transformation was due in no small degree to Britain's skilful and patient handling of the dispute through the World Court and the United Nations, refraining from the use of force. Perhaps the decisive element can be found in the gradual convergence of the views of American and British oil interests, whose major concern shifted from competition for concessions to the recognition of the common danger that such concessions could be nationalized. A compromise in the form of an international consortium was a successful and lasting solution.

The Suez Canal problem was much more central. Besides the important strategic and commercial interests it involved, it has a high symbolic value for both sides—for the British it was the lifeline of the Empire, for the Americans a notorious item of British imperialism. Thus the background to the 1956 events was uneasy. The Americans had persistently refused to support Britain in her negotiations with the Egyptians and to become associated with the joint security arrangements she proposed; eventually, in 1954, the British were forced to agree to withdraw their forces. The nationalization of the Canal was precipitated by the abrupt withdrawal of American support for building the Aswan Dam. The break in the alliance relationship over Suez had, however, additional reasons, lying within the faulty reciprocal perceptions of mutual reactions. Although the facts are generally known (see pp. 133ff.) a few details are discussed here because they shed light on the basic difficulty of Anglo–American relations: unwarranted illusions about the efficiency of the underlying social communications.

Undoubtedly Eden's perceptions of the reactions in Washington were blurred—he was aware that the Americans were eager for a peaceful solution while he was determined to remove Nasser by force. He construed the situation in Washington in a sense consistent with his design without realizing that for the Americans, in terms of their own politics, the policies he chose would have been about the hardest to endure. Eden's basic idea was that Eisenhower would 'lie doggo' until the elections, would remain conscious of analogies to the Panama Canal, and would acquiesce in a *fait accompli*. This rather muddled perception was largely due to stifled communications—not only was Dulles not in sympathy with Eden, but he too had to be careful, as he was not the principal, while Eden was exceptionally inhibited by engaging on a course of action which he was determined to keep secret at home. It was therefore possible for Eden to misperceive the constraints operating upon Eisenhower, notably by the false analogy between an American and a British pre-electoral situation. Inevitably, the result was a disappointed expectation —an occurrence which is much more acute in a close alliance than in a hostile relationship, as the disappointment is aggravated by the frustrations of assumed competence and of misplaced confidence.

The reconstruction by Professor Neustadt[28] of Eden's thinking is not based upon full evidence but it is convincing. The idea brought from Washington by Macmillan that Eisenhower would do nothing before the elections was based upon the traditional British interpretation of the importance of the Jewish vote in New York, which would ensure American passivity in an action in which Britain was associated with Israel. The basis of this interpretation was flimsy. It stems from the widely believed explanation of Truman's overruling of the State Department's advice in favour of an immediate recognition of Israel in 1948, by his concern with this Jewish vote, although possibly, as he himself averred, this explanation was wrong. In 1956, in any case, the electoral situation was entirely different. As a Republican, Eisenhower was not dependent on the Jewish vote in New York, which usually supports the Democrats, and much of which could have been expected to do so under any circumstances. The electoral arithmetic in this case was complex. Eisenhower was not really concerned with losing the New York vote which constituted 10 per cent of the Electoral College, as he was quite sure of a majority within it. What he wanted was as large an individual vote as possible— he wanted the support of the Jewish vote in New York but no more than the support of any other group and here the appeal of 'peace' seemed to offer the strongest general advantage.

The second misperception concerned the relations between Dulles and Eisenhower. Throughout the crisis, Eden seemed to draw some comfort from his interpretation of nuances in the thinking of the two and to hope that, in the last resort, he could rely on Eisenhower's personal friendship and make him disavow Dulles. In fact, Dulles was very conscious of his dependence upon the President and exerted himself to retain his confidence; he apparently cleared with him in advance every major move throughout the crisis.[29] The third misperception related to the Panama analogy. Undoubtedly the Americans would intervene there if any serious fighting started near the Canal, but, for them, the analogy with Suez was shaky; the British explanation of intervention was too thin, it could not be squared with the Tripartite Declaration which the Americans had invoked and, in its slow motion, it was something quite remote from American ideas of defence. Finally, and decisively, Britain could not complete the intervention owing to the impending collapse of the pound. The Cabinet had to call the operation off without having the opportunity to find out whether, despite all the misperceptions mentioned, the Americans might not, after all, have acquiesced in a completed intervention: Dulles's alleged remark to Selwyn Lloyd: 'Why did you stop?', seems to indicate this possibility.[30]

Thus the Suez affair showed, both in Britain's relations with the United States and in general, how difficult it is to exercise influence over another state: this involves diverting the other party from its own domestic concerns to matters which may be of very unequal priority for it. Misperceptions played a large part in leading to the failure, and Neustadt suggests two possible ways in which Dulles might have avoided the clash: either by putting teeth into the Suez Canal Users' Association (SCUA) or by sending to London a contingent form of the 'ultimatum' about the pound which Britain received only after the event. It is rather telling that he cannot suggest a way in which Britain could have avoided it —except, of course, by completing the action swiftly, for which she lacked capability, or by not undertaking it at all.

# 10 Britain's Major Relationships II: The Commonwealth, Western Europe, and the United Nations

FOR a complete account of British policies towards the individual regions and states, the reader must be referred to history books.[1] The three areas of policy in this chapter have been selected as much on the basis of their relevance for illustrating the argument of this book as of their intrinsic importance; this explains the exclusion of such obviously important topics as British relations with the Middle East or with France. The choice of the first two areas is self-evident: the Commonwealth was the major element in the conceptions of Britain's world role and in her foreign policy during the first fifteen postwar years; Western Europe has been the dominant issue of her foreign policy since then and is likely to constitute its major element in the future. The choice of British United Nations policy which, in itself, is rather unimportant, requires a brief explanation. As far as possible, this discussion has not been limited to actual policies but has been extended to their alternatives, to the 'what might have beens'. As many of the critics of British foreign policy regard the United Nations as a major unutilized alternative, the inclusion of a section on it seems logical.

The three following accounts are limited to the essentials relevant to the main argument of this book. This explains their inclusion in one chapter which, as a result, becomes heterogeneous.

## The Commonwealth Idea
Even in the heyday of the Empire, imperial ideas were not a coherent nation-wide orthodoxy but were criticized and opposed by many Englishmen. Nevertheless, the national involvement in the Empire was an important reality at all social levels and was by no means limited to the upper and the upper-middle classes. Not only was the Empire the source of Britain's military and economic power and of national pride, but it also provided many individual Britons with a good income, with

outlets for their energy and with opportunities for their careers. All these gains were not without a cost. Already early in the twentieth century the British military planners had become thoroughly alarmed at 'the strategists' nightmare' posed by the problems of imperial defence; after 1945 the economists began to appreciate the opportunity cost of having developed the Empire while neglecting to modernize Britain's own industry and economic infrastructure; during the 1960s an increasing number of Britons became convinced of the dangers of what gradually became called 'the Commonwealth myth' which had helped to mask Britain's loss of power, diverted her energies, and delayed her adjustment to the postwar world.

In the interwar period, the White Dominions successfully moved towards greater political independence by means of graduated constitutional change, and were defined by the Balfour formula of 1926 as 'autonomous communities equal in status' in the British Commonwealth. They refused to contribute to imperial defence but operated as a serious restraint upon constructive British policies in Europe. However, the tightening of the economic ties in the Commonwealth by the establishment of imperial preferences in 1932 and the entry of each of the Dominions into the second world war on Britain's side—although this time by individual decisions—helped to prolong the British belief in the Commonwealth's usefulness; India's successful incorporation in it helped to obliterate the memory of the persistent refusal of the Congress Party to participate in the war effort. Despite all the troubles in India, Burma, Egypt, and Palestine, most Britons unconsciously continued to think about the immediate postwar world in terms of a *Pax Britannica*. Britain was expected to continue bearing her responsibilities on the assumptions of a basic solidarity and identity of interests and of the ultimate desirability of maintaining the Commonwealth. The Commonwealth seemed to be the most promising way of resolving Britain's dilemma of having to choose between either becoming ineluctably reduced to the status of a mere European power (which had been noted already by Seeley) or accepting some form of American hegemony. The Commonwealth became the foundation of Churchill's influential doctrine of the 'three circles' (see above pp. 150ff.), which replaced his unattainable idea of a union of the 'English-speaking peoples'. It successfully incorporated Southern Asia; the rest of the Empire was stable and the strategic communication lines remained intact; it was a major trading area in the world, within which, in 1951, Britain was the largest customer and the largest supplier of all the member countries except Canada. No wonder it appealed to the imagination of many as a unique inter-racial, rich/poor brotherhood of nations. Public opinion in Britain and almost all the leaders in other member-countries—except perhaps Malan and his supporters—fully agreed with the British leaders about the value of the Commonwealth. The picture was not without clouds as there were troubles in Malaya, Kenya, the Gold Coast, Nigeria, and British Guiana, and racial discrimination in South Africa, but, for a whole decade after the emancipation of the Indian sub-continent, the Commonwealth remained intact.

Fifteen years later the situation had completely changed. Britain had turned decisively to Europe and, after a whole decade of trying, eventually joined the EEC; she had emancipated some 600 million people and had retained from her vast Empire a residue of nineteen small scattered territories with a total population of some 5 million, 4 million of whom lived in Hong Kong the independence of which was precluded by its relationship to China; the Commonwealth had disappointed earlier high hopes in its role as a successor to the Empire, both in actual practice and in the estimate of the British political elite and public. The beginning of this fundamental transformation of British foreign policy is generally found in the Suez affair in 1956. The decision to withdraw from east of Suez in 1967, the Duncan Report in 1969, and the entry into the EEC on 1 January 1973 were the major formal expressions of the logic of the end of empire.

Needless to say this was a painful process, undertaken reluctantly, to all appearances inevitably forced upon the British by the evolution of Commonwealth affairs. For analytical purposes we can recognize within the flow of events four major strands: the role of the Commonwealth in the conduct of British foreign policy; economics; events within individual Commonwealth countries; events within the Commonwealth. In reality, of course, all these were closely connected.

The first and most directly relevant strand lay in the gradual diminution in the practical uses to British diplomacy to which the Commonwealth could be put; instead of being a potential asset which could at least occasionally be used, the Commonwealth became a liability and was therefore seen increasingly in terms of Commonwealth responsibilities rather than opportunities. In the earlier 1950s, links proved useful in implementing British policies in the Far East: a Commonwealth division took part in the Korean action and India was closely associated with it; at the Geneva Conference in 1954, India and Canada became members of the International Control Commission while Britain became co-Chairman with the Soviet Union; Australia, New Zealand, and Malaya had been co-operating with Britain in maintaining the security of South-east Asia since 1955 which facilitated the British withdrawal from east of Suez from the end of the 1960s, leaving residual security arrangements even into the 1970s. In the Suez affair, however, the Commonwealth was of no use as, with the exception of Australia, its members were highly critical of Britain's action. Moreover, remaining dependencies were becoming an embarrassment once other Empires had disintegrated, and, as Ian Macleod, who himself greatly hastened the process of emancipation in British Africa, was reported to have said, his, as well as subsequent British governments had no intention of remaining the last colonial power in Africa alongside Portugal. The disposal of the remaining dependencies frequently proved difficult, as was exemplified in the affair of Anguilla rebelling against St Kitts. Even more serious were British commitments when emancipated Commonwealth members became embroiled with outsiders (the Sino-Indian War in 1962 and the Confrontation), among themselves (the two 1965 rounds of the Indo-Pakistani conflict), or split by civil war (Nigeria). In the 1960s it became increasingly clear that, far from being a support, the Commonwealth was a liability.

The economic importance of the Commonwealth to Britain rapidly decreased as British business did not adjust itself to the changing trading conditions within it. Between 1951 and 1961 the Commonwealth proportion of Britain's exports dropped from 50 to 39 per cent whereas her exports to the EEC countries grew from 25 to 32 per cent. Moreover, most of the British foreign investment which was directed to the Commonwealth through the arrangements of the sterling bloc proved to be relatively unremunerative. Finally, Commonwealth immigration provided a useful reservoir of labour but the rapid growth in the number of immigrants became a source of domestic difficulties, leading to a series of increasingly restrictive Immigration Acts, which affected Britain's popularity in the Commonwealth.

Events within individual Commonwealth countries were highly discouraging. The original constitutions did not last long and were frequently removed by military coups d'état, beginning with Pakistan in 1960; with the signal but only partial exception of India, parliamentary democratic institutions disappeared. Racial problems arose—first through the treatment of the non-whites in South Africa and then in that of the Indians, Pakistanis, and whites in East Africa.

The structure of the Commonwealth came under severe strain owing to the combination of three factors: the multiplication of membership, the slackening of British leadership, and the growing determination of its members to discuss the domestic affairs of other members, which forced

South Africa to withdraw in 1961. The 'management' of Commonwealth affairs shifted from Whitehall to the Commonwealth Secretariat established in 1965, and in 1968 the Commonwealth Relations Office was wound up, symbolizing the growing limitation of close informal relations. The Commonwealth Prime Ministers' Conferences degenerated into a forum for acrimonious public debates until, at the tense Conference at Singapore in 1971, which centred on the British decision to resume arms sales to South Africa, Heath announced what may be regarded as a declaration of independence for Britain from the Commonwealth.

Naturally, at many points Commonwealth affairs were linked with issues of the central strategic balance, but they were conducted and thought about to a large extent autonomously and it is not, therefore, easy to incorporate them in an analysis of foreign policy. Rather characteristically, in the early wartime planning efforts discussed by Lord Gladwyn in his memoirs, the question of the priority to be accorded to imperial and Commonwealth interests was put without integrating it with the broader issues of global strategy; it was never satisfactorily answered. Although a rational appreciation of the Commonwealth was difficult, the emotional attachment of the British to the idea of it could not be doubted. Both Attlee and Churchill expressed their preference for the Commonwealth over Europe during the House of Commons debate on 5 May 1948, after the signature of the Brussels Treaty; it was the Commonwealth attachment which made Sir Anthony Eden exclaim, when discussing the European Defence Community four years later, that joining a European Federation was something the British knew, in their bones, they could not do; the Commonwealth was the centre of Gaitskell's image of one thousand years of British history. As John Strachey put it, the Commonwealth served as a transitional system which facilitated the emancipation of the Empire and helped the British to assuage a 'sense of personal loss—almost an amputation' which occurred whenever a part of it was granted independence.[2]

Until the early 1960s, almost the entire British political elite shared these sentiments and their attitudes changed fairly slowly. According to the survey published by *The Times* on 1 October 1971, even those listed in *Who's Who* (who included a much larger number of converts to Europe than others) in 1963 still gave the Commonwealth the highest rating for being 'very valuable' among the international groupings—69 per cent against 63 for NATO and 42 per cent for the Common Market; by 1971 however, the percentage had dropped to 31, well below the 62 per cent rating for the Common Market and the 52 per cent for NATO.

Motivations differed widely. Labour supporters were interested mainly in the New Commonwealth, while Conservative supporters were more concerned with imperial defence, British investments, and imperial preferences. For a long time the accusation of 'scuttling' was politically dangerous. For instance, when Lord Salisbury resigned from the Cabinet in 1957 over Lord Home's decision to free Archbishop Makarios from exile as an essential prelude to granting Cyprus independence. Macmillan had to tread warily in yielding to Macleod's pressures from the Colonial Office for rapid grants of independence in Africa, and his famous 'wind of change' speech in Africa in 1960 was deliberately vague and ambiguous; his turn to Europe was undertaken in an extremely low key. The argument questioning the utility of the Commonwealth to Britain was first authoritatively raised in public only in April 1964 by an anonymous 'Conservative'—widely believed to have been Enoch Powell—who, in an article in *The Times*, graphically described the Commonwealth as 'the ghost of the British Empire sitting crowned upon the grave thereof'. The Labour government elected in 1964 attempted to revive British faith in the Commonwealth, attributing the strains within it, as well as within the domestic economy, to Tory mismanagement. By 1967, however, the economic problems had proved resistant to Labour policies and the government felt impelled to abandon the idea of any sizeable British military presence east of Suez and to turn once more to Europe.

It is harder to estimate the changing attitudes of the British people. Public opinion polls show that a high percentage continued to regard the Commonwealth as valuable, but one cannot determine to what extent their opinions were considered and lasting. Undoubtedly there existed a vague general emotional attachment, on the lines simply expressed by Field-Marshal Montgomery: 'Bottled up in men are great emotional forces which have got to be given an outlet which is positive and constructive and warms the heart and excites the imagination'.[3] The imperial and then the Commonwealth idea provided just such an outlet, although, when Britain was preoccupied with domestic troubles, Commonwealth affairs were readily forgotten. Perhaps the most telling example is that furnished by Hugh Dalton about the granting of independence to India: 'I don't believe that one person in a hundred thousand in this country cares tuppence about [India] so long as British people are not being mauled about out there.' The Act granting independence was passed without division in both houses of parliament; there was little sense of occasion.[4] Perhaps this apparent discrepancy is explicable in terms of a differentiation between a Commonwealth idea as an aspiration, and operational Commonwealth policies. With the majority of the people the aspiration seems to have been much stronger than interest in actual policies. To some extent this seems also to apply to the political elite; it helps us to understand why interest in the Commonwealth, both in scholarly writings and in Hansard, relates mainly to the period of British rule rather than to the post-independence relations in the context of which actual policies are determined.

Although the Commonwealth idea was thus occasionally forgotten and was gradually losing lustre, there was no alternative to replace it. The turn to Europe which sounded its death knell was not clearly connected with the Commonwealth in political argument. Britain's three successive applications to join the EEC were presented to the British public in a deliberately low key, as involving mainly commercial and technological rearrangements, and not as a complete substitute of the lofty Commonwealth idea. Other Commonwealth members had reservations, generally very grave ones, about Britain's proposed European alignment, but the aspirations and wishes of the majority of the Commonwealth countries and those of Britain which clashed most violently, leading to the impasse at the Commonwealth Prime Ministers' Conference at Singapore in January 1971, were not over Europe but over the governmental decision to resume sales of arms to South Africa which, for Britain, is clearly of only marginal importance.

## Commonwealth Politics

The basic and so far not clearly answerable question is whether the Commonwealth was an asset or a liability in postwar British foreign policy or, more precisely, to what extent was it the one or the other. As recently as 1968, the late Leonard Beaton argued that imperial ambitions could be legitimately construed as a rational part of national interest, and that the contributions to the standing of the imperial power and to its prestige were real even though some economists now disputed the reality of imperial economic contributions.[5]

Even if there was some substance in this argument, although scarcely as late as 1968, the concomitant notion that the Commonwealth constituted some part of a meaningful general sub-system of the world system in which Britain could not only be a leader but could also find her major role in the world, was no more than an illusion. There was not much in foreign or defence policies that the independent Commonwealth countries could agree upon even in the 1950s. The situation was highly anomalous for Britain, who was expected to govern her foreign policy not only by her own, British interests, but also by those of the other members and who was incapable to agreeing with them about most interests, and was not in a position to mobilize the resources of the other members even to pursue such interests as they had agreed to be in common.[6] This is, in general, a tenable proposition but the evaluation of the individual cases is frequently dubious. Thus one of the major reasons why Britain felt impelled to press on with the recognition of the communist government of China seems to have been the fear of a racial split within the Commonwealth, as India and Pakistan were determined to recognize it, whereas Australia and New Zealand decided not to do so. But another major reason was Britain's desire to preserve Hong Kong and her Chinese trade and investments. Conceivably, far from curbing Britain's freedom of choice in the matter, the Commonwealth pressures provided her with a convenient excuse to the Americans for doing what she felt was in her interests, but was strongly opposed by them.

Under the circumstances, the idea put forward by some anti-Europeans that it would have been possible to extend and strengthen Commonwealth links to the point of making the Commonwealth a meaningful alternative to Europe was illusory. This somewhat romantic notion of the Commonwealth becoming the sole or the major mainstay of British foreign policy was impracticable and, in fact, contravened the prevalent broader ideas of the three circles and of Britain's world role, as has been well expressed by Professor Bruce Miller:

At best the Commonwealth can be a weapon in Britain's diplomatic armoury, but not the armoury itself. It can be a resource which Britain employs for certain of its purposes but not for all. As such, its utility may not be great and will certainly not be universal.[7]

In retrospect, to many critics of Britain's postwar foreign policy, especially to those who are ardently pro-European, the continuing belief in the Commonwealth appears to have been a way of dodging the unpalatable realities of the postwar world which enabled the Foreign Office to continue pursuing a world role and the Treasury to defend sterling long after the basis for these two policies had been finally shattered by the Suez expedition. The loss of opportunities in Europe was the heavy price paid. Peter Calvocoressi justifiably claimed:

The intellectual and emotional resources which had gone into thinking about world affairs—whether about running the Empire or getting rid of it—could have been switched to thinking about Europe's affairs and to deciding a role for Britain in Europe.[8]

The Commonwealth made severe demands on the time and energy of British Prime Ministers. During the financial crisis early in 1961, the issues of South Africa and of Southern Rhodesia were highly distracting for Macmillan; Wilson spent an inordinate amount of time on the Commonwealth Prime Ministers' Conference in June 1965.[9] In more general terms, the Commonwealth could be regarded as a misleading and pernicious myth. According to one outspoken critic of British politics, the public image of the Commonwealth was presented 'to the British people and in our diplomacy as being some special political and moral entity and, worst of all, be invoked as yet another excuse for not taking decisions.'[10] Although many members of the establishment were well aware of the realities of life and of the contradictory ambitions of the Commonwealth leaders, they too 'joined in maintaining a pretence which in the end created more problems than it was covering up'. More specifically, 'the Commonwealth Myth, substituting for the imperial role, imposed limits on British policy in the hope of pleasing her Commonwealth associates'. It became inextricably intertwined with the maintenance of the international currency role of sterling, blurring and confusing the feasibility parameters of British policy, and resulting in an international economic policy which was detrimental to British national interests.[11]

All these negative *ex post* verdicts about the value of the Commonwealth to Britain seem to be largely justified, but only in application to the latter part of the postwar period. For a whole decade, between 1947 and the Suez affair and the new spate of grants of independence beginning in 1957, Britain remained relatively undisturbed in control of a large part of Africa. The complexity of the international issues and the uncertainty about the role of the Commonwealth unavoidably baffled the policy-makers and the various experts involved. But it is nevertheless true that, particularly in the early 1960s, when clarification of the issues became easier, an element of inertia and of wishful thinking seems to have reinforced the powerful imperial traditions; and it was not restricted to the politicians and the civil servants. For instance, the Confederation of British Industry endeavoured, in its own commentary, to gloss over an important negative conclusion of the Reddaway Report on investment overseas (which it had itself commissioned); that the chronic balance-of-payments deficits should outweigh the long-term benefits of such investment.[12]

The political problems of the Commonwealth can be conveniently divided under three headings: issues of Commonwealth organization, of British influence over other members, and of the influence of other members over Britain.

The two linked major organizational issues lay, first, in the adaptation of Britain's position as *primus inter pares* to one of equality with the members and, second, in the enlarged membership. In the interwar period, Britain's historical leadership and undisputed position of being the hub of Commonwealth communications enabled her to reconcile her position with that of the 'sovereign equality' of the Dominions. The new Asian members fitted reasonably well into this pattern, once a compromise formula had been devised to allow India to join under a republican regime. In the later 1950s, however, Africa provided the new members. New tensions arose through the 'British' character of the Commonwealth, through Britain's gradually losing her central role, and through the Commonwealth now including a number of very small states. Britain adapted herself to her new, less dominant position relatively successfully—the paternalistic attitudes to African territories were rapidly shed.[13] The Commonwealth Secretariat headquarters was established in London, but its Secretary-General, Arnold Smith, former Canadian Ambassador and Minister, deliberately sought to stress its multinational and multiracial character and the fact that it was no longer Anglocentric.

Some problems of the enlarged, heterogeneous Commonwealth proved to be intractable. Perhaps one should single out the complex dilemma arising from its racial composition and from the inclusion of many small states.[14] Britain took a clear stand for equality between individuals, regardless of race; this can be regarded as the main reason which compelled the South Africans to withdraw from the Commonwealth in 1961. She was, however, unable to resolve the problem of Southern Rhodesia after the disintegration of the Central African Federation. From the British point of view, the economic sanctions on which she embarked proved costly and yet they did not ensure adequate recognition from the Commonwealth; on the contrary, its African members consistently accused Britain of lacking the will to act decisively, i.e. by using military force. The desire to avoid accusations of racial bias forced the British to be attentive to the wishes of the non-white small members of the Commonwealth. Thus the racial problem made it impossible for the Commonwealth to accommodate its working to the existing inequalities of power within it and constituted a kind of restraint which did not operate in a racially homogeneous organization like the EEC.

Another major problem arose from the mutual inability of the members to control one another's domestic policies. On the one hand, the British were unable to prevail upon the other members either to maintain parliamentary institutions and to prevent the rise of military dictatorships, or to uphold the federations established by the British in Central Africa, the West Indies, or Malaysia; on the other hand, the Commonwealth partners were extremely sensitive to Britain's behaviour, and expected her to observe a stricter code of conduct than that of some of their own number. Hence mutual irritations—of the British over the 'dual standards' and of the others over their inability to prevail—in cases like that of Suez, which was partly comparable with Goa, or of British regulation of immigration which, in a way, could be compared with the treatment of the Asians in East Africa.

The unlimited right of Commonwealth citizens to enter Britain acted as an important stimulus in turning the Commonwealth into an extremely sensitive issue of British domestic politics which reduced its attractions for part of the British public. The rapid influx of Commonwealth immigrants to Britain in the 1950s, and their high birth-rates soon increased the numbers of the new settlers to over a million, and gave rise to racial tensions accentuated by their concentration in a few major urban areas and by the general shortage of housing. This resulted in increasingly restrictive immigration regulations through the 1962 Act and the 1965 and 1968 reductions in quotas. The successive governments set themselves the tasks of eliminating racial discrimination and of creating conditions for the assimilation of the immigrants into British society. These proved difficult to achieve but did not seem to be seriously hampered by the involvement of the individual immigrant groups in major policy differences between Britain and their countries of origin.

Furthermore, the Commonwealth did not, as might be superficially expected, exactly facilitate the relations between Britain and the individual members. On the one hand, Britain was drawn into taking a stand on almost all the intra-Commonwealth disputes, whether arising from domestic issues, like the Biafran breakaway movement, or from inter-state conflicts, like that between India and Pakistan. On the other, through the obligation to make arrangements embracing the whole Commonwealth, Britain's intimate relations with Australia and New Zealand were not developed to the full and were even adversely affected, for instance when she applied irritating immigration restrictions to their citizens, even though these rarely wished to settle permanently in Britain. She jeopardized her relations with South Africa, even though this is an important market and area of investment.

In foreign policy, major, occasionally overlapping differences arose, first, about colonialism, second, about attitudes to communism, and third through the tension between membership of the Commonwealth and the regional pulls to which the individual members were subject. The issue of colonialism resulted in a fairly general alignment of the new members behind the increasing anti-colonial pressures of the Afro-Asian bloc and its various manifestations in the United Nations. It also lingered in the minds of many Americans, who somehow did not draw a clear distinction between the Commonwealth and the Empire and continued to suspect Britain of covert imperialism. Allied with this was the American reluctance to accept, and to respond to, the British anxieties over the spread of communism in Malaya and over the communist threat to the Indian Ocean (a reluctance reciprocated by Britain regarding Vietnam). The Americans changed their minds only when the British retreat from east of Suez was decided upon in 1967 but the anxieties of the Afro-Asians on that score were given new nourishment by the British decision to resume the sale of arms to South Africa in 1970.

Major fissiparous tendencies in the Commonwealth arose through a variety of regional forces acting upon the individual members and the great and originally unexpected profusion of regional groupings on all continents. For some time, Britain had not been able to guarantee the security of the outlying members, first Canada and then also Australia and New Zealand. The 'special relationship' between Britain and the United States eased the transition of these Old Dominions from British to American protection, but not without some friction, especially over the exclusive ANZUS agreement. While Australia's dependence upon the United States led to foreign-policy postures on issues such as non-recognition of the Peking government and participation in the Vietnam conflict which coincided with those of the Americans and not the British, Australia's growing identification with Asia created some additional divergencies. Thus she pursued an independent line on Indonesia, as when, despite British misgivings, she supported United Nations involvement in 1948–9 and participated in the Good Offices Committee initiated by the Security Council. As Britain gradually became less important as a provider of security, capital, and immigrants, relations with her, including the new Five-Power-Security-Agreement and the Commonwealth as such, were increasingly likely to provide no more than a sort of intermittent backdrop for Australia's Asian policies, which were bound mainly to be determined by the policies of the great powers and of the major local powers.

India frowned upon regional security arrangements in Asia such as SEATO and pursued a path of non-alignment which brought her into close relations with the communist powers, first China and then the Soviet Union. The African states were torn between the Commonwealth and the Organization for African Unity (OAU). Some members of the latter raised questions about the compatibility of being members of both and occasionally tried to determine the policy positions within the OAU for the Commonwealth members: 'the situation eased off only with the weakening of Africanism in the later 1960s, by which time the Commonwealth itself had been greatly weakened'.[15]

As may well be expected, Britain's turn to Europe in 1960 imposed the greatest strain. In 1961 the idea of Britain's becoming a member of a close European regional grouping was unpalatable to all the members of the Commonwealth and united the old and the new ones in disliking the British move. Previously, the two groups had frequently disagreed—Australia, especially, pursued a different line from the new members on such important divisive issues as the Suez intervention or South African membership. The Commonwealth loomed large in British negotiations with the EEC for two main reasons. First, there were the specific individual interests of each Commonwealth member for which accommodation had to be sought; this was an important and time-consuming issue, particularly during the first round of EEC negotiations in 1961. Second, up to the end of the 1960s, even more fundamentally important was the damaging effect of the Commonwealth upon the credibility of Britain's commitment to Europe. Alongside the 'special relationship' it was the Commonwealth link which induced de Gaulle to oppose Britain's entry on the grounds that she had not become sufficiently European. Ultimately, by 1971, the Commonwealth members had become reconciled to the apparent inevitability of Britain's entry and the weakening of the Commonwealth; they restricted themselves to endeavours to prevail upon Britain to see to the protection of their special interests—particularly New Zealand dairy produce and West Indian sugar. Only the government of Australia declared itself dissatisfied with Britain's final arrangements; this is characteristic of the degree to which the significance of the Commonwealth had been eroded, both for Britain and for the other members. Conceivably, the Commonwealth, which has survived some severe crises, will also survive that entailed by Britain's membership of the EEC. At a meeting of the representatives of thirty Commonwealth members in April 1972 to review the possibilities open to them on British accession to the EEC, the Secretary General, Arnold Smith, saw the future of the Commonwealth links in preventing South North polarization:

'At all costs', [he said,] 'I think, we must, in the common interests of humanity, avoid the tendency to polarization of the world in terms of Continental, ideological and economic groupings. I hope, therefore, that the enlarged Europe and the countries which come to be linked with it organically will be outward-looking so that the EEC itself can become one of the powerful influences against polarization.'[16]

## British Attitudes to Western Europe

How are we to explain Britain's neglecting to take a lead in Western

European affairs when it was open to her in the later 1940s and in the 1950s? In retrospect, this seems to be the fundamental and most costly mistake in postwar policies; moreover, it cannot be attributed to the un-controllable nature of the changes in Europe; its causes must be sought in the faulty perceptions, anticipations and priorities of the successive British Governments.

Like all negative questions, this one cannot be answered conclusively. It certainly cannot be tackled solely in terms of the continental-oceanic dichotomy which dominated the issue in the 1960s and early 1970s. The postwar Labour government cannot be accused of devoting itself to the Commonwealth or the United States links at the expense of neglecting Europe; on the contrary, the issues of European security and economic rehabilitation, which clearly affected Britain's most vital interests, not only intimately involved the United States but were as salient for the government as the most important Commonwealth affairs, even the emancipation of India. The roots of the relative neglect of Europe and of the excessive concentration upon the Commonwealth later on can be sought partly in the immediate postwar policies, interpreted against their more remote historical background, but mainly in the attitudes which the political leadership and public opinion in Britain adopted to European integration.

History lends itself to the support of opposed arguments. The pro-ponents and the opponents of Britain's entry into the EEC readily found evidence to support their respective views, although, in most cases, it can be regarded as a mere rationalization of preconceived attitudes. During the debate on the first British application in 1962, Hugh Gaitskell claimed that Britain could not turn her back on 'one thousand years of history'; to Roy Jenkins, Britain had always been a European state and her major wars and diplomatic efforts had always centred upon Europe. Similarly, the argument about the intimate links with the 'English-speaking people' can be readily balanced by one that Britain has preserved some major common historical traditions with Europe, such as those of a settled community and of politics at local level, and also a similar class structure.

In terms of her historical experience, Britain's intensive and exhausting participation in the second world war should have been followed by a period of withdrawal from European affairs, once the challenge to the balance of power had been decisively removed and a new balance had been established. The sustained British efforts to establish a postwar balance could be interpreted as being no more than the preparation of conditions for such a withdrawal, a parallel for which could be found in the past after every major European war. Therefore, British and continental outlooks, although based upon the identical immediate broad objectives of security and of economic rehabilitation and on the acceptance of American assistance in both, differed in their time-scale—for Britain these arrangements were meant to facilitate as early as possible a withdrawal, for the Continental nations, they had to constitute a long-term order. Another, even more significant difference lay in the power positions of the individual nations. Britain was a victorious nation and one of the Big Three, whereas all the continental nations had been either defeated or occupied and humiliated, and their power was non-existent or very low. Although co-operation across the Channel proceeded smoothly both on the Marshall Plan and on NATO, both on British initiatives, the United States, and not the depleted Continental nations, was Britain's main partner; the depleted nations of Western Europe were as much an object of British foreign policy as partners in it.

Under these circumstances there is little wonder that full co-operation did not continue beyond the immediate postwar tasks. By continental standards, Britain's position was eccentric and therefore, in the long run, her foreign policy could not but be 'out of phase' with those pursued on the continent: when Britain proved unwilling to take part in the early European integration moves, which she could have done on her own terms, she disappointed European hopes that she would continue her wartime leadership; when she became ready to join, de Gaulle stood opposed to her entry. Roy Jenkins tellingly sums up the British political debate over Europe as one 'about whether our relations with the countries of the continent should be more akin to America's with continental European countries or to their own with one another'.[17] Immediately after the war, however, the conditions for such a debate scarcely existed. The relative advantages of an American alignment against a closer alignment with Europe seemed colossal. Despite a temporary disruption, the British felt much more at ease co-operating with other English-speaking people, sharing a common cultural background, stable democratic institutions, and the many channels of intimate co-operation established during the war; the United States was the only visible source of sorely needed military and economic support. To the British, who emerged from the war with the foundations of their national state intact, the decisive American intervention in the war seemed to confirm the value of Britain's oceanic orientation. A return to some approximation of pre-war 'normalcy' could be reasonably expected with the support of the Americans, of an Empire partly transformed into the Commonwealth, and of a revived domestic economy and a revitalized social structure.

Although sharing Britain's immediate policy objectives, the continentals, with their fundamentally different war experiences, did not share Britain's outlook. The very foundations of their national states had been shattered by the war and by the defeat or humiliation inflicted through it; the war record showed the tardiness and the limitations of overseas help, and a return to normalcy appeared much more uncertain to nations threatened by a communist revolution. The old order seemed to have been decisively destroyed, and, against this background, the historically divisive issue of Germany readily served as a focus for integrationist ideas. The French followed the patterns of their post-1918 policies while trying to avoid their costly failure. They started again with the object of weakening Germany permanently and of co-operating with the Russians in an attempt to dismember her; when they failed to convert their Western allies to their ideas, they deliberately engaged in a policy of conciliation and integration which had been proposed in the Briand-Stresemann plans in the late 1920s but had never been implemented.

The problem of speeding up but effectively controlling the rehabilitation of Germany became the common German–French issue for which integration offered a logical way out. Britain, of course, was also intimately involved in the German issue, which was central for European security and prosperity and which directly involved her as one of the occupying powers. The British interest was not, however, nearly as strong and urgent as that of the French and the Germans themselves. The voluminous debate on the German problem in Britain in the late 1940s tended to fall between the two extremes of the immediate problems arising from occupation and of the vague general aspiration to prevent the possibility of the revived threat of a German aggression. There was no such urgency as on the continent to think about mid- and long-term solutions.

Not unexpectedly, the European integration movement had only a marginal impact upon British politics. It was taken up by Churchill, who, being in opposition, was deprived of the opportunity for direct action and became the chairman of the all-party committee to launch the European campaign, on the basis of Western civilization organizing itself against communist barbarism; this was well in line with his 1940 proposals for an Anglo-French Union. It was supported for quite different reasons on the Left, by prominent intellectuals like G. D. H. Cole and R. H. S. Crossman, who sought a 'Third Force' which would secure for Britain a freedom to abstain from the two military blocs and to pursue socialist freedom and rational planning at home. To some, integrated

Europe appeared as a solution for Britain's balance-of-payments problems, others saw in it the logical result of the brotherhood of man and
of the absurdity of national divisions.

Although firm governmental action could easily have turned Britain
to lead the European integration movement, the successive governments
had insufficient incentives to do so; the Attlee Government did not go
beyond Bevin's vague proposals for a Western Union in January 1948,
which laid the foundations of NATO but not of European integration;
Churchill, when in power, did not pursue the idea of a United States of
Europe which he had proclaimed when in opposition. It seems clear that,
with very few exceptions, neither the politicians nor the officials found
much attraction in the European idea, and many, including Attlee and
Eden, were positively antipathetic to it. Even the pro-Europeans tended
to support only the weaker, functionalist version of an integrated
Europe and to oppose the stronger, federalist one which had a greater
appeal on the continent and was the foundation of the actual successive
moves towards integration. Moreover, to the British, the issue of integration did not appear to be urgent, and the decisions to abstain from the
negotiations about the Schuman and Pleven Plans were based upon the
expectations that the plans would not succeed, combined with confidence
that if they did, Britain would have another chance to join the integration
movement at a later stage. In the early 1950s neither expectation seemed
to be unjustified.

Although the British political system permits the political leadership
a great degree of freedom in the conduct of foreign policy, as its decisions
are readily accepted, it does so because the leadership takes into account
and generally reflects public opinion. Public opinion on Europe has been
repeatedly sampled by public-opinion polls, but owing to the complexity
of the issue, one may surmise that the commitment of individuals to their
opinions may not be particularly strong and that their opinions may
readily change. Nevertheless, the general drift was clear—although the
public generally approved of European co-operation (a traditional
feature of British foreign policy), Britain's participation in any form of
integration, especially leading to a federation, was politically dangerous.
Characteristically, in a Gallup Poll taken on the eve of the first British
application, in July 1960, 49 per cent declared their support for joining,
against 13 per cent opposed to it; but only 22 per cent favoured joining
'with political implications' with 35 per cent dissenting. Public opinion
was subject to wild fluctuations. It reached the peaks of 60 per cent in
favour in November 1962 and 70 per cent in May and July 1966, but
hovered around a mere 20 per cent from December 1970 till June 1971.

Then it climbed steadily to around 50 per cent in the early part of 1972 but dropped again in 1973.[18]

Public and governmental attitudes tended to be influenced by the major characteristics of the British national character which have been discussed above—by traditionalism and pragmatism, which strongly reinforced British nationalism and attachment to national sovereignty. In the quarter of a century of intermittent debate about Britain and Europe, the arguments both for and against can generally be traced to one of these roots or to their combination.

Traditionalism, inertia, fear of reversing well-established policies strongly obstructed a change of policy as drastic as the decision to join Europe in any form. It seemed to go against many time-hallowed traditions of British foreign policy and also to threaten many of them in domestic politics. Some of these traditions may have become unreal, obsolete, and counterproductive, but they were still politically potent and a good case and much effort were required for their abolition. There was the question of the oceanic orientation of British foreign policy and of the intimacy of the Commonwealth and the United States links; the issue of parliamentary sovereignty; the place of monarchy; the probable interference with Britain's cheap food policy, her welfare-state arrangements and the control mechanisms in domestic economy.

Nationalism was much stronger in Britain after the war than on the continent. Lingering insularity and a divorce from continental politics were reinforced by the sentiments of superiority engendered within the Empire which was now being successfully transformed into the Commonwealth. In contrast to the crisis of nationalism among the defeated and divided Germans, and among the French, who were hopelessly split between the Resistance and the Collaborationists, British patriotism had been reinforced by wartime experiences and victory. The traditional British sentiments of national superiority obstructed a union with a weakened and disorganized Europe in 1945; once the Europeans had sufficiently recovered to become dangerous competitors, they created a feeling of acute unease. To the continental politicians working for integration, the British naturally appeared to be nationalistic, parochial, and generally uninterested.

Although the frequently stressed distinction between the 'empirical' or 'pragmatic' British and the 'doctrinaire' continental approaches does not stand a close examination, and amounts to little more than an emotionally tinged description of different national styles, it played an important part in determining British attitudes. Many British people were put off by the frequent European references to federal and supranational goals, by the open-ended commitment to the European idea, and, later, also by the ideological zeal of many European officials. In fact, although this passed largely unnoticed, especially among the anti-Europeans in Britain, European integration developed in an essentially pragmatic way and the far-reaching aspirations were not translated into actual policies without the consent of the participants; the compromise of Luxembourg is the epitome of this spirit of pragmatism, and one may argue that it was rather the British who were doctrinaire by remaining committed to a number of doctrines with increasingly less bearing on political reality, particularly regarding the place of parliament, the Commonwealth, sterling, and their world role. Moreover, empiricism readily led to scepticism about the long-range economic benefits which were said to be sure to accrue from the European link and to offset the immediate costs. Britain's domestic experiences did not encourage trust in long-range governmental promises and, by the time the EEC had shown itself to be highly successful, the immediate costs of admission had risen accordingly.

The lingering British belief in the 'doctrinaire' nature of continental politics encouraged an unimaginative evaluation of the political trends in Europe while both tradition and pragmatism encouraged British policy-makers to concentrate on single European states and issues rather than pay attention to unrealistic-sounding ideas of integration. The British were slow to realize that the integration movement was a real political force, that the EEC would materialize and that it would grow very fast. This frame of mind was further reinforced by a degree of wishful thinking, coupled with efforts to divert the integration movement into institutionally more innocuous forms, or to neutralize it by not including but merely associating Britain. Most striking of all was the general failure to comprehend de Gaulle's policies. In the later 1950s, the British could justifiably be convinced that the official estimates of European integration had proved right: it had got bogged down in one solitary institution—the European Coal and Steel Community with which Britain had a satisfactory commercial arrangement; the subsequent plans for the European Defence Community had been trimmed down to an extension of NATO, following a British initiative, while all the other integration proposals had died. The officials were convinced that the *relance européenne* had no prospects, and that there was no point in engaging in another confrontation between the irreconcilable ideas of the European integrationsists and of the British. Hence the British did not participate in the Messina talks but merely sent a 'representative', characteristically not from the Foreign Office but from the Board of

Trade, whose contribution was limited to a repeated expression of doubts as to whether Britain could possibly accept the ideas of the emerging agreement. Until the Treaties of Rome were actually signed in March 1957, the issue of European integration was not apparently regarded as sufficiently salient to call for action. In vain did Lord Gladwyn warn from the Paris Embassy that vital British interests were at stake and that Britain should make a real start towards Europe; they were dismissed by the argument that the Commonwealth took 43 per cent of Britain's exports and supplied her with cheap food.[19]

The last stages of the European negotiations coincided with Britain's post-Suez crisis when she was at the nadir of her strength—suffering from the psychological shock and from the subsequent strains in her relations with the United States and the Commonwealth. Until further information is divulged[20] all that we can surmise is that the still non-existent Community was simply deemed insufficiently important to receive full attention in Britain. As soon, however, as the Treaties of Rome had been signed, Macmillan publicly sounded an alarm: 'Let us be under no delusions, by far the biggest danger would be if this great European unit came into being and we did nothing about it and were left outside.'[21]

However, the political logic of European integration which appealed to the Germans and the French was insufficiently recognized by the British, who futilely continued their attempts to extend the EEC into a free-trade area open to all the members of the OEEC. Such a development would have diluted the integration movement and was therefore unacceptable to the ardent continental federalists. In the early, fluid days of the Community it seemed politically possible but the members of the Community were too preoccupied with inter-community adjustments to be able to cope with the additional problem of free-trade extension; after de Gaulle's coming to power, it was politically obstructed.

The alternatives open to the British were not very promising; a trade war seemed out of the question owing both to Britain's limited capacity to wage one and to the political dangers of aggravating the division of Europe. The expedient eventually adopted of organizing the European Free Trade Association (EFTA) with six small non-members of the EEC (Finland later became an associate) was an insufficient lever to make the EEC accept a general Western European free-trade association. Although EFTA proved to be unexpectedly successful in stimulating trade amongst its own members, its economic impact upon the EEC was limited; the French did relatively little trade with its members, while Germany's substantial exports to low-tariff Switzerland and the Scandinavian countries were not seriously affected. Politically, EFTA embarrassingly associated Britain with a number of neutral states, divorcing her trade and defence policies.

Even more serious than the economic division was the political threat of the EEC becoming politically integrated. The Adenauer–de Gaulle link established in September 1958 thoroughly alarmed the British, especially Macmillan. According to leaked press reports, he went to the length of stating to President Kennedy, when in Washington in March 1960, that, in the event of a Franco–German Union, Britain would have no choice in the long run but to lead a peripheral alliance, and he even recalled the historical parallel of the alliance with Russia to oppose Napoleon.[22]

By the summer of 1960, Britain's precarious economic and political position persuaded Macmillan and a few of his close associates and top civil servants that ultimately Britain should join the EEC, although the majority of the members of the government still believed that an arrangement short of membership should be sought. Macmillan is vulnerable to the frequently made accusations that he failed to acquaint the nation more fully with the extent of its economic difficulties until the summer of 1962, and that he tenaciously clung to the ideas of a world role and of close links with the United States. He certainly did not attempt to revise and reappraise British interests but rather to preserve them as far as possible. He did not try to sell the European idea to the people and the party but, on the contrary, he gave all the appearance of trying to persuade them that nothing of fundamental importance was involved, that the EEC was largely a commercial affair; he tried, as it has been put, to sidle into Europe. It is, however, difficult to think that he could have acted otherwise in the light of the severe constraints imposed by domestic politics. He justifiably suspected that a strong lead would have split his party and given an electoral advantage to Labour on an anti-European base, damaging not only the narrow conservative Party interests but also the national interest of getting into Europe.

Macmillan's ambiguity and equivocation were successful in neutralizing domestic opposition to the proposed drastic alteration in the direction of British foreign policy. The issue was handled in a low key. As proposed by the British, the negotiations dealt with making satisfactory arrangements to meet the special needs of the United Kingdom, especially of its agriculture, of the Commonwealth, and of the EFTA partners. It is hard to escape the impression that the British government was preoccupied with these concrete issues to the point of somewhat neglecting the fact that de Gaulle was swayed by much broader policy considerations

—namely how to ensure that he would retain the political lead in the Community and would continue being able to assert the maximum degree of independence *vis-à-vis* the United States. Interpretations of de Gaulle's motivations vary, but it seems likely that he made up his mind to veto Britain's application only after his re-election in the autumn of 1962, and that Macmillan's Nassau link with the United States and his general ambiguity about Britain's continental commitments were convenient excuses rather than the reasons for his veto. In fact, Macmillan's position regarding French nuclear weapons was, apparently, open when, in a seeming contradiction to Macnamara's Ann Arbor speech, he spoke in support of French nuclear policy. At the same time it is hard to assume that a more determined British commitment would have prevented de Gaulle from dragging on the negotiations until after his re-election, or that his decision would have been different. France was then surging into a period of economic strength and, with the ending of the Algerian strife, was building up a position of real strength in the EEC; Britain in her economic weakness, and with the uncertainties facing her in her oceanic orientation, was again entirely out of phase with France.

The effects of the rejection were serious—perhaps most of all on the British, whose national morale had been raised by the expectations of entry and who had been lulled into confidently expecting it, upon the Commonwealth, the old and new members of which agreed in disapproving of Britain's move, and upon Britain's standing with the United States and with the rest of the world. Only EFTA survived the crisis relatively well. The British did not pursue the unpromising strategy of enlisting the aid of the other five members of the EEC who favoured Britain's entry, mainly because Dr Adenauer clearly set a greater priority on preserving his close links with France. They adopted a policy of waiting for the right moment to enter the Community later while devoting themselves to such interim measures as helping to reduce the tariffs in the Kennedy Round of the GATT negotiations and trying to increase trade with their Commonwealth and EFTA partners—very successfully with the latter. In 1967 domestic and external developments converged further to weaken Britain's position, to the point of persuading the leadership of the reluctant Labour Party also to decide in favour of Britain's entry. On the other hand, Britain's balance-of-payments crisis, leading to the devaluation of sterling and the withdrawal from east of Suez, undermined her world role; while on the other, the future of the 'special relationship' with the Americans had been becoming increasingly dubious ever since the Cuban missiles crisis and the Macnamara doctrine, especially once the Americans were seriously engaged in developing direct bilateral relations with the Russians. Also, the institutional shape of the EEC was less intimidating after the Luxembourg compromise, as the supranational ambitions of the Commission seemed to have been decisively defeated and the unacceptable Common Agricultural Policy of the Community was in some jeopardy. Britain was, however, still too much out of phase with France; de Gaulle, at the height of his influence, could confidently hope to firmly establish French leadership in the EEC before allowing Britain's entry.

Britain's inability to play a meaningful role as an individual state in the international negotiations dealing with the major issues of international trade and finance, which had become obvious already in the 1960s in the Kennedy Round, became even more pronounced in the prolonged series of international financial crises later on. Once the adamant stand of France had been mitigated by the disorders of 1968, by the retirement of de Gaulle, and by the rapid rise in Germany's power, the major political obstacle to Britain's entry was removed. With Britain for once in phase with France, Edward Heath, much less emotionally devoted than his predecessors to the 'special relationship' and to a broad world role, successfully resumed the negotiations and brought Britain into Europe by the agreement signed on 22 January 1972.

While the governmental commitment to membership remained firm throughout the period of negotiations and after entry, Britain's EEC policy became caught up in the movements of public opinion and in the internal politics of the Labour Party. Public opinion, though still divided, was at first slowly moving towards favouring Britain's entry, but it turned sharply in the opposite direction under the impact of galloping inflation and of the rising unpopularity of the government in the first months of 1973. This change of direction was particularly pronounced within the Labour Party. Britain's entry had been rejected by the party in 1961–2 mainly owing to Labour suspicion of Germany and attachment to the Commonwealth, and had been only temporarily accepted in 1967 as subordinate to the issue of technology. It was now rejected again, with much stronger emphasis, having become an integral part of Labour opposition to the whole complex of governmental domestic policies, especially industrial-relations legislation and wages restraint. Great bitterness arose within the party against the sizeable group of pro-marketeer rebels, and Wilson came under strong pressure to commit a future Labour government to a British withdrawal from the EEC; he took great pains to preserve party unity and found a formula for it in a programme of 'renegotiating' the terms of entry.

This non-committal formula preserved Wilson's freedom of man-oeuvre. Theoretically it could lead to the next Labour government quitting the EEC, but Wilson gave the impression of acting merely as a responsible leader of his party whose primary task was to preserve its unity, rather than as a convinced anti-marketeer. 'Renegotiation' of the terms of entry is likely to differ in style rather than in content from the battle the Conservatives waged after entry to secure as much in favour of Britain's national interests as possible, One may surmise that Wilson has not gone back on his conversion to Europe in 1967, as he gave the impression that he fought hard to protect himself from a party mandate to withdraw unconditionally. One may also surmise that the majority of the political elite who, according to *The Times* survey discussed on pp. 45–6, favoured Britain's entry in 1970 has increased rather than de-creased. Despite the last-ditch battles in the House of Commons and then during the autumn annual conference of the Labour Party in 1972, the majority of the people at least passively accepted that Britain would become a member of the EEC. There was no disagreement between the pro- and the anti-Europeans that Britain's main task within the enlarged Community would be to pursue and protect her national interests. The White Paper on *The United Kingdom and the European Communities* forecast: 'our country will be more secure, our ability to maintain peace and promote development in the world greater, and our economy stronger, and our industries and people more prosperous'.[23] Although many may not have agreed with the statement as a forecast, more regarded it as a distinct hope; it would appeal to all as a reasonable aspiration.

## Britain and the United Nations

One cannot generalize about the British style of behaviour within international organizations as it is determined by the function of each particular organization. NATO and its lesser imitations, SEATO and CENTO, created no special problems as they were based upon the traditional alliance patterns, and British diplomats were very happy operating within their contexts—as long as they had the opportunity of advance consultation with the Americans. The international economic organizations were not integrated into the general pattern of foreign policy, and British postures in them were governed by specifically economic reasoning. The United Nations, however, created a new set of problems and hence requires a brief separate analysis. It is the focus of many alternative conceptions of a world order. It is, at the same time, one of the channels through which Britain pursues and defends specific national interests; and it is also of some importance as a channel for communication with other states. The first three weeks of the annual session of the General Assembly are particularly important, when Foreign Ministers and Heads of Government convene and are at leisure to meet while the general debate goes on. At all times, it is a major operation forum for small states—and it gives British diplomats the opportunity to establish contacts with their representatives, who often rise to positions of central power, although less frequently now than in the past. It is also a source of information, although one of declining importance.

There is a great discrepancy between the aspirations frequently expressed and the policies actually pursued by Britain in the UN. The confusion is increased by the fact that the UN, as a major forum of multilateral diplomacy, is relevant for two distinct major strands of Britain's foreign policy: first, as a venue for her endeavours to build a stable world order and for playing a world role, and, second, as an instrumentality for her pursuit and defence of specific national interests.

However much the proponents and the critics of the UN disagree about the place that this organization could or should have taken in British foreign policy, they agree that this has been rather insignificant. The reasons can be found partly in the relatively poor record of the UN, which has shown itself incapable of efficient action in many major matters of international concern, especially on the central issues of peace and security. Partly, however, they lie also in the position of Britain in the world and in British attitudes and actions. The history of the establishment of the UN provides the background. Throughout the preparatory negotiations, Britain supported the American plans, although not very enthusiastically and often with reservations about detail. The League of Nations experience of the two countries had been different—it is possible to see in Cordell Hull's fervent advocacy of international organization a desire to atone for America's abandonment of the League. Britain's record in the League had been much less clear. On the one hand, it is possible to regard her failure to support the League in its collective-security efforts as a major error in calculations due to her traditional confidence in military self-sufficiency and to her reluctance to get involved in continental politics. On the other hand, from the power-political point of view, the League loomed large as a dangerous myth which had prevented the country in the interwar years from conducting a realistic foreign policy.

The main British objective was to continue, as far as possible, the wartime arrangements of intimate consultations among the Big Three, with France added. Plans for a world council on these lines were discussed in the Foreign Office during 1942, and were embodied in its basic planning document for the postwar international system, 'The Four-Power Plan'. According to Lord Gladwyn, who headed the Economic and Reconstruction Department involved in the planning, a revival of the League of Nations, located in Washington rather than in Geneva, was unlikely and probably undesirable, although a successor organization would not be inconsistent with the general Four-Power idea.[24] The origins of the British commitment to a universal international organization embodied in the Moscow Declaration of 30 October 1943 must therefore be attributed mainly to the desire to please the Americans. The British were not, however, fully united on the details of their objectives. Whereas Churchill strongly favoured regional councils, the Foreign Office had doubts about his idea of a United States in Western Europe which would be regarded by the Russians as a hostile bloc and could in any case fall under German domination.[25]

Ultimately, the British played a constructive role in the actual establishment of the UN. In line with their World Council ideas, they insisted on a meeting of the great powers prior to a general conference, and played a central role in persuading first the Americans and then the Russians to limit the great power veto to enforcement procedures alone; in view of the great difficulties of the San Francisco Conference, even after this compromise, it must appear doubtful whether the conference would have had any chance of success had the compromise not been previously reached. At San Francisco Britain again played a cautious but constructive role; the worst of the British fears about the new Organization were assuaged by the Charter. The UN was barred from encroaching upon the Empire by the weak provisions regarding the 'non-self-governing territories' and by the 'domestic jurisdiction clause'; Britain's interests could be protected in the Security Council by her power of veto and under the collective self-defence arrangements, whereas in the General Assembly there was an assured majority in support of the United States. It was impossible to envisage in 1945 how short-lived all these guarantees would prove.

The Labour government continued the policies of the wartime coalition, although its protestations of internationalism were much stronger, in deference to the traditional internationalist streak in Labour ideology. To the professional diplomats it was clear that the Charter of the United Nations was realistically based upon the recognition of the physical power of states and that the traditional diplomatic harmonization of the interests of the major powers was the only promising method to ensure peace.[26] To them, the avowed Labour objectives of the UN acting as a substitute for power politics sounded utopian. However, in

1946, Attlee himself put on record in the House of Commons his belief that the UN should be the first step towards a world government, and, at the first session of the General Assembly, that it 'must become the overriding factor in the exercise of foreign policies so that the Rule of Law will everywhere prevail'. The Minister of State for Foreign Affairs, Philip Noel-Baker, spoke of 'Britain's determination to use the institutes of the United Nations to kill power politics'. All these were merely vague expressions of aspirations, but, apparently under the influence of the Legal Adviser, Eric Beckett, the Foreign Office became critical of the limitations of the Charter and, by the end of November 1946, both the government and the opposition were committed to the views, first, that important and urgent world problems of a political nature should as soon as possible be confided to the UN for settlement, second, that it would be highly desirable to abolish the 'veto', and third, that it would also be desirable, at an early stage, to take some preliminary steps towards the constitution of a world state.[27] Nothing concrete emerged from these ideas but the government continued to pay lip-service to the UN, whenever a suitable occasion arose: it stressed NATO's conformity with Article 51 of the Charter; it declared its reluctance to take any action which might have the effect of weakening the UN, when it decided to forgo the use of force in the Anglo-Iranian dispute, although it was motivated more strongly by the realization that the use of force was inexpedient and that it was opposed by President Truman.

Support for the UN was, and to some extent has remained, a major aspiration of Labour Party activitists who, in this respect, are far ahead of the general run of public opinion. An analysis of the electoral addresses in the 1970 election revealed that as many as 18 per cent of the Labour candidates referred to the UN against a mere 2 per cent of the Conservatives. The UN Association, however, was only a pale shadow of its interwar predecessor, the League of Nations Union; there was no public enthusiasm for the new organization and, as the cold war evolved and as anti-colonialist criticisms of Britain within the UN mounted, the public mood of scepticism and pessimism over the UN deepened. When, in the aftermath of Suez, ideas of a world government became common currency for a while, both in the Labour and the Conservative Parties, the logic of the arguments for such a government did not disguise the utopian nature of the proposals entertained. The UN was not necessarily regarded as the most promising road to a world government; frequent criticisms were voiced of its ineffectiveness, the intrigues within it, and of what, to some, appeared rather lavish expenditure. Worse than criticism, the organization rapidly lost its news value and public opinion had no opportunity to become readily informed about its work. Only limited humanitarian activities, especially UNICEF, occasionally appealed to the broad public. Nevertheless, potential support for the UN persisted. The Gallup Poll recorded that 75 per cent of the public regarded it as 'very important' in November 1960 and 70 per cent in January 1962. In July 1966, 63 per cent supported the idea of a permanent UN peacekeeping force, and 66 per cent British participation in it. In contrast to France, British public opinion was sufficiently alert and favourable to restrain any contemplated negative governmental actions towards the UN. It could also be expected to support positive governmental action within the framework of the UN; and some of these actions could even serve as an admittedly limited source of popularity at home. A major opportunity in this direction opened in the early 1970s in the field of pollution, which affects many British economic interests. The British Government played a constructive part in the early stages of UN involvement in this field and in the Stockholm Conference in 1972.

The Conservative governments were more sceptical than Labour. The most outspoken British criticism of the UN was voiced by Sir Alec Douglas-Home, at a meeting of the Berwick-upon-Tweed United Nations Association on 28 December 1961. He summed up all the shortcomings of the organization but wound up with a statement that Britain, being 'a most vulnerable island', wanted peace and the rule of law abroad, 'where we have to earn our living', and co-operation with all without exception. Although he posed a serious question about the value of UN activities, he concluded that its aims and aspirations remained valid: 'I come down decidedly on the side of hope', Britain must 'neither sail off into the blue of Utopia nor founder upon the reef of cynicism'.[28] Despite the mounting criticism of the organization and the increasing anti-colonial pressures within it, the Labour government elected in 1964 made an attempt to revitalize Britain's contribution to it. At the United Nations Association, on 14 April 1967, Wilson said:

We say without equivocation that the United Nations must go forward with resolution towards the goal of world authority. If it ever allows itself—or if we allow it—to lose sight of this goal, then what should have been a proud and noble enterprise will be swallowed up in the desert of national self-seeking and indifference.

He went on to admit that translating this declaration of purpose into action was by no means a simple task. He made, however, a determined attempt to do so. In the first instance, he made an important gesture of goodwill by appointing as British Permanent Representative to the UN Sir Hugh Foot, who had previously resigned from his New York post in protest against the Conservative government's African policies. Sir Hugh was elevated to the House of Lords as Lord Caradon and was given the position of a Minister of State in the Foreign Office. His liberal reputation, his position in the government, and his close relationship with the Prime Minister, all contributed to his success. By then, however, the atmosphere in the UN was highly unpropitious to Britain owing to the Rhodesian crisis. When Wilson addressed the General Assembly on 15 December 1965, twenty African delegates walked out. The British initiative to give an auspicious start to the work of the newly established Committee of Twenty by offering logistic support for up to six battalions of peacekeeping forces was thus blocked.

The Heath Government elected in 1970 is likewise on record as being in support of the UN, although somewhat less emphatically and unreservedly. Even on the august occasion of the twenty-fifth anniversary of the organization, when addressing the General Assembly on 23 October 1971, Heath looked critically at its record and stressed the point that his government was committed to 'vigorous policies in the interests of the security and prosperity of the British people' which were fully in accordance with the country's commitments under the Charter. The call for 'greater energy and realism' in the work of the organization was coupled with one for greater growth in trade and aid, but was accompanied, not by a promise to increase the latter, but by a mere statement that Britain had been contributing generously to development for many years.

For a variety of reasons, the UN environment was not particularly congenial to the British diplomats. In the first instance, Britain's position within the UN was rather weak. Although, as one of the Permanent Members of the Security Council, she commanded the power of veto, she did not enjoy adequate support among the membership to enable her to act with ease in the General Assembly. The Commonwealth group was in no sense a voting bloc which would automatically support Britain, as the Latin-American bloc originally supported the United States, and and Soviet bloc the Soviet Union. In the early years of the UN, before Suez, the Commonwealth group met regularly and, except on Kashmir, prevented acrimony when intra-Commonwealth issues reached the UN or when the members differed in their stands on other issues. Moreover, the Group jointly nominated candidates for 'Commonwealth seats' in the Security Council and in other agencies. Gradually, however, the group became swallowed up in the Afro-Asian group, and, in the tide of anti-colonialism, its members took part in lambasting Britain.

Furthermore, the other members of the UN were not, on the whole, particularly friendly to the British. During the early period of American predominance, Britain came under repeated communist attacks over her actions and commitments arising from the aftermath of the war—in Syria and Lebanon, Greece, Indonesia, and also Egypt; in the Palestine case, the UN could not get further than the partition decision which, in the eyes of the British government, was unrealistic and therefore unacceptable; in the Anglo-Iranian dispute, the organization was quite ineffective. Britain's close alignment with the United States was unhelpful in the UN context. Lord Gladwyn records how, following his forensic successes in the UN in criticizing communist aggression in Korea, he found it difficult to voice his misgivings about American coercion attempts through majorities in the General Assembly, because the Foreign Office was apprehensive about the effects upon American public opinion.[29] Moreover, the support of the Americans could not be counted upon, and the British occasionally suffered from their tergiversations and pressures. For instance, the Americans suddenly refused to support the Palestine Trusteeship plans, and they exercised severe pressures upon the Dutch to give up their struggle in the Dutch East Indies. The 'dual standards' of the UN over Suez and Hungary, the handling of the Congo Crisis, and the mounting attacks on British 'colonialism' by the Afro-Asian majority which were supported by the Communists, especially over the South Rhodesian issue, further aggravated Britain's situation.

Part of the trouble, however, lay in Britain's own behaviour. The climate of multilateral diplomacy and the histrionics of the General Assembly and of the Committee of Twenty-Four did not correspond with her traditional notions of classical diplomacy, and, open diplomacy can prove awkward when a specific issue affecting a vital interest of a major power is being considered. A problem which might be solved by the old-fashioned method of private, non-publicized diplomacy, often becomes intractable when debated in the UN. The press of the world takes a hand. A relatively minor problem becomes magnified out of proportion to its true significance, simply because great powers are involved, and owing to the clash of differing views in the debate at the UN. The pressure of international public opinion is useful only in some cases, especially in 'preventive diplomacy of which Britain generally approved. On the whole, however, she preferred a parallel private diplomacy.

The first British Permanent Representative to the UN, Sir Alexander Cadogan, who was appointed by Attlee, set the cautious tone which could be expected from a professional diplomat not particularly enthusiastic about the organization. The UN handled several British problems which were extremely delicate, and Trygve Lie had some justification for his complaint that Britain was not very co-operative, especially over Palestine. By the time a real international enthusiast, Lord Caradon, was appointed by Wilson, Britain had lost too much power and popularity among the anti-colonial majority of the UN to play a major role in the organization.

Britain's attitudes towards the interpretation of the Charter are indicative of her hesitant, vacillating attitudes to the organization itself. The 'domestic jurisdiction' clause (Art. 2[7]) served Britain as the legal basis for staunchly denying UN jurisdiction over her own and others' colonial and domestic matters, but was conveniently ignored when, in 1947, Britain supported the anti-Franco resolution which over-rode the clause. Gradually and reluctantly, Britain accepted that the General Assembly would constantly encroach upon the clause, and adopted a political rather than a legalistic attitude to each vote. Even more serious was Britain's use of force in the Suez affair, which could not be reconciled with the Charter even through a far-fetched legal interpretation; this was, however, an isolated occasion which was not repeated. It gave rise to Britain's using her powers of veto twice; the only other issue which involved repeated use of the veto, five times, was the prolonged crisis over Southern Rhodesia.

In view of all this, it is not surprising that throughout the period, especially at the beginning, Britain was unenthusiastic about issues of her foreign policy coming under UN scrutiny. She used the organization whenever it appeared to provide a convenient instrumentality—e.g. when the Palestine issue had become intractable, or in the Anglo-Iranian dispute in 1951, but otherwise she did not, on the whole, favour UN action in matters directly affecting her, especially concerning colonialism. She agreed only reluctantly to UN intervention in the Indonesia issue in 1948, and to the dispatch of UN Missions to North Borneo and Sarawak in 1963 and to Aden in 1967. In the Suez affair, Eden's plan was to use the UN merely as a smokescreen; his strategy was to proceed with the conference of the Maritime Nations, then, after its likely failure, to appeal to the Security Council which would be paralysed by the Russian veto, and so to have the excuse for using force. Dulles upset the timetable by introducing the meaningless SCUA proposals. It was characteristic of the confusion of thinking in Britain about the UN, that when Eden reluctantly complied with Dulles, Labour MPs attacked him, demanding a direct resort to the UN, regardless of the near-certainty of a deadlock there. Ultimately the image of the UN in Britain greatly suffered from the accusation against it of holding 'dual standards', owing to the Organization's strong discriminatory condemnation of the Suez action, which contrasted with its leniency towards the Russians in Hungary. Insufficient recognition was paid to the value of the UN Emergency Force in enabling Britain to extricate herself from a politically and militarily untenable position.

A crude yardstick for measuring the importance Britain attached to the various activities of the UN can be sought in her financial contributions to them. Against about a $7\frac{1}{2}$ per cent share in the general administrative budget, she contributed an average of around 10 per cent to the budgets of the Food and Agricultural Organization, the International Labour Organization, and the Civil Aviation Organization, and nearly 13 per cent to the Inter-Governmental Maritime Consultative Organization. This faithfully represents Britain's interests as a large importer of food and an industrial, maritime, and air power. Logically, one of Wilson's major UN initiatives was to raise some of the questions of maritime law and practice which were relevant to the wreck of the Torrey Canyon. Earlier in the work of the UN, Britain contributed as much as 15 per cent to the budgets of both the Relief and Rehabilitation Administration (UNRRA), which dealt with postwar relief work, and to the United Nations Relief and Works Agency for Palestine Refugees, which reflected her residual Middle Eastern responsibilities.

On the widest world issues, including those of international peace and security, Britain's initiatives within the UN were not fully commensurate with her tradition as a world power. This may be attributed to a combination of the inhibiting impact of the rather uncongenial atmosphere and to the official British reluctance to use the machinery. For instance, if one takes the issue of disarmament, up to the end of the 1950s Britain was in a strong position to lead the middle and small powers in exercising joint pressures upon the superpowers. She was, however, concentrating upon the superpower level, partly because she was herself a nuclear power and therefore felt that she shared an interest with them, partly owing to her traditional attachment to a 'seat at the top table,' and partly in deference to American sentiments.

Undoubtedly Britain's most negative experience with the UN was, as Sir Alec Douglas-Home put it, being constantly 'put in the dock' on colonial issues. Up to a point this was inevitable, as the UN simply reflected the mounting tide of anti-colonialism in the world, and Britain was in control of the largest Empire in 1945 and had remained responsible for more dependent territories than any other member. At the same time, however, the antagonism might have been reduced by an earlier British attempt to accommodate the new forces. The original difficulty lay mainly in Britain's legalistic approach. There was not the slightest difficulty in the way the British liquidated the trusteeship relationship on the basis of the Charter by emancipating the few territories concerned. For a long time, however, they insisted on a strict interpretation of Art. 73 (e), which merely provided for reports from other dependent territories for 'information purposes', and did not include information on political matters. Britain consistently opposed the mounting pressures to widen the terms of reference and to establish bodies to deal with the information and to make recommendations. She also insisted that the 'domestic jurisdiction' clause should apply to specific colonial matters, notably to the issues of Algeria and of apartheid.

At the end of the 1950s, Britain began to accept the seemingly inevitable extension of UN powers but still remained generally opposed to such moves as the setting of timetables for independence or the taking of measures against Portugal, although she stopped supplying Portugal and South Africa with arms in compliance with UN resolutions. The paradoxical position in which Britain found herself is best exemplified by the way the Committee of Twenty-Four favoured Spain against Britain on the Gibraltar issue while it removed Hong Kong from the list of colonial territories in March 1972 at the request of China, who pointed out that the colony is a Chinese territory, occupied by Britain, with which China would deal 'in an appropriate way when the conditions are ripe.[30]

The major bone of contention was the issue of Southern Rhodesia. After the Unilateral Declaration of Independence, Britain dropped her previous 'domestic jurisdiction' objection to repeated UN recommendations and exercised her initiative in the Security Council to reaffirm a previous Council resolution calling upon all states to refrain from recognizing the illegal regime and to break off economic and diplomatic relations, and specifically calling on Britain to take all the appropriate measures to end the rebellion. Although Britain resorted twice more to the Council for authorization to use force to prevent oil supplies from reaching Southern Rhodesia by sea and, after the failure of the *Tiger* talks, for the sanctions to be made mandatory, the UN remained highly critical of the ineffectiveness of the economic sanctions and of the three successive attempts by British governments to reach an accommodation bilaterally.

The prolonged application of economic sanctions against Southern Rhodesia led to a complete impasse. On 30 December 1971 Britain had again to cast her veto against a Security Council resolution asking her not go give a free hand to the South Rhodesian government, on lines very similar to a resolution proposed in 1963. After the ultimate failure of the Pearce Committee attempt in 1972, no solution was in sight. And yet, did Wilson have a real alternative? He rated the issue as the most complicated and insoluble of all that a British government had ever had to face—Ulster came only later. He distinguished four relevant constituencies: (1) Rhodesian public opinion, which was not uncomplicated; (2) British public opinion, with the Conservatives insisting that Britain should retain her responsibility; (3) the Commonwealth, which condemned the lack of decisive action while Zambia was vulnerable to a pre-emptive strike by the Rhodesians and refused to accept British troops unless they had orders to occupy the Kariba Dam within days; and (4) the strong anticolonialist pressures within the UN.[31] The idea of passing responsibility entirely to the UN—which Wilson omitted to discuss in his retrospective account—evoked the spectre of a 'red army in blue berets' and, like the use of force, would have been unacceptable at home. The uneasy, costly, and ineffective compromise of economic sanctions was an expedient which satisfied nobody but seems to have been the least costly way out. As in the case of Suez, however, the role of the UN in offering this unwelcome but face-saving course remained largely unrecognized in Britain.

# 11 International Economic Policies

*The Politics of International Economics*
BRITAIN was the first country to industrialize and to depend upon international exchanges, but she did not include economic issues squarely within her foreign policy; *haute politique*, issues of war and peace, predominated in her diplomacy as much as in those of other major powers. Some of the economic problems were solved through imperial expansion, through the extension of British sovereignty over major sources of supply and major markets; others were left to the autonomous operation of free trade. Only in the disturbed conditions of the twentieth century did economic issues become clearly political, notably when problems of exchange and of tariffs bedevilled the international scene in the interwar period. The last war was an all-out national effort in which security completely overrode economic considerations; security continued to overshadow them during the early period of the cold war and they gradually shifted to the foreground of British foreign policy only in the 1960s. Characteristically, in 1962, the Plowden Report recommended that 'The work of our representatives overseas must be increasingly dedicated to the support of British trade', while in 1969 the Duncan Committee repeatedly stressed that commercial priorities should be given clear precedence over other diplomatic activities except those pertaining to Britain's security[1]

It was much more than a question of additional diplomatic support for the promotion of British exports. Major economic issues, such as those of trade preference blocs or of international exchange, assumed central political importance. Less central but equally difficult was the problem of dealing with the developing countries for whom economics is *haute politique*, especially in the United Nations setting.

For a long time Britain's economy has been inextricably enmeshed in the international economy. No autarkic alternatives are available to a small island with a dense population enjoying an exceptionally high standard of living, which depends on the importation of nearly half of its food and of most of the raw materials needed, and on sufficient exports to pay for these. Britain's degree of political autonomy in economic matters is clearly slight. Her dependence upon the international order and upon the rules of behaviour enforced by it is not a new thing; what has greatly changed is her capacity to cope with the situation if it develops against her interests. Roy Jenkins recalls how a meeting of the Group of Ten which he attended as Chancellor of the Exchequer affected his thinking about Britain's position—he had to wait patiently during long adjournments to allow the Ministers of the Six to thrash out a joint view.[2] The United States Secretary of the Treasury was likewise somewhat impatient but he was not worried 'because he then thought that he could live with whatever decision emerged from the Six'; Jenkins was by no means sure that he could do so'.

Britain's post-war difficulties were increased by the historically evolved unique pattern of her international economic policy. She maintained an international reserve currency and a pattern of preference for not immediately profitable Commonwealth investments and, as her trade was based on the free-trade principle, exports and imports to and from individual countries and blocs could not be readily reduced to conform to the tendencies of the postwar period. In a position of rapidly diminishing economic weight, it became increasingly difficult for Britain to be confident that her own patterns would be acceptable to others. It was a question of compatibility with others and not of abstract rationality; for instance, both for purely economic and for social reasons, Britain's policy of free imports of cheap food, established after the fierce battles to repeal the Corn Laws in the last century, is not only preferable for Britain but constitutes a more rational policy than the protectionist food policy adopted by the EEC. Standing out, however, has proved, in the long run impossible.

Britain's economic recovery after 1945 was speedy and her subsequent average growth rate higher than ever before in her history. Nevertheless, owing to wartime disinvestment at home and the sale of assets abroad, the greater success of other countries, and the emancipation of her colonies, she slipped back from her former position as the dominant world trader and the second-wealthiest country in the world. In some ways, the economic and the security issues inherent in Britain's changed position were similar—she started with a leading position acquired during her imperial past but had to adjust her policies to her more limited capabilities; she could not conceivably assure her vital interests on her own, and she became dependent on outside support and/or some form of internationalization; the most promising source of support being the United States. There were, however important differences. Britain's main defence problems, despite nuclear weapons, could still be meaningfully reduced to the traditional forms—the government identifying the main enemy and organizing its defences and alliances against him. The international economic system is much more complex; the forces of the market which exercise a kind of political power are to a large extent uncontrolled, although we cannot regard them as fully uncontrollable.

Immediately after the war, when the economies of her future successful commercial rivals were shattered, Britain, together with the United States, was the main architect of the original economic arrangements. Naturally her policies were based upon her traditional ways of thinking about international economics, which go quite far back in history; they fall into two broad streams—the free traders and the protectionists—reflecting two perennial arguments: about the nature of the international system and about the relations between economics and politics. The free traders assumed a basic harmony of economic interests between nations and a separation of economics and politics; the protectionists, that nations behave basically in a selfish manner and that economics and politics are inextricably connected. These two sets of assumptions were connected only in the course of the historical evolution of the two schools of thought, but they are not logically inseparable: one can conceive of an international economic system based upon harmony of interests in which economics and politics are integrated rather than separated, and possibly the powerful tradition of free trade obstructed constructive innovations on these lines.

The ideas of free trade, which faithfully reflected the prevalent ideas about the management of the domestic economy on the basis of the *laissez faire* principle and supported the diplomatic principle of 'harmonization' (see pp. 122ff.), temporarily won the day. They were successful; in the last half of the nineteenth century the British economy grew, helping to double the standard of living of the workers, securing domestic peace, and also apparently contributing to international peace. The German economy, however, operating on a protectionist basis, began to advance much more rapidly. Towards the turn of the century British diplomacy was forced to negotiate with other states about the consequences of their divergent economic, domestic, and colonial policies, and some British imperialists decided in favour of an imperial conception of British trade. They did not manage to advance a coherent commercial conception of the Empire but in fact this gradually grew up as the result of currency and investment links.

As long as Britain retained some of the initial advantages of being the first country to industrialize, she pursued, in the main, a free-trade policy, even though other nations did not follow suit. The protectionist school, represented by Joseph Chamberlain's drive for imperial preferences early in the twentieth century, was unsuccessful; it triumphed, however, in the face of the intractable Great Depression; in 1932, the Commonwealth accepted a protectionist imperial-preferences policy. The idea of free trade remained, nevertheless, powerful as an aspiration, and persisted in the postwar period. Protectionism continued to be considered as a deviation, temporarily necessary, and the image of Britain as a free-trade country lingered among the majority of the British even though she had, in fact, become heavily protectionist.

The implications of the free traders' assumptions about the nature of the international system can be conveniently discussed in connection with the actual policy issues, but the doctrine of the separation of economics from politics is best analysed separately. Already in 1939 E. H. Carr[3] powerfully attacked this doctrine in application both to domestic and to international economics, pointing to the inextricable links between economics and politics; whether trade had followed the flag or the other way around, they were intimately connected; Palmerston may have advanced the principle of the autonomy of foreign investments which could not rely upon governmental protection, and the City may have operated autonomously, without direct links with foreign policy, but this was made possible only by the power of the British Navy. Carr's influential analysis helped to clarify thinking about the basic connection between economic and political power and objectives in general and to evaluate the lessons of the interwar period; it is also helpful in approaching the postwar period.

Carr quotes Hitler's observation in *Mein Kampf*: 'Is it not precisely the hallmark of British statesmanship to draw economic advantages from political strength and to transform every economic gain into political power?' This aptly sums up the period of Britain's imperial expansion and power. In the twentieth century, especially since 1945, the issue frequently arose in a negative form: how to avoid the transformation of the loss of political power into economic losses, and, *vice versa*, of economic losses into political ones. There seemed a valid *prima facie* case for keeping the economic and the political domains fairly separate in order to avoid this happening—to maintain Britain's political influence despite her waning economic capabilities and, likewise, to maintain her economic interests despite her waning political and military power to back them. Both in 1919 and in 1945 the major underlying assumption was that Britain would, at least to some degree, recoup her fortunes, in the latter case with American assistance or through some form of international arrangements. Purchasing time, therefore, by maintaining positions of power, however temporarily endangered, might prove profitable. Retrenchment, shedding of overcommitments, was therefore restricted to the immediately urgent cases; anyway, there were more than enough of these to keep governments working at full stretch.

Carr's criticism of this policy of separation is valid only because the assumption of recovery did not hold; as a result, the lack of full integration of policies in the economic and political spheres proved costly. Immediately after the war there was a political case for refusing to scale down the sterling balances as the Americans advocated, and for retaining the sterling bloc as a cementing factor in the Commonwealth, but certainly not by the mid-1960s. The phenomenon of the separation of economics and politics and the dire cost paid for it when the state loses power is not uniquely British. Similar shortcomings can be noted among American decision-makers in the postwar period, who usually saw economic issues as 'distasteful interruptions from matters of high policy', although in contrast to their British counterparts, they employed economic policies as an instrument of national security.[4]

The divorce between economic and political thinking also played a part in delaying Britain's joining the EEC. Economic and political expertise and power were lodged in separate ministries, which contributed to the apparent inability of the policy-makers to assess the implications of the fundamental clash between the commercial logic governing the British moves and the political logic of the French attitudes. De Gaulle may not have fully understood economics but he integrated it with and subordinated it to politics. Probably the national interests of the British and the French could not have been reconciled, and the strategy adopted by the British, in the main aiming at establishing a commercially reasonable position and at securing the support of the other members of the Community in the hope that they would prevail upon the French, was the most promising one. It seems likely, nevertheless, that, had the British policy-makers appreciated earlier and more clearly the inextricable links between the political and the economic issues at stake, negotiations might have proved easier or, at least, would have been shorter and their adverse effects may have been somewhat reduced on both sides.

The stand taken on the American balance-of-payments deficit in the late 1960s is another example of Britain's refusing to face the political aspects of an economic issue. There were sound political reasons for supporting the Americans, on the general grounds of being in close alliance with them, and on the specific ones of the solidarity of British and American interests in defending their currencies as vehicles of international exchange; there was no case for supporting the French attack. Was it, however, necessary to refute the political logic of the French arguments by insisting that the issues were purely economic? Conceivably, it would have been healthier for the British to substitute for what, in effect, was a futile *dialogue des sourds* with the French, a more straightforward confrontation of national interests. Instead of minimizing the conflict, the British refusal to admit the political implications of the issue seems to have aggravated it. It is hard to avoid the feeling that the British economic specialists involved genuinely failed fully to appreciate the political aspects of the American balance-of-payments deficit.

It seems futile to endeavour to answer in general terms the question which is occasionally put, whether the political or the economic aspects of British foreign policy are or should be dominant. Security and prosperity are its constant twin objectives and one is given precedence over the other in the light of the perceived necessities of any given situation. Differences of opinion about timing are sometimes of great importance but, in the long run, neither aspect can be neglected. Even during the great divisions of opinion following the 1914–18 war, Keynes concentrated on food, coal, and transport but only after Germany had been deprived of her fleet and colonies; and despite his preoccupation with security, Lloyd George thought about economic rehabilitation, in the Fontainebleau Memorandum for instance. On the whole, British foreign policy in the interwar period can now be seen as having been based upon an excessive belief in the importance of economic considerations, due to the mistaken assumption that security was not endangered. Fascism and Nazism were considered as predominantly economic phenomena; Lloyd George in his dealings with Lenin, and Neville Chamberlain in his dealings with Hitler relied excessively on the economic motivations of their opponents.

Seemingly, some of this excessive attribution of economic motivations to others persisted in the postwar period, particularly in British relations with de Gaulle and with some developing countries. This time, however, no government could avoid being aware of a basic security threat to Britain, a fear of which matched and often surpassed the continuing concern with her ailing economy, which was occasionally augmented by the fear of an American recession. The Attlee Government devoted its full energies both to security and to the economy; its successors could not fail to follow suit. Politics since 1945 were not, therefore, based on economic myths, as in the interwar period; on the contrary, one may argue that in the 1960s they were partly based upon political myths of a world role for British forces east of Suez and for sterling, myths which operated against economic priorities.

An important factor in perpetuating the traditional divorce between economics and politics can be found in the divided expertise and power in the two fields. The Board of Trade worked on its own. Although the Foreign Office was naturally concerned with many economic matters, it traditionally accepted without question the expertise of the Treasury on international finance. From the perspective of the 1970s, we can understand better the central role played by the defence of sterling in Britain's postwar policies in general but, until the end of the 1960s, sterling remained the responsibility of the Treasury and of the Bank of England. On the whole, sterling problems did not play a significant direct part in determining major foreign-policy objectives, although the run on sterling was the decisive factor in hastening the declaration of the Suez cease-fire in November 1956. The situation changed only in the later 1960s when the aggravated balance-of-payments problems began to loom large. These problems provided the rationalization rather than a direct reason for the decision to withdraw from east of Suez but they certainly played a crucial part in curtailing Britain's traditional attachment to the wide scope of her world role. By then, the co-ordination of economic and political moves was improving. Consultative machinery between the agencies involved was established and a greater degree of economic expertise in the Foreign Office was ensured by suitable training. Nevertheless, competition for being the centre of economic expertise still inevitably arises, for instance, between the Treasury and the Procurement Agency of the Ministry of Defence. We still do not fully understand the implications of the links between economics and foreign policy, but we are at least well aware of their existence and importance.

*Main Postwar Economic Strategies*
Despite the conceptual and institutional separation between economics and politics, Britain's postwar external policies in the two fields, not unexpectedly, show close parallels. In the first place, the international economic system reflected the divisions of the political system on the two separate lines of the cold war and the differences between the developed and the developing world. Second, Britain was closely enmeshed in both systems, and, in the immediate postwar years, played a leading part in both, second only to the United States. Third, all the successive governments were acting on the basis of a similar appreciation of Britain's political and economic interests and position in the world. Their acute awareness of Britain's dependence upon the stability of the international system, reinforced by the habit of playing a central part within it, bred a sense of international responsibility both in economics and in politics.

Fourth, both Britain's economic world role focusing on sterling and her political role as a policeman east of Suez were simultaneously undermined owing to insufficient capabilities, leading to their abandonment in the late 1960s.

When one looks at the record as a whole, it is clear that, through her co-operation with the United States and her membership of such organizations as the OEEC (later OEECD), the GATT, EFTA, and the Group of Ten, Britain firmly joined the capitalist, anti-communist camp of the developed, rich countries. It is possible to assert that, in the main, Britain had here no alternative. Whereas in the political/strategic domain it was possible at least theoretically to conceive of a 'Third Force', Britain's utter dependence upon American economic assistance made co-operation with the United States imperative; this was the only hope for an effective policy towards the twin basic British objectives—to restore and expand world trade and to establish a stable system of international finance. In 1945 there was no alternative to the American link; without the loan which was negotiated on what, in the eyes of the British, were extremely stiff terms, Britain would have been bankrupt. This dependence meant that the international economic and financial systems were established largely according to American ideas; Maynard Keynes had the foresight to plead for an integrated international financial system with set obligations for surplus countries, but he was defeated. The Americans were confident that the dollar could serve adequately as an international medium of exchange with sterling in support. Subsequently, Britain's economy was continuously ailing under this secondary burden—eventually, in the late 1960s, the dollar also came to grief.

Apart from sterling (see below pp. 268ff.), Britain's eccentric position within the international system had deleterious effects also upon her trade. As she started in a seller's market with a considerable advantage over her devastated continental rivals and Japan, she had little incentive to renew her obsolete equipment and was in a poor position to compete when her rivals entered the markets later on. The periods of expansion in international trade rarely coincided with the periods of expansion in Britain's economy and hence she did not fully profit from them; notably, owing to her exceptional rearmament effort, she missed many of the opportunities of the post-Korean boom. From the late 1950s she began to suffer from a chronic imbalance of her external accounts and from repeated runs on the pound for which the standard orthodox economic advice and governmental reaction was to deflate and thus reduce economic growth. Her poor domestic performance was variously attributed to structural defects and to misguided policies, and only towards the end of the period did policy-makers and experts become fully aware how far they were due to the structural defects of the international system and the excessive responsibility Britain held within it. As shown by the Keynes–White controversy in 1945, Britain could not exercise a decisive influence upon the international system; she was even less capable of doing so in the early 1970s, when the Six had become a leading factor.

The basic dichotomy confronting Britain in international economics can be subsumed under the traditional one between free trade and protectionism: the former offered a model of a global system based upon non-discriminatory multilateralism, the latter one of protectionist regional trading blocs. Both models were of an ideal type and, in real life, any system would have had to find a compromise between the two. British policies oscillated uneasily in between. Free trade was the principle governing the system jointly worked out, in the main, by the Americans and the British at Bretton Woods and Havana but, as this system would have favoured the most powerful trading nation, namely the United States, Britain stubbornly defended her imperial preferences. Attachment to free trade was one of the major reasons why Britain rejected the early European integration plans and explains why the unrealistic ideas of a North Atlantic Free Trade Area (NAFTA) were occasionally voiced in the EEC debates; it provides one of the stock arguments of the anti-Marketeers against Britain joining the EEC.

Simultaneously, Britain continued imperial preferences, established EFTA and, finally, decided to replace both with membership of the EEC. Within the Community, however, it is likely to suit British interests to press for free trade again. Liberalization of the remaining restrictions on international trade would help to safeguard more of the traditional patterns of Britain's trade, notably cheap food supplies. Moreover, by reducing the potential sources of friction, free trade would also ease future political relations both with the Commonwealth countries and with the United States.

It is possible to distinguish a parallel, although not fully simultaneous, evolution of British economic and political strategies; their essence can be summed up as a gradual acceptance of the growing limitations of Britain's independent power, accompanied by a change of emphasis from the global to the regional context and from an alignment with the United States to one with Western Europe. The early global and American orientation was expressed in the joint proposals for a non-discriminatory multilateral system which have been trenchantly analysed by Professor R. N. Gardner. According to him, the system established was deficient owing to the absence of three essential preconditions: a tolerable system of political equilibrium; a reasonable state of economic equilibrium; and adoption of appropriate external and domestic policies by both creditor and debtor nations. The difficulties were further increased by three major errors in national policies: first economism—the belief that economic policy could be made in a political vacuum and that the principal approach to world peace could be through economic co-operation; second, universalism—the belief in the possibility of a universal order without alliances and special arrangements; and third, legalism—the tendency to think that outstanding international problems could be resolved by drafting codes of formal rules of behaviour.[5] Despite all these short-comings, the Bretton Woods system worked reasonably well until the end of the 1960s, and it assisted, or at least did not seriously obstruct, economic growth. However, as it did not have the makings of a permanent system, it can be added to the other 'masking factors' which prevented the British from realizing their real weaknesses after 1945 (see chs 4 and 5); and it can be seen as a major cause of the acuteness of the sterling problem in the late 1950s and of the troubles which bedevilled the whole international economic system in the early 1970s.

The British were not governed by a doctrinal attachment either to free trade or to a close alignment with the United States, but were pursuing specific interests. Much more realistically than the Americans, they were more sceptical of the prospects of a tolerable political balance and were apprehensive of chronic imbalances of payments; they were not at all sure that the United States, the main creditor nation, would always uphold the system sufficiently, and they therefore persisted in safeguarding as far as possible their interests as a debtor nation. Keynes proposed large overdraft facilities, amounting to $25,000 million, with additional credits for emergency, against the American proposal to limit these facilities to the amounts actually subscribed, first $5,000 and then $8,000 million. The British also insisted that imperial preferences should be maintained, and that their major domestic priorities, elimination of unemployment and ambitious economic growth should, if necessary, override the rules established to govern international trade. Last but not least, they were determined to keep the World Bank and the Fund as purely financial institutions, in order to ward off the possibility of institutional interference in members' domestic affairs.

The World Bank and Fund were duly established with a fairly limited scope and the proposed International Trade Organization did not materialize at all, leaving behind only the residual General Agreement on Trade and Tariffs (GATT). Although Britain took an active part in the successive rounds of the GATT negotiations for tariff cuts, ever since the European Recovery Programme her major efforts have been directed not towards the global system but towards the Commonwealth and Western Europe. The post-Korean trade boom decisively tilted the balance of importance towards the developed countries; in the 1951–5 period British exports to these rose by some 60 per cent against a mere 13 per cent rise in exports to the members of the sterling bloc, the primary products of which did not rise in price equally to industrial products. Subsequently, Britain was unable to increase Commonwealth trade rapidly and, following the formation of the EEC, her main efforts were directed towards Europe—to forming a free-trade association with the EEC, then entering the Community and, in the meantime, to developing EFTA.

It was in the late 1960s that the full implications of Britain's relative loss of economic power became increasingly clear—she found it difficult to effectively pursue her trade interests in the so-called Kennedy Round of the GATT negotiations, in which the EEC emerged for the first time as a common trading bloc; acute balance-of-payments difficulties forced her to devalue, and her policy-makers discovered that the cost of keeping sterling as an international exchange currency at an overvalued rate was extremely heavy and the benefits dubious; as a single state on its own she could not play a major role in the dollar crisis of the summer of 1971. For all these reasons, Britain returned to the idea of a thorough reform of the international system, this time not acting by herself but through the EEC. The Heath Government not only unconditionally accepted the new somewhat attenuated structure of the Community but firmly indicated that it intended to work towards the goal of a common currency and a common economic policy. The Community should also offer Britain a firm base for pursuing her traditional free trade and global interests, for taking a full part in the establishment of a new international financial system, and for moving further towards the objective of global free trade under the GATT.

This decisive shift towards Western European alignment was not exclusively due to the fact that Britain's policy-makers had realized her increasing inability to pursue her vital economic interests on her own. Simultaneously Britain's economic interests began to coincide with those of Western Europe rather than with those of the United States or the Commonwealth. The United States is much less dependent on world trade than either Britain or her continental neighbours; Britain's dependence is equalled by that of Germany, surpassed by Austria and Switzerland and about doubled by that of the Netherlands and Belgium; even France is not very far behind. Moreover, all Western European countries are more or less equally vulnerable in respect of their vital imports of oil.

Statistical tables often, perhaps usually, serve as mere rationalizations of policies decided for political reasons, but, particularly when the magnitudes are sizeable, they do express important realities which cannot be ignored by governments. The following table sets out the basic similarity of the role of trade in Britain and in Western Europe:

| | | *Percentage Ratios of Exports (X) and Imports (I) to GNP* | | | | |
|---|---|---|---|---|---|---|
| | | *1955* | *1960* | *1965* | *1967* | *1968* |
| Austria | X | 16·9 | 18·1 | 17·2 | 16·9 | 17·5 |
| | I | 21·4 | 22·8 | 22·6 | 21·6 | 22·0 |
| Belgium | X | 30·2 | 36·7 | 37·5 | 34·5 | 39·1 |
| | I | 37·4 | 38·5 | 38·1 | 35·2 | 39·9 |
| France | X | 10·1 | 11·8 | 10·1 | 10·4 | 10·0 |
| | I | 9·7 | 10·8 | 10·4 | 11·3 | 11·0 |
| Italy | X | 8·4 | 11·4 | 12·6 | 13·0 | 13·6 |
| | I | 12·3 | 14·8 | 12·9 | 14·5 | 13·7 |
| Japan | X | 8·9 | 9·5 | 9·6 | 9·1 | 9·1 |
| | I | 10·9 | 10·5 | 9·2 | 10·1 | 9·2 |
| Netherlands | X | 33·7 | 35·8 | 33·4 | 31·9 | 33·1 |
| | I | 40·2 | 40·3 | 39·0 | 36·9 | 36·8 |
| Switzerland | X | 20·6 | 21·9 | 21·2 | 21·8 | 23·3 |
| | I | 23·5 | 26·0 | 26·5 | 25·7 | 26·5 |
| UK | X | 15·0 | 13·8 | 13·7 | 13·2 | 15·1 |
| | I | 20·1 | 17·6 | 16·1 | 16·2 | 18·6 |
| USA | X | 3·8 | 4·0 | 3·9 | 3·9 | 4·0 |
| | I | 3·1 | 3·2 | 3·4 | 3·7 | 4·1 |
| W. Germany | X | 14·4 | 17·0 | 15·8 | 17·9 | 18·7 |
| | I | 13·2 | 15·0 | 15·3 | 14·3 | 15·2 |

The direction of a country's trade is, of course, of great, though by no means decisive political importance. Politicians only slowly realize the implications of figures and even more so those of trends; political rather than economic arguments generally prove decisive. The unexpectedly great trading successes of EFTA could not prevail in saving it, as its importance as a political base was slight. The fact that 43 per cent of British exports went to the Commonwealth in 1957 was not the decisive reason why the British government rejected the pleas of the British Ambassador in Paris for a positive move towards the nascent EEC. In the longer run, however, the trade trends prevail. The economic logic of Britain's joining the EEC is demonstrated by the magnitude of the redirection of her trade from the sterling area to Western Europe which is shown in the following table:

### The Trends of British Trade
### (in £ million)

| | 1962 | | 1970 | |
|---|---|---|---|---|
| | *Imports* | *Exports* | *Imports* | *Exports* |
| Sterling area | 1,580 | 1,367 | 2,460 | 2,218 |
| W. Europe | 1,394 | 1,488 | 3,412 | 3,313 |
| N. America | 838 | 580 | 1,857 | 1,231 |
| USSR & E. Europe | 168 | 132 | 364 | 258 |
| L. America | 298 | 163 | 326 | 283 |
| The rest | 351 | 332 | 614 | 722 |

*Source*: General Statistical Office, *Annual Abstract of Statistics* No. 108, 1971, tables 274, 275.

Finally, Britain has been governed only to a limited extent by purely political considerations in the direction of her trade. She followed the strategic embargoes on exports to communist countries, but only with modifications; after a considerable Cabinet division, Wilson accepted the United Nations embargo on the sale of arms to South Africa, but excluding standing contracts. Rhodesia is only a partial exception— insisting on her primary responsibility, Britain disrupted her trade with Southern Rhodesia by applying sanctions more scrupulously than other countries. This policy can, however, be explained not only by political considerations but by the desire to avoid commercial losses elsewhere. Britain lost her rather insignificant trade with Southern Rhodesia, running at £30,000 in 1965, but managed to retain her much more important trade with South Africa without disrupting that with black Africa, exports to which now exceed those to South Africa. Especially important was trade with Nigeria, greatly increased by British oil purchases. The 1970 figures were: (in £ million)

| | Imports from | Exports to | Balance |
|---|---|---|---|
| South Africa | 258 | 333 | +75 |
| Nigeria | 124 | 114 | −10 |

*Source*: ibid.

Many aspects of international economic policy have only recently come to be somewhat better understood; the operations of the City, for instance, and of the multinational companies.[6] No clear policy line seems to exist on these except the very general one that economic operations are allowed to proceed autonomously, subject to the laws of the land, until and unless the political implications become obvious. For instance, the successive governments allowed, and frequently encouraged, the investment of American capital in Britain, but they had reservations about the Americans acquiring full control of the British Ford Company and purchasing Rootes, as the car industry is central to the country's economic life. The take-over in the ball-bearing industry proposed by the Swedish firm, S.K.F., raised governmental opposition because of the strategic importance of this industry. It is unthinkable that an American or other foreign acquisition of the British computer or any other important industry would ever be permitted. Investment of British capital abroad broadly followed the country's major political alignments: at first it concentrated on the sterling area, where it was free from any restrictions, later, after Britain's entry into the EEC, more of it went to the Community.

Three specific aspects of Britain's international economic policy are sufficiently central to foreign policy in general to warrant a brief separate discussion: sterling, oil, and aid.

*Sterling*

In the wake of the continuous balance-of-payments crises in the 1960s and of the subsequent gold and dollar crises, we have now become extremely conscious of the significance of sterling as a major, perhaps the major, factor in determining Britain's fortunes since 1945. While disagreement continues about other areas of British foreign policy, especially her relations with Europe, no dissenting voice has been raised against the present negative evolution of postwar sterling policies.

*The Economist*, long one of the most ardent critics of the traditional sterling policies, thus evaluated the whole record in 1971:

No country has sacrificed more to the great delusion of the old monetary order than Britain. In order to keep sterling standing in the front firing line of fixed exchange rates, for far longer than the Americans have now bothered to keep the dollar there, the average British family must have lost thousands of today's pounds in thwarted income over the whole decade 1957–67. In November, 1956, it was largely in order to maintain sterling's status that we marched into the Suez war, and it was wholly in order to maintain it that we then hurried out again. Ten years later the same fetish of worship round the $2.80 totem pole turned Britain's first Labour government for 13 years into the most conservative government that Britain has known since Stanley Baldwin declined a bit in his old age.[7]

Apart from the somewhat cryptic ascription of the origins of the Suez action to sterling, this evaluation is quite reasonable. In more general terms, the history of sterling, which has been critically and cogently assessed by Susan Strange, in *Sterling and British Policy*[7] can be briefly stated as follows. Preoccupation with sterling's reserve role led Britain's policy-makers to ignore economic reality and to defend its parity at the cost of keeping it grossly overvalued, thus damaging export prospects, incurring deficits in the balance of payments, and being repeatedly forced into wasteful spells of deflation.

Sterling policy is a clear demonstration of several phenomena of broader application: the slow growth of our understanding of international economics, of the divorce between economics and politics, and the growing inability of the individual state to determine its own policies. Several factors are generally mentioned as the major reasons for the prolonged defence of sterling parity: the conservatism of the Treasury and the Bank of England, the enormous difficulty of Britain's changing her policy owing to her pivotal position in the international financial system, her dependence upon the United States, the close links between British sterling and Commonwealth policies, and the attachment to sterling as an important aspect of Britain's international role. It would, however, be impossible to segregate the impact of the individual factors with any precision, as they coincided and overlapped and they were appreciated differently in different periods and by different individuals. Macmillan mentions how the exchange rate of sterling seemed to be beyond Britain's power to decide unilaterally in July 1961. In a common sense way he states that he himself would have preferred a floating rate because this 'would be a barometer and any weakness of the market much more quickly detected than by Government statisticians.[8] He does not explain why he thought the idea to be impossible—one surmises that, not having any economic expertise himself, he felt it unthinkable to try to override the Treasury and the Bank of England on an issue of central importance, especially as the Americans and the whole international financial community (not to mention orthodox academic advice) were all opposed to devaluation.

Why, however, did Wilson defend sterling in 1967? Being himself an economist he fully understood the increasing academic advocacy for devaluation. It is hard to judge to what extent he was governed by official orthodoxy, by American pressures, or by his attachment to a world role. And, in spite of the comfortable majority he had won in 1966, he may also have had a political motive: that Labour should not be held responsible for the pound losing its value. Britain, however, was not alone in her conservatism. The Commonwealth countries too, although affected by the weakness of sterling and ultimately suffering losses through the devaluations of the pound, behaved similarly. They continued to accept the postwar arrangements for Britain's managing the reserves of the sterling area for some time even after they had resolutely asserted their freedom to alter their constitutional arrangements and to conduct independent foreign and commercial policies.

Sterling troubles did not arise out of complete lack of foresight. In fact, had the 1944 Keynes plan for a clearing union been adopted by the

Americans, with its heavy obligations upon surplus countries, all the subsequent troubles would have been avoided. But the Americans, with their apparently impregnable position and massive trade surpluses, thought otherwise. Sterling, which became the auxiliary reserve currency, was in trouble from the beginning. Britain's economy was too small and weak to support such a responsibility—the early convertibility crisis following the American loan could, however, have been attributed to her passing weaknesses, and the full extent and chronic nature of the problem became clear only in retrospect. As the first line of defence for the dollar, Britain was carrying a heavy responsibility both to her ally and bene-factor and to the international system as a whole. In Roy Jenkins's words, the Americans adopted an attitude 'both sympathetic and admonitory' to Britain's troubles[9] and encouraged her in this policy on the—justifiable —grounds that the collapse of sterling parity would precipitate the col-lapse of the whole postwar international financial system as, indeed, it did. The Americans were not alone in wishing to keep sterling stable; all the major financial states were also involved. About 50 per cent of the international transactions immediately after the War were conducted in sterling, and even in the early 1970s, some 20 per cent may have continued to be so. All the users of sterling wished to keep it stable. The holders of sterling balances were naturally even more interested in keeping up the value of their holdings, which in 1967 amounted to £3,800 million. Britain was thus fulfilling a major international responsibility which she could not easily shirk; she continued to fulfil it at an increasingly heavy cost to herself.

In fact, the great speculative waves of the 1960s arose from movements of private funds and were not really altered by the reserve-currency nature of the pound.[10] The latter was only their indirect cause by dis-couraging Britain from devaluing the pound, which had been visibly overvalued from the beginning of the decade. As the maintenance of the parity of sterling was in their interest, the Group of Ten readily assisted Britain in her difficulties, helping her to continue with an overvalued and unstable currency which undermined her competitive position.

Postwar sterling policies cannot be understood otherwise than on the basis of their historical background. Acquiring an international currency had been a slow and cumulative, not a deliberate process. It was parallel to, and it interacted with, the acquisition of the Empire—within which sterling was an important asset; in a circular way, Britain's imperial power supported and extended the international use of sterling. After 1945, sterling as an international currency was thus an inheritance from the Empire as much as was the chain of overseas strategic bases, about both of which it was extremely difficult to strike a clear balance of advantages and disadvantages (see pp. 297–303). First of all, it was difficult to grasp the situation adequately. Economic analysis was still rudimentary. The ominous results of the burden of sterling became apparent only during the 1957 sterling crisis, which was due entirely to international pressures as the domestic economy at the time was quite sound. Although, already in 1959, the Radcliffe Committee Report[11] had spelt out the implications, the advice of the Treasury and the Bank of England remained orthodox and external support enabled sterling to survive. Only the major international currency crises in the later 1960s brought a fuller appreciation of what was involved.

The second reason was psychological; it lay in the politicians' attachment to sterling as a vague but powerful instrument and also as a symbol of power and influence. This was particularly true of Wilson in his dogged last-ditch defence of sterling against increasing pressures and advice from the economists to devalue. According to Lord Longford, he forbade his associates even to talk about devaluation or to seek advice about it.[12] In his admittedly uncommunicative but extensive memoirs he clearly indicates that he closed his mind in this respect and ultimately accepted devaluation only under extreme duress. The accusation sometimes made that he regarded the pound as a symbol of Britain's international virility, even more important than the H-bomb, seems to be warranted.

The historical paradox about sterling is that, although the international use of the currency was associated with the acquisition of the British Empire, the sterling area, which loomed large in the postwar years, had been established only a short time before, when Britain's Empire and her economy were both in decline. The sterling system used to be loose and only in 1931, when Britain abandoned gold parity, were other countries forced to choose between sterling and gold; the sterling area was formally established in 1940 as a means of extending exchange controls, and was maintained after 1945 owing to the accumulation of sterling balances. At first the system ran smoothly owing to the complementarity of the trade interests of Britain and the other members of the area—Britain was running a deficit with the non-sterling countries but a surplus with the overseas sterling areas, whereas the trade pattern of the latter tended to be the reverse. Substantial visible trade deficits for the areas as a whole arose, however, after the Korean war, and were only met by sales of the gold produced, while growing deficits in Britain's invisible account were covered by imports of capital.

Although the overall balance of the sterling area was thus temporarily maintained, the economic links between Britain and the sterling area were simultaneously weakened. The changes between 1958 and 1967 were especially dramatic.[13] The overseas sterling area became dependent for two-thirds of its capital inflow on the non-sterling world, and its trade with the latter increased by 100 per cent against a mere 25 per cent increase in its trade with Britain; its share of United Kingdom imports fell from about 50 to 25 per cent and its share of United Kingdom exports fell from about 41 to 30 per cent. The general position of Britain thus greatly deteriorated, in relation not only to the non-sterling world but also to the overseas sterling area.

Probably, even while Britain was at the height of her power, sterling was not only an asset but, to a limited extent, also a liability—apparently, during the financial crises which recurred about every decade between 1763 and 1914 the Bank of England was[14] subordinating domestic growth to international economic stability. In a situation in which Britain's power was rapidly receding and the economic basis of the sterling area arrangements was being rapidly eroded, the balance of payments became increasingly negative. The adverse effects of the sterling mystique can be traced in governmental activities in general, as well as, more specifically, in a foreign policy unduly biased towards the Commonwealth, and in an obstructed economic growth.

Throughout the 1960s sterling was a chronic and at times predominant issue: whenever there was a serious run on the pound, its defence received the highest priority, inevitably at the cost of attention to other issues. This was a serious drain on governmental time and energy. In addition, the sterling arrangements and the constant preoccupation with the balance of payments with the non-sterling world created an artificial division between expenditure in the two, and dual standards of husbandry. Successive Governments allowed and encouraged British investment in the overseas sterling area, although the sums were excessive to what the economy could afford, and although the prospective returns were not as alluring as they could often have been elsewhere; nor was overseas governmental expenditure in the sterling area nearly as vigorously curbed as outside it.

Expenditure within the overseas sterling area was insufficiently curbed partly because the policy-makers were not alerted to its implications through the balance of payments as they would have been with non-sterling countries, but partly also because it was tied up in a circular way with the Commonwealth. On the one hand, as the sterling-area arrangements were the only commonly agreed substantial Commonwealth policy, the British were encouraged to maintain and buttress them as a major contribution to the Commonwealth links; on the other, the continuance of the arrangements was instrumental in obscuring the loosening of other Commonwealth links. Thus one myth reinforced the other one—sterling could not have survived quite as long as an international currency without the Commonwealth, while the widespread belief that the Commonwealth links had more substance than they had in reality was reinforced by the sterling-area arrangements.

The most detrimental effect of the myth of sterling was upon domestic economy. As the French pointedly stated in their criticisms of the United States dollar policy in the late 1960s and early 1970s, the countries which are willing to hold increasing quantities of the international currency issued by another country, finance the latter's balance-of-payments deficits. This, however, applies to a country in a financially strong position. Britain, by contrast, was notoriously weak throughout the postwar period and, far from profiting from sterling being an international exchange currency, she was burdened with high costs. In order to ensure the maintenance of the sterling balances in London, international confidence had to be maintained and attractive terms had to be offered. The burden of interest on the balances grew as the international interest rates grew and confidence in Britain's economy waned. Even worse, a realistic devaluation of sterling was further impeded as it could be regarded as a breach of trust towards the holders of sterling balances. Most importantly, the effects of the recurrent balance-of-payments crises were aggravated by the fear that they would result in a run on the pound. Maintenance of sterling parity was the main reason for the 'stop-go' policies; no sustained period of vigorous growth was possible as the resulting deterioration in the balance of payments immediately led to deflation, often savage; Britain's ailing economy was the price of keeping the pound up. The cost was particularly heavy under the Wilson Government when it was fighting the last losing battles, between 1964 and the devaluation in 1967; according to some admittedly speculative findings, Wilson's last-ditch defence of parity cost the country some 2 per cent of lost economic growth, while the cumulative cost over the whole period of the Labour government was some £5,000 million.

After the 1967 devaluation, the importance of sterling rapidly dwindled both for the British and for the world. Sterling became much less important in the world economy: by 1972 its holdings, though slightly increased in absolute terms, amounted only to some 7 per cent of the total reserves; the financial crises of the early 1970s centred on the D-mark and the dollar. Sterling issues gradually faded out as a problem confronting British governments. The sterling area lost its cohesion when a substantial number of members refused to follow Britain's 1967 devaluation, in contrast to the general devaluation in 1949 in which Pakistan was the only exception. Under the Basle Agreements of 1967, Britain received international guarantees against a new sterling crisis; and, in the bilateral agreements with the holders of sterling balances in the following year, she guaranteed 90 per cent of the holdings in dollars or gold. Finally, in the negotiations to enter the EEC, the British side—in the wording of the White Paper of July 1971—agreed 'to envisage an orderly and gradual run-down of official sterling balances after our accession'. In June 1972, when a run on the pound resulted in the stupendous loss of reserves of $2,500 million within one week, the government did not defend sterling's parity, but decided to float it. This final break from the prolonged and costly defence of sterling was this time further obstructed by the recent international agreements about exchange rates and the obligations undertaken to keep fluctuations within narrow limits; the government, however, acted decisively and successfully pleaded necessity despite the embarrassment caused to others, especially the United States and France. It was clearly following the national interest and, in the process, it administered the final blow to the international exchange role of sterling. The orthodox believers in the need for Britain to carry on international responsibility rather than to pursue her own interest were paid mere lip-service in the Chancellor of the Exchequer's original announcement of the floating of the pound, which stated that the previously agreed rate of $2.60 to the pound was realistic; it was quite clear from the outset that floating would end in a substantial devaluation.

The rapid decline in sterling's international role and its floating exchange rate did not, by themselves, restore the health of Britain's economy or foreign confidence in it; but they did free the government from one extremely restrictive constraint. This is best demonstrated by the contrast between the Conservative attempts to maintain a substantial rate of economic growth in 1964 and in 1973. In the first case, the determined policy pursued by Maudling, which resulted in a growing deficit in the balance of payments, ended in an immediate crisis and in a Labour electoral victory; a situation similar in structure, although different in its detail, arose in 1973 but the Heath Government felt in a position to persevere in its determination to avoid a restrictive period of deflation.

## Oil[15]

Even before the reversal of British and Arab roles in 1973 both oil experts and foreign-policy experts were agreed that oil would become an increasingly complex issue in the later 1970s and the 1980s, owing to the combined effects of increasing consumption demands and of increasing difficulties with the major producing countries in the Middle East. Oil had become fully internationalized because, as in international finance, there existed a distinct international system although there was no truly international management. Oil issues had appeared somewhat easier to understand and to integrate into foreign policy than issues of currency parity, as we had at least some intelligible hard data; but the differences of opinion on future oil requirements, on the reserves available, and on the likely policies both of the producer and of the consumer countries were bewildering.

To start with, was consumption likely to rise at the rate of 7–8 per cent per annum, as from the early 1950s, or even faster, if developing countries rapidly increased their consumption? What were the likely changes in the patterns of consumption? In the short run, Britain—and Western Germany—had stopped substituting oil for coal, and Britain was beginning to exploit natural gas from the North Sea; in the longer run, nuclear energy would be more utilized. Would the use of the car continue to rise or would it be curtailed?

Nor were we quite clear about oil reserves. There was a fair agreement that there were over 360 milliard barrels of exploitable oil in the Middle East but we did not know whether the deposits which were being rapidly discovered in the North Sea amounted merely to the cautious estimates at the end of 1972 of some 6 milliard barrels or were very substantially higher, perhaps as much as 30 or 40 milliard.[16] Was there exploitable oil on the European continental shelf, in Baffinland, in North Canada?

In their general structure, British oil policies have resembled sterling policies in two respects: first, the successive governments have allowed a fairly autonomous management of both and, second, in both cases British policies have been closely linked with American ones, Britain starting as the senior and ending as the junior partner. On the other hand, there was no parallel between the management of sterling by the Bank of England and of oil by the oil companies; ever since the first world war oil had been directly involved in foreign policy and had very largely determined its conduct in the Middle East. British oil policy was therefore interesting in two respects—as an illustration of the general theme of adaptation to the loss of a dominant position and of internationalization, and as an important area of public policy with unique characteristics. Of special interest is the question to what extent the traditions evolved in the past were likely to affect Britain's future management of oil issues as a major Western European producer.

The basic objective of British oil policy has been consistent ever since Winston Churchill, as the First Lord of the Admiralty, proposed to the

House of Commons on 7 June 1914 the purchase of the controlling interest in the Anglo-Persian Company for £2,200,000. A secure supply of oil in war and peace, he prophetically foresaw, was vital; it was even more so later when, apart from its strategic use for the Navy, oil had become the major fuel for civilian purposes. The government did not attempt to control the oil business and did not exercise its dominant interest in the Anglo-Persian Company (later renamed Anglo-Iranian and finally British Petroleum Company) to control its commercial policy. It did, however, use its political power in the Middle East throughout the interwar period to encourage British oil interests and to exclude American competitors.

The fierce British-American competition for Middle Eastern oil ended only some time after the war when, through a series of complex interlocking arrangements, the interests of all the major Anglo-American groups were brought into a happy state of harmonization. In Iran, the last Middle Eastern country where the oil interests remained exclusively British, it became obvious how dangerous such a monopoly had become —by 1951 the resentment against the company's monopoly and its stubborn refusal to accept a 50/50 profit-sharing agreement, which had become standard elsewhere, spilled over into antagonism against the British government, as, in the eyes of the Iranians, the two were virtually indistinguishable. The British government naturally tried to protect the company, but decided not to proceed with the unpromising idea of military intervention and was unsuccessful in referring the case to the World Court. The settlement was ultimately forced upon Iran by slow strangulation through an embargo upon her oil which no country was prepared to break. This was ensured politically by British intervention with President Truman, but success would have been unthinkable had not the major oil companies established beforehand a great degree of solidarity.

The settlement in Iran was through an international consortium taking over and compensating the Anglo-Iranian Company. The pattern of interdependence among the major producing companies, mainly American and British, was thus finally established. Co-operation between them was fully internationalized, increasingly so in the face of the growing solidarity and hence bargaining power of the oil producers, now organized in OPEC. British companies remained the leaders in Kuwait, Iran, and Iraq, but all moves were internationally agreed. On its part, the British government treated all the oil companies with studied impartiality in order to avoid reprisals. The recognition of interdependence and the resulting solidarity among the major producing companies was matched by the growing recognition by all the Western European countries of the identity of their interests as regards oil imports. Britain's consumption, formerly outstandingly large, well over one-quarter of Western European total consumption in 1950, was surpassed by that of Western Germany by 1965 and, by 1970, was under one-sixth of the Western European total.

| | Oil Consumption ('000 tonnes) | | | |
|---|---|---|---|---|
| | 1950 | 1960 | 1965 | 1970 (prelim.) |
| UK | 18,300 | 47,000 | 72,600 | 103,000 |
| Total W. Europe | 62,000 | 196,350 | 387,000 | 628,000 |

Source: Institute of Petroleum, Information Service Oil, world statistics, 1971

The problems of ensuring a steady flow of supplies and of thinking about their protection in case of hostilities, thus appeared to have become a common Western European problem.

The economic and strategic importance, as well as the complexity of the politics of oil, was recognized by the establishment of a separate oil department in the Foreign Office. Britain had been extremely vulnerable to a disruption of oil supplies, for instance, when the Arab producers stopped supplies following the Suez action, her dependence upon alternative supplies from American-controlled sources gave the American government an uncomfortably great leverage in influencing the winding up of the action. The situation had greatly improved because the international oil business became further integrated and had better conceptualized the interconnectedness of events in single countries, while the sources of supply were more diversified and the solidarity of the producers still remained incomplete. Significantly, in the recent reorganization of the FCO, in 1971, the Oil Department disappeared.

The internationalization of the commercial operations of the oil industry did not, however, amount to the elimination of the political element. Ever since the beginning of the century the British government had been involved in the protection of Middle Eastern oil supplies. And as recently as 1971, British forces went to the aid of Kuwait; jeopardy to the stability of the area was a major argument against the withdrawal of the British forces from the Persian Gulf in the early 1970s; the withdrawal actually took place despite this and despite the wishes of the oil companies, because, once the intention to withdraw had been announced, the nationalist forces let loose in the region made continuation of the slender British military presence ineffective and politically hazardous.

Even though short of gunboat diplomacy and of military presence, which are now a matter of the past, the British—and the other Western governments—were inevitably involved in determining what can be termed the macro-economic background to the deals negotiated by the oil companies, national interest was involved and sometimes problems arose in a form in which governmental decisions were crucial.[17] For instance, during the Biafran breakaway movement, the unenviable choice for the British lay between recognizing that the Biafrans controlled the oilfields and paying them the royalties—and thus jeopardizing the future of the concession in the event of a federal victory—or suffering a disruption of supply in the expectation of a federal victory. Here, as in all the supplying countries, the major British interest lay in maintaining political stability. The oil issue was undoubtedly given full consideration in determining the British policy of support for the federal government; until, however, the full history of the war has been divulged, it is possible only to speculate how British oil interests were taken into account alongside the political interests. In less dramatic circumstances, British oil companies needed occasional diplomatic support; for instance, when they were obstructed in their efforts to break into the American market by the application of anti-trust laws. Apart from political troubles and occasional issues of high oil policy, the oil companies carried out their day-to-day commercial operations autonomously (including BP in which the government holds the major interest) and dealt directly with the local governments. The companies were naturally in close contact with the local British diplomatic outposts, exchanging information and seeking advice. In view of their own resources, however, they were in fact much less dependent upon local diplomatic support than smaller commercial concerns.

A dramatic change was expected in the later 1970s, when Britain would become a major oil producer. The stringency of her oil needs would be drastically reduced, especially as estimates of reserves available in the North Sea were constantly rising. Even if the reserves lasted only a fairly short time, they were likely to extend over the period of the greatest anticipated oil shortage, before nuclear energy was harnessed, and would drastically improve Britain's position *vis-a-vis* her major suppliers. The question arose, however, how well the traditional patterns of Britain's oil policies could be adapted to her policies as a producer. Owing to the uncertainty about the quantities involved, the technological problems of exploitation and the desire for speed, the successive governments adopted a policy of exploitation by the established oil firms, leasing blocks demarcated in the North Sea. The system proved highly successful in speeding up exploration and discovery and in bringing the fields into production. Dilemmas would, however, arise in Britain's interests as a major consumer and simultaneously a major producer of oil, in what was increasingly becoming a seller's market. The questions of the division of profits between the government and the oil companies and of ensuring priority of supplies to Britain were bound to loom large in the mid- and late 1970's.

On one crucial issue Britain showed real foresight: she was highly successful in taking the initiative with her neighbours about the demarcation of the continental shelf surrounding Britain, while this was relatively easy, before the major oil finds had taken place. For instance, had the two sides known that major oilfields straddle the demarcation line between their portions, the Anglo-Norwegian agreement would undoubtedly have been much harder to reach. Britain laid the foundations for this policy as early as the 1958 Geneva Conference on the Law of the Sea, when she secured Norwegian goodwill by abandoning, for the purposes of demarcation, the rather dubious legal claim to take into account the so-called 'Norwegian trench', a discontinuity on the Norwegian side of the continental shelf which dips below the 200 metres line. The goodwill thus secured enabled Britain to attain the desirable momentum in the demarcation negotiations. As soon as the Convention on the Continental Shelf[18] had come into force in 1964, the British government approached all the governments concerned with a view to reaching demarcation agreements. Having previously resolved the major issue with Norway, Britain concluded an agreement with her in the same year, setting the pattern of a treaty which was followed by subsequent agreements with the Dutch, the Belgians (who had some difficulty with their municipal law), the Danes, and the West Germans. So far, only in two cases have no agreements been reached. The difficulty with the French lies in the importance of the exact location of the demarcation line, which would be extended into the Atlantic if exploitable oil were found there. The Irish, apparently diffident about their legal expertise, have proved hesitant in finalising an agreement on what, in view of the likely oil deposits in the South Irish Sea, could be their major national asset.

### Aid[19]

Britain's economic policies towards developing countries were strongly affected by the existence of the Commonwealth and by the overwhelming size of the problems encountered with in. Her primary responsibility was, of course, to the emancipated units, all of which were in dire need of some economic assistance, although not to the same degree. She had a responsibility towards all the units, and she was not at liberty to concentrate aid upon selected countries, as did the Russians in their aid programmes; such a choice could not have been justified by any reasoning, and would have been politically inexpedient, as the satisfaction of the few chosen states would have been purchased at the cost of the dissatisfaction of the many passed over. Nor did she have the choice available to the French of maintaining a constant flow of aid at a fairly high level. The French could do this in relation to the relatively smaller population of their ex-colonies—and with the substantial support of the other members of the EEC which they had secured. The more than 600 million British Commonwealth citizens emancipated could not possibly be adequately provided for from the war-shattered economy of the 50 million inhabitants of the British Isles, even with the assistance of the wealthy ex-Dominions. The other effect of the existence of the Commonwealth was that Britain's major aid efforts were concentrated within it and remained relatively unknown to other developing countries. Therefore it was even harder for the British to defend themselves against the rising anti-colonial pressures; their aid policies were judged largely on the basis of their performance within the United Nations.

Aid is dispensed for a dual purpose. One, stressed in many British official announcements, is an altruistic, humanitarian one—to help others to raise their standards of living, to promote economic and social development, in general, to improve their lot. The other one is self interested —to secure influence, to promote one's trade. Needless to say, the two objectives do not fully coincide, as each imposes different priorities.They do not, however, necessarily clash. It cannnot be said that British aid either satisfied the recipients or secured Britain much influence; moreover, it became more of a liability than an asset in the United Nations forum, where Britain's record was compared with those of other donors in terms which made it appear slighter than it actually was.

The first question which poses itself concerns the size of the aid given.

*Aid in £ millions net*

|  | 1966 | 1967 | 1968 | 1969 | 1970 |
|---|---|---|---|---|---|
| Official aid | 183·2 | 179·0 | 178·5 | 178·5 | 188·9 |
| % of GNP | 0·48 | 0·45 | 0·42 | 0·39 | 0·37 |
| Private flows | 142·1 | 118·3 | 128·1 | 298·8 | 336·8 |
| % of GNP | 0·37 | 0·30 | 0·30 | 0·65 | 0·67 |

Source: Overseas Development Administration, *British Aid Statistics 1966-1970* (*1971*).

In terms of her limited resources and of her great domestic needs, Britain's effort was not insubstantial, although it is not fully reflected in the figures of transfers of assets figuring in statistical tables. It included the most extensive technical-assistance service offered by any country, which enabled the recipient countries to employ highly skilled professional

British personnel, and also education facilities for Commonwealth students, up to 25,000 of whom were studying in Britain. The transfers of assets however, were, modest and, moreover, included an increasing element of private investment.

In a general way, the Labour Party favours the substitution of economic for military instruments in the conduct of foreign policy, and greatly favours foreign aid. A really massive transfer of resources is, however, hard to envisage. In September 1951 the *Tribune* pamphlet *Going Our Way*? pleaded that £1,400 million should be transferred from the 'extra' military expenditure to the Colombo Plan, but this was not practical politics at the height of the cold war—even if the political support of the recipient countries could have been ensured and relied upon, it would have been of extremely limited value in a confrontation with the Soviet Union. The Wilson Government expressed its will to increase aid by establishing a separate Ministry for Overseas Development—which was incorporated in the FCO by its Conservative successors—but was held back by Britain's increasing economic difficulties.

The motivation for channelling some 80 per cent of the aid to the Commonwealth, rather than favouring United Nations agencies, are similar to those of giving aid. First, as is frequently stated officially, Britain's first duty is to the Commonwealth; the Colombo Plan and bilateral arrangements with single countries offer much cheaper and more efficient means for administering aid than the United Nations. Second, there is also an unspoken assumption that this is the best method to maximize Britain's influence. The aid is dispensed too thinly to offer the British government a leverage in any single country comparable to that available to the French, who completely control the economies of their African associates. With the exception of her residual dependencies and of a very few successor states which are very small, Britain does not give any single Commonwealth country sufficient money to make it closely dependent upon her. The compensating factor is that no odium of neo-colonialism is incurred, while the Colombo Plan machinery minimizes the danger of disappointed applicants becoming resentful about the distribution of largesse. Thus, for a modest outlay, not only is a duty discharged but general goodwill is secured although this cannot be translated into direct influence.

This concentration upon the Commonwealth and the Colombo Plan is reflected in, and adversely affects, Britain's position in the United Nations. Britain has been traditionally sceptical of ambitious United Nations initiatives like the establishment of the Special United Nations Development Fund or the setting up of fixed targets for aid—first 1 per cent of the Gross National Product and then 0·7 per cent for the governmental contribution. She has been critical of what she sometimes regards as the extravagant costs of United Nations administration, and chary of diverting much of her aid into United Nations channels. By and large, Britain follows United Nations proposals, although rather reluctantly and with delay. She has been surpassing the 1 per cent aid target for a number of years only because of private investment, which used to be encouraged to go to the developing countries within the sterling area. The governmental contribution, however, has not come up to the United Nations target of 0·7 per cent of the Gross National Product and has actually dropped from 0·53 per cent in 1964 to 0·37 per cent in 1970. At the UNCTAD Conferences which have become the major forum of confrontation between the developing and developed countries, Britain's representatives advocated liberalization of trade, but her actual trade policies did not follow suit. Britain played a cautious part, never taking bold initiatives herself.

The unresolved relation between the benefits of the recipient and the interests of the donor require a new interpretation in the present situation. The Commonwealth links have been weakened, the EEC may require reorientation, and the UNCTAD forum seems to be growing in importance. Should Britain enlarge her governmental aid to come closer to the 0·7 per cent of GNP advocated by the United Nations? Should she reconsider an increase in the proportion channelled through the United Nations, especially through the allocation to it of any proposed increase? Should she undertake initiatives on 'untying' the loans through an international agreement, following up an official announcement by the then Minister of Development soon after the present government had taken office? Although, as the Minister stated, Britain could not do this alone, she has room for liberal initiatives, as apparently she now contributes only some 7 per cent of total world aid but gets some 11 per cent of the orders generated by it.[20] In 1970 as much as 64 per cent of Britain's bilateral aid was tied; this was in favour of British exports but could reduce the effective value of aid by as much as 25 per cent.

Whichever solutions are chosen for each of these questions, it seems clear that a more articulate and more vigorous policy with regard to aid could play a more important part in Britain's foreign policy. It is, however, rather dubious whether more than a small portion of Britain's aid could be channelled to the advantage both of the recipients and of Britain, either through the United Nations or through the EEC.

# 12 Defence Policy

*Defence and Foreign Policies*

DEFENCE policy has never been effectively divorced from foreign policy like the economic policies discussed in the preceding chapter. Nevertheless, the place of security in the conduct of foreign policy remains nearly as obscure as that of its twin objective prosperity. Defence is one of the most expensive items of national expenditure; until 1970 it was *the* most expensive one, costly not only in monetary terms but also in its demands upon manpower. Conscription and competition for resources between defence needs and social expenditure and consumption affect the lives of every citizen. Nevertheless, although public opinion occasionally concentrates upon comprehensible single issues, especially those involving actual fighting, it follows fairly passively the less comprehensible changes in the broad policies pursued and strategies chosen, annually announced in the White Papers on defence. Technological complexities have, in fact, rendered ineffective any attempts to investigate military procurement. According to the 1965 computation by Julian Critchley, Parliament devoted only some 4 per cent of its time to defence matters, on which between one-third and one-quarter of the governmental expenditure was spent.[1] Moreover, the Defence and External Affairs Subcommittee established by the House of Commons in 1969 felt itself hampered by what appeared to it to be an 'unnecessarily restrictive' security classification of the documentation. The parliamentary system seems even less capable of dealing adequately with defence than with general foreign-policy issues—divisions over topical subjects, such as German rearmament, various aspects of nuclear policy, or conscription, tend to occur within the two major parties rather than between them.

This phenomenon is by no means limited to Britain, as it stems from a confusion about the exact purpose of a nation's defence efforts—they aim at security (i.e. protection from physical attack), at maintaining national independence, and at providing a position of strength from which the country's foreign policy can be more confidently conducted. For Britain, the problems of pursuing all these objectives under postwar conditions were exceptionally acute. The basic need of security of the realm required the organization of Western defences and a substantial American contribution; the Brussels Pact and NATO were the logical outcomes. At the same time, however, Britain also wished to maintain her world role: to ensure the maximum degree of national independence and the means for honouring a variety of overseas commitments. Her resulting defence efforts in developing a nuclear deterrent and in maintaining defences east of Suez not only detracted from her ability to contribute to the defences of Europe but, in some instances, contravened the basic policy of interdependence with the United States.

The postwar governments adopted an essentially military response to Britain's security problems. This can mainly be attributed to the gravity of the perceived military threat in Europe, especially as the recent lessons of appeasement made policy-makers very sensitive to the dangers of becoming defenceless. The left-wing critics of Attlee and Bevin sometimes contended that this was a major stumbling-block in the way of East–West accommodation. However, even if one allows for the possibility that a less military Western response might have prevented the confrontation taking the stark form of the 'cold war', one must question whether Britain was in a position to play a decisive role. Admittedly, Bevin played one in hastening the process of American involvement, but he could scarcely afford to take the risks of acting otherwise (see ch. 7). It is obvious, however, that the Russians, faced as they were with American nuclear monopoly, could scarcely have responded otherwise than in military terms, independently of whether their designs were expansionist or not. Although it is possible to argue that the British were afterwards hampered in their repeated efforts to reduce international tensions by their basically military appreciation of the issues, their importance in the eyes of the Russians was in any case insufficient for them to carry decisive weight.

Defence policies cannot be interpreted without due regard to the intricate links between defence, economics, and politics. This is especially so since 1945 as the costs of defence have been growing exponentially, while, simultaneously, the subtleties of nuclear strategy and of guerrilla warfare have politicised military policies and, in a parallel way, foreign policy has been militarized. These interconnections became obvious much earlier than those between international economics and politics. The economic aspects of defence, which will be referred to in greater detail on pp. 288ff., came up in the form of two fundamental issues which confronted all the successive governments. First, expenditure on defence imposed such a burden on the British economy that a compromise had to be found between domestic needs and a powerful defence force, especially as the freedom of the Germans and Japanese from defence burdens gave these countries a great competitive advantage over Britain. Second, at any level of expenditure chosen, there was always much too little to satisfy all the defence needs and commitments. The recurrent problem of all defence reviews was how to choose priorities well below the minimum level of requirements: meeting the minimal demands of one Service inevitably amounted to cuts in the minimal demands of the other two; new weapons systems could be planned and developed only very selectively, without any freedom to keep other options open; and the military backing of many commitments had to be left well below the minimal threshold of military security.

Defence is, in theory, an instrument of foreign policy; in practice the roles can be mixed up or even reversed. Inevitably, many short-term contingencies, sometimes of a predominately military nature, have played a large part in British foreign policy since 1945. From the detached perspective of the 1970s, it is possible to judge that the widespread defence commitments shaped or even distorted British foreign policy for frequently ephemeral reasons, notably for the maintenance of bases shortly to be evacuated. The views of those directly involved at the time were different—contingencies inexorably arose from historical involvements, sometimes military commitments followed political ones and sometimes the maintenance of military bases contributed to, or even determined, political commitments. Warner R. Schilling hypothesized about the 'gyroscopic effect' of defence budgets upon the contents of American foreign policy, since both the Executive and Congress tend to continue at the level of expenditure decided upon, despite startling international developments. It would be difficult to apply this hypothesis to Britain—in each single case inertia could be due either to a political or a traditional defence commitment or to some combination of both—the size of the defence budget is not nearly as important a determinant of foreign policy as in the United States. Whichever way we choose to evaluate the links, the Forces were called upon to pursue a variety of operational tasks which stretched their limited capacity to the full; and, incidentally, they generally acquitted themselves extremely well.

Institutional tensions inevitably arise in the co-ordination of defence and of foreign policies in the realm of planning. Modern technology requires the planning of new weapons systems a long time ahead, to allow some ten years or so for the time-lag between the decision to develop them and their final coming into use, in which they can be expected to remain for quite a time—in the case of ships some twenty years.

Therefore defence policy is, by necessity, subject to continuous scrutiny and to planning ahead, an operation which is not and, indeed, cannot be undertaken for foreign policy in equal measure. The annual White Papers on Defence, despite their limitations due to security reasons and to the inevitable time-lag between the conception of a policy and of its public announcement, state the major defence tasks as conceived every year, and thus offer a continuous insight into the evolving security aspects of British foreign policy in a much more systematic way than general debates on foreign policy can ever achieve. The Foreign Office cannot provide the military planners with any convincing appreciation of the relevant political commitments likely to arise during the expected lifetime of the new weapons systems planned, or, indeed, even ten years ahead. Another significant divergence arises over costs. In a way, it is the defence budget which constitutes the cost of the country's foreign policy. Although the policy-makers, both in the Foreign and Commonwealth Office and in the Ministry of Defence, agree in their desire to secure as large appropriations for defence as is feasible, the economic pressures come directly to bear only on the defence planners. In a country with as widespread foreign commitments as Britain, it was inevitable that a gap would arise between the reappraisal of these commitments from the defence and the diplomatic angles. That political objectives which need not be immediately costed can persist much longer than economically untenable defence objectives was best shown in the last stages of the defence policy east of Suez, especially with regard to the evacuation of Aden, which appeared much more pressing to the military than to the diplomats.

The relationship between economics, defence, and foreign policy was thoroughly ventilated under the Labour government of 1964–70. Denis Healey, the Minister of Defence throughout the period, combined the unique advantages of continuity of office and of a thorough understanding, not only of defence problems but also of those of foreign policy, in which he had long been specializing. Moreover, as pressure from the Treasury to economize was growing, while the country was undergoing a series of increasingly severe economic crises, the Minister of Defence was in a strong position to win any argument with the Foreign Office, which, during his tenure of office, was headed by four successive Secretaries, none of whom could match Healey's expertise. As Healey himself put it at a seminar at the Royal United Services Institute for Defence Studies on 4 November 1970: 'in 1965 the Treasury wanted me to cut the bill and the Foreign Office wanted me to keep all the commitments. There was a great struggle and finally the Foreign Office gave in'.[2] Much the same thing had happened before, when Dalton ultimately prevailed over Bevin and, in February 1947, persuaded the Cabinet to withdraw from Turkey and Greece. This time, however, more was at stake than a withdrawal from one specific commitment. Limited in his expenditure to £2,000 million in 1964 value, and supported by rigorous defence-cost examination methods developed by the Americans (Planning, Programming, and Budgeting), the Minister of Defence was in a position to demand a full examination of the political objectives and of their military and financial implications. The trimming of defence expenditure had gone too far to allow both for the required contribution to NATO and for a wide scope of extra-European commitments. In 1966 the White Paper on Defence admitted that Britain would 'not undertake major operations of war except in co-operation with allies',[3] which meant that the independent world role would no longer be underwritten. Logically and inexorably this led to the subsequent decision to withdraw from east of Suez.

Although the gradual elimination of Britain's overseas defence commitments was occasionally strongly objected to by the Foreign Office, the completion of the withdrawal laid a sound foundation for the co-ordination of defence and foreign-policy planning. Lord Carrington, who became the Minister of Defence in the Conservative Government elected in 1970, said, lecturing at the Royal United Services Institution, on 21 October 1970, that he was strongly impressed by the favourable change. He recalled that when he had been First Lord of the Admiralty in 1959, the members of the Foreign Service used to think of the Services as their servants, whereas to the Services the main objective of the Foreign Office seemed to be to keep everybody happy rather than to look after important British interests; by 1970 a close co-operation and consensus had developed between the two.[4]

British defence policy evolved in the same direction as British foreign policy, i.e. from a broad conception of a world role to a narrower conception of the primacy of regional interests. The two policies were not, however, synchronized. The general pattern of defence policy can be easily summed up, despite the baffling complexity of its detail. From the very beginning of the period Britain remained committed to the defence of Western Europe, and her overseas commitments were gradually reduced until the withdrawal from east of Suez in 1971 brought them nearly to an end. The pattern is complicated, however, by the continuation of a nuclear policy, which is the major residue of the world role, and by the intrusion of the heavy military involvement in Ulster, the implications of which have not yet been fully incorporated into the conception of the defence of the realm.

Although the exact nature of the individual linkages is hard to understand, defence, being an important aspect of the world role, clearly played a significant part in Britain's foreign policy. It was the pivot of the 'special relationship', and consequently, throughout the 1970s, the major obstacle to Britain's friendship with France and to her admission to the EEC. The links between Britain's defence and economic policies were equally close but even more complex. It is possible, nevertheless, to state in general terms that economic weakness underlay the contraction of Britain's defence commitments which were part of her world role, the landmarks being the decisions to abandon the main responsibility for Greece and Turkey in 1947 and to withdraw from east of Suez in 1967.

## The Costs of Defence

In our statistically minded age, the sums spent on defence and the percentage of the GNP devoted to it are frequently regarded as a fair index not merely of the nation's appreciation of its security problems but also of its determination to assert its will internationally. In fact, the political value of defence expenditure is not much more obscure than its military value. National expenditure is only a rough index of the nation's military power, as money can be spent in a more or a less satisfactory manner; it is nevertheless a useful index, because the military worth of strategies and of advanced weapons systems cannot be fully ascertained until they have been tried out in combat.

Strong arguments have been advanced about the insufficiency of Britain's defence expenditure to maintain levels commensurate with her extended world role. Some American writers have been particularly struck by this. One of them graphically described the issue as 'the dilemma of rising demands and insufficient resources'. In a society which has become as democratized as contemporary Britain, defence demands become electorally 'soft' whereas competing demands for consumption and social welfare are electorally 'hard'.[5] There comes a point, however, where the need for expenditure on defence does have to be recognized. Even as hard-headed an advocate of restrictions upon governmental spending as The Economist could put the issue in the form of the question whether Britain wished to be reduced to an 'Iceland with fifty-five million people'.[6]

It is true that social expenditures in Britain have been rising much faster than defence expenditures—in 1970 the cost of education for the first time surpassed that of defence. Both parties are responsive to social pressures and, failing sufficient resources to meet them, save on defence.

At the same time, however, defence expenditures have never come under serious public attack. At the end of 1950, when convinced that a real emergency had arisen, the government of the day dramatically raised expenditure at an extremely heavy social cost. The linear progression towards a relatively reduced defence expenditure which was resumed after the ending of the Korean war has been steady but slow and can be regarded as a function not only of social pressures but also of a relatively more settled international environment and of the more reduced role Britain has decided to play in it.

The issue is best illuminated by the record of the reaction of the Attlee Government to the Korean war. On the eve of the conflict the government seemed to be on the point of stabilizing the country's defence expenditure when, after consistently severe cutbacks from wartime levels, it was set at £780 million, a sum fully within the capacity of Britain's economy. There were powerful arguments in favour of keeping the expenditure at this level. The economy had been only precariously restored and the people were still subjected to severe rationing. Moreover, it is in the British national tradition not to save effort in wartime but to reduce the defence establishment to a minimum in peacetime; during the peak of her power in the 1860s, Britain had been spending no more than some £30 million a year on defence, and the peacetime average for the nineteenth century had been scarcely 2 per cent of the GNP. The Labour Party was particularly reluctant to increase the defence effort, as it is ideologically opposed to power politics and its left wing was strongly pressing for the substitution of economic instruments for military ones. The government, however, perceived a danger of communist aggression in Europe which amounted to a national emergency, and therefore, considered it vital to halt the running down beyond recovery of the defence establishment which had been built up at a high cost during the war. The existing weapons systems could be regarded as serviceable for some time, and the full cost of their replacement by newer systems could not be fully anticipated.

The original governmental reaction was slow. On 26 July 1950 the Minister of Defence, Emmanuel Shinwell, announced in the House of Commons that the government had decided to increase the defence estimates by £100 million, in the full awareness that this would not ensure adequate defences in the new situation in which the communist threat seemed much more acute, but that Britain could not by herself afford more than merely to start an adequate programme. Within ten days, however, the government prepared a large-scale three-year rearmament programme which was later increased by a further £200 million. The Prime Minister described this in the House of Commons as the maximum that Britain could afford without reverting to the drastic expedient of war-economy, and warned that rearmament would inevitably slow down economic recovery and would require substantial sacrifices from the British people. Nevertheless, on 29 January 1951, he announced a further increase of the programme to £4,700 million over the next three years, warning the House that this would cut deeply into the export drive.[7]

The emergency to which Attlee responded was the increasing fear of a communist military drive in Europe and, more immediately, the risk of alienating the Americans and of losing their military support; the latter had meanwhile doubled their own defence effort and were pressing Britain for ever higher expenditures. Attlee's decisions were taken in the full knowledge of the grave effects upon the British economy. Indeed, although the programme was not completely fulfilled, its results were crippling, especially as in the second part of 1950 the turn in the terms of trade caused by the Korean war transformed the substantial British foreign-exchange gain of £438 million in the second quarter to a loss of £638 million in the third one. The pre-emption of capital and skill for defence severely handicapped British export industries in competition with the rapidly recovering industries of Western Germany who, at the time, incurred no defence expenditure at all. As a percentage of the GNP, in 1952 Britain's defence expenditure surpassed that of France, at that time engaged in the ruinous war in Indochina.

In the next few years defence expenditure was only slightly reduced, until, under the pressure of the post-Suez economic crisis, Duncan Sandys was appointed Minister of Defence with a specific mandate to secure a substantial reduction in expenditure and manpower. Again, compared with Western Germany, in 1957 Britain was spending roughly twice as much per capita on defence, $8\frac{1}{2}$ per cent of the GNP against Germany's $4\frac{1}{2}$ per cent, while she used only 15 per cent of the GNP for capital investment against Germany's 22 per cent. The government decided to cut expenditure to 7 per cent of the GNP which still did not go nearly as far as the 40 per cent reduction to continental levels advocated by PEP.[8]

These proposed substantial, though not drastic economies were largely achieved, and the subsequent White Paper (1957) announced the abolition of National Service, a drastic cut in the number of troops, and the establishment of the nuclear deterrent as the foundation of British defence policy. The latter was made possible cheaply through a resumed close co-operation with the Americans, but the demands of other advanced military technologies remained crippling. According to Sir Solly Zuckerman, right into the mid-1960s the defence effort required some 1,400,000 of the nation's manpower, about one-fifth of the scientists and engineers, and about two-fifths of the total expenditure on research and development.[9]

Conflicting arguments can be advanced about the economic consequences of this defence effort. Buying weapons systems from the United States would have been much cheaper, but there was the question of maintaining national independence in advanced technologies and of domestic employment. On the one hand, there was the 'spin-off' effect into civilian industry, which, for instance, enabled Britain to produce civilian aircraft more cheaply thanks to technology developed through Air Force production expenditure but, on the other, the defence and export industries competed for resources. Whatever the merits of the arguments, the effort was over-ambitious and beyond Britain's resources, especially as it was impossible to calculate in advance the rapidly rising costs of new technologies and to devise adequate governmental financial control on expenditure.

Inevitably, the research and development programme got into increasing financial trouble. According to some calculations, had all the programmes of the later 1950s continued, they would have required about double the research and development funds available in the early 1960s.[10] Many programmes had therefore to be cancelled, sometimes at a fairly advanced stage. Confusingly, governments began to calculate defence savings in terms not of actual savings but of the costs which they expected to incur in the future—Healey's cancellation of three major aircraft projects, including the controversial TSR-2, was said to have saved £1,200 million, that of the aircraft carrier demanded by the Navy and its substitution by fifty American F-111's (which were later cancelled in turn), some £1,000 million in capital costs and also substantial running costs.

The Wilson Government decided to lower the ceiling of defence expenditure by substituting the fixed sum of £2,000 million in 1964 value for the Conservative 7 per cent of the GNP. As the GNP slowly grew, the defence expenditure was thereby gradually reduced to 4·9 per cent spent in 1970, a percentage still much higher than the 3·3 per cent spent by Western Germany and surpassing the 4 per cent spent by France. However, as the British GNP had not risen nearly as rapidly as that of other industrialized nations—it was surpassed by the West Germans in 1961 and by the French in 1965—Britain, despite her relatively much higher national effort, spent in 1970 a sum slightly below those available to Western Germany and France. The figures were $5,960 million for Britain, $5,982 million for France and $6,188 million for Germany.[11]

Ever since the 1957 White Paper on Defence, British defence policy has pursued the philosophy stated therein that Britain's influence in the world depends first and foremost on the health of her internal economy and the success of her export trade. Her defence effort remains greater than that of Germany or France but does not produce a fully commensurate expenditure. One may assume that, as long as the East–West detente continues, social pressures in Britain, as in other Western countries, will lead to further inroads into defence expenditure to satisfy domestic needs and wants, and will further reduce it in terms of a percentage of Britain's GNP—a Labour government especially, could easily reduce it by perhaps as much as one-third. It cannot be said that Britain obtained influence in NATO quite commensurate with her defence effort, which was proportionately larger than that of her European allies. The question of how much influence is likely to be gained or forfeited by a given level of defence expenditure is bound to remain uncertain although it should be the governing factor in policy decisions. While the minimum military requirements—which obviously are also somewhat uncertain—prescribed the lowest parameters below which no government is likely to go, actual expenditure is bound to be increasingly influenced by the defence efforts of others. The minimum will probably be the percentage of the GNP spent by Germany and France, but the actual absolute size of the expenditures of these two countries may induce Britain to spend somewhat more in order to avoid falling too far behind them.

A substantial saving has been effected by the British withdrawal from east of Suez where, by 1973, only residual traces remained. The direct costs of overseas defence commitments were not particularly high, only 7 per cent of the defence budget in 1958,[12] but there were heavy indirect costs. Moreover, as military requirements in Europe and overseas generally differed, attempts to design weapons systems, especially aircraft, for both theatres were inescapably costly and frequently not very satisfactory. Finally, while Britain was maintaining an exceptionally wide range of defence responsibilities, the choice of priorities between the conflicting demands of the three Services was extremely difficult. The general easing of the overseas defence burden coincides, however, with a probable increase in the demands on Britain within the European theatre. While Britain remains primarily responsible for ensuring the continuation of as substantial an American commitment to NATO as possible, she can be required to increase, rather than allowed to reduce, her own contribution. The danger of Soviet expansionism has receded, only to be replaced by that of a much greater exposure to it through American withdrawal. The prospects of economies through the joint procurement of weapons with Britain's European partners are remote, although some beginnings have been made by the Air Force and the Army. Joint procurement may eventually evolve, but, by enabling Britain and her allies to develop weapons systems not within their individual capacities, it could become a source of additional expenditure rather than of saving.

A major unknown factor lies in the impending change of generations among those in power. During the 1970s and 1980s, people will come into power who have not personally experienced the last war and for whom Munich and Hitler are remote history. The younger men know that Britain was not occupied during the last war and that she has no serious quarrels with anybody; the British are not constantly reminded, as are the Germans, of the exposure of the West to the Communist menace. It is therefore conceivable that the pressures to give priority to the electorally 'hard' domestic demands will prove overwhelming, especially if the rate of economic growth does not greatly improve. At the same time, while in the past defence expenditure was vulnerable to the criticism that some of it was wasted on ultimately cancelled programmes or served ephemeral overseas tasks, at present defence relates mainly to seemingly vital, irreducible, and hence not unpopular national interests: the defence of the homeland and the maintenance of law and order, especially in Ulster, and sustaining a substantial role in Western Europe.

## Defence of the Homeland

Britain traditionally employed two parallel strategies: a maritime one based upon her naval power, to defend her imperial and commercial interests, and a continental one, based upon the maintenance of a balance of power in Europe. Despite recurrent arguments about priorities, the two strategies were parallel and complementary rather than alternative: both aimed at warding off threats to the British Isles and the Empire and at protecting vital interests. Naturally, each strategy had its proponents and opponents, especially within the individual Services involved, and, according to the current external and domestic pressures, one of them would become temporarily dominant. On these traditional lines, two strands can also be distinguished in Britain's postwar defence policy; that of the defence of the homeland and its immediate approaches, and that of overseas commitments and interests. The former, although clearly more basic, is relatively simpler and hence requires less analysis.

As Michael Howard has convincingly argued,[13] throughout this century Britain has been unable to maintain a predominantly maritime outlook and has been largely preoccupied with the balance of power in Europe. This has led to her participation in two wars against Germany, and her postwar involvement in the defences of Western Europe. It seems clear that Chamberlain's doctrine of 'limited liability', which he adopted for economic reasons in 1937, immediately after he had come to power, was untenable. The doctrine presupposed that Britain would never again send a major expeditionary force to Europe and that she would rely on her Navy and Air Force alone. Only two years later Chamberlain had to admit his mistake; an expeditionary force was indispensable to persuade Britain's allies, especially the French, of the seriousness of her intentions. Britain's present commitment to the defence of Western Europe can thus be regarded as a direct continuation of her defence policies earlier in this century. The general purpose of this commitment has remained identical —to maintain the balance of power in Europe. In the changed circumstances of the postwar world, however, the form of this commitment has greatly changed, and its military, diplomatic, and institutional aspects require a brief analysis.

At the military level, the most striking difference between the postwar commitment and its historical antecedents lies in its seemingly permanent nature—as the 1954 White Paper on Defence rather mournfully remarked: 'against our previous dispositions'. It has been a major feature of Britain's defence policy since 1945 that substantial British contingents are required on the continent to ensure her defence; continuity of this purpose has been fully maintained although the contingents changed their institutional form from being occupying troops on the territory of a defeated enemy state into becoming part of a collective NATO force in which they are fully associated with the Germans. The grave military and political drawbacks involved in sending an *ad hoc* expeditionary force at the last moment have been so clearly manifested on the eve of both world wars that a return to the doctrine of 'limited liability' seems most unlikely. Until and unless the international system has become fundamentally reformed, we may expect that Britain will retain substantial forces on the continent, as her obligation under the 1954 arrangement is to do so until the end of the century.

At the diplomatic level, when the probable challenge to the balance of power becomes overwhelmingly strong and Britain cannot counteract it by a flexible policy of playing the balancer, alignments become fixed. After the war, this happened earlier and more deliberately than in the past. The postwar security arrangements reflect a further hardening of alignments, such as had already characterized the situations preceding the two world wars. Already during the last stages of the war the British had recognized that the major threat would come from Russia, that Western Europe must organize itself to face it and that this would depend upon United States participation in the West European defence effort; later on, the ultimate protection under the American nuclear umbrella became essential. The initial uncertainties and hesitations had already completely disappeared by the spring of 1947, whereas before the two world wars the British had continued their efforts to compose their differences with Germany—in the case of the first world war right up to its outbreak. This major difference can be largely attributed to the fact that this was the first time the Americans proved willing to play a permanent part in Europe's balance of power thus obviating the search for unpromising alternatives to an alignment with them.

Furthermore, Britain's major defence partners in 1945 were no longer the same as they had been earlier in the century. As the Russians had now replaced the Germans as the most likely challengers to the international order, and as the Americans were the only nation capable of balancing them, it was the latter who became Britain's foremost ally, replacing the French in a role which they had occupied since the beginning of this century. The Germans now became firm allies, whereas the French were seriously estranged by their continuing opposition to the American predominance within the alliance. The major problems of British defence policy in Western Europe were bound to revolve around ensuring a continuing American participation, an adequate German contribution to the future form of defence, likely to include some form of German militia perhaps on the Swiss pattern, and the reconciliation of France, perhaps an important country geographically but unable to make an equally important manpower contribution. Militarily, the French were the least important and therefore, unless major political reasons intervened, the British were likely to set a higher priority upon American and German contributions.

Finally, in contrast to the earlier, vague, and therefore unreliable diplomatic understandings with the French, the major area of Britain's defence policy had now been firmly institutionalized in the North Atlantic Treaty Organization (NATO) which went far beyond the traditional patterns of even tightly arranged alliances. Ever since Bevin had succeeded in his initiatives to establish and to consolidate the Organization, NATO had remained the pivotal institution of British homeland defences and the major guarantee of a continuing United States military involvement in Europe. The basic strategy of the Organization was fairly clear and consistent—to deter and, if necessary, temporarily stem any possible communist advance into Western Europe, working in concert with other Western European states and securing the participation of the United States as well as its ultimate nuclear guarantee. NATO never commanded conventional forces capable of stemming a major communist thrust; its capabilities were limited to coping with minor emergencies and, in any major confrontation, to purchasing time for a diplomatic solution to be sought. Its strategic role was meaningful only under the ultimate protection of the American strategic nuclear force, which was ensured by the 'hostage effect' of the presence of American troops on the ground in Europe and by the additional risks for the attacker in the American tactical nuclear weapons allotted to NATO. NATO's much greater stress on conventional weapons since 1963 did not alter the essence of this strategy. The scope of the alliance was basically limited to the central front in Europe, with some ambiguity about the northern and the southern flanks. It did not extend beyond the area of its European members and attempts to establish replicas in the Middle East and South-east Asia resulted in organizations which were both militarily and diplomatically ineffective.

Not only was Britain NATO's initiator, but she remained its faithful supporter throughout a succession of strategic and political troubles. In the course of the public debate in Britain during the 1960s over economies in defence and the priorities of European as against overseas demands, the utility of NATO was occasionally questioned, not only by its adamant leftist opponents.[14] The governments were, however, determined to remain fully committed to the Organization, and the debate was finally sealed by the 1967 decision to withdraw from east of Suez. The British military contribution remained solid, despite its heavy foreign exchange costs and the recurrent difficulties of achieving acceptable off-set arrangements with the Federal Republic of Germany.

NATO is also an extremely important channel for British diplomatic activities. It is a convenient venue for discussing all the major issues of Western relations with the Soviet Union, so that, ultimately, all members arrive at similar perceptions, or, at the very least, a thorough under-standing of the perceptions of others. NATO secures not only American participation in the defences of Western Europe, but also a solid footing on the continent for Britain. British initiatives were, for instance, im-portant in securing the integration of the German forces through the London Agreement of 1954, and then in associating Germany with NATO's nuclear planning through joint Anglo-German drafting of the proposals for guiding lines for the use of tactical nuclear weapons, for NATO's Nuclear Planning Group.

Working within NATO served Britain well, particularly thanks to the 'special relationship,' which ensured what its French critics regarded as, in effect, an 'Anglo-Saxon' directorate. The repercussions on Anglo-French relations during the 1960s were, accordingly, adverse, as the

British refused to support French ambitions to join the Anglo-Saxon states in their leading position and to form a tripartite directorate. Although NATO thus contributed to Anglo-French friction, the fact that in 1966 the French withdrew only from the military alliance, but decided to remain a member of the Organization and to continue to take part in its political activities helped to prevent the division from assuming a military form and resulting in a complete break. For a while the Western European Union (WEU), a historical subdivision of NATO, was the only forum where the six members of the EEC and Britain met as a group.

At the time of writing, the institutional future of Western European defences remains uncertain. The choice lies between the Western European Union, the Eurogroup inside NATO, and the enlarged Community. Each choice has a drawback. The Western European Union has a well established machinery but is outmoded. The Eurogroup has the advantage of keeping European defence as a substructure of NATO, which it must remain, but it has no formal machinery; its greatest disadvantage is that the French have remained adamant in their refusal to participate in the military structures of NATO, although they have continued to recognize the validity of the alliance. The EEC has no machinery at all, but, along the guidelines explored in the Davignon Report for consultation among Foreign Ministers, similar consultations between Defence Ministers could evolve; this would ensure French participation and would be in line with Britain's entry into the EEC. A recent report[15] has advocated the last solution, but this appears to be promising only in the unlikely case of the French being accorded the highest priority and consideration. In fact, NATO seems to be a more promising candidate. Not only does it ensure the essential integration of the United States in European defence but, on the basis of the so-called Harmel Report accepted by the North Atlantic Council in December 1967, the Organization has begun to evolve the foundations of political solidarity not only for deterring a threat but also for engaging in detente negotiations. The Eurogroup, although still informal and established on British initiative only in 1969, played in 1971 an important part in resolving the issue of an increased European contribution made necessary by the pressure of American demands. Whether, however, the focus of Western European defence stays within NATO or shifts to the enlarged Community, it seems unlikely that NATO will reach its twenty-fifth anniversary in 1974 without a major change.

*Overseas Defence*

Here the postwar record is entirely different from the steady continuity of the strategies governing the defence of the homeland. In 1945, the British started with a congeries of world-wide commitments in their Empire, but, by the end of 1971, they had nearly shed them altogether. They did not endeavour to preserve their Empire by force of arms as did the French, the Dutch, and the Portuguese; substantial military actions against independence movements were fought in some colonies, Kenya, Aden and Cyprus, for instance, but none was of long duration and all ended in fairly early grants of independence. The British did, however, unquestionably accept a residual responsibility for the defences of the Commonwealth—Australia and New Zealand remained reluctant to provide a sizeable contribution and were scarcely capable of doing so, while the developing countries were fully extended in financing their own development. Britain also endeavoured to preserve her leading position in the Middle East.

It would be pointless to enter into the legal complexities of the various defence commitments, the political significance of which cannot be judged by legal forms, as is clearly shown by the absence of any legal commitment to Australia and New Zealand—the only one which, early in the 1960s, could still conceivably have led to a sizeable British military involvement overseas and which was based entirely upon emotional ties and moral obligations. The commitments were untidy and also clearly untenable. Already in 1953 John Strachey warned the House of Commons:

This country is getting into the general condition of the Austrian Empire in 1914, a position hopelessly extended, ramshackle, indefensible because of a conditioned habit of mind leading to dispositions totally out of touch with the new reality which had supervened.[16]

The very basis of British defence policies east of Suez was greatly weakened by India's independence from 1947. India's security was no longer Britain's full responsibility and she ceased to be a secure base and a reservoir of manpower, although Gurkhas continued to be recruited. However, British commitments were not drastically revised. Serious adjustment started only in 1954, and only in 1968 did Britain finally declare the decision to withdraw.[17]

Britain undoubtedly persisted so long with her military involvement east of Suez because of its close connection with conceptions of a world role, and of the Commonwealth as one of the 'three circles'. The mystique of the Empire was a powerful element in shaping the ways of thinking of the political elite and of all persons in positions of responsibility, as they had been brought up while the Empire was a reality. Both the Labour supporters, who were generally motivated by their attachment to the New Commonwealth, and the Conservatives, who were concerned with the military bases and British investments, generally agreed on maintaining Britain's defence responsibilities. The traditional way of thinking operated among the general public, too, as shown in its strong reaction to Britain's exclusion from the ANZUS Treaty, which merely reflected the fact that Australia and New Zealand would now have to look for their security primarily to the United States.

These traditional ways of thinking were reinforced by several factors which made it possible to continue the traditional policies. By sheer luck, apart from the Sino-Indian war in 1962, no member of the Commonwealth faced a major outside challenger, and no two major engagements coincided. Britain was thus equal to all the numerous successive defence tasks, despite her overstretched military capacity. The sterling-area arrangements meant that the cost of maintaining troops overseas did not add to the growing British difficulties with the balance of payments,and was not, therefore, as noticeable as that of the British forces in Germany. There was also an element of economic aid through local expenditure— the negotiations for withdrawal from Singapore and Malta demonstrated the importance for the local economies of employment on British bases. Finally, like the sterling arrangements, the British defence commitments could be regarded as elements of strength which buttressed the Commonwealth and secured Britain a strong military standing in world affairs. Only as her general power waned did the negative aspects of the commitments clearly outweigh the positive ones.

The officially stated rationale of the overseas defence undertakings changed as time went on. Immediately after the war they were a simple function of Britain's great-power position. The 1948 White Paper[18] stated: 'The objectives of our defence policy derive directly from our obligations and commitments as a Great Power.' and the 1950 White Paper[19] that 'The Middle East is a vital strategic area and the maintenance of our position in the Far East is essential for the security and economic well-being of the Commonwealth.' Britain's only major military overseas operation not arising from her post-imperial commitments, her participation in the Korean conflict, was also based on her world role— the need to support the United States, Britain's major ally in Europe, and thus to ensure the continuance of American support there.

The Korean action shifted the emphasis of the overseas defence efforts to the containment of communism in areas of Britain's responsibility. This task, already pursued in Malaya, was strongly emphasized by the Conservative governments of the 1950s. The 1955 White Paper[20] claimed: 'We must play our part with the other countries of the Commonwealth and with our allies in resisting the spread of Communism throughout the world.' This claim was repeated in subsequent years but by 1961 the task was reduced to local peace-keeping: 'many of our most important responsibilities are not concerned with the direct deterrence of all-out global war, but rather with the checking of small outbreaks which could grow into nuclear war by accident or design.'[21] The Labour government elected in 1964 decisively changed the stated objectives of British overseas defences. In the 1965 defence debate Denis Healey told the House of Commons:

The justification of our military presence east of Suez is not the building of a wall against Communism. Nor is it the maintenance of selfish British economic interests. It is essentially the maintenance of peace and stability where the sudden withdrawal of colonial rule has often left the local people unable to maintain stability without some sort of external aid.

If one examines the actual defence activities, the early postwar claims that they arose from Britain's great power status were fully justified. Especially during the first decade (but, to an increasingly limited extent, also later), British guarantees and links were of real value to other states and secured substantial influence for Britain. The organization of armed forces, the provision of equipment and of training facilities in British staff schools, and the secondment of British officers constituted some of the most important links between Britain and many Commonwealth and Middle Eastern countries. These links often survived the replacement of the original post-independence regimes; and it was only by the mid-1950s that they began to weaken and, in many cases, were replaced by other connections or by a degree of self-reliance.

Military threats from without to the newly emancipated countries were relatively rare and did not unduly strain the credibility of British protection. The only substantial exception was the Sino-Indian War in 1962, which China conclusively won but which she ended with great self-restraint; here Britain's assistance was limited to prompt supplies of arms. Elsewhere, however, for instance, against the threats of Iraq and Saudi Arabia to British protégés in the Persian Gulf or the claims of Guatemala to British Honduras (now Belize), or of Spain to Gibraltar, occasional British military demonstrations proved sufficient. The only massive and successful operation was the Confrontation with Indonesia between 1963 and 1966, which cost some £250 million and at the height of which as many as 66,000 troops were involved. This was more an issue of delimitation and of determining the most suitable political unit than a straightforward attempt at territorial expansion by a neighbour.

Similar issues arose with many other units of the Empire which had evolved historically in forms rather unsuited for independence: some were too big, most were too small, many were racially or tribally too heterogeneous. The simple expedient wisely accepted by the United Nations and the Organization for African Unity was to accept the established administrative boundaries. This simple policy was not always possible but no ready alternative principle for delimitation was available. Consequently, British forces became involved in a number of military actions, notably in the partition of the Indian subcontinent, in Palestine, and in Cyprus. On several occasions Britain attempted to overcome the problem of small or heterogeneous units by establishing federations. These invariably disappointed, and were dissolved; sometimes violence broke out, but British military interventions were extremely rare in these as well as in other domestic disturbances. Although, at the request of the local governments, British forces successfully intervened in Jordan in 1958 and in East Africa in 1964 to quell military rebellions, no interventions took place in Nigeria during the Biafran uprising, or in Malaysia during the troubles which led to the expulsion of Singapore or the racial riots in 1969. This restraint increased Britain's political credit in the eyes of the Third World, but her refusal to undertake a military intervention in Southern Rhodesia more than counterbalanced it.

The responsibilities to the newly emancipated units as well as opportunities to exercise influence over them gradually dwindled, but British economic interests east of Suez remained important, and, in the public debate over the proposed withdrawal in 1967, they were often quoted as a good reason for staying there. In fact, the connection between military presence and the protection of economic interests was always somewhat tenuous, especially after the successful conclusion of the Anglo-Iranian dispute in 1951–2 without the employment of force. The presence of British troops in the Persian Gulf was highly desirable for British oil companies, but only as long as it increased the stability of the region; hence they did not endeavour to prolong this presence after the announcement of the withdrawal in 1967. There is little doubt that, in a very vague and general way, the presence of large British investments served as a general justification for the presence of British troops, particularly in the Middle East with its oil and in Malaya. It was no accident that the two major overseas military operations, the Emergency in Malaya and the Confrontation on behalf of Malaysia, took place in a country where British investments were very high—during the Confrontation they were variously valued at up to £800 million.

The strategic/military reasons for British overseas deployment and actions seem, however, to have been much more significant. Imperial defences had been centred on India, as she was both a main centre and a source of supply of abundant manpower, and on the imperial lines of communication through the Suez Canal. This pattern of British overseas defences persisted, although its rationale had been undermined by India's independence; already in 1946 British military operations in the Dutch East Indies were crippled when Indian troops were withdrawn. However, the lingering British concern with the defence of Australia and the fact that India stayed within the Commonwealth disguised the futility of continuing the strategic task.

The Suez Canal Zone, correctly called, in the Anglo-Egyptian Treaty of 1963, 'the essential means of communication to the different parts of the British Empire', could not be effectively defended against growing Egyptian nationalism and had to be abandoned. The nationalization of the Canal in 1956 precipitated the only major British military action, which futilely attempted to reverse the pattern of British withdrawal from the Empire. Even had it been successful, however, the Canal Zone base could not possibly have been effectively reactivated. Already in the immediate postwar years, substitutes for the Suez base had come under discussion; Attlee's own favourites were Mombasa, Haifa, and Cyprus (the Middle Eastern Headquarters was eventually shifted to the latter), but these alternatives were all less central and were threatened either by nationalism or by communal strife. Once Britain had lost political control over the Canal and, even more decisively, once the Canal had been closed in 1967, the chain of strategic bases east of Suez lost its *raison d'être* altogether, especially as it was irrelevant for the new major Asian strategic problem of dealing with Communist China. Nevertheless, many rearguard actions were fought. The existing chain of bases reinforced the accustomed ways of thinking and established vested interests in the Services, all of which delayed an earlier evolution of a new, post-imperial strategy for Britain.[22]

Britain's overseas defence commitments did not fully disappear with the completion of the official withdrawal from east of Suez at the end of 1971. Some forces still remained in the area, about 8,000 men in Hong Kong, a battalion group with some air support and an occasional naval support in Singapore, and some seconded troops and officers in the Persian Gulf. It was, however, unthinkable that any of them could involve Britain in a major action. The Hong Kong force merely served the purpose of maintaining law and order and of dealing with very minor threats; the Five Power Security Pact in South-East Asia was merely consultative and entailed no automatic British obligation to use the troops stationed there or to reinforce them. It had a largely symbolic significance but it contributed to the stability of the region and it helped the Australians to maintain their own larger contribution on which the Pact was clearly contingent. The handful of British military personnel in the Persian Gulf had a clearly defined operational role, to organize local defences and to enable them to deal with rebel activities, which were on a limited scale.

With the abolition of the bases and the diminution in the size of the British Navy, British capacity to engage in even minor overseas operations greatly decreased. The possibilities of involvement, too, had decreased to such residual issues as a serious threat from Guatemala to Belize or racial disorders breaking out in Fiji. Logically, the remaining two British overseas bases were both West of Suez, on the southern flanks of NATO, in Cyprus and Malta; both of them had become the concern of NATO as was shown by the Organization's intervention in the negotiations between Britain and Malta in 1972 over the terms of continuing the formally purely British base on the island.

There existed, nevertheless, some lingering traces of the policy of containing communism and of Britain's world role. The Simonstown Agreement, which the Heath Government buttressed by its controversial decision to resume the sale of arms to South Africa, served this broad objective, although the reduced British naval capacity could not contribute much to the containment of the Soviet Navy which in the early 1970s had penetrated into the Indian Ocean and the Persian Gulf.

A few elements of strategic thinking in Britain remained partly geared to the defence of the Indian Ocean, the strategic reserve, for instance, or the debated through-deck cruiser on the discussion on whether NATO should depart from its limited objectives of central defence. At the same time, new possible strategic interests were slowly emerging, especially Britain's interest in maintaining the freedom of the open seas, which was coming under an increased threat of encroachment by the litoral states. This was an interest which Britain shared with other members of the international society, including the Russians. It was therefore conceivable that, in addition to her few remaining limited local tasks, Britain would retain a part in major maritime strategies to be conducted internationally. Participation in them would be fully within Britain's capacity, her commitments would be limited, she would be running few political risks, and they would clearly serve British interests not of the past but of the present and the future.

*Nuclear Strategy*
Nuclear strategy has played a central part not only in Britain's defence policy, particularly since 1957, but also in her diplomacy, buttressing her conceptions of her world-power status and affecting her relations with the

United States, France, and Western Europe. Moreover, the problems of British nuclear strategy shed some light upon scientific and technological policies in general and illuminate some important facets of domestic politics, especially the relations between the officials, the military, and the scientists, and the party and parliamentary system. As the new field only opened in 1941, we can also see how quickly major involvements generate inertia and build up supporting forces which establish a new tradition. Finally, at the date of Britain's entry into the EEC her nuclear strategy remained one of the few unrevised links with the United States, which would inevitably require reconsideration within a fairly short time.

A convenient starting-point is found in the motivations underlying the major decisions in the field.[23] To start with the decision to engage in the development of nuclear weapons in 1941, the major motive was of course strategic, the fear that the Germans might develop a decisive weapon. The Maud Committee of scientists therefore applied itself to two primary questions, whether the weapons were scientifically possible, and, if so, whether Britain could produce them before Germany; both questions were answered in the affirmative. Apart, however, from the immediate war need, the Committee also considered a long-term strategic risk:

If the war should end before the bombs are ready, the effort would not be wasted, except in the unlikely event of complete disarmament, since no nation would care to risk being caught without a weapon of such decisive possibilities'.[24]

A whole additional report dealt with the use of uranium as a source of power. The long-term military and civilian aspects were both duly noted in the subsequent official deliberations on the project.

The next major decision was made by the Defence Sub-Committee of the Cabinet in January 1947, to manufacture a national deterrent. Again, the strategic issues was dominant—the Russians appeared threatening and the Americans unreliable, and the international attempts at the regulation of atomic weapons had reached a deadlock; moreover, hurt national pride and the desire to obtain bargaining power and influence over the United States played an important additional part.[25] The possibility of savings on conventional weapons contributed; it became the dominant reason for the decision to establish the deterrent as the basis of the national defence policy, which was embodied in the White Paper on Defence in 1957. There was no easy alternative and the Labour opposition soon rejected the idea of a unilateral abandonment of the weapon, pressed for by the Campaign for Nuclear Disarmament; after the French atomic test early in 1959, it adopted only the more limited compromise proposal for a non-nuclear club.

The British deterrent was partly based upon close co-operation with the United States, which was restored in the later 1950s and was deepened at Nassau in 1962, through the *Polaris* agreement. As the only economically possible way of continuing the British deterrent, the American link appealed not only to Macmillan but also to his successor, Wilson, who came into power with an electoral undertaking to renegotiate the agreement but soon discovered that the nuclear weapons were cheap. Moreover as was pointed out by the late Leonard Beaton in his influential pamphlet *Would Labour Give Up The Bomb?*[26] to make a unilateral renunciation move effective, the government would have had to destroy not only its nuclear stockpiles and research establishments which were also used for the development of nuclear energy for peaceful uses, but also all the existing and planned delivery systems, both the aeroplanes and the submarines. This would have amounted to a massive unilateral disarmament and the loss of a major technology. Moreover, by that time the programme for the four *Polaris* submarines was sufficiently advanced to make cancellation costs prohibitive; it was arguably cheaper to proceed with the programme than to cancel it.

The bomb was developed against the background of the strategic insecurity and uncertainty of 1940–1 and 1945–7, well before any strategy could have been thought out, but the limitations of Britain's arsenal were instrumental in making her strategists conceptualize nuclear strategy even before their American counterparts. Churchill was the first Western statesman to decide to base national defence policy upon a declaratory policy of nuclear deterrence. The 'Global Strategy Paper', prepared on his direction by the three Chiefs of Staff in 1952, revolutionized the strategy not only of Britain but also of the United States and of NATO. Britain could not, however, keep pace with the proliferation of American and Soviet armoury and the subsequent sophistication of nuclear strategy. She remained dependent upon the primitive counter-city strategy and was not in a position to evolve a meaningful strategy of graduated deterrence. Moreover, her dependence upon declaratory policies involved a certain unreality—nuclear deterrence became the basis of national defence around 1955, but the first squadron of Victor bombers was not operational until 1958. Finally, some supporters of the deterrent, but not the governments themselves, attributed to it some kind of general effectiveness, even against non-nuclear challengers. This rhetoric disguised Britain's weakness in conventional weapons after the abolition of National Service and encouraged unrealistic and wishful thinking, notably about the reliability of the American Skybolt project, despite repeated American warnings about its poor prospects.

Although the credibility of the British deterrent was limited and diminishing, one cannot deny it a certain strategic value in introducing an element of risk which could act at least as a partial restraint on some potential Soviet actions. It could also in some circumstances have a catalytic or 'trigger' effect upon American action. Finally, in relation to other small nuclear powers, France and China, the credibility of the British deterrent could be regarded as higher. Moreover, the deterrent was the catalyst in introducing civilian control over the military and in the resulting rationalization of the British defence system. The transition from a co-ordination of Services to a system based upon central control coincided with the final adoption of the deterrent as the basis of British defence in 1957.

The diplomatic effects of the nuclear strategy were both far-reaching and contradictory. There were benefits—a degree of prestige, a standing in the international nuclear negotiations which allowed Britain to play a leading role in the Partial Test Ban and the Non-Proliferation Treaties, and, more importantly, a basis for close nuclear co-operation with the United States; the unexpectedly successful British thermonuclear explosion in 1957, in particular, opened the door for her at the convenient moment when the Americans needed nuclear bases in Britain.

At the same time, there were also severe diplomatic drawbacks. In Anglo-American relations the nuclear relationship was not only a link but also an irritant which caused several acute crises, notably over the cancellation of Skybolt. Moreover, the British deterrent could be regarded by other middle powers, especially France, as an incentive to develop their own national deterrents. The most insoluble problems arose from Britain's dependence upon the United States, although, with great diplomatic skill, Macmillan managed to obtain at Nassau what was to amount to full control for Britain over her *Polaris* submarines, a matter of vital importance in a case of emergency. This dependence became a major element in de Gaulle's determination to keep Britain out of Europe; the Nassau Agreement may not have been decisive in causing his first veto, but, at the very least, it fully confirmed his basic assessment that British strategy with its dependence upon the United States clashed with a European orientation of Britain's economic policy; it also provided him with a convenient opportunity to reject Britain's application.

Apart from political considerations, there was an overwhelming economic case for preferring Britain's American alignment in nuclear matters to French independence in them. The British acquired their weapons at a much lower cost estimated at some $5,000 million against France's $12,000 million. Between 1966 and 1971 France spent about one-quarter of her defence budget on nuclear weapons, whereas Britain spent a mere 4·1 per cent; the expectations for 1975 were 20 per cent and 2 per cent respectively. Moreover, after Britain's first two *Polaris* submarines had been laid down in 1964, within four years Britain had all four of them operational, whereas it took the French some four and a half years to make their first submarine operational.[27]

The credit and debit account of Britain's deterrent has partly to be evaluated in the light of its 'spill-over' effect on nuclear-power technology. Here Britain at first led the world; but having chosen gas-cooled reactors, which became uncompetitive as against the later-developed American water-cooled reactors she found herself in a cul-de-sac in the early 1970s. The evolution of the nuclear-power programme demonstrates the limitations of a rational appraisal and the colossal power of inertia in major technological involvements. Once the programme had been embarked upon, at each stage when a decision had to be made there appeared to be no attractive alternative to maintaining co-operation with the United States. A full continuity of nuclear policy can therefore be observed throughout the changes of government, although it came near to becoming an electoral issue in 1964. The same continuity can be discerned in the smooth and efficient co-operation between scientists and scientific administrators ever since the war. The nuclear programme also demonstrates the inability of Parliament to control a situation in which the government and the civil service are determined to proceed: for several years Parliament was kept entirely unaware of the very existence of the nuclear project.

Inertia may remain the determining factor in keeping the British deterrent going for a long time ahead. Its strategic utility, limited as it is, is unlikely to become immediately undermined as a result of the SALT agreement between the Americans and the Russians in 1972, under which the Anti-Ballistic Missile Systems (ABMS) in both countries will remain limited, leaving their territories fairly penetrable. It is hard to think that the advances in Anti-Submarine Warfare (ASW) will be sufficiently rapid to render the *Polaris* submarines vulnerable to attack in the very near future.

Thus the nuclear issue, which constituted the core of Britain's major diplomatic alignment with the United States and formed an integral part of her past conception of her world role, may conceivably continue to occupy a central place in her policy, at least over the next decade. The rationale of the national deterrent will have to be adjusted to the new conception of Britain's status as a middle power and to her membership of the EEC. The occasions demanding a policy decision already exist:

there are the issues of the next generation of nuclear weapons and of the Anglo-American nuclear agreement, which has become subject to termination in 1974.

In theory, Britain has three possible choices: first, to assume complete national independence in nuclear matters; second, to extend the present links with the United States; third, to establish co-operation with France. None of these is readily manageable. The first choice seems quite unlikely. For both economic and technological reasons, Britain clearly cannot retain even the present degree of her credibility as a nuclear power by her own effort. An individual national nuclear policy could only therefore take the form of either a unilateral nuclear disarmament (but the considerations which prevailed against this in the past are likely also to continue in the future), or of the untenable short-term policy of maintaining the present deterrent as long as it is even marginally credible, without deciding about its replacement.

Extending the present arrangements with the Americans to the next generation of nuclear weapons has the great advantages of cheapness and of relative simplicity—all that is needed is to continue the present relationship and renegotiate the existing agreement. The obstacles are, however, clear. From Britain's point of view, continuing her dependence upon the United States means that her major strategic alignment would continue to cut across her rapidly developing major political and economic alignment with Western Europe. From the American point of view, the extension of the nuclear relationship is bound to be contingent upon the state of the SALT negotiations, and also upon the evolution of American relations with the French. It is easily forgotten that already in the past the Americans had, to a limited extent, helped the French in their nuclear efforts;[28] they may be unwilling to continue to accord Britain a more privileged position in the future.

The third theoretical possibility, some form of nuclear co-operation with the French, advanced ever since 1965 by Heath, was included in the foreign-policy programme of his government. *Prima facie*, such co-operation has great technological and economic attractions. Moreover, politically, it would cement Anglo-French relations and would contribute to the integration of Western Europe. The policy has, however, made no headway. There is a fair technological case for Anglo-French co-operation, as the British are much more advanced in the technology of nuclear weapons, while the French have developed ballistic missiles. The French are facing an immediate and apparently increasing economic burden in the final stages of their development of nuclear warheads, which could be greatly reduced by their having access to British nuclear technology;

the future needs of both states from 1974 onwards will become more symmetrical, as both will need to carry the heavy cost of developing a new generation of weapons. Is an agreement possible, however, on the equity of contribution when the French spend some 0·65 per cent of their much larger GNP on nuclear technology against Britain's 0·18 per cent? It is doubtful whether the French would accept the British valuation of Britain's greater technological contribution.[29]

The political difficulties are greatest. Although, in the improved climate of mutual relations, the French would be ready to explore exchange of technological information which would be to their advantage, they have remained fully attached to a policy of completely independent national defence which seems to preclude the most promising co-operation, that is, in the deployment of the two national submarine forces, which would require an agreement upon joint targeting. Immense difficulties would also arise in securing the agreement of the United States, the Federal Republic of Germany, and other Western European states to any form of Anglo-French deterrent. Consequently, the hopes that Anglo-French nuclear co-operation will resolve the British dilemma and will make an immediate contribution to the cohesion of the West are obviously far-fetched. This does not, however, preclude the obvious long-term attractions of such co-operation in both respects.[30]

# Part Three
# Conclusion

# 13 Summary and Conclusions

*The Record*

In an analysis as brief as this it would be impossible to account in detail for the motivations of the major policy decisions and for the appreciation of the alternatives considered, even if they were fully known. Policies therefore tend to appear to have been near-inevitable. Every single decision could, indeed, be considered as near-inevitable, but only within the narrow terms of the then definition of the situation. The record and its brief summary which follows should not be read as conveying the author's belief in determinism, as they may superficially indicate. The reasons for the major policies and decisions were compelling, but, when they are considered in perspective, not overwhelmingly so. This includes the turn to Western Europe which inevitably dominates the concluding phase of the accounts of each major area of British foreign policy.

This section will briefly summarize the general trends noted and the situation reached by the end of 1972 in the major areas discussed in the text; the subsequent ones will evaluate the record in terms of the propositions advanced in chapter 1 and of some broader explanations, and will briefly look into the future.

Continuity is the most striking characteristic of British political as well as social life, some aspects of which were discussed in chapters 2 and 3. It is possible to see the first twenty-five postwar years as a prolonged attempt to sustain this continuity both in Britain's domestic arrangements and in her foreign policy, on the basis of a general political consensus which preserved it despite the changes of government. The Attlee Government moulded postwar Britain. At home it introduced the non-selective welfare state and a mixed private-nationalized economy; in foreign policy it decided to withdraw from the Empire, it inaugurated Britain's nuclear and NATO strategies, and it rejected the leadership of Europe. The Conservative governments between 1951 and 1964 did not deviate from this programme except in details; the Labour government between 1964 and 1970 merely tried to restore and complete the details of the 1945 Labour programme. The political rhetoric inherent in party competition therefore bore an air of unreality, obstructing a clear appreciation of the degree of adaptation and change which actually took place, though in opposite ways, in domestic and foreign policies: both parties found it electorally advantageous to exaggerate the degree of change and of the differences between them in domestic matters, while the rhetoric of Britain's continuing independent world role disguised the degree of her gradual adaptation to a reduced international status. The homogeneity of the political elite and the well-organized bureaucratic system, the two-party system which discourages radicalism, public opinion which is fundamentally conservative, all worked in favour of a consensus and discouraged a fundamental reappraisal and drastic innovation.

During the 1960s, the basis of the consensus was gradually eroded. While at home dissatisfactions grew owing to insufficient economic growth and the shortcomings of the welfare state and industrial relations, in foreign policy, the rejection of Europe, the excessive dependence upon the United States, and the belief in the Commonwealth as a real element of power became less and less tenable. Britain was emerging from her postwar adaptation process in a shape which was not really satisfactory—she was rapidly falling behind other advanced industrial states both in economic growth and in the degree of her world influence. By 1970 the situation was ripe for ending the consensus. The Heath Government was elected in June 1970 with a mandate for change—to reorganize and rationalize the administrative machine, taxation, the social services, and industrial relations; and to bring Britain into Europe. Moreover, the new Prime Minister did not believe that a real consensus had ever existed; in an interview with Anthony Sampson in March 1971,[1] he said: 'There never was . . . a deliberate effort of will and thought to create a particular situation', although he agreed that something akin to a consensus arose over collectivism as the result of the First World War losses and of the Great Depression. The change in Britain's political climate was accentuated by the Prime Minister's abrasive personal style and by his determination to adopt what may be called an 'aggressive strategy' against the workers on the basis of public reverence for Parliament and Law, and his determination to get Britain into the EEC. The governmental policies, which the Labour opponents justifiably regarded as deliberately divisive, antagonized the working class and increased the influence of the left wing in the Labour Party sufficiently to impel Wilson to dissociate himself from several major policies on which a relative consensus had previously prevailed, notably the need to control industrial relations by law and Britain's entry into the EEC.

Within two years after the 1970 election a severe bout of inflation, increasing industrial unrest, and renewed pressures on sterling which led to its being floated, all darkened the domestic scene; advanced British technologies were ailing, notably the nuclear power and computer industries, and Concorde was becoming a white elephant; the Ulster troubles which had started in 1969, continued to require a substantial military intervention; the problems of absorbing the Commonwealth immigrants remained unresolved. Public morale accordingly suffered. The malaise of the middle class engendered by the succession of setbacks at home and abroad was increased by rising disappointment with the promises of managerial efficiency and of cost effectiveness on which the Conservative government had based its programme of reform. Faced with inflation and a steep rise in the cost of living the workers became convinced that the government was determined to reverse the advances they had made in their social and economic position.

The Industrial Relations Act and Britain's entry into the EEC became the main issues around which the political and social divisions crystallized. They could, however, easily become the basis of a new political and social consensus in the 1970s. The national tradition that Britain should be governed on a basis of consensus obstructs innovation but is also a great element of strength. It enabled the British to weather without a major rift the dissolution of the Empire and social reform after 1945; it could readily be restored around a new programme to tackle Britain's lingering problems within the new EEC setting.

Although Britain entered the EEC in the throes of yet another economic crisis, this time accompanied by a serious social one, her basic condition was by no means unsound. The stirrings of reform had extended to all major areas of the political and social systems, the need for innovation had been generally accepted. The Plowden Report dealt with the Civil Service and the Duncan Report with the Foreign Service, and governmental structure underwent several reorganizations. The Maud Report covered local government, the Crowther Commission the Constitution, the Donovan Report the trade unions, the Law Commissioners engaged in the codification and reform of law, and the Heath Government in the reform and simplification of taxation. Needless to say, many of the proposed reforms were insufficient or not implemented, and others proved ineffective, notably the Industrial Relations Act. They showed, however, at least a willingness to accept the necessity for reform, a departure from unquestioning traditionalism. At the very least, they established warning signs against some policies, in most cases they laid the foundations of reform. Some areas had actually been reformed; by the early 1970s, agriculture had been fully modernized to the point of being the most efficient in Western Europe, the structural inefficiencies of industrial management had largely been removed, industrial productivity had begun to improve, and much redundant labour had been shaken out. Most importantly, perhaps, after the growth of social malaise following previous disappointments, national expectations were reduced to more manageable proportions, making the people more receptive to an even moderate turn for the better in Britain's fortunes. Although in 1972 dissensus manifested itself more violently than ever in the workers' opposition to the government, society seemed firmly set on the path to reform. A hopeful sign lay in Wilson's sustained endeavour to avoid a firm commitment to full repeal of governmental policies.

As has been discussed in chapter 4, Britain undoubtedly lost much of her power and influence between 1945 and 1973. The parameters of her actions considerably narrowed in a world in which the power of several other states had grown proportionately much faster, and many issues had become internationalized. She emerged, however, from the process with a much clearer perception of her own power and one which also corresponds more closely with the perceptions of other nations. The greatest source of ambiguity and of illusions was removed with the withdrawal from east of Suez. Before that it was difficult to evaluate the various bases, military presences, and commitments which had served as elements of strength but were increasingly becoming grave liabilities. Within the context of the EEC, Britain is clearly in an advantageous position as one of the three leading countries in terms of her territory and population. Through the cumulative effect of a consistently slower economic growth, her per capita GNP dropped well below that of France and Germany, but the gloomy extrapolations of past trends into the future are unconvincing. She is likely, as has been argued, to have nearly completed the painful process of economic and social reorganization, in which she has lagged behind other advanced industrial states, but which, once it is successfully completed, may not only make her competitive but give her some distinct advantages over her rivals in terms of social and political organization. Her resource base will dramatically improve once the fuel supplies from the North Sea are fully exploited—if they prove to be as substantial as the increasing estimates indicate, they will fundamentally transform her economy. Britain can confidently be expected to remain a leading military power in Western Europe, although at the cost of a continually sustained economic effort. Most important of all, if the EEC evolves into a more closely integrated political unit, she will be less and less required to act on her own and will be less constrained by her limited resources within the broad international context, whether political, strategic, or economic.

This shift of the fulcrum of British foreign policy into the Western European context is likely to indicate an increasing growth in the importance of what the modern sociologists sometimes call 'identitive' power—the use of diplomacy within the enlarged Community to persuade the partners to accept as far as possible British interpretations of Western European interests and to make the best possible use of Britain's residual close links with overseas, which, if carefully preserved and developed, could constitute an important element in the influence both of her self and of the Community in the world.

The process has been facilitated by the gradual revision of the basic assumptions and perceptions which governed British foreign policy in 1945 (ch. 5). The central assumption, that Britain could and would continue as an independent political unit in the traditional sense, and that her position and her place within the international system would return to some sort of prewar 'normalcy', proved untenable. The assumptions underlying British policies towards the Soviet Union, the United States, and the Commonwealth were drastically revised. With a considerable time-lag, the perceptions governing British policies were adjusted to postwar realities; and those which had degenerated into dangerous myths, especially concerning the role of sterling and the central importance of the Commonwealth, were discarded. This provided a sound basis for a more rational choice of feasible objectives and of suitable means for their pursuit.

British entry into the Community may be expected to force the decision-makers to question and to revise some well-established traditions of the political processes, both at home and in foreign policy. In the first instance, membership will shift the focus of attention from the various problems and issues of the global system with which Britain cannot cope by herself as an individual nation-state to the more manageable regional system. Moreover, as was already partly noticeable during the 1971 negotiations for entry, the need to consider individual policies in respect to their bearing upon Britain's central EEC policy imposes a rational scrutiny and a fairly clear criterion of evaluation on practically the whole range of British foreign policy. Continuity cannot be expected to be broken, but 'thinking European' will at least create an opportunity for a far-reaching revision of traditions. How far the actual revision will go will depend on circumstances, and, to a large extent, on the political will brought to bear. This rational scrutiny will be further encouraged by the increasing abandonment of the United States as the usual paradigm and yardstick for British policies, in favour of the more appropriate comparisons with France and Western Germany. Finally, the retraction of the exceptionally wide scope of British foreign policy is bound to make it less vulnerable to the inevitable vagaries of chance and to erratic preoccupations justified only by the inevitable urgency of problems which are not really important in themselves.

Turning to elements of the national style (ch. 6) one can confidently expect that pragmatism will remain the major characteristic of British politics. However, whereas pragmatism was a distinct disadvantage so long as it obstructed a fundamental revision of foreign policy when Britain's power was rapidly waning after 1945, it may become a source of strength if and when entry into the Community engenders a new sense of purpose. The traditional virtues of pragmatism—flexibility, lack of ideological commitments, recognition of hard facts—will all come into their own. There is no reason to doubt that Britain's geographical position can be fruitfully interpreted as a justification for her membership of Western Europe, as in the past, it was a justification for her abstention. Her tradition of harmonizing her policies with those of others provides a good foundation for her relations with her fellow members, for taking a positive part in shaping Community relations with the outside world, and for helping to progress towards a realistic integration of the Community.

The traditional principle of balance of power governed the perceptions and the appreciation of the major strategic/political aspects of world politics by British policy-makers as much as those of most other states. Within the restraints of Britain's diminished power, the principle could not serve as a basis for a fluid and flexible foreign policy, because the balancing arrangements inflexibly determined an alignment with the United States and NATO. Although the concept of the 'balance', and the allied one of a 'power vacuum' which would be filled by an expansionist communist power dominated British foreign policies throughout the period, they are likely to remain fully relevant for Britain only in relation to the issues of the security of Western Europe. Parallel development can be seen in Britain's rapidly decreasing ability and wish to use force for major foreign-policy purposes, certainly since Suez. However, in view of her traditions of 'gun-boat diplomacy' and of the residual power of her surface navy, it is possible that, within the more promising context of membership of the EEC, Britain could readily attempt once more in the future to provide the nucleus of an international force, which she unsuccessfully tried to organize in 1956 and 1967.

British attitudes to the norms of behaviour prevailing within the international system underwent an important evolution owing to the combination of two factors: the rise of a new international order and the fundamental change in Britain's power position. Britain's traditional support for these norms stemmed partly from the fact that they were generally in conformity with her interests and even sometimes of her making, and partly from the important place of moral and legal issues in domestic political debates. Occasionally confusion would arise between Britain's actual interests and the broad moral principles she was supporting.

With the narrowing of the scope of Britain's foreign policy, this confusion is likely to disappear. Within the postwar international order, Britain found herself in rather a handicapped position. International law now proved incapable of protecting her established interests, and the evolving new rules of international morality forced her to recognize important changes in law to her detriment—notably she had to accommodate the forces of anti-colonialism and of opposition to established ways of exploiting natural resources. Tensions inevitably ensued. Only in the Suez action did the British openly defy the emerging new order; but for some time they proved reluctant to accept the General Assembly's anti-colonial norms; and when they were incapable of meeting existing commitments, they were occasionally forced to repeal their obligations.

The tensions are bound to persist, with regard to Southern Rhodesia, for instance, but they can be expected gradually to abate, as the scope of the British interests involved has greatly narrowed. As a country traditionally enmeshed in the international system and clearly recognizing her vital interest in order, Britain will probably retain her national tradition of being concerned with, and upholding and developing, the rules of international behaviour both in their legal and in their moral forms; public interest in Britain in these aspects of foreign policy is an additional incentive. In some areas, especially the law of the sea, Britain is likely to continue to play a leading part, as in the past, both in her own interests and in those of others.

The major changes in Britain's foreign policy can be summed up as a gradual erosion of her successive conceptions of an individual world role, and her growing concern with her own national interests (ch. 7). Britain's own role conception became increasingly out of tune with her capabilities, and also with the more limited roles prescribed as suitable for her by other nations. However, through a combination of the complexity of the situation, of wishful thinking, and of the psychological and electoral difficulties of admitting that Britain's status had diminished, the revision of the conception took place only in the 1960s. Ideas of the extent of Britain's actual power were inflated by the conception of the 'three circles' and by an exaggerated view of the influence gained by British moral leadership, by her nuclear weapons, and by her diplomacy. Within the Community, Britain must channel her major efforts to influence world politics through the EEC; this is what her interests require but the amount of energy she will be able to bring to bear is likely to prove decisive. Another important factor lies in a clear definition of what precisely these national interests are. Although the British national system makes it possible to arrive at their formulation without major sectional distortions, some clarification of the confused relationship between the aspirational and the operational levels of these interests is required, in order to make really meaningful the transition from Britain's concern with her world role to one with her own national interests.

The situation with which Britain was faced at home and abroad in 1945 (ch. 8) combined with the successive conceptions of her independent world role to orientate her foreign policy strongly towards the central power balance and the two superpowers (ch. 9). Although British policies towards Russia were concerted with the American ones, they were arrived at on the basis of an individual appreciation of Soviet behaviour and of British interests; they were not decided by ideological antagonism either. The British were the first to take alarm at Soviet intentions and to work towards a Western alliance, but also the first to work for a detente in the early 1950s and, after the Suez disruption, in the late 1950s and the 1960s, although the major policy decisions were made within the context of NATO. Towards the end of the 1960s, as the dialogue between the United States and the Soviet Union gathered momentum, British strategic interests in relations with the Soviet Union began to correspond more and more with those of her Western European allies, rather than with those of the United States, and the basis for an independent British role in relations with Russia became finally eroded.

While the British relationship with Russia was, in the main, limited to the major strategic balance issues, that with the United States extended to the whole range of Britain's political/strategic and economic problems. Its intimate nature, expressed in the name 'special relationship', was based exclusively on the common perception of the Communist danger. Before the war, the relationship had never been so close or so 'special' as during the brief period of the common struggle against Hitler; it again became much less 'special' in the 1950s; and, after a revival at the end of the decade, largely because nuclear co-operation suited both sides at that time, it gradually became attentuated, as the major British strategic interests shifted towards a closer Western European alignment.

The 'special relationship' was asymmetrical in terms of power and of the influence of the two partners upon each other; but the record of British policies in Europe and outside it clearly shows that Britain preserved her independence in pursuing her interests, particularly in areas of special interest like the Middle East; she conformed with American wishes mostly in Asia, where her interests were most limited. In the process, despite the intimacy of mutual relations, misperceptions arose on both sides, notably in the case of Suez. The intimacy greatly diminished with the advent of the Heath Government, and the merger of the historical Anglo-American partnership into a broader Western European-American partnership seemed likely.

British Commonwealth relations (ch. 10) played the next most important part in British foreign policy. The Commonwealth idea was a powerful, and psychologically necessary, transitional idea while the Empire was being wound up. Owing to the increasing divorce between Commonwealth aspirations and political realities, the idea gradually became a myth. By the end of the 1960s, the overwhelming majority of the political elite and of the people had relinquished their exaggerated ideas about the Commonwealth, frequently falling into the opposite extreme of completely discounting its importance. The major misperceptions which were later abandoned arose from the tendency to regard the Commonwealth as a meaningful political sub-system, a basis of the 'three circles', and to attribute to it excessive importance as an element of Britain's political influence. After the Indian sub-continent had become smoothly emancipated and India was successfully retained within the Commonwealth, the rest of the Empire remained stable for a further decade. This encouraged illusions about its political cohesion, despite the fact that Britain did not manage to resolve the problem of its political organization or to exercise influence over the domestic or foreign policies of its members, whereas, on their side, the Commonwealth countries exercised restraints upon hers. Suez, Southern Rhodesia, and finally the British entry into the EEC, destroyed any lingering illusions about the cohesion of the Commonwealth, but the association of some of its developing members with the EEC may reinforce the bonds. The loosening of the bonds with Canada and Australia has been more final.

If, in retrospect, Britain's Commonwealth policies appear as a prolonged clinging to unrealities, her Western European policies appear as a refusal to face reality. In fact, in both cases, the situation immediately after the war was sufficiently confused to account for the wrong anticipations, although an element of wishful thinking also played its part. In the later 1940s and early 1950s Western Europe was not a promising partner; and British anticipations that its integration would not get off the ground and that, in case it proved successful, Britain would have a later opportunity to join, were justified. The fatal mistake was committed when Britain refused to join the crucial Messina talks in 1955. The subsequent conversion of the majority of Britain's political elite to the European idea was obstructed by the obstacles encountered in de Gaulle's vetoes as well as its own reluctance to turn to Europe unreservedly, at the expense of Commonwealth and American ties, and the opposition of public opinion to the idea. Only after the gradual erosion of Britain's non-European links and of her position in the world system did the EEC appear as the most promising venue for the pursuit of vital British political as well as economic interests—to the prevalent majority of the political elite but not to the general public.

The United Nations served as a focus for alternative, radical conceptions of world order and also as a forum where Britain pursued and defended some specific national interests and maintained communication with other, especially developing, states. But the organisation constituted only a minor strand of British foreign policy. Continuing declarations of general support both by Labour and, though less enthusiastically, by Conservative governments and general support by public opinion cannot disguise the fact that Britain was an unenthusiastic participant unsupported by any voting bloc, and ill at ease in the climate of open diplomacy, especially under the fire of anti-colonialists. Britain's behaviour was loyal—she used the United Nations whenever it was a convenient instrument of her foreign policy and she generally abided by the unpalatable recommendations of the General Assembly even where they stretched the Charter and encroached on her domestic jurisdiction. Often she did so reluctantly. Against this background, it is difficult to envisage that Britain could or would try to play a significant role in any future attempts to revive and strengthen the activities of the United Nations, even in the unlikely case that this would prove possible.

Despite the traditional intellectual and institutional divorce between economics and politics (ch. 11) the evolution of Britain's postwar external policies in both fields showed close parallels. In both, she was acting on the basis of a deep appreciation of her interdependence and her inability to pursue her interests on her own, but in her uniquely exposed post-1945 position she was unable to control developments and to anticipate their direction; in both she became dependent upon the United States but gradually discovered growing solidarity with Western Europe. While in the important field of oil policies the major British oil companies, with their autonomous economic operation and the minimum of governmental interference, managed to establish international solidarity with other major oil companies, Britain's crucial sterling policies became inextricably linked with the maintenance of her world role in general and, specifically, east of Suez, and with their concentration on the Commonwealth. The evolution of sterling policies showed a close parallel with that of the conceptions of her independent world role—the full extent of their cost and their untenable nature became clear only in the late 1960s. Britain only abandoned her responsibility for maintaining an international currency in 1967, and her interests in the field of international finance gradually came closer to those of Western Europe rather than to those of the United States. British aid policy was also closely linked with the Commonwealth through its major instrumentality, the Colombo Plan. It was limited in scope and extent; it could in future play a much more important role in British foreign policy, either through the United Nations or through the EEC.

Finally, a considerable advance was made in the co-ordination of British defence and foreign policies and the control of their economic aspects (ch. 12). The constant of the defence policy was a substantial military contribution to the defence of Western Europe, institutionalized in NATO. Britain's contribution was instrumental in securing American participation in NATO and ensured her a leading role in its operation. From the later 1950s, however, when Germany was rapidly becoming NATO's main European contributor of forces, it became more and more questionable whether Britain's burden of defence, which remained heavier than those of France or Germany, brought proportionate diplomatic returns. The overseas defence commitments proved to be more ephemeral. They were the aftermath of imperial and wartime responsibilities and were connected with the ideas of Britain's world role and with the Commonwealth. They were gradually reduced, side by side with the latter, until the withdrawal from east of Suez at the end of 1971 brought them to an end, with very few residual exceptions. The rationale of these defences was changing throughout the period, but it is clear that historical commitments were the major reason for the involvement east of Suez. Britain's nuclear policy also was closely connected with her world role— as a major military capability and as the basis for her advanced power technology. The policies were relatively speaking cheap but entailed dependence upon the United States and estrangement from France.

### The Changes between 1945 and 1973

Changes in British policies were matched and frequently surpassed by those in the international environment. To sum up very briefly the outstanding ones: the cold war had evolved into a detente; China, an integrating EEC, and Japan were in the process of becoming major actors on the international stage; decolonization had been almost completed; world industry, technology, and trade had greatly expanded; the population explosion and pollution had become major international concerns. How do the propositions advanced in the first chapter, formulated with special relevance to 1945, relate to the changed circumstances of 1973, especially the British entry into the EEC?

To start with the domestic-foreign links (pp. 13ff.) there is no reason to revise the first proposition, that there is a degree of continuity and congruence between domestic and foreign policies. The repercussions of actions and of their outcomes, of strength and weakness, of successes and failures in one sphere continue to affect the other.

The ways in which the governments pursue national interests and formulate policies in both fields remain different, as stated in the second proposition, but membership of the EEC substantially affected them both owing to the consequent blurring of the boundaries between what is domestic and what is foreign. Even before Britain's actual entry, EEC issues became enmeshed in domestic ones.

The third proposition, that one cannot postulate in general terms which priorities prevail when domestic and foreign policy objectives clash, remains fully valid. Although the objectives stemming from Britain's membership of the enlarged Community are bound to play an increasingly prominent role in the definition of her national interests, it is unlikely that this will, to any significant extent, stop governments from according customary priorities to urgent domestic demands. The prompt floating of sterling in the summer of 1972, in spite of an undertaking to the contrary given a short while beforehand, clearly indicates the trend of things at least for some time to come. The situation only will change if and when the enlarged Community achieves closer integration and any decisive shift of competence from domestic to Community processes must be slow. The calls upon the time and energy of British governments which arose in the past from Britain's world-wide commitments are bound to diminish. Governments will thus be freer to attend to domestic priorities, but there is no reason to think that these priorities will necessarily receive a higher allocation of resources than in the past whenever they compete with foreign-policy objectives, especially with defence expenditure.

The debate over Britain's entry into the EEC confirms the fourth proposition, that the more a foreign-policy issue encompasses society's resources and relationships, the more it is drawn into the domestic system and the more important and difficult becomes the problem of securing a consensus. Any progress towards an integrated Community economic policy, which is the avowed objective of the British government, will further blur the boundaries between what is foreign and what is domestic. The result will be that areas of public policy will become both, and the general public will be as intimately involved in them as in any domestic issue of general concern.

Finally, does the record confirm the judgement that Britain is a 'penetrated political system', i.e. one in which others have become direct participants? In many respects the freedom of action of the successive British governments of the postwar period was severely circumscribed, frequently by the views and attitudes of the Americans but also by those of the other advanced industrialized nations who participate in the organization of international finance and trade. Nevertheless, the powerful constraints and influences did not amount to a *force majeure* and did not involve direct foreign participation in Britain's political processes. After coming to power in 1964, Wilson was free to devalue the pound or to sever the nuclear links with the United States; Heath could have decided to show his loyalty to the EEC by defending sterling in the summer of 1972 instead of floating the pound. Throughout the period, despite growing interdependence and their awareness of it, British policymakers did not forfeit their ultimate freedom of decision, although within constantly narrowing parameters. Entry into the EEC is unlikely to change the situation. Increasing areas of national policy are likely to become Community policy but, for some time at least, national autonomy is likely to survive to an extent similar to that which Britain has enjoyed since 1945. International influences and constraints may become stronger and may affect her political processes at an earlier stage of policy formation, but certainly for a number of years British governments will retain the ultimate freedom of decision, including, as a last resort, the decision to leave the Community, however inexpedient and costly this might prove.

Turning to the impact of the international environment upon British foreign policy (pp. 11ff.), the first proposition, that this impact was exceptionally strong, loses much of its validity. By 1973 Britain's foreign policy has become much more limited in scope than in 1945 and membership of the EEC—as well as her continuing membership of NATO— cushions her from the direct impact of international developments in the most crucial fields of her foreign policy.

Second, the historical conception of British involvement in the international system, in terms of Britain's responsibilities, has been fundamentally revised. The Heath Government has firmly declared its basic approach to world order in terms of national interests. British awareness of interdependence, of the need for harmonization, and of the importance of maintaining an orderly international system continues, but the welfare of the international system is no longer directly equated with serving national interests, and Britain's responsibility to contribute to the international system is no longer accorded primary importance. The floating of the pound in 1972 strongly contrasts with its stubborn defence in 1966–7.

Third, the gross imbalance between Britain's capabilities and her international responsibilities in the immediate postwar years has now been largely rectified. Although at home, her technological ambitions and defence procurement are still in the process of adjustment and the conditions for an increased economic growth are by no means certain, abroad, her commitments have been drastically reduced as the result of the withdrawal from east of Suez and the limitation of her role in the central strategic balance. Her capabilities for playing a leading role in the enlarged Community are fully adequate and the chances of her maintaining a reasonable balance in the crucial area of the defence of the homeland are quite reasonable.

Fourth, parallel with all these developments, Britain's international position cannot any longer be regarded as 'eccentric' in relation to other comparable states. The ending of the Empire and of the 'three circles' doctrine, the abandonment of Britain's idiosyncratic positions in international trade and finance, and, ultimately, her membership of the EEC, have brought her interests increasingly into line with those of her continental neighbours.

Finally, in contrast to 1945, Britain's position in 1973 offers prospects of stability for some time to come. The converging ephemeral factors which obstructed a clear appreciation of the limitations of her power have all disappeared; the assumptions held in 1945 which were proved wrong have now been abandoned; the mistaken perceptions which lingered in the form of misleading myths have been corrected.

### General Evaluations

As foreign policy is not a coherent field, a general explanation of its record requires a broad approach. Many writers and thinkers who have been searching for reasons for Britain's loss of power since 1945 find them mainly in her loss of Empire. The following brief account of some of these explanations is therefore grouped around the theme of the decay of empires and, by analogy, also of civilizations. A recent symposium[2] which attempted to identify the common factors in the decline of eight empires fell short not only of formulating a general theory but even of indicating the key factors involved. Given the complexity of the problem and the degree of factual uncertainty, it is impossible to judge the relative importance of the factors identified, or indeed, their relevance. The recurrent major factors are the extravagance and irresponsibility of the ruling class, pathological bureaucratization, inadequate manpower, insufficient agricultural production, high taxation, inflation, resistance to change. All of them can, to a varying degree, be applied to postwar Britain.

Arnold Toynbee's theory of the rise and fall of civilizations cannot be fully applied to empires and nations, but his basic ideas offer a fruitful, although only partially applicable framework for explanation. In general terms, we can say that the challenges of the contemporary international system were excessive for the British Empire to survive, but the immediate challenges to postwar Britain were insufficient to force her fully to engage in the necessary drastic adjustments. More detailed explanations are less satisfactory. For instance, the analogy with the Roman Empire and its decay through the Toynbeesque challenge of the internal proletariat, as presented by Paul Einzig,[3] is not very persuasive: 'Britons have become so thoroughly pampered and spoilt that they want to have everything at once, regardless of what the country can afford at present. Neither the public nor its rulers seem capable of self-denial or self-restraint.' Free spectacles and unemployment benefits may carry a partial analogy with the Roman *panem et circenses* but otherwise the analogy scarcely holds good—there is no parallel between the stability of the social arrangements in contemporary Britain and in fifth-century Rome, nor does the sophisticated contemporary international environment resemble the menace of the barbarian Goths. Interesting partial parallels can be found in comparing postwar Britain with Renaissance Venice.[4] Not only is it a case of two maritime powers engaged in a choice between maritime and continental orientations, but both of them lived on myths, although quite different ones—the Venetians deluded themselves about the unique excellence of their society, and the British about the extent of their world role and the linked conceptions of the Commonwealth, sterling, and their military function east of Suez.

More specific is the explanation that decay is caused by society's neglect of economic activities. Not only historians but practising politicians also are struck by the importance of the economic base and by the broader social significance of its being neglected. For instance, President Nixon, who, in 1971, became thoroughly anxious lest the United States might be becoming economically decadent, referred occasionally to the decay of the Roman Empire, and undoubtedly saw the connection between economic decline and moral decadence.[5] An elaborate theory developed by Shepard B. Clough[6] is, however, on the whole reassuring as far as Britain is concerned. She may be somewhat lacking in the essential factors necessary for economic growth which he distinguishes, notably in the right ideology, but the principal five reasons he identifies for which civilizations have declined are not all presented: except for Ulster, the central government has not broken down and internal disorders have not occurred; neither is invasion imminent. Excessive and unproductive consumption, and the successful adoption by others of British industrial techniques need not by themselves lead to real decay.

The last point coincides with explanations tracing Britain's loss of power to her educational and governmental systems. Correlli Barnett[7] attributes the decline to sixty years of increasing backwardness and uncompetitiveness, mainly due to an educational system which had a strong literary and moralistic bias and offered an extremely poor technological preparation. Already before the first world war Britain was on the way to becoming a technological colony of the United States and of Germany. In the three consecutive versions of his *Anatomy of Britain*, Anthony Sampson broadens this explanation to include the indecisiveness and backwardness, the amateurishness and nepotism of the whole ruling class, reared mainly in public schools. These explanations point to what may be regarded as important although scarcely decisive elements of social weakness. However, the educational system has been reformed since the war and Sampson's strictures on the civil service, the interconnected business empires, the old Etonians in the Tory Party, the absentee House of Lords, and the snobbishness of the Guards, were much more justified at the time of the first edition of his book in 1962, than at that of its third in 1971, when some of the institutions singled out for criticism were being reformed while the significance of others had dwindled.

Imperial decay is frequently attributed to the loss of political will. Duncan Sandys's celebrated remark to Roy Welensky about the loss of the will to govern by the English has been elaborated into a major explanation by many thinkers. The decline of confidence is particularly marked when one compares the postwar period with Victorian Britain, whether one attributes it to the decrease of optimism and to the loss of the Victorian belief in the will and progress, based on the then contemporary rationalism, or to the loss of 'self-righteousness' i.e. the sense of moral justification and purpose.[8]

The whole social structure of contemporary Britain is, in some respects, the fundamental cause of her weakness. Being the first nation to industrialize, she has developed institutions and customs which favour a conservative outlook in social matters. Particularly important is her backwardness in the organization of industrial relations. The historical multiplication of competing trade unions, the ineffectiveness of the TUC leadership, and the militancy at the shop-floor level all strike many observers as the major reason for the uncompetitiveness of British industry when compared with its Japanese or German rivals. [9]

Another important aspect of the postwar period may be called, in Friedrich von Hayek's terms [10] 'the muddle of the middle'. The welfare state was an attempt to find a middle way between capitalism and socialism, avoiding the excesses of either; nationalization was to establish a working relationship between state activities and private enterprise; equalization of incomes was to work simultaneously with the retention of economic incentives. The compromises have not been fully successful. They have shaped a society with some of the defects although without the main benefits of either authoritarianism or liberal democracy based upon free enterprise. Preserving continuity and a basic political consensus, the successive governments have proved indecisive on the central issue of allocating values, uneasily fluctuating between relief for poverty and creation of economic incentives.

The unpropitious nature of the international environment for maintaining Britain's dominant position is referred to in many of these explanations, although generally it is not given sufficient emphasis. Britain's industrial and commercial predominance and her extensive Empire were acquired in particularly advantageous circumstances. Any full explanation of the decline of Britain in the twentieth century has to take full account of the increasingly adverse environmental conditions and not only the elements of internal weakening which are singled out as the main factors. Therefore none of the approaches mentioned fully explains what has happened although each contributes to a general picture of a pragmatic and energetic nation which had made good use of the opportunities available in the world in previous centuries but could not maintain its position in the twentieth century when conditions became much more adverse. It is unthinkable that, even if free from the weaknesses singled out by the various thinkers, Britain could possibly have retained much of her previous power for any length of time. Some of the argument in this book has revolved around the confused nature of capabilities and the uncertainty about their positive and negative value in times of change. The loss of imperial will was a handicap in maintaining the Empire, one which, with considerable exaggeration, is sometimes singled out as the main reason for its abandonment. Was it not, however, also a great asset in smoothing the colonial emancipation process? Britain's record in this respect, especially under Attlee and Macmillan, was outstanding. The grants of independence were something more than yielding to force, as Britain's critics sometimes claim; they were much earlier and more un-grudging than those of any other colonial power. It was largely owing to this loss of will that the process was not prolonged, and that Britain was saved from an equivalent of Napoleon's 'Spanish Ulcer' or of the French involvement in Indochina and Algeria, or of the American debacle in Vietnam. Admittedly, the absence of a real shock, the masking effects of the Commonwealth, and their reluctance to embrace the ideas of Euro-pean integration left the British in a spiritual void, without a new focus for a renewed political will.

Similarly, some of the main social causes of Britain's relatively low rate of economic growth which have greatly contributed to her recent loss of power may lose their negative effect and even turn to positive assets if, as seems possible, economic growth recedes as the dominant social ob-jective in the world and is replaced by some broader objectives, now vaguely referred to as the 'quality of life'. In the immediate future, it is imperative for the British economy to achieve the maximum com-petitiveness after her entry into the EEC and all its structural deficiencies require adjustment. In the longer run, however, traditional national attachment to non-economic priorities and the forces of continuity which gravely obstruct this achievement may prove a great asset.

Explanations inevitably merge into evaluations. It would be highly misleading to say simply that Britain has lost much of her power and influence; we must take fully into account the change in the circumstances between 1945 and 1973. Other middle powers, France, for instance, were not in a strictly comparable position; and hence comparison with them is bound to be rather confused and controversial. In any case, we can make only highly speculative guesses about long-term trends. If we limit ourselves to the evaluation of the speed and method of the postwar ad-justments, the only judgements about major policy decisions which seem to be reasonably warranted from the short perspective of 1973 are that the decolonization process was a success, while the Suez action and, even more clearly, the decision to abstain from the Messina talks, were failures. Even as severe a critic of Britain's performance as Professor Waltz admits that Britain's adaptation to the postwar world was relatively successful:

The world has changed more than Britain. Gracefully withdrawing from Empire, phasing out one base while jumping to another, muddling towards Europe, climbing summits in pursuit of a world influence for which the material basis is lacking, substituting the myth of Commonwealth for the reality of

Empire; most of these are not inspiring ways of adjusting to decline in a country's international status, but they are benign. Quicker response and bolder movement have often produced worse results. External manner parallels internal procedure: though growth rates have lagged—whether in the economy generally, in the field of education, or in the construction of roads—employment is nevertheless full, the political system stable, and the administration of programs humane.[11]

## The Outlook

This concluding section is not an exercise in crystal gazing, but merely an attempt to assess, inevitably in a rather speculative and tentative manner, the assumptions upon which Britain's foreign policy seemed to be based when she joined the EEC on 1 January 1973, and the direction of this policy as it stood at that date.

The first, basic assumption is about the future of the international system—that it will not be subjected to cataclysmic upheavals within the foreseeable future, although it is likely to undergo major changes and transformations. All the subsequent assumptions follow from this.

Second, the evolution of international relations since 1945 has reinforced rather than undermined the assumption then held that, again within the foreseeable future, national states are likely to remain the most significant agencies dealing with the nation's needs and wants. Interdependence as well as its awareness have grown greatly since, but there is no sign of the British or any other government of a major Western country abdicating its leading role in its nation's affairs. No rapid progress towards any supranational arrangement seems likely.

Third, pace the Meadows Report, the existence of mankind will not suddenly be undermined by the exponentially growing dangers of overpopulation, pollution, or depletion of natural resources. All these issues, however, are becoming an important and constant governmental concern, and each of them may require drastic action which may, to a large extent, weaken the second assumption, as this action would have to be international.

Fourth, a fairly stable equilibrium is likely to continue in the central strategic balance and a nuclear war will remain unlikely, but disturbances from a variety of causes are still possible.

Fifth, the Western developed world will be striving for a stabler international economic system. This is, however, threatened by a parallel reversion to economic nationalism which could lead to a major economic crisis.

Sixth, the developing countries will continue to press for higher prices for the commodities they export and for aid. Although it is extremely hard for the developed countries to respond adequately, their failure to do so may result in a South–North rift which could endanger international order.

As long as these assumptions remain more or less tenable, the general direction of British policy can be anticipated with a fair degree of confidence, although the speed of its evolution and its general effectiveness will, to a great extent, depend upon the success of Britain's domestic arrangements, which, in a circular fashion, will be influenced by her successes or failures abroad.

The postwar British governments were painfully aware that foreign policy is 'the art of the possible', and did not get the country involved in prolonged attempts to defy insuperable difficulties, as did the French or the Americans. Nevertheless, they often accepted reality reluctantly, and occasionally rather slowly. In retrospect, it is quite clear that Britain suffered many setbacks because she attempted too much and adjusted too late. Although, in relation to other major powers, Britain's power base is much weaker in 1973 than it was in 1945, her foreign policy has become much more commensurate with it and hence more realistic. In general terms, this transformation of the basis of British foreign policy can be summed up as the resolution of uncertainties and the abandonment of untenable policies. The British have revised the underlying assumptions and got rid of the misleading myths; they have replaced ideas of an independent world role by the pursuit of 'national interest'; they have made considerable progress in integrating defence and international economic policies with diplomacy, and have shifted the emphasis from strategy to economics, from high diplomacy to low diplomacy, from the global system to 'the area of concentration', from relations with the superpowers to those with Britain's continental neighbours. Some major constraints upon British foreign policy have now been finally removed: the defence of sterling, the decade-long negotiations to enter the EEC, and the defences east of Suez. Consequently, the national effort can now be more concentrated, the objectives kept more manageable and the tasks better defined. British foreign policy can now look more to the future than to the past. The country is entering this new phase with few illusions left, without doctrines or grand designs, without pretence that foreign policy is the product of autonomous intellectual processes and of moral judgements. This pragmatic approach could become a source of strength and could enable Britain to respond effectively to her external problems, provided a general sense of purpose is recaptured; this may well be found in the now fashionable ideas of the 'quality of life'.

Turning to the major policy areas, the transformation of the prevalent ideas about Britain's world role is best shown by Sir Alec Douglas-Home, the senior member of the Heath Government, who was actively involved in its pursuit in the past. In 1963, in his 'political testament', Sir Alec stated:

I believe that Britain has a fine part to play on the world stage. Not as a 'trimmer' in international politics but as a country standing for true values.

But to carry weight we must be in the First XI and not only that but one of the opening batsmen.

It is fashionable to think that power can be discarded but those who think that way are moving unconsciously towards neutralism and there should be no such word in the English vocabulary.

It is not in the British character. We cannot lead from behind or from the middle ranks—we must be in front.[12]

As Foreign Secretary in the Heath Government in the 1970s, Sir Alec fully associated himself with the Prime Minister's emphasis upon national interest, which is now increasingly interpreted as demanding a fair degree of integration with the Community. The high-sounding phrases of the traditional world role sounded hollow when Sir Alec referred to Britain's responsibility in the Indian Ocean in the face of Soviet penetration as the reason for the government's decision to resume the sale of arms to South Africa. A more fundamental reason for this decision could be sought in the government's narrower objective of not being pushed around by the Africans or, for that matter, by the Americans, or the French, or anybody else.

The traditional British oceanic orientation seemed to have come to an end. Exaggerated expectations about the Commonwealth had faded out, sterling had been phased out as an international currency, the 'special relationship' had degenerated into dependence of a questionable value, the British Navy had been severely reduced in size. By the 1960s European orientation seemed to be the only realistic alternative, but many of its opponents preferred some form of isolationism or a 'Little England' position. To view the issue in a broader perspective, it is necessary to get away from the acrimonious debate over the EEC in the early 1970s; the division of opinion was real but not at a very deep level. At first, many of the pro-Europeans shared the anti-Europeans' doubts about the future of the Community, some of them allowing it no more than a fifty/ fifty chance of survival; there was no doubt in the minds of either side that the Common Agricultural Policy of the Community was retrogressive and contrary to British interests. Independently, however, of the future of the Community, Britain's turn to Europe seemed to be irreversible: European orientation in defence had been established by NATO and completed by the withdrawal from east of Suez; trade with

Western Europe had grown much more rapidly than with any other trading partners; and the solidarity of British and of Western European interests had become apparent in many fields.

Despite the division between the parties over the EEC, the validity of the European orientation is disputed largely for emotional reasons, as was the defence involvement in Europe in the late 1940s, similarly without a practical alternative being available. The actual policies proposed by the two parties may not prove to be as fundamentally opposed as they sounded at the beginning of 1973. The Heath Government clearly indicated its determination to set the national interest first, before Community agreements, in its decision to float the pound in July 1972; it is bound to defend this interest on other occasions, especially if the Common Agricultural Policy survives to the end of the period of transition and the burden falls fully upon Britain. If Wilson came back to power and managed to maintain the flexibility of policy which he showed full determination to defend against party pressures, his promised renegotiation of the agreement, to accommodate British interests, will differ in form and style rather than in substance from what Heath would do to protect the national interest.

In the world of large trading blocs and of militarily dominant superpowers, Britain clearly cannot adequately pursue her interests by her own efforts; provided her vital interests are accommodated, she can probably act most effectively through the enlarged Community. The political differences between the two parties are not based upon fundamentally different definitions of Britain's vital interests or upon very different assumptions about the future of the Community. While Heath may not unreservedly assume the success of Britain's membership, although he is determined to work for it, Wilson does not fully exclude the possibility of success. The validity of the European orientation would not be undermined even if Britain's vital interests are not adequately accommodated; it would be open to the British to defend them as the French have done on many occasions; the Community may suffer a setback but not necessarily disintegrate or stagnate.

Even ardent proponents of the European idea and the theoreticians of integration have, at least for the time being, abandoned the neat schemes of federal integration. Within the foreseeable future, the more likely evolution of European integration seems to lie in some untidy pattern of co-operation in which the EEC will not necessarily play a focal role and the centres of power may remain diffuse. The traditional British pragmatism, in which, one may presume, the assumptions of future British foreign policy will remain embedded, is a sound basis for Britain's playing a successful role in this process.

Whatever happens in Europe, it seems unlikely that British foreign policy will seriously depart from the European reorientation indicated by Heath in his Godkin lectures in 1967, when he complained about 'the instinctive tendency among some British officials . . . to ask first and foremost what the United States will think and how it will act' and in his subsequent directive, when he was in office, for the officials to 'think European'. It is, of course, true that Britain could survive, and even moderately prosper, outside the Community, as even Roy Jenkins[13] admits. She would, however, forfeit any opportunity to play a significant role in world affairs, and would thus become fully dependent upon the decisions of others on a wide range of her vital interests. NAFTA, a revived 'special relationship', or the Commonwealth are not realistic options.

Opposition to Britain's joining Europe is based partly on an appraisal of the difficulties and costs involved, but largely upon an emotional attachment to national sovereignty and freedom of decision which has, in actuality already been greatly eroded. The international oceanic outlook often serves as a thin disguise for 'Little Englanders' with a xenophobic aversion to Europe. There is a pronounced inward turn, a moral disengagement from foreign affairs, accompanying the physical disengagement across the seas. In the words of Professor Bruce Miller:

Britain is experiencing a turn inwards such as may not have occured before . . . in the past few years Britain has become much more concerned with domestic matters and much less with what happens or might happen abroad. This is partly a result of disappointments—the humiliating difficulties of sterling, the misbehaviour of the Africans, the preoccupations of the United States, and the rejection of Britain's application to join the EEC. It has been also caused by a concentration on domestic careers and development following the final dissolution of the Empire and the disappearance of many of the jobs which used to flow from it. It is connected with higher standards of education in Britain and the levelling up of incomes and opportunity. One can argue that Britain looked overseas too much in the nineteenth and early twentieth centuries.[14]

The psychological processes involved are best exemplified in the transformation of the views of Enoch Powell, who was so filled with admiration for the Indian Empire that, a year after India's independence, he still thought about recapturing her. When, after the abandonment of the Suez base, the imperial cause had finally been lost, he abruptly switched over to being a 'Little Englander' and one of the most outspoken partisans of opposition to Europe. Characteristically, as on other political issues, notably Commonwealth immigrants, Powell faithfully reflects the deep-seated sentiments of the British public, but, at the same time, champions a lost cause. As an American, David Calleo, shrewdly observes, 'Britain is too big for her island. There almost seem to be too many people, too much industry, too much finance, and possibly too much talent for the narrow base of food and raw materials.'[15] Little England is an emotional attitude but not an actual option.

## Postscript[16]

Thus, by the end of 1972, it appeared that more realistic foundations for Britain's foreign policy were emerging both at home and abroad; a stable and effective foreign policy was no longer obstructed by the convergence of unfavourable trends and of obscuring circumstances as in the years following 1945. The early months of 1973 indicated that Britain was likely to be successful in adjusting her foreign policies both within the Community and in her outside relations. Her first one hundred days as a member proved a success and there seemed to be no real obstacle to her achieving a reasonable working relationship with the Community as a whole as well as with its members. Equally encouraging were the signs that Britain's relations with non-members would not suffer unduly. While what remained of the 'special relationship' at the administrative level was bound to smooth out bilateral Anglo-American relations, at the political level there were no important specific issues, as in the major spheres of American foreign policy Britain had squarely become part of Western Europe. The main issues of American foreign policy, such as the detente negotiations with the Soviet Union, proposals for an Atlantic Charter to include Japan, and arrangements for a new international economic order, would be dealt with by the Community as a whole rather than directly by Britain. Heath's visit to Washington in February 1973 firmly established Britain as a useful member of the Community who was likely, first, to press for the formulation of a Community policy, and, second, to understand and, up to a point, try to meet the American point of view.

As regards the Commonwealth, in stark contrast to the turbulent 1971 Commonwealth Conference of Prime Ministers, the Ottawa Conference in August 1973 passed off relatively unperturbed. The improved prospect for the survival of the Commonwealth is encouraging for the future evaluation of the difficult postwar period of British foreign policy. Perhaps to future generations, an analogy may be found between the evolution of the Commonwealth and that of the League of Nations in the 1930s; although both organizations failed signally in their major political objectives, they developed unspectacular but by no means unimportant economic and social activities which benefited all the members. Outside the United Nations, the Commonwealth is the only organization which is broadly international and which crosses the regional, racial and economic divisions of mankind. Although sharing the League of Nations experience, the Commonwealth need not share its ignominious end. The British Empire was said to have been born in a fit of absence of mind, but developed, in its golden age, a unique political structure. The Commonwealth has likewise developed pragmatically, item by item. Having survived its early teething troubles, it may still come down in history as another monument to British political genius. In accordance with the spirit of our times, it is no longer based on fixed political structures like its imperial predecessor, but on a functional network of co-operation which works regardless of national boundaries.

The domestic outlook remained uncertain but hopeful. As has been argued, conditions existed for improved economic growth. The Heath Government had at least achieved the high rate of 5 per cent *per annum* in reasonably propitious international conditions, although this growth was accompanied by alarming balance-of-payments deficits and inflation. In the longer run, the coming into full production of the North Sea oilfields offered a sound prospect for a fundamental improvement in the British economy. Conditions existed for social stability and for a new consensus, although some of the problems which had been bedevilling the whole postwar period had remained acute and unresolved, notably in industrial relations.

The major unpredictable variable was psychological. Following the exhaustion with the war effort and the loss of the Empire, the British had not yet generated the social dynamism necessary to overcome the grave domestic and foreign problems that are facing them today. It has been notoriously difficult to rouse the nation in peacetime, but with the exception of the first postwar government, which pursued the constructive goal of a welfare state, leadership was weak; subsequent slogans, 'you never had it so good', or the 'technological revolution' and appeals to the 'spirit of Dunkirk' all proved ineffective. Political will is not, however, something constant; it comes in bursts and waves and it could be rapidly revived in more propitious circumstances.

The European idea had not inspired the British; now it had become somewhat tarnished. The British regarded their entry into the EEC as a matter of expediency; membership could not possibly replace the lofty imperial and Commonwealth ideas. The European idea was not devoid of dangers in the opposite direction either; it may be regarded by some of its proponents as a panacea exonerating the British from greater domestic efforts or by offering a new base for an extended world role. It was also conceivable that Britain could yield to pressures within the Community and abandon her traditional striving for multilateralism and for international co-operation; if Western prosperity, which is based upon these, were undermined, Britain would face renewed dangers like the Great Depression and the totalitarianism of the 1930s, in a much more exposed position.

More optimistic expectations seemed, however, fully justified. Joining Europe, despite its costs and unpleasantness, could play the role of the Toynbeesque 'challenge', sufficiently severe to stimulate social forces, but also reasonably manageable. If really successful, entry could become analogous to the stimulus of the industrial revolution,[17] enabling Britain to rejuvenate her domestic system and to find a new world role, after the series of postwar frustrations and disappointments. Even if only moderately successful, Britain's membership should at least halt the gradual deterioration of her position in comparison with her continental neighbours.

By the autumn of 1973, the emerging foundations of the new foreign policy appeared to be shattered both at home and abroad. No solution was in sight for the growing disruption of the international financial system and the world-wide inflation when the Middle Eastern war in October brought in its wake the energy crisis and the sudden steep rise in the price of oil; rises in the prices of other commodities and further inflation could be expected. Britain was additionally affected. Reversing orthodox economic advice in favour of continuous economic growth, her government got caught by the rapidly worsening terms of trade which, augmented by the drop in the value of the pound by some 20 per cent from its 1971 levels, resulted in a colossal deficit in the balance of payments for 1973 of over £2¼ billion or as much as 4 per cent of her GNP, which the higher oil prices could be expected to increase by a further half. The growing industrial strife culminated in the miners' overtime ban and in a severe shortage of coal which induced the government to limit the supply of power. Political dissent grew accordingly.

In January 1974 the prospects of the government managing to control inflation through its incomes and prices policy, and of the country resuming full industrial production and restoring a balance of payments were uncertain. While public opinion turned still further against the EEC associating all Britain's troubles with her membership, the government, too, seemingly reversing the basic direction of its foreign policy, put its main efforts into pursuing an individual, national policy of dealing directly with the oil producers instead of trying to work towards a Community policy, seriously weakening the Community and estranging its members—other than France—as well as the United States.

It is conceivable that we are facing a period of decline and near-anarchy both at home and abroad which will make nonsense of any ideas of a future British foreign policy on the lines suggested in the last section. In the longer run, however, the assumptions stated at the beginning of that section and its mildly optimistic outlook may prove tenable. The industrial strife and the political division of present day Britain cannot be expected to disappear quickly, but may be no more than the last phase of the painful process of the postwar adjustment which has been the subject of this analysis, although this phase is proving to be unexpectedly difficult and prolonged. The present upheaval in the international system, faced with the end of cheap energy and the seemingly insoluble problems arising from the new imbalances of payments, may not last very long; incidentally, it will help to safeguard mankind from looming dangers of ecological disasters inherent in a continuous economic growth at the high postwar rates. In the new system, with her oil and coal resources, Britain will enjoy a sufficient advantage over her Western European and Japanese commercial rivals to expect an adjustment in the growing disparities of their national incomes which, in turn, will improve the conditions for domestic peace. Her relative failure in the postwar economic growth league is likely to make her adjustment to limited or nil growth relatively easy. For the time being, the prospect for Britain's playing a constructive international role in western Europe and, through the Community, in the world, has seriously receded but has by no means fully disappeared.

# Select Bibliography[1]

BARKER, ELISABETH. *Britain in a divided Europe 1945–1970.* London, 1971.

BARTLETT, C. J. *The long retreat: a short history of British defence policy 1945–1970.* London, 1972.

BELL, CORAL. *The debatable alliance.* London, OUP for RIIA, 1964.

BELOFF, MAX. *The future of British foreign policy.* London, 1969.

BOARDMAN, ROBERT & A. J. R. GROOM. *The management of Britain's external relations.* London, 1973.

CAMPS, MIRIAM. *Britain and the European Community 1955–1963.* Princeton, NJ, 1964.

DARBY, PHILLIP. *British defence policy east of Suez 1947–68.* London, OUP for RIIA, 1973.

EDEN, ANTHONY (1st Earl of Avon). *The memoirs,* vol iii: *Full circle.* London, 1960.

GEORGE-BROWN, LORD. *In my way.* London, 1971.

GLADWYN, LORD. *The memoirs of Lord Gladwyn.* London, 1972.

GORDON, MICHAEL R. *Conflict and consensus in Labour's foreign policy 1914–1965.* London, 1969.

HUGO, GRANT. *Britain in tomorrow's world.* London, 1969.

KAISER, KARL & R. MORGAN, eds. *Britain & West Germany: changing societies and the future of foreign policy.* London, OUP for RIIA, 1971.

KITZINGER, UWE. *Diplomacy and persuasion.* London, 1972.

LEIFER, MICHAEL, ed. *Constraints and adjustments in British foreign policy.* London, Acton Society Studies, 1972.

LIEBER, R. J. *British politics and European unity. Parties, elites and pressure groups.* Berkeley, Calif., 1970.

MACMILLAN, HAROLD. *Memoirs,* i. *Winds of change 1914–1939;* iii *Tides of fortune 1945–1955;* iv. *Riding the storm 1956–1959;* v. *Pointing the way 1959–1961;* vi. *At the end of the day 1961–1963* (1966–73).

MAYHEW, CHRISTOPHER R. *Britain's role tomorrow.* London, 1967.

MILLER, J. D. B. *The Commonwealth in the world.* 3rd. ed. London, 1965.

NORTHEDGE, F. S. *Descent from power; British foreign policy 1945–1973.* London, 1974.

PIERRE, ANDREW J. *Nuclear politics; the British experience with an independent strategic force 1939–1970.* London, 1972.

ROSECRANCE, R. N. *Defence of the realm.* NY, 1968.

---

[1] Only includes general books on British foreign and defence policies and the major memoirs of the period.

STRANG, LORD. *The Foreign Office.* London, 1955.
— *Home and abroad.* London, 1956.
THOMAS, HUGH. *The Suez affair.* London, 1967.
VITAL, DAVID. *The making of British foreign policy.* London, 1968.
WALTZ, KENNETH N. *Foreign policy and democratic politics; the American and British experience.* Boston, 1967.
WILSON, HAROLD. *The Labour government 1964–1970; a personal record.* London, 1971.
WOODHOUSE, C. M. *British foreign policy since the second world war.* London, 1961.
YOUNGER, KENNETH. *Changing perspectives of British foreign policy.* London, OUP for RIIA, 1964.

# Notes

## PART ONE: THE BACKGROUND OF POLICY-MAKING

*Notes[1] to pages 1–19*

### Chapter 1. Introductory

[1] Hugo, *Britain in tomorrow's world* (1969), p. 23.
[2] George Modelski, *A theory of foreign policy* (1962), p. 7.
[3] Vital, *The making of British foreign policy* (1968), p. 11.
[4] J. Frankel, *Contemporary international theory and the behaviour of states* (1973).
[5] Arnold Wolfers, 'The Anglo-American tradition in foreign affairs', in Stanley Hoffman, ed., *Contemporary theory of international relations* (1960), p. 242.
[6] Sir Charles Webster, 'British foreign policy since the second world war', in RIIA, *United Kingdom Policy: foreign, strategic, economic* (OUP for RIIA, 1950), pp. 11–12.
[7] This study is not concerned with the operation of the 'foreign-policy machine', which has been described in detail in a number of books, for instance Boardman & Groom, eds. *The management of Britain's external relations* (1973); and Strang, *The diplomatic career* (1962); *The Foreign Office* (1955). The subject will also be treated in a forthcoming book by Dr William Wallace.
[8] Lord Butler, *The art of the possible* (1971), p. 162.
[9] Charles O. Lerche & A. A. Said, *Concepts of international politics* (2nd ed., 1970), p. 22.
[10] Hugo, p. 74.
[11] S. S. Nilson, 'Measurement and models in the study of stability', *World Politics*, Oct. 1967.
[12] Butler, pp. 133, 174.
[13] Macmillan, *Winds of change* (1966), p. 24.
[14] Butler, pp. 238–9.
[15] This has been elaborately and convincingly conceptualized by the Princeton Professor, Harold Sprout and his wife Margaret in 'The dilemma of rising demands and insufficient resources', *World Politics*, July 1968.
[16] J. N. Rosenau, ed. *Linkage politics* (1969).

*Notes to pages 20–46*

### Chapter 2. The Political System

[1] *The Guardian*, 21 Apr. 1963, quoted by Richard Rose, *Politics in England* (1965), p. 229.

[1] The following acronyms are used in these footnotes: ISS=Institute for Strategic Studies; RIIA=Royal Institute of International Affairs; RUSI=Royal United Services Institute for Defence Studies.

[2] This has been forcefully argued by P. H. Partridge in *Consent and consensus* (1971).
[3] Waltz, *Foreign policy and democratic politics* (1967), p. 65.
[4] Ibid. pp. 28, 31–2.
[5] Younger, *Changing perspectives of British foreign policy* (OUP for RIIA, 1964).
[6] D. C. Watt, *Personalities and policies, studies in the formulation of British foreign policy in the twentieth century* (1967). (Opening essay).
[7] G. L. Guttsman, *The English ruling class* (1969), p. 1.
[8] Guttsman, *The British political elite* (1963).
[9] Vital, p. 83.
[10] Anthony Sampson, *Anatomy of Britain* (1962), p. 638. In the third version, *A new anatomy of Britain* (1971), the author did not change his opinion.
[11] Max Nicholson, *The system; the misgovernment of modern Britain* (1967); Thomas Balogh, 'The British elite', *Listener*, 15 Mar. 1973.
[12] Strang, *Home and abroad* (1956), p. 303.
[13] Strang, *Britain in World Affairs* (1961), p. 335.
[14] Graham P. Allison, 'Conceptual models and the Cuban missile crisis', *Amer. Polit. Sci. R.*, Sept. 1969; Richard E. Neustadt, *Alliance politics* (1970).
[15] Cf. Watt, p. 185.
[16] Cf. Neustadt, pp. 91–2.
[17] Lord Wigg, *George Wigg* (1972), p. 312.
[18] F.M. Lord Montgomery of Alamein, *Memoirs* (1958), p. 541.
[19] Gladwyn, *Memoirs* (1972), p. 354.
[20] George Thayer, *The British political fringe* (1965).
[21] Robert Mackenzie, *British political parties* (2nd ed. 1963); and Samuel Beer, *Modern British politics* (1965).
[22] Robert T. Holt & J. Turner, 'Insular politics', in Rosenau, ed., *Linkage politics*, pp. 212–14.
[23] Piers Dixon, *Double diploma* (1968), pp. 179, 183–4.
[24] Alan Watkins, *Spectator*, 11 June 1965.
[25] Rose, pp. 122–3.
[26] Clement Attlee, *The Labour Party in perspective* (1937), pp. 226–7.
[27] Stephen Haseler, *The Gaitskellites* (1960).
[28] Denis Healey, *Power Politics and the Labour Party* (1961).
[29] A. J. P. Taylor, *The Trouble Makers* (1957), p. 13.
[30] *The Economist*, 26 May 1973, p. 15.
[31] Younger, 'Public opinion and foreign policy', *British J. of Sociology*, June 1955, p. 169.
[32] Abrams, 'Social structure, social change, and British foreign policy', in Kaiser & Morgan, eds, *Britain and West Germany* (1971), pp. 138–9.
[33] *Evening Standard*, 7 Oct. 1971.
[34] Peter Calvocoressi, 'Britain in the world', *Polit. Q.*, Jan.–Mar. 1969.
[35] G. M. Young, *Stanley Baldwin* (1952), p. 229.
[36] Sampson, *Macmillan, a study in ambiguity* (1967), p. 119.
[37] Eden, *Full Circle* (1960), p. 36.

## Chapter 3.  Economic and Psychological Factors

[1] Sprout & Sprout, *World Politics*, 4 July 1968.
[2] Quoted by Peter Jay, *The Times*, 3 Mar. 1972.
[3] Andrew Shonfield, *British economic policy since the war* (1959), pp. 56–8.
[4] W. Beckerman, ed. *The Labour government's economic record 1964–70* (1972).
[5] Brinley Thomas, *Migration and economic growth* (2nd ed., 1973).
[6] Herman Kahn & B. Bruce Briggs, *Things to come* (1972), p. 233.

[7] Macmillan, *Pointing the way* (1972), p. 378.

[8] Ibid. p. 360.

[9] So many workers were unemployed and productivity was so low that, with some exaggeration, the late American management consultant, Bill Allen, had called Britain a 'half-time country'. Cf. *The Economist*, 29 Jan. 1972, pp. 11–12.

[10] P. M. S. Blackett, *Military and political consequences of atomic energy* (1948), p. vii.

[11] For instance, in a recent book, *Comparative foreign relations, framework and methods* (1969), David O. Wilkinson devotes one of his nine chapters entirely to this phenomenon.

[12] Sir R. Welensky, *Welensky's 4,000 days* (1964), p. 319.

[13] Sir David Kelly, for instance, in *The hungry sheep* (1955); also in a highly exaggerated fashion by Christoper Booker in the temporarily popular book, *The Neophiliacs* (1970).

[14] Beloff, *The future of British foreign policy* (1969), pp. 2ff.

[15] Sampson, *Macmillan*, p. 159.

[16] Sampson, *New Anatomy*, p. 104.

[17] R. H. S. Crossman, *The Times*, 5 July 1972.

[18] Sampson, *New Anatomy*, p. 91.

[19] 'England, whose England?', *Encounter*, July 1963, p. 14. This whole issue, under the title 'Suicide of a nation', aptly expressed the malaise. The derision of social institutions in *Private Eye* was another manifestation of it.

[20] Arthur Koestler, *Encounter*, July 1963.

[21] G. K. Young, *Masters of indecision* (1962), esp. pp. 135, 153.

*Notes to pages 70–87*

## Chapter 4.  Power, Influence, and Capability

[1] This section is partly based upon the author's *International politics: conflict and harmony* (1969), ch. 6.

[2] Montgomery, *Memoirs* (1958), p. 542.

[3] W. L. Burn, *The age of equipoise* (1964).

[4] Wilkinson, p. 111.

[5] L. Gelber, 'Britain, Soviet sea-power, and Commonwealth connections', in Paul Streeten & H. Corbet, eds, *Commonwealth policy in a global context* (1971), p. 43.

[6] Sir Oliver Franks, *Britain and the tide in world affairs* (1955, Reith Lectures 1954) p. 7.

[7] Wilkinson, p. 60.

[8] F.O. 371/257. 'Memorandum on the present state of British relations with France and Germany', in G. P. Gooch & H. W. V. Temperley, eds, *British documents on the origins of the war, 1898–1914*, iii. 397–440.

[9] *The Economist*, 14 Aug. 1971, pp. 54–5.

[10] Gooch & Temperley, iii. 402–3.

[11] Cf. Hugo, pp. 103–5.

[12] Discussed in detail by James Cable in *Gunboat diplomacy* (1971).

[13] *The Times*, 30 Mar. 1972.

[14] Quoted by H. Corbet, 'Commercial realignments and Commonwealth connections', in Streeten & Corbet, p. 61.

[15] Cmd 9138 (1954).

[16] Cmnd 4107 (1968), pp. 106–14.

[17] British Council, *Annual report*, 1969/70, p. 17.

*Notes to pages 88–111*

## Chapter 5. Perceptions and Sources of Behaviour

1 K. Young, *Arthur James Balfour* (1963), p. 279.
2 This term is taken from Michael Brecher's extremely well researched and thought out book, *The foreign policy system of Israel* (1972).
3 Beloff, *Future of British foreign policy*, p. 7.
4 Bruce M. Russett, *Community and contention* (1963), p. 51.
5 Neustadt, *passim*.
6 G. MacDermott's strictures in *The Eden Legacy* (1969), esp. pp. 73, 98, 127ff., are largely justified despite their exaggerated form.
7 Wilson, *The Labour government 1964–1970* (1971), pp. 610–12.
8 Cf. the most recent well-documented account, Kitzinger, *Diplomacy and persuasion* (1973), pp. 45–88.
9 Waltz, p. 252.
10 Talcott Parsons, *The structure of social action* (1937), p. 58.
11 Rose, 'England the traditionally modern culture', in L. W. Pye & S. Verba, eds, *Political culture and political development*, quoted by Abrams, in Kaiser & Morgan, p. 132.
12 This was in various ways manifested in the novels of Evelyn Waugh, in T. S. Eliot's *The Cocktail Party*, in the escapism of Christopher Fry's plays, or in Angela Thirkell's novels.
13 Waltz, p. 65.
14 Kelly, p. 1.
15 Quoted by Sir H. Nicolson, 'Men and circumstances', *Foreign Affairs*, Apr. 1945, p. 476; see also Frankel, *The making of foreign policy*, pp. 159–62.

*Notes to pages 112–50*

## Chapter 6. The National Style

1 Sampson, *Macmillan*, p. 89.
2 Strang, *Home and abroad*, p. 304.
3 George-Brown, *In my way* (1971), pp. 140, 162–3.
4 Ibid. p. 164.
5 Shonfield, 'The pragmatic illusion', *Encounter*, June 1967; Vital, pp. 98ff; Frankel, 'The intellectual framework of British foreign policy', in Kaiser & Morgan, pp. 88–9.
6 Waltz, pp. 31–2, quoted on p. 23, above.
7 Strang, *Home and abroad*, p. 154.
8 Dixon, p. 98.
9 *Sunday Times*, 23 Apr. 1972.
10 Quoted by James Eayrs, *Fate and will in foreign policy* (1967), p. 39.
11 Gooch & Temperley, iii. 402.
12 430 HC, 18 Nov. 1946, cols 577–90.
13 Eden, *Full Circle*, p. 36.
14 Nicolson, *Diplomacy* (3rd ed., 1963), pp. 53–4.
15 Gooch & Temperley, iii. 402–3.
16 Central Office of Information, *British foreign policy: a brief collection of fact and quotation* (1961), p. 22, in a passage omitted from the 1964 edition.
17 Dixon, pp. 231 and 214.
18 HC 531, 29 July 1954, col. 811.
19 D. Read, *Cobden and Bright: a Victorian partnership* (1968), p. 110.
20 Mayhew, *Britain's role tomorrow* (1967), pp. 29–31.
21 Gooch & Temperley, iii. 403.

[22] Strang, *Britain in world affairs*, p. 154.
[23] Henry Brandon, 'A chance to take on a world role', *Sunday Times*, 2 Jan.1972.
[24] This view is confirmed by J. F. Byrnes, *Speaking frankly* (1947), pp. 175–6; see below, pp. 196–8.
[25] K. Young, *Sir Alec Douglas-Home* (1970), pp. 89, 191.
[26] Macmillan, *Pointing the way*, pp. 266–7.
[27] HC 423, 24 May 1946, col. 788.
[28] Cable, pp. 175–229.
[29] Vital, p. 14.
[30] Strang, *Britain in world affairs*, p. 141.
[31] Lord Morrison of Lambeth, *Autobiography* (1960), pp. 281–2.
[32] Hugh Thomas has summarized the evidence in *The Suez Affair* (1966), on which this account is largely based.
[33] L. Henkin, *How nations behave: law and foreign policy* (1968), p. 294, n. 12.
[34] Eden, *Full circle*, p. 437.
[05] Dixon, p. 278.
[36] Wilson, pp. 179–81.
[37] George-Brown, pp. 136–7.
[38] Gordon Walker, *The Cabinet* (2nd ed. 1972), pp.
[39] Lord Trevelyan, *Worlds apart* (1971), p. 186.
[40] E. H. Carr, *The twenty years' crisis* (2nd. ed., 1946), pp. 79–80.
[41] Nicolson, *Diplomacy*, p. 139.
[42] James Joll, ed., *Britain and Europe* (1950), p. 179.
[43] Woodhouse, *British foreign policy since the second world war* (1961), pp. 211–12.
[44] Richard West, *Rivers of tears* (1972).
[45] George-Brown, p. 171.
[46] Maurice Challe, *Notre révolte* (1969), quoted by Hugh Thomas in N. Waites, ed., *Troubled neighbours* (1972), pp. 309–10.
[47] Bruce Reed & G. Williams, *Denis Healey and the policies of power* (1971), p. 113.
[48] E.g. Professor Georg Schwarzenberger classifies the rules of international law into those of power, of reciprocity, and of co-ordination, *Power politics* (3rd ed., 1964), ch. 13.
[49] Henkin, pp. 18, 21–2, 35, 86, 89.
[50] Carr, pt. iv.
[51] Lord McNair, *International law opinions* (3v., 1956).
[52] *General Assembly Official Record*, 667 plen. mtg, p. 1284.
[53] HC 747, 31 May 1867, cols 106, 122–3, 198.
[54] Henkin, p. 188.
[55] Ibid. p. 189.
[56] Ibid. p. 200.
[57] Cmd 151 (1919); Cmnd 6666 (1945).
[58] HC 441, 6 Aug. 1947, cols 1469–71.
[59] Henkin, p. 50.

*Notes to pages 151–73*

## Chapter 7.   World Role and National Interest

[1] On the theory of 'roles' in foreign policy, see K. J. Holsti, 'National role conceptions in the study of foreign policy', *International Studies Q.*, Sept. 1970, pp. 233–309.
[2] Gladwyn, pp. 111ff., 117ff.
[3] Quoted by Abrams, in Kaiser & Morgan, pp. 141–2.
[4] Sir Winston Churchill, *Europe unite! Speeches 1947–1959* (1950), pp. 417–18.
[5] Franks, p. 2.
[6] *The Times*, 18 Jan. 1957.

[7] Macmillan, *Spectator*, 20 May 1955.
[8] Quoted in Sampson, *Macmillan*, p. 61.
[9] Macmillan, *Pointing the way*, pp. 456, 71; *At the end of the day* (1973), pp. 194, 198ff., 215.
[10] Macleod, *Spectator*, 23 Apr. 1955.
[11] Wilson, esp. pp. 48, 80, 345ff., 489; George-Brown, p. 146.
[12] Cmnd 2901 (1966), p. 7.
[13] George-Brown, p. 141.
[14] Ibid. pp. 209–11.
[15] This section is largely based upon the author's *National interest* (1970); see also Hugo, chs 2 & 3.
[16] *Foreign Affairs*, Oct. 1969.
[17] Brookings Institution, *Major problems of United States foreign policy* (1954), p. 373, quoted by Feliks Gross, *Foreign policy analysis* (1954), p. 53.
[18] Hugo, chs 2 & 3, esp. pp. 73–4.
[19] Ibid. p. 39.

## PART TWO : MAJOR POLICY AREAS

*Notes to pages 174–88*

### Chapter 8.  The Setting in 1945

[1] Younger, *Changing perspectives*, p. 261.
[2] Roy Jenkins, *Afternoon on the Potomac?* (1972), p. 23.
[3] Sir Llewellyn Woodward, *British foreign policy in the second world war* (3 v. 1970–1).
[4] Gladwyn, ch. 8.
[5] Ibid. p. 117.
[6] Ibid. p. 117–18.
[7] Ibid. pp. 167–8.
[8] Ibid. p. 120.
[9] Guttsman, *British political elite*, pp. 241ff.
[10] Strang, *Home and abroad*, p. 287.
[11] Hugh Dalton, *High tide and after* (1962), pp. 73, 83.
[12] Sir R. Harrod, *The British Economy* (1963), p. 25.
[13] Strang, *Home and Abroad*, p. 290.
[14] HC 413, 20 Aug. 1945, col. 312.
[15] Report of the Annual Conference of the Labour Party (1945), p. 117.
[16] Francis Williams, *A Prime Minister remembers* (1950), p. 149.
[17] Jenkins, 'Ernest Bevin', *The Times*, 7 June 1971.
[18] George F. Kennan, *Memoirs, 1925–1950* (1968), pp. 107–9.
[19] Dalton, p. 190.
[20] HC 446, 22 Jan. 1948, cols 383–410.

*Notes to pages 189–220*

### Chapter 9.  Britain's Major Relationships I: The Superpowers

[1] Macmillan, *Pointing the way*, esp. p. 265.
[2] *The Economist*, 28 Apr. 1973, p. 85, see also below, pp. 202–3.
[3] HC 484, 15 Feb. 1951, col. 733.
[4] Trevelyan, p. 185.
[5] Donald Maclean, *British foreign policy since Suez 1956–1968* (1970).
[6] Norman Davies, 'Capitalist ramps and Soviet cavemen', *The Times*, 21 Mar. 1973.
[7] Afterwards published anonymously as 'Sources of Soviet conduct', *Foreign Affairs*, April 1947.
[8] Woodward, iii. pp. 561–4.
[9] *The Diaries of Sir Alexander Cadogan* (1971), p. 321.

[10] Strang, *Home and abroad*, pp. 206–8.
[11] K. Young, *Douglas-Home*, p. 124.
[12] Gladwyn, pp. 209–10.
[13] Dalton, pp. 57–8.
[14] Gladwyn, p. 204.
[15] Williams, *Ernest Bevin* (1952), p. 265.
[16] Gladwyn, pp. 185, 204.
[17] Dalton (pp. 206–9) records that the communication was initiated by him and was accepted by Bevin partly, perhaps, owing to a moment of physical weakness.
[18] *Report of the Annual Conference of the Labour Party* (1950), p. 243.
[19] Gladwyn, p. 117.
[20] Churchill, *Speeches. In the balance* (1951), p. 243.
[21] Dalton, p. 327.
[22] Eden, *Full Circle*, p. 363, see also p. 289.
[23] Maclean, pp. 117–19, 260.
[24] H. C. Allen, *The Anglo-American relationship since 1783* (1959), p. 27.
[25] Dalton, p. 74.
[26] *Spectator*, 25 July 1958.
[27] Wilson, pp. 356ff.
[28] Neustadt, pp. 83–8.
[29] Ibid. pp. 103–6.
[30] Ibid. pp. 29, 94, 113.

*Notes to pages 221–54*

Chapter 10. Britain's Major Relationships II: The Commonwealth, Western Europe, and the United Nations

[1] For an up-to-date account see Elisabeth Barker, *Divided Europe* (1971).
[2] John Strachey, *The end of Empire* (1959), p. 204.
[3] Montgomery, p. 195.
[4] John Higgins, 'Partition in India', in Michael Sissons & P. French, eds, *The age of austerity* (1963), p. 191.
[5] *The Times*, 20 Sept. 1968.
[6] Miller, *The Commonwealth in the world* (3rd ed., 1965); Max Beloff, 'Does Britain need the Commonwealth', *The Times*, 10 Aug. 1970.
[7] Miller, *Commonwealth in the world*, p. 91.
[8] Calvocoressi, *Polit. Q.*, Jan.–Mar. 1970, p. 91.
[9] Macmillan, *Pointing the Way*, ch. 18, esp. p. 298; Marcia Williams, *Inside Number 10* (1972), p. 55.
[10] G. K. Young, *Masters of indecision*, pp. 27–8.
[11] Susan Strange, *Sterling and British politics* (OUP for RIIA, 1971), p. 336.
[12] Ibid. pp. 152–4.
[13] It is interesting to recall that as lately as 1952 the Commonwealth Relations Office had objected to the marriage of the Bechuanaland chief Tseretse Khama to a London typist.
[14] Ali A. Mazrui, 'Geographical propinquity versus Commonwealth cohesion', in Streeten & Corbet, eds, pp. 16–19.
[15] Ibid. pp. 19–22.
[16] *The Times*, 16 Apr. 1972.
[17] Jenkins, *Afternoon on the Potomac?* p. 25.
[18] See Kitzinger, ch. 12; Waltz, pp. 254–5.
[19] Gladwyn, pp. 291ff.
[20] The fullest accounts of Britain's first application to the EEC (Camps, *Britain and the European Community, 1955–1963* (1964) and Richard Mayne, *The recovery of*

*Europe* (1970)) do not refer to the effects of the Suez affair.
[21] *The Times*, 23 May 1957.
[22] Ibid. 31 Mar., 1 Apr. 1960.
[23] Cmnd 4715 (1971), p. 2.
[24] Gladwyn, ch. 8, esp. p. 113.
[25] Woodward (abd ed., 1962), pp. 453–6.
[26] Gladwyn, p. 169.
[27] Ibid. pp. 179–81.
[28] K. Young, *Douglas-Home*, pp. 139.
[29] Gladwyn, pp. 179–81.
[30] *The Times*, 18 Mar. 1972.
[31] Wilson, pp. 178–83.


*Notes to pages 255–82*

## Chapter 11.   International Economic Policies

[1] Cmnd 2276 (1962), p. 3; Cmnd 4107 (1969).
[2] Jenkins, *Afternoon on the Potomac?* pp. 34–5.
[3] Carr, esp. pp. 114–20.
[4] H. B. Malmgren, 'Managing foreign economic policy', *Foreign Policy*, 6/1972, p. 56.
[5] Richard N. Gardner, *Sterling–dollar diplomacy* (rev. ed., 1969), p. 383.
[6] Michael Hodges, *Multinational corporations and national government; a case study of the United Kingdom's experience 1964–70* (1974).
[7] *The Economist*, 18 Dec. 1971, p. 13.
[8] Macmillan, *Pointing the way*, p. 378.
[9] Jenkins, *Afternoon on the Potomac?* pp. 47–8.
[10] *The Economist*, 12 June 1971.
[11] Cmnd 827 (1959); see also Shonfield, *British economy since the war*.
[12] Reed & Williams, p. 226.
[13] Geoffrey Maynard, 'Sterling and international monetary reform', in Streeten & Corbet, pp. 140ff.
[14] Judd Polk, *Sterling; its meaning in world finance* (1956), quoted in Strange, p. 48.
[15] Cf. C. Tugendhat, *Oil: the biggest business* (1968).
[16] RUSI, *Oil—strategic importance, and future supplies. Report of a seminar ... on 21 March 1973*, pp. 7–8, 10.
[17] Ibid. p. 15.
[18] Cmnd 2422 (1964); see also Cmnd 584 (1958).
[19] The statistical data and most of the other details in this section can be found in Overseas Development Institute and Society for International Development, *Britain's role in the second development decade* (1972).
[20] *The Times*, 21 Apr. 1972.


*Notes to pages 283–309*

## Chapter 12.   Defence Policy

[1] *The Times*, 9 July 1965.
[2] RUSI, *Does the strategy of flexible response need modifying?* (1971), p. 13.
[3] Cmnd 2901, p. 7.
[4] RUSI *Journal*, Dec. 1970, p. 4.
[5] Sprout & Sprout,*World Politics*, July 1968; see also Waltz; and W. Goldstein, 'British defence and alliance strategy: the quandary of a middle power', *Polity*, Winter 1970.
[6] *The Economist*, 16 Dec. 1967.
[7] HC 478, 26 July, 12 Sept. 1950, cols 479, 959; HC 483, 29 Jan. 1951, cols. 584–5.
[8] Bartlett, *The long retreat* (1972), pp. 133, 276.

9 Sir S. Zuckerman, *Scientists and war* (1966), p. 45.
10 A. C. L. Day, 'And the cost of defence', *Polit. Q.*, Jan.–Mar. 1960, pp. 81–2.
11 ISS, *The military balance 1971–2*, table 4, p. 62.
12 See n. 10, above.
13 Michael Howard, *The continental commitment* (1972).
14 Cf. 'Is NATO becoming irrelevant?', *The Times*, 6 Apr. 1964.
15 Sir Bernard Burrows & C. Irwin, *The security of Western Europe; towards a common defence policy* (1972).
16 HC 512, 5 Mar. 1953, col. 633.
17 For an authoritative account see Darby, *British defence policy east of Suez* (1973).
18 Cmd 7327 (1948), p. 11.
19 Cmd 7895 (1950), p. 3.
20 Cmd 9391 (1955), p. 6.
21 Cmnd 1288 (1961), p. 3.
22 J. L. Moulton, *Defence in a changing world* (1964), pp. 102–3; Howard, 'Britain's strategic problems east of Suez', *International Affairs*, Apr. 1966, p. 181. Darby, who devoted several sections to the base strategy, fully confirms this view.
23 Margaret Gowing, *Britain and atomic energy 1939–1945* (1964) is the official account of the wartime period. In *Nuclear Politics 1939–1970* (1972) Andrew J. Pierre conveniently summarizes it, and presents a comprehensive and plausible account of postwar developments.
24 Pierre, p. 17, quoting Gowing, p. 78.
25 Pierre, pp. 73–7, 121.
26 Published by the *Daily Telegraph* in August 1964.
27 *The Economist*, 24 June 1972, pp. 44–5. For details which add up to similar, though not fully identical, totals, see Ian Smart, *Future conditional: the prospect for Anglo-French nuclear co-operation*, ISS, *Adelphi Papers*, no. 78, 1971, pp. 12–13.
28 Smart, p.37.
29 Ibid. p. 21.
30 Ibid. pp. 22ff., esp. p. 45.

PART THREE: CONCLUSION

*Notes to pages 310–36*

## Chapter 13. Summary and Conclusions

1 Sampson, *New anatomy*, p. 100.
2 Carlo M. Cipolla, *The economic decline of empires* (1971).
3 Paul Einzig, *Decline and fall? Britain's crisis in the sixties* (1969).
4 J. R. Hale, ed., *Renaissance Venice* (1973).
5 *The Economist*, 18 Sept. 1971.
6 Shepard B. Clough, *The rise and fall of civilization* (1953).
7 Correlli Barnett, *The collapse of British power* (1972).
8 Peter Wiles, 'The declining self-confidence of the super-powers', *International Affairs*, Apr. 1971, p. 289.
9 Dr Joseph Luns in an interview with Kenneth Harris, *Listener*, 3 May 1973, p. 584.
10 F. von Hayek, *The road to serfdom* (1944).
11 Waltz, pp. 306–7.
12 K. Young, *Douglas-Home*, p. 191.
13 Jenkins, *Afternoon on the Potomac?* p. 40.
14 Miller, 'Britain and the Commonwealth', *South Atlantic Q.*, 59/2, Spring 1970, p. 203.
15 David P. Calleo, *Britain's future* (1968), p. 89.
16 Postscript written at the end of January 1974.
17 W. W. Rostow, *Politics and the stages of growth* (1971).

# Index

Abrams, Philip, 25, 40
Acheson, Dean, 151
Adenauer, K., 162, 241f.
Aid, 279–82, 299, 320
Alignments, postwar, 92–3, 184–8, 195, 317; wartime origins, 174–9
Allison, Prof. G. P., 28
Anglo-Iranian oil dispute, 132, 148–9, 218, 247, 250f, 276, 301
Anguilla, 16, 110, 224
Anti-colonialism, 280, 316; UN &, 91, 142, 246ff., 316, 319; international law &, 143; in Commonwealth, 231–2; see also Imperialism
ANZUS Pact, 128, 216, 232, 299
Appeasement, 14, 43, 125f., 197, 284
Aron, Raymond, 8
Assumptions, basic, 88–93, 314, 323; origins of Br., 90; postwar, 90–3; reappraisal, 92; rationality, 100; in 1973, 328–33; see also Myths
Atomic energy, see Nuclear energy
Attlee, Lord: policy & attitude, 16, 24, 36, 91, 118, 142, 148, 152, 185–6, 215, 260; on Churchill, 21; & India, 130, 158; international organization & UN, 169–70, 247; & Commonwealth, 225; & Europe, 225, 237; & defence, 289–90, 302
Australia, 91, 183, 224, 228, 232, 298f., 302–3; see also ANZUS Pact

Bagehot, W., 102
Balance of payments, 48, 51, 54ff., 262, 264f., 272ff., 290, 335
Balance of power, 118, 124–7, 179, 197, 293–5, 315
Baldwin, Lord, 42
Balfour, Lord, 88, 93
Bank of England, 261, 269, 271f.
Barnett, Correlli, 325
Beaconsfield, Lord, 140

Beaton, Leonard, 227, 305
BBC, 83, 93
Beckett, Sir E., 178, 247
Beer, Samuel, 32
Belgian neutrality, 140
Beloff, Prof. Max, 60, 90
Benn, A. Wedgwood, 202
Bevan, Aneurin, 135, 159, 181, 190
Bevin, Ernest: character & policy, 16, 24, 91, 126, 128–9, 185–8, 205, 284; & Left wing, 22, 37, 186f., 192, 197; continuity & bipartisanism, 22f., 34, 185; & officials, 28, 103, 186; & USSR, 89, 126, 192, 196–8; & USA, 94, 205; & powers of UN, 148; on coal exports, 182; & Europe, 187–8, 197, 237; & France, 188, 197; & NATO, 295
Brandt, Willy, 154, 202
Bretton Woods, 262–4
Brown, George (Lord George-Brown), 103, 113, 137f., 141, 165f.
Bulganin, N. A., 200f.
Bureaucracy, see Civil Service
Bureaucratic politics, 28
Burn, Prof. W. L., 72
Butler, Lord, 12, 17, 22

Cabinet government, 29–30
Cable, James, 131
Cadogan, Sir A., 194, 250
Calleo, David, 333
Calvocoressi, P., 41, 228
Capability, 4, 8, 71–87, 326; related to responsibilities, 12; psychological, 47; economic, 47, 79–82, 86–7; defined, 71; Br. perceptions & relative position, 74ff.; overestimates & lost opportunities, 75–6; non-British estimates, 76–7; geographic/demographic, 79–80; military, 82ff.; diplomatic, 83f.; 'identitive', 83, 314; cultural, 83–4, 87;